"A Temple Not Made with Hands"

"A Temple Not Made with Hands"

Essays in Honor of Naymond H. Keathley

EDITED BY
Mikeal C. Parsons
AND
Richard Walsh

FOREWORD BY
J. Randall O'Brien

☙PICKWICK *Publications* · Eugene, Oregon

"A TEMPLE NOT MADE WITH HANDS"
Essays in Honor of Naymond H. Keathley

Copyright © 2018 Wipf and Stock Publishers. All rights reserved. Except for brief quotations in critical publications or reviews, no part of this book may be reproduced in any manner without prior written permission from the publisher. Write: Permissions, Wipf and Stock Publishers, 199 W. 8th Ave., Suite 3, Eugene, OR 97401.

Pickwick Publications
An Imprint of Wipf and Stock Publishers
199 W. 8th Ave., Suite 3
Eugene, OR 97401

www.wipfandstock.com

PAPERBACK ISBN: 978-1-5326-1697-6
HARDCOVER ISBN: 978-1-4982-4131-1
EBOOK ISBN: 978-1-4982-4130-4

Cataloguing-in-Publication data:

Names: Parsons, Mikeal C., editor. | Walsh, Richard, editor. | O'Brien, J. Randall, foreword.

Title: "A temple not made with hands" : essays in honor of Naymond H. Keathley / edited by Mikeal C. Parsons and Richard Walsh.

Description: Eugene, OR: Pickwick Publications, 2018 | Includes bibliographical references.

Identifiers: ISBN 978-1-5326-1697-6 (paperback) | ISBN 978-1-4982-4131-1 (hardcover) | ISBN 978-1-4982-4130-4 (ebook)

Subjects: LCSH: Bible. New Testament—Criticism, interpretation, etc. | Bible. Acts—Criticism, interpretation, etc. | Bible. Luke—Criticism, interpretation, etc. | Baptists—History. | Keathley, Naymond H.

Classification: BS2280 T33 2018 (print) | BS2280 (ebook)

03/07/18

Contents

Foreword | ix
  —J. Randall O'Brien

Editors' Preface | xi
  —Richard Walsh and Mikeal C. Parsons

Biography of Naymond Keathley | xv
  —Craig Keathley, Kevin Keathley, and Kristen Keathley Riggsby

Curriculum Vitae of Naymond Haskins Keathley | xix
  —Derek Hogan

List of Abbreviations | xxix

I. Interpreting the Bible

Enemies and Evildoers in Book V of the Psalter | 3
  —W. H. Bellinger, Jr.

Matthew's "Messianization" of Mark | 15
  —Lidija Novakovic

St. Peter's Crisis of Faith at Harvard: The Scarsellino Picture and Matthew 14 | 28
  —Heidi J. Hornik

Jewish Purification Practices and the Gospel of John | 43
  —Frank Wheeler, Sr.

The Knowledge of God: Prophetic Vision and Johannine Theme | 56
—R. Alan Culpepper

Romans 6:1–14: The Case for a Chiastic Q&A | 71
—Rudolph D. Gonzalez

Slave and Free: Ideal Ideologies in Vesuvian Villas
and in Galatians 3:28 | 85
—Bruce W. Longenecker

The Ideal King in Hebrews: The Exemplary and
Empowering Rule of the Son of God | 102
—Jason A. Whitlark

II. Interpreting Luke and Acts

Luke, Metalepsis, and the Deuteronomistic History | 119
—James M. Kennedy

"Filled with the Spirit": Improvisational Speech in Acts 4:5–31 | 129
—William D. Shiell

The Ethiopian Eunuch Unhindered: Embodied Rhetoric in Acts 8 | 146
—Mikeal C. Parsons

Recalling the Mount of Olives: Sleeping and Praying in Acts 12:1–7 | 161
—Andrew E. Arterbury

Dream-Visions in the Plot of Acts | 174
—Derek S. Dodson

Cinematic Acts and the Triumph of Christianity | 186
—Richard Walsh

III. Interpreting Christian and Baptist Life

The Bible as Spiritual Friend | 203
—Charles H. Talbert

Restoring the New Testament Church? Baptist Self-Perception(s) in America from the Mid-Nineteenth to the Early Twentieth Century | 214
—*C. Douglas Weaver*

Discipleship as Participation in Christ's Death to Sin | 230
—*Sharyn Dowd*

The Abolitionist Pastor Who Left Providence "To Serve the Devil": Rev. James B. Simmons of the First Baptist Church of Indianapolis (1857–1861) | 240
—*Travis L. Frampton*

Fidelity | 260
—*Daniel G. Bagby*

Foreword

ASKED FOR AN APT description of Naymond Keathley, from the Bible to which he has given his life teaching, one has no hesitation: *". . . love, joy, peace, patience, kindness, goodness, faithfulness, gentleness, and self-control"* (Gal 5:22). These are the fruit of the Spirit; this is Naymond Keathley. Other descriptors include: exemplary Christian gentleman, model servant-leader, faithful scholar, gifted administrator, dedicated churchman, loving family member, devoted friend!

My introduction to Naymond came in 1991 as I arrived at Baylor as an Associate Professor of Religion. Holding the rank of Full Professor, along with the highest regards of his colleagues, Naymond stood out as a much-loved, clearly-respected member of the department.

By the time I met him, Naymond had already distinguished himself as a religion professor in other places, having served as religion chair at Palm Beach Atlantic College in Florida, then as Associate Professor of New Testament and Greek at the Golden Gate Theological Seminary in California. In addition, he was well known in the Society of Biblical Literature, the American Academy of Religion, and the National Association of Baptist Professors of Religion. I would come to understand why.

Naymond's person and work illustrates Robert Greenleaf's classic book, *Servant Leadership: A Journey into the Nature of Legitimate Power and Greatness*. Greenleaf notes, "The great leader is seen as servant first." Who wants to be great? We all do. Who wants to be a servant? Only the greatest in our midst. That's Naymond, who embodies the words Jesus shared, "Whoever wants to be great among you must be your servant . . . For even the Son of Man came not to be served, but to serve" (Matt 20:26).

An exemplar as a servant-leader, Naymond has served Baylor as a professor and in several administrative capacities as well. These include: Director of Undergraduate Studies in the Religion Department, Associate Dean of the College of Arts and Sciences, Co-Director of the Baylor in Great

Britain Program, and Senior Vice-Provost of the university, among others. In each of these positions, Naymond's character, competence, and social skills benefitted Baylor, but also me directly.

After having been named Interim Chair of Religion in 1998, Chair in 2002, and Provost in 2005, I knew without hesitation to whom I needed to turn for help with the administrative tasks and other leadership challenges inherent in the work. Frankly, Naymond was a mentor to me. For starters, his character, competence, caring, collaborative approach, and commitment to friendly service and excellence provided a model for my new administrative self. Moreover, in any tense situation involving multiple parties, Naymond's gentle nature inevitably "lowered the temperature and elevated the spirit."

Apparently, there is an organizational and administrative gene on our hereditary code of life, our DNA. If so, Naymond has the gene. In his work as Director of Undergraduate Studies in a department where every undergraduate student in the university is required to enroll in two courses and where the teaching schedules of more than thirty professors must be arranged in a Rubik's Cube fashion, Naymond breezed through the assignments.

As Associate Dean of the College of Arts and Sciences, his impressive people skills and problem-solving skills allowed the university's largest college to operate smoothly without incapacitating student traffic jams. As Co-Director of the Baylor in Great Britain Program, Naymond adroitly navigated logistical labyrinths to the grateful relief of those of us less patient. Then, his service as Senior Vice-Provost proved an immeasurable gift to the university, and to me personally. Rather than attempting to reproduce the job description of his office, suffice it to say, as he and I served together, Naymond did "everything else." Truth be known, he did "everything."

I do not believe I would have become a college president had it not been for Naymond. First, as an administrator, a mediator, and a diplomat, he was my teacher. Second, as a Christian servant-leader, he was my mentor. Third, without Naymond's help, I would have failed. He graciously, generously, providentially gave me what I lacked: example, wisdom, support, confidence, experience, and time.

Kay and I count Naymond and Carolyn among our dearest friends, our years together some of our sweetest memories, and our hopes for their current joy and blessed future our loving prayer.

J. Randall O'Brien
Carson-Newman College

Editors' Preface

NAYMOND H. KEATHLEY HAS devoted his life to his family, the Baptist church, and Baptist higher education, to what might quite literally be described as "a temple not made with hands." As most readers will know, this phrasing appears twice in the book of Acts. It occurs first when Stephen defends himself (7:48) against the charge that he spoke against the law and temple (6:11–14). The phrasing appears again in Paul's attack on Athenian idolatry (17:24). In both cases, the speakers reject attempts to confine the sovereign Creator they serve to human dimensions. In fact, both speakers quickly segue to heavenly, not human, matters. Stephen speaks of Jesus's heavenly glory (7:56) and Paul speaks of Jesus's resurrection (17:31).

This collection of essays honoring Naymond's academic career rightly bears this phrasing as its title for several reasons. First, of course, Naymond has devoted himself throughout his life to the transcendent deity Stephen and Paul describe through this phrase as humanly unconfinable. Second, and consequently, Naymond's life and vocation bespeaks the character of one who has devoted himself to such a Creator. Stephen quotes the prophet upon whom he relies for the phrase, "not made with hands," only far enough to capture the description of this deity (Isa 66:1–2a, cited in Acts 7:49–50). If Stephen's speech had been eulogistic, instead of polemical, he might have continued the quotation:

> But this is the one to whom I will look,
> to the humble and contrite in spirit,
> who trembles at my word. (Isa 66:2b)

The quotation is extended here because Isaiah's words, now introduced by Stephen's "temple not made with hands," succinctly describes Naymond's character. Despite his many accomplishments, some of which are summarized in the foreword by J. Randall O'Brien, the biography by Naymond's children (Kevin, Craig, and Kristen), and the list of Naymond's publications, Naymond is deeply humble, self-aware, kind, and generous of spirit. This collection testifies above all else to that character, and many of the essayists here refer specifically to their regard and admiration for Naymond on precisely this point.

Third, the title phrase is apt because it comes from Naymond's cherished Bible. Naymond has not only "tremble[d] at my word," he has also made the Bible's study and explication his life-long career. Not surprisingly, many of the essayists here are Naymond's students and speak glowingly of what his teaching has meant to their own lives and careers. Because of Naymond's biblical study and his personal and pedagogical influence on others in this regard, the first part of this collection is essays that roam quite widely through the Bible, for Naymond's own teaching has extended throughout the Christian Bible, teaching survey courses on the entire Protestant Bible as well as the New Testament and any number of upper-level and graduate seminars on the Gospels, Paul, and the General Epistles (see the essays by Bellinger, Novakovic, Hornik, Wheeler, Culpepper, Gonzalez, Longenecker, and Whitlark).

Fourth, "a temple not made with hands" appropriately describes this volume and Naymond's academic career because it comes from Naymond's beloved book of Acts. Naymond's dissertation and some of his publications deal specifically with that book, so this volume's second part collects essays devoted specifically to Luke/Acts. The essays come both from experts in the area and also from those who have chosen to write specifically in the area in order to honor Naymond's own scholarly interests (see the essays by Kennedy, Shiell, Parsons, Arterbury, Dodson, and Walsh).

Finally, the title phrase is appropriate because it suggests a "spiritual" house or community. In a different, but complementary way, the cover art depicting the scene of Peter's attempt to walk on water (Matt 14:22–33 and the subject of Heidi Hornik's contribution to the volume) is a visual depiction of this understanding of the temple not made with hands. In that scene, Peter represents the faithful but fragile human community that Jesus gathered around him. The church to which Naymond has devoted his life is such a temple/house. Accordingly, the third and final section of this volume contains essays devoted to the Baptist life and church that Naymond loves so deeply (see the essays by Talbert, Weaver, Dowd, Frampton, and Bagby).

The contributions in this volume reflect but a fraction of the colleagues, students, church members, and community friends who have been deeply and positively impacted by Naymond Keathley. They too represent the "temple not made with hands," which Naymond, by God's grace, has dedicated his life to build. Christopher Wren is the famed architect who designed St. Paul's in London. The visitor to St. Paul's will search in vain to find a tomb erected in his memory. Rather there is a plain stone plaque on the main floor beneath the center of the dome. On it is an inscription which reads: "LECTOR SI MONUMENTUM REQUIRIS CIRCUMSPICE" ("Reader, if you seek his monument—look around you"). So, too, dear reader, if you would see the monument honoring the life and work of Naymond Keathley, look to these writers—family, friends, former students, colleagues—who represent living memorials of a life well lived.

We wish to thank Dr. Bill Bellinger, Chair of the Religion Department, for providing funds to assist in defraying expenses associated with production costs for this volume. Also, we are grateful to Greg Barnhill, Baylor graduate assistant, for his excellent work in readying the various contributions for publication.

Richard Walsh

Methodist University

Mikeal C. Parsons

Baylor University

Biography of Naymond Keathley

When Naymond Keathley's name comes up in various settings with Baylor alumni, inevitably people describe a warm, caring professor. Each person shares a story of enjoying his class and several discuss how his class helped shape their spiritual lives. The same is true for those that knew him while at Southern Seminary, Palm Beach Atlantic College, or Golden Gate Seminary; there is an admiration for Naymond Keathley that has followed him throughout his career.

Naymond Keathley was born in Memphis, Tennessee in 1940 to Rubye and Maurice Keathley. The youngest of four boys, Naymond developed a predilection for ministry at a young age. He preached his first sermon at the age of 5 when one of his brothers broke an ankle and the family was unable to attend Sunday services. Naymond decided that even though they were staying home, they still needed to have a service. One can imagine the pride that Maurice and Rubye as good Southern Baptists would have had watching their youngest son in that moment exhibiting a desire to be a preacher, only to have it broken at the conclusion in which Naymond instructed his "congregation" to turn in their hymnals to "Pistol Packin' Mama."

In 1958, Naymond graduated at the head of his class at Central High in Memphis and headed to Baylor University where he majored in history and minored in Religion, German, and English. In 1961, he met Carolyn Griffin, an incoming freshman, also from Memphis, who contacted him about sharing rides home for school breaks. They were engaged by Christmas and married in August of 1962. They have three grown children and are proud grandparents to five granddaughters and one grandson.

Naymond graduated cum laude from Baylor in May 1962. That fall, he started at Southern Baptist Theological Seminary in Louisville, Kentucky, where he earned his Bachelor of Divinity in 1966 and his PhD in 1971. Under the mentorship of William Hull, he successfully defended his dissertation, "The Concept of the Temple in Luke-Acts." During his journey in religious education, Naymond began to realize a call to be an educator rather than a pastor. He had served as a student assistant both at Baylor and at Southern as well as serving as the Garrett Teaching Fellow in the New Testament Department at Southern from 1967–1969. He felt called to help reach into the hearts and minds of students as they learned about the Bible and Christian religion.

Naymond's formal teaching career began in 1972 at Palm Beach Atlantic College (now Palm Beach Atlantic University) in Florida where he joined the faculty of the young institution as an Assistant Professor of Religion and Philosophy serving as the chair of that department from 1975–1976. As is the case with many professions, the early years are often a trying, learning experience. If you speak to students from those years, they may recall that Naymond lectured as if the material were fresh and at the top of his mind. In some cases, this was because his new responsibilities included teaching courses that he had not only never taught, but in some cases had never taken. He would spend hours reviewing and learning material that he would then present in lecture in the ensuing days. It was a commitment to do his best work and to do right by his students.

In 1976, Naymond was approached by Golden Gate Baptist Theological Seminary in Mill Valley to join the New Testament faculty. The call came in large part due to the recommendation of a Baylor contact, Jack Flanders. Naymond and Carolyn accepted that call and made the decision to move their young family from east coast to west coast. The California years were a time of growth and professional development for Naymond as he advanced in academic rank from Assistant Professor to Associate Professor of New Testament and Greek. Beloved and respected by his students, Naymond would frequently invite them into his home where they would become, in many cases, like members of the family. Naymond and Carolyn enjoyed close relationships with colleagues that included dinner clubs and social outings not to mention the close ties developed through the church community as well. The collegial respect that others hold for Naymond is reflected in his being invited on three separate occasions to return to his previous institutions as a visiting professor, twice at Golden Gate and once at Southern.

In 1981, it was Jack Flanders again who was instrumental in a professional move for Naymond. This time he was not simply making a recommendation, but was calling to request Naymond to come to Waco and consider a position in the Department of Religion at his alma mater. It was not a forgone conclusion that Naymond and Carolyn would accept the move; they had built significant relationships in California, had school age children to consider, and in many respects had established some roots in the Bay Area. It was really their oldest son who helped sway the decision. Kevin was in 9th grade and when asked by his parents about what he thought his college plans might be in a few years, his answer was Baylor. So again, Naymond and Carolyn packed up the family and set out for the Lone Star State, a decision that has proven to be the right choice both professionally and personally.

Naymond has proven his commitment to Baylor over and over again throughout the past 37 years. He has served the Department of Religion first as an associate professor then as a full professor and has also served the department as Director of Undergraduate Studies, and Interim Chair. He served Baylor as Associate Dean of the College of Arts and Sciences, Special Assistant to the Dean of Truett Seminary, Co-Director of the Baylor in Great Britain Program, Senior Vice Provost, and most recently as Interim Director of the Center for International Education (Jo Murphy Chair), before returning to the classroom to conclude his career where it started and where his passion has remained.

Through the years he has served on the Faculty Senate and numerous committees and councils. He has represented Baylor at college and seminary inaugurations and on recruiting trips from Anaheim to Nashville. He has been a faculty sponsor for student honor societies and has written numerous articles and study guides for professional and denominational publications as well as authoring or contributing to three books. He has always done what was asked of him and more.

In addition to service to the University, service within the church community has always been a significant part of the life of Naymond Keathley as well. He was ordained in his home church, Temple Baptist in Memphis. He and Carolyn were active members of Crescent Hill Baptist in Louisville and First Baptist in West Palm Beach. In California, they joined Tiburon Baptist where Naymond served as interim pastor in 1977 and 1978. Since 1981, Naymond and Carolyn have been active members of Seventh and James Baptist. Naymond has served as deacon, Sunday school teacher for both adult and youth, has chaired multiple church administrative committees, and been a member of the sanctuary choir, church cabinet, and worship council. He has filled the pulpit not only at Seventh but also numerous other churches throughout Texas, Oklahoma, Tennessee, Florida, Kentucky, and California and served three different churches as interim pastor.

It goes without saying that to honor Naymond Keathley is also to honor Carolyn Keathley for she has been an integral part of not only of his personal life, but also his career. Every decision along the way has been a partnership between Naymond and Carolyn who will soon enter their 57th year of marriage. They have exemplified what it is to be committed husband and wife and partners along the journey of life and have served as an example to many young couples in the church and in the community at large.

Naymond Keathley has enjoyed a long career of significant impact on those that have known him, learned from him, and worked with him. Some of the younger generation of faculty consider him to be an institution at Baylor. He has been and continues to be an influential example of integrity, professionalism, and faith. Over the years he has been known by many titles: Professor, Director, Chairman, Deacon, Interim Pastor, Associate Dean, and Senior Vice Provost, to name a few. Many have been fortunate to know him in these roles, but no role has he filled better than the one he has filled for the three of us who have been exceptionally blessed to know him simply as Dad.

Craig Keathley

Kevin Keathley

Kristen Keathley Riggsby

Curriculum Vitae
Naymond Haskins Keathley
By Derek Hogan

Personal

Birth: September 25, 1940, Memphis, Tennessee

Parents: Maurice F. and Rubye H. Keathley (both deceased)

Marriage: Carolyn Jeannine Griffin, August 4, 1962

Children: Kevin, born June 15, 1966
    Craig, born January 7, 1970
    Kristen, born December 20, 1974

Educational

Public schools, Memphis, Tennessee 1946–58

B.A., *cum laude*, Baylor University, Waco, Texas, 1962
    Major: History
    Minors: German, English, Religion

B.D., The Southern Baptist Theological Seminary, Louisville, Kentucky, 1966

Ph.D., The Southern Baptist Theological Seminary, Louisville, Kentucky, 1971
    Dissertation: "The Concept of the Temple in Luke-Acts"

Areas of Specialization: New Testament Literature, New Testament Language, New Testament Theology, Old Testament Literature

Vocational (non-academic)

Manager, Campus Baptist Book Store, The Southern Baptist Theological Seminary, Louisville, Kentucky, 1969–72

Academic

Student Assistant, Department of Religion, Baylor University, 1960–61

Student Assistant, New Testament Department, The Southern Baptist Theological Seminary, 1965–67

Garrett Teaching Fellow, New Testament Department, The Southern Baptist Theological Seminary, 1967–69

Assistant Professor of Religion and Philosophy, Palm Beach Atlantic College, West Palm Beach, Florida, 1972–76

Chair, Department of Religion and Philosophy, Palm Beach Atlantic College, 1975–76

Assistant Professor of New Testament and Greek, Golden Gate Baptist Theological Seminary, Mill Valley, California, 1976–79

Associate Professor of New Testament and Greek, Golden Gate Baptist Theological Seminary, Mill Valley, California, 1979–81

Associate Professor of Religion, Baylor University, 1981–89

Visiting Professor of New Testament and Greek, Golden Gate Baptist Theological Seminary, Mill Valley, California; July, 1984

Visiting Professor of New Testament, The Southern Baptist Theological Seminary, Louisville, Kentucky, June–July, 1989

Professor of Religion, Baylor University, 1989–present

Visiting Professor of New Testament and Greek, Golden Gate Baptist Theological Seminary, Mill Valley, California; June, 1994

Associate Dean, College of Arts and Sciences, Baylor University, 1996

Director of Undergraduate Studies, Department of Religion, Baylor University, 1999–2006.

Co-convener, Department of Religion, Baylor University, 1999

Special Assistant to the Dean, George W. Truett Theological Seminary, 2000–2001

Senior Vice Provost, Baylor University, 2006–2011

Jo Murphy Chair and Interim Director of the Center for International Education, Baylor University, 2011–2014

Professional Development (since coming to Baylor)

Participant, Annual Meetings of the Society of Biblical Literature, 1982, 1983, 1986, 1989, 1990, 1991, 1992, 1994, 1995, 1996, 1997, 1998, 2000, 2001, 2002

Participant, Annual Meetings of Association of Baptist Teachers of Religion, 1982–85

Participant, Annual Meetings of the National Association of Baptist Professors of Religion, 1983, 1986, 1989, 1990, 1991, 1992, 1994, 1995, 1996, 1997, 1998, 2000, 2001, 2002

Presented paper, "Introduction to the Epistle of James," Annual Meeting of National Association of Baptist Professors of Religion, Southwest Region, 2000

Participant, Annual Meetings of Society of Biblical Literature, Southwest Region, 1982–85, 2000–2002 (In 2000, presided at one of the New Testament sections.)

Participant, Seminar on the Development of Early Catholic Christianity, 1985–1998. (This ecumenical seminar, composed of representatives from a dozen private and public universities and seminaries, meets four times each year to discuss scholarly papers related to historical and theological developments in the second century. In 1987–88, served as co-host for the group at Baylor.)

Participant, Biblical Seminar, 1986 to present. (This seminar, composed of representatives from a dozen institutions, meets four times a year in the Dallas area for discussion of scholarly papers.)

Participant, Seminar on the Gospels, Southern Methodist University, 1986

Participant, Summer Teaching Institute, Baylor, 1982

Participant, Retreat for Fellows of the Summer Teaching Institute, Baylor, 1988, 1989, 1990, 1991, 1994, 1995

Participant, Brown Bag Computer Workshop, Baylor, 1982

Participant, Faculty Workshop on the Computer and the Humanities, Baylor, 1983

Participant, Instructional Technology Workshop, Baylor, 1996

Member, Nominating Committee, National Association of Baptist Professors of Religion, 1983; Nominating Committee for Editorial Board, 1994

Participant, Tours of Israel, 1985; 1989 (leader)

Tour leader, Journeys of Paul Tour (Greece and Turkey), 1998

University Service

Faculty Sponsor, Graduate Theological Fellowship, 1982–84

Faculty Sponsor, Alpha Lambda Delta (Freshman Honor Society), 1986–1990

Faculty Sponsor, Theta Alpha Kappa (Religion Honor Society), 1988–89

Colloquium leader, Honors Program, 1982–83, 1987–88, 1996–97

Seminar leader, Welcome Week, 1982, 1983, 1984, 1985, 1986, 1987, 1988, 1989, 1990, 1991, 1992, 1993, 1995

Speaker, Pastor's Bible Conference (January Bible Study), 1983, 1986, 1990, 1999, 2001

Faculty Marshall, Spring, Summer, Winter Commencements, 1984–1999

Speaker at Academic Sessions for the Religion Department at the Fall, Winter, and Spring Premieres, 1999–present

University representative:

Inauguration of the President of Golden Gate Baptist Seminary, Mill Valley, California; October, 1983

Inauguration of the President of Georgetown College, Georgetown, Kentucky; October, 1984

Inauguration of the President of Golden Gate Baptist Seminary, Mill Valley, California; April, 1987

Annual meetings of Baptist Associations, 1984-1995

Speaker for Baylor Parent League Rallies (recruiting)

- Albuquerque, New Mexico, 1994
- Memphis, Tennessee, 1995
- Little Rock, Arkansas, 1995
- St. Louis, Missouri, 1996
- Memphis, Tennessee, 1997
- Little Rock, Arkansas, 1997
- Nashville, Tennessee, 1998
- St. Louis, Missouri, 1999
- Denver, Colorado 2000
- New Orleans, Louisiana 2001

University Committees:

- University Library Committee, 1983-87 (Chair, 1985-87)
- Planning Group on Academic Support, University Self-Study (Chair), 1984-86
- Book Store Manager Advisory Committee, 1986
- Calendar, 1998-
- Committee on Committees, Graduate School, 1986, 1992
- Faculty Advisory Committee on the Book Store (Chair), 1987-1990
- Religious Affairs Committee (Chair, Subcommittee on the Faculty Retreat), 1987-1991, 1993-94
- Faculty Senate, 1988-1994 (Secretary and member of the Executive Committee, 1993-94)
- Steering Committee, United Way Campaign, 1989
- Curriculum Committee, Graduate School, 1989-1992 (Chair, 1990-91)
- Compensation, Benefits, and Personnel Committee, 1991-94 (Chair, 1992-94)

Faith and Learning Discussion Group, 1992–93

Graduation Task Force, 1993

Administrative Committee of the BU Retirement Income Plan and Group Health Insurance Plan, 1993–1998

Steering Committee and Chair, Committee of Mission, Governance, and Organization, University Self Study, 1994–96

Search Committee for Religion-Philosophy Librarian, 1994

Technical Standards Board, 1996–present

Curriculum Committee, College of Arts and Sciences, 1996 (Chair), 2000–present

Committee for Selection of the George W. Truett Distinguished Church Service Award, Baylor Alumni Association, 1996

Campus Master Plan Committee (ex officio), 1996

University Grievance Committee, 1997–2000

Calendar Committee, 1999–present (Chair, 2000–2002)

Beall Russell Humanities Lecture Committee, 2001–present

Computer Technology Committee, Arts and Sciences, 2002–present

Committees in the Department of Religion:

Brochure, 1982–83

Faculty Additions, 1982–83

Goals and Objectives, 1982–83

Graduate Student Evaluation, 1982–83

Language Committee (Chair), 1983

Undergraduate Curriculum Revision (Chair), 1984–85

Audio-Visual Committee (Chair), 1985–86

Coordinator of Library Acquisitions, 1986–93

Coordinator of placement of Ph.D. graduates, 1986–93

Relation to the Seminaries (4-2 B.A./M.Div. Program), 1986–89

Resources, 1990–93, 1995–1998 (Chair, 1990–91, 1995–98)

Personnel, 1992–94 (Chair, 1993–94)

Coordinator, Annual Alumni Breakfast at AAR/SBL meeting, 1989–present

Merit Pay, 1993

Undergraduate Studies, 1994–97, 1998–present (Chair, 1999–present)
Religion/Truett Liaison Committee, 1999–present (Chair, 2000–2001)
Search Committee (2000–2001)

Community Service

Speaker, Occupational Investigation Class, Midway Junior High School, Waco; January, 1983

Speaker, Inner City Ministries' Christmas Luncheon for Senior Citizens, December, 1988

Church and Denominational Service

Youth Director, Temple Baptist Church, Memphis, Tennessee; 1961–62

Interim Pastor, First Baptist Church, Jupiter-Tequesta, Florida; 1975

Interim Pastor, Tiburon Baptist Church, Tiburon, California; 1977

Interim Pastor, Berea Baptist Church, Stockton, California; 1977

Interim Pastor, Tiburon Baptist Church, Tiburon, California; 1978

Bible Study Leader (January Bible Studies, Doctrinal Surveys, etc.) for fourteen conferences in South Florida Baptist, Methodist, and Presbyterian churches; 1973–76

Bible Study Leader for twenty-seven conferences in California Baptist churches, 1977–81

Bible Study Leader for thirty conferences in Baptist and Methodist churches in Texas and Tennessee; 1981 to present

Pulpit supply in numerous Kentucky, Florida, California, Oklahoma, Tennessee, and Texas Baptist churches

Participant, Baptist General Convention of Texas, Waco; 1982 (Speaker, Alumni Luncheon for Golden Gate Baptist Theological Seminary)

Messenger, Baptist General Convention of Texas, 1983, 1984, 1985, 1986, 1989, 1990, 1991

Speaker, Serendipity (BSU), February 16, 1983

Teacher, Seminary Extension Course in Revelation, Fall 1983, Spring 1990

Messenger, Southern Baptist Convention, New Orleans, Louisiana, June, 1990

Participant, Cooperative Baptist Fellowship, Fort Worth, Texas, May 1992

Participant, Cooperative Baptist Fellowship, Birmingham, Alabama, May 1993

Participant, Cooperative Baptist Fellowship, Fort Worth, Texas, July, 1995

Participant, Cooperative Baptist Fellowship, Houston, Texas, June, 1998

Participant, Cooperative Baptist Fellowship, Orlando, Florida, 2000

Local Church involvement (Seventh and James Baptist Church)

> Deacon, 1984–present; chair, 1991–92
>
> Sunday School Teacher, Adult Division, 1982–86, 1988–93; Youth Division, 1986–88 (Frequent substitute teacher to the present)
>
> Member, Sanctuary Choir, 1982–present (Vice-President, 1999)
>
> Member, University Committee, 1988–92 (Chair 1989–90, 91–92)
>
> Chair, Education Council, 1987–88
>
> Chair, Adult Education Committee, 1985–87
>
> Chair, Search Committee for Minister of Education, 1983
>
> Moderator, 1985–86, 1988–89
>
> Chair, Denominational Relations Task Force, 1990–91
>
> Member, Administrative Council, 1994–1996
>
> Member, Pastor Search Committee, 1994–95
>
> Participant/host, Texas Baptists Committed Dinner, 1996
>
> Member, Minister of Music Search Committee, 1999
>
> Member, Worship Council, 1999–present (Chair, 2001)
>
> Member, Church Cabinet, 2000–2001

Publications

"The Concept of the Temple in Luke-Acts." PhD diss., Southern Baptist Theological Seminary, 1971.

"First-Century Birth Rituals," *Sunday School Lesson Illustrator* 3.1 (1976) 78–79.

"The Jewish Sabbath and the Christian Lord's Day," *Sunday School Lesson Illustrator* 5.1 (1978) 64–66.

"Paul's Missing Epistles," *Sunday School Lesson Illustrator* 5.2 (1979) 73–74.

Review of *The Revelation of Jesus Christ*, by Ray Frank Robbins. *Journal of Church and State* 21 (1979) 140–41.

"To the Praise of His Glory: Ephesians 1," *RevExp* 76 (1979) 485–93.

"Growing in Faith and Love." In *Adult Life and Work Lesson Annual 1982–83*, 1–49. Nashville: Convention Press, 1982.

Review of *The First Urban Christians*, by Wayne A. Meeks. *Journal of Church and State* 26 (1984) 142.

"God's People in a Changing World." In *Adult Life and Work Lesson Annual 1985–86*, 116–77. Nashville: Convention Press, 1985.

Discovering Romans. Carmel, NY: Guideposts, 1986.

Review of *The Jewish and Christian World 200 B.C. to A.D. 200*, by A.R.C. Leaney and *Pagan Rome and the Early Christians*, by Stephen Benko. *Journal of Church and State* 29 (1987) 336–38.

Review of *The Origins of Christianity: A Critical Introduction*, by R. Joseph Hoffmann. *Journal of Church and State* 30 (1988) 146–47.

Editor, *With Steadfast Purpose: Essays on Acts in Honor of Henry Jackson Flanders, Jr.* Waco: Baylor University, 1990.

"The Temple in Luke and Acts: Implications for the Synoptic Problem and Proto-Luke." In *With Steadfast Purpose: Essays on Acts in Honor of Henry Jackson Flanders, Jr.*, 77–105. Waco: Baylor University, 1990.

"Discipline." *Mercer Dictionary of the Bible*, edited by Watson E. Mills, 215–16. Macon, GA: Macon University Press, 1990.

"Confession." In *Holman Bible Dictionary*, edited by Trent C. Butler, 285–86. Nashville: Holman Bible, 1991.

"Lord's Day." In *Holman Bible Dictionary*, edited by Trent C. Butler, 891–92. Nashville: Holman Bible, 1991.

"Repentance." In *Holman Bible Dictionary*, edited by Trent C. Butler, 1175–76. Nashville: Holman Bible, 1991.

Review of *A Theological Introduction to the New Testament*, by Eduard Schweizer in *Baptists Today* 10 (19 March 1992) 19.

Review of *Reading Matthew: A Literary and Theological Commentary on the First Gospel*, by David Garland in *Baptists Today* 12 (6 January 1994) 17.

The Church's Mission to the Gentiles: Acts of the Apostles, Epistles of Paul. Macon, GA: Smyth & Helwys, 1999.

Organizational

Alpha Chi, National Honor Society

Society of Biblical Literature and Exegesis

National Association of Baptist Professors of Religion

AAUP, Baylor Chapter

Honors and Awards

Outstanding Young Men of America, 1976

Most Outstanding Professor, Palm Beach Atlantic College, 1976 (selected by students)

Who's Who in Religion, 3rd ed., 4th ed.

Who's Who in Biblical Studies and Archaeology, 1st ed., 2nd ed.

Who's Who in the South and Southwest, 24th ed.

Who's Who in American Education 1992–93

Professor of the Month, Panhellenic Council, 1996

Abbreviations

All abbreviations of primary texts have followed SBLHS 2nd ed. Those primary texts that are not listed in that style guide have also been included below.

AB	Anchor Bible
ABD	*Anchor Bible Dictionary*. Edited by David Noel Freedman. 6 vols. New York: Doubleday, 1992.
ACNT	Augsburg Commentaries on the New Testament
AIL	Ancient Israel and Its Literature
AJEC	Ancient Judaism and Early Christianity
AnBib	Analecta Biblica
ANTJ	Arbeiten zum Neuen Testament und Judentum
ANRW	*Aufstieg und Niedergang der römischen Welt: Geschichte und Kultur Roms im Spiegel der neueren Forshcung*. Part 2, *Principat*. Edited by Hildegard Temporini and Wolfgang Haase. Berlin: de Gruyter, 1972–.
ANTC	Abingdon New Testament Commentaries
AOAT	Alter Orient und Altes Testament
BAR	*Biblical Archaeology Review*
BBR	*Bulletin for Biblical Research*
BECNT	Baker Exegetical Commentary on the New Testament
Bib	*Biblica*

BibInt	Biblical Interpretation Series
BJRL	*Bulletin of the John Rylands University Library of Manchester*
BSac	*Bibliotheca Sacra*
BTB	*Biblical Theology Bulletin*
BZ	*Biblische Zeitschrift*
BZAW	*Beihefte zur Zeitschrift für die alttestamentliche Wissenschaft*
BZNW	*Beihefte zur Zeitschrift für die neutestamentliche Wissenschaft*
CBQ	*Catholic Biblical Quarterly*
CIL	*Corpus Inscriptionum Latinarum*. Berlin, 1862–
Contr.	*Controversiae* (Seneca the Elder)
HNTC	Harper's New Testament Commentaries
HTR	*Harvard Theological Review*
ICC	International Critical Commentary
I.Eph.	*Die Inschriften Von Ephesos*, edited by Hermann Wankel and Reinhold Merkelbach (Bonn: 1979–1990)
Int	*Interpretation*
ITC	International Theological Commentary
JBL	*Journal of Biblical Literature*
JLS	*Journal of Literary Studies*
JSHJ	*Journal for the Study of the Historical Jesus*
JSJ	*Journal for the Study of Judaism in the Persian, Hellenistic, and Roman Periods*
JSNT	*Journal for the Study of the New Testament*
JSNTSup	Journal for the Study of the New Testament Supplement Series
JSOTSup	Journal for the Study of the Old Testament Supplement Series
JTI	*Journal of Theological Interpretation*

JTS	*Journal of Theological Studies*
KJV	King James Version
LB	*Linguistica Biblica*
LCL	Loeb Classical Library
LNTS	Library of New Testament Studies
MLBS	Mercer Library of Biblical Studies
MNTC	Moffat New Testament Commentary
NAC	New American Commentary
NCB	New Century Bible
NIB	*The New Interpreter's Bible*, edited by Leander E. Keck. 12 vols. Nashville: Abingdon, 1996.
NICNT	New International Commentary on the New Testament
NICOT	New International Commentary on the Old Testament
NovT	*Novum Testamentum*
NovTSup	Supplements to *Novum Testamentum*
NPNF	*A Select Library of Nicene and Post-Nicene Fathers of the Christian Church.* Edited by Philip Schaff and Henry Wace. 28 vols. in 2 series. 1886–1889.
NTL	New Testament Library
NTS	*New Testament Studies*
OTG	Old Testament Guides
OTL	Old Testament Library
PCNT	Paideia Commentaries on the New Testament
PNTC	Pillar New Testament Commentaries
PRSt	*Perspectives in Religious Studies*
RB	*Revue Biblique*
RevExp	*Review and Expositor*

RIC	*Roman Imperial Coinage*
RSQ	*Rhetoric Society Quarterly*
RSV	Revised Standard Version
SBLDS	Society of Biblical Literature Dissertation Series
SBLMS	Society of Biblical Literature Monograph Series
SBLSBS	Society of Biblical Literature Sources for Biblical Study
SBT	Studies in Biblical Theology
SHBC	Smyth & Helwys Bible Commentary
SEÅ	*Svensk exegetisk årsbok*
SNTSMS	Society for New Testament Studies Monograph Series
SP	Sacra Pagina
ST	*Studia theologica*
TDNT	*Theological Dictionary of the New Testament*
TDOT	*Theological Dictionary of the Old Testament*
TNTC	Tyndale New Testament Commentaries
TS	*Theological Studies*
TynBul	*Tyndale Bulletin*
VC	*Vigilae Christianae*
WBC	Word Biblical Commentary
WUNT	Wissenschaftliche Untersuchungen zum Neuen Testament
YCS	*Yale Classical Studies*
ZECNT	Zondervan Exegetical Commentary on the New Testament
ZNW	*Zeitschrift für die neutestamentliche Wissenschaft und die Kunde die* älteren *Kirche*

I. Interpreting the Bible

Enemies and Evildoers in Book V of the Psalter

W. H. Bellinger, Jr.

ONE OF THE CENTRAL shapers of modern study of the Psalms, Claus Westermann, has famously suggested that there are three dimensions to lamentations:

> A characteristic of the lamentation ... is that it usually has three dimensions. It is directed toward God (an accusation or complaint against God), toward others (a complaint against an enemy), and toward the lamenter himself (I-lament or We-lament).[1]

We might summarize that there are three characters in the laments: God, the enemies, and the lamenters. The enemies are persistent in the Psalter. They are especially present in the complaint psalms and so seemingly ever-present in Books I and II of the Hebrew Psalter. I will attempt to be consistent with the term "complaint" as the label for the genre. The Psalms describe the actions of those who seek to harm the righteous in a variety of ways. I have been working on Book V of the Psalter, but I have not really done much with the enemies in these texts. What I want to do in this brief preliminary essay is to say a bit about the history of scholarship on the enemies and to describe the basic data on the enemies in the psalms of Book V and then to see if there are a few conclusions we can draw in terms of how we might deal with the presence of enemies in these texts.[2]

---

1. Westermann, *Praise and Lament*, 267.

2. I am delighted to dedicate this essay with gratitude to Naymond Keathley who has for more than three decades demonstrated to me (and many others) the biblical ideals of collegiality and friendship. As a New Testament teacher and scholar, Naymond

History of Scholarship

Much of scholarship has understandably investigated the identity of these enemies. Early critical scholars identified the conflicting enemies in terms of opposing parties in early Judaism.[3] Mowinckel understood the evildoers as sorcerers, as practitioners of an evil magic who placed a curse on the righteous person.[4] This curse has brought about illness or some other trouble, and the lamenter prays for healing and restoration. The term Mowinckel focuses on is פעלי און with און understood as that which is sinister and obscure, the secret power of a curse to ruin someone. The English translation of Kraus's Psalms commentary amusingly translates the term as "practitioners of all that is weird."[5] These workers of iniquity are characterized in sinister and even twisted ways. I do not think, however, that they are magicians casting spells in the way many contemporary readers would hear that language. Some psalms describe the enemies as false accusers or as persecutors.[6] The enemies in the community complaints are usually national enemies, and some scholars have understood the enemies in the individual complaint psalms in the same way.[7] Gunkel argues that the complaints related to disease and distress so that illness was the primary crisis behind many of these texts.[8] It is reasonable to think that would be the case in any society. A number of these texts seem to reflect the view that illness was judgment because of sin, and so contemporary readers can imagine the theological tensions and strained relationships these crises brought. In such contexts the psalms portray two stereotypical groups, the righteous and the wicked—worshipers who prayed the complaint psalms and those who opposed them, characterized in these texts as wicked enemies.

I think most interpreters would agree that the enemies are painted in rather broad strokes and so are difficult to identify with any specificity. The descriptions also vary from psalm to psalm. Most scholars would suggest

---

has always cherished the Older Testament also as part of the Christian Scriptures. There is irony in dedicating to a friend an essay on enemies, but I would suggest that the texts on enemies and evildoers in the Psalter actually commend to us the hope of friendship. My thanks to Chwi-Woon Kim for his editorial assistance with this essay.

3. Bellinger, *Psalms*, 17.
4. Mowinckel, *Psalmenstudien I*.
5. Kraus, *Psalms 1–59*, 99.
6. Schmidt, *Das Gebet des Angeklagten*; Beyerlin, *Die Rettung der Bedrängten*.
7. Birkeland, *Die Feinde des Individuums*; Birkeland, *Evildoers in the Book of Psalms*. This view is also an implication of John Eaton's interpretation of many complaint psalms as royal texts (*Kingship and the Psalms*).
8. Gunkel, *Introduction to the Psalms*, 121–98.

that the enemies in the individual complaint psalms are different from those in the community complaints. In some individual complaints, the enemies are characterized as false accusers and in others as those who mock those who are perceived to be under divine judgment. There does not seem to be one single answer to the question of the identity of the enemies in the Hebrew Psalter. George W. Anderson uses the terms "conventional monotony" and "confusing variety" in describing the psalms' portrayal of the enemies.[9] In addition, these poetic texts use a variety of images to portray the enemies. Lions, bulls, wild oxen, and dogs are but some of the animal images used (e.g., Ps 22:12–13, 16–21). Other psalms use images of hunters seeking to catch their prey or images of a besieging army. With poetic imagery like that, it is no wonder that it is difficult to identify these characters with any precision. The opponents become representatives of the power of Sheol, the realm of the dead. Death has invaded life and diminished it in some way. These opponents are part of that trouble and woe for the petitioners in the Psalms. These issues have long troubled Psalms scholars but I would suggest that it is the open poetic language that makes the complaint psalms adaptable for life and its many contexts of trouble and woe and so available for continued use by communities of faith through the centuries.

This brief survey of scholarship on the enemies reflects the standard form-critical view in Kraus's summary excursus on the enemies.[10] The first matter in his list is the distinction between enemies of the nation and foes of individual petitioners. Similar terms are used to identify both. External enemies are forces of death for both the community and for individuals. In some cases, the opponents are false accusers and persecutors who seek to manipulate the poor and powerless, oppressors and extortioners of the poor. These enemies are people in ancient Israel and represent death and oppression. Those who are persecuted seek divine justice. Their opponents are wicked people, but the image of the opponents moves beyond that to a stereotypical image of evil and opposition to the divine. This stereotypical image points to the opposite of the poor and righteous person.

Scholars have sought the identity of enemies in the Psalter and have done so in a global way often tied to the genre of complaint psalms. I want to take a bit of a different tack and look at the particular terms and texts characterizing the enemies in Book V to see what we might discover about these characters in the concluding book of the Psalter.

---

9. Anderson, "Enemies and Evildoers," 18–21.
10. Kraus, *Psalms 1–59*, 95–99.

Enemies in Book V

The lengthy fifth book of Psalms is comprised of several clusters of psalms (Pss 107–10; 111–18; 119; 120–37; 138–45; 146–50). This list takes into account the collections determined by superscriptions. Psalms 146–50 serve as the five-fold doxology to close the Hebrew Psalter. Every cluster includes occurrences of terms for enemies/evildoers; the primary terms are צר, איב, and רשע. These terms are no respecters of genre. Hymns, complaints, royal psalms, and wisdom psalms all use the terms. In psalms of praise, terms for enemies appear in sections that recount past salvific acts of YHWH (107:2; 136:24), express confidence in deliverance from enemies by YHWH (138:7), and praise YHWH's defeat of the wicked (146:9; 147:6). Psalm 139, often taken to be a hymn, petitions God to remove the wicked. Individual complaint psalms characterize the lamenter's accusers as wicked. Psalm 109 is an individual imprecatory psalm against enemies characterized as wicked. Psalm 140 pleads for deliverance from the wicked, and the crisis in Psalm 143 is closely related to "my enemies." Communal complaint Pss 123 and 137 use other terms to refer to enemies and evildoers. Psalm 108 refers to an enemy of the community. Royal Pss 110 and 132 use איב to name the king's enemies from whom YHWH brings deliverance. Enemies oppose the righteous and YHWH's instruction in the wisdom texts of Pss 112, 119, and 127.

We need to consider the terms for enemies and evildoers in the context of the poetics of Book V. The book begins with the context of return from exile, as elucidated in the conclusion of Ps 106 (see v. 47) and the opening of Ps 107:

> O give thanks to the Lord, for he is good; for his steadfast love endures forever.
>
> Let the redeemed of the Lord say so, those he redeemed from trouble
>
> and gathered in from the lands,
>
> from the east and from the west, from the north and from the south. (vv. 1–3)

The term translated "trouble" in v. 2 of the NRSV is more specifically "the hand of the foe." The root צרר is used to characterize trouble and woe. It connotes something oppressive and constricting. That may well be the reference in v. 2 but it may also speak of the power of the enemy in the "hand of the oppressor." Similar language is used in vv. 6 and 39 to characterize distress or trouble. The psalm reflects on a variety of distresses from which YHWH has delivered; the language suggests the connotation of a community under oppression and is tied to exile and return. The foe of the community is identified with the same term in Ps 108:13–14. God is the trustworthy one who delivers from such oppression. The participial form איב suggests those who act with hate or enmity and so adversaries. Psalm 110:1–2 uses the term to refer to the king's (and YHWH's) enemies as those who will be defeated. This first cluster of psalms suggests that the trouble is oppression by the community's foes. The exception is Ps 109 which is a parade example of an imprecation from an individual who has been accused by those characterized as wicked (רשע):

> For wicked and deceitful mouths are opened against me,
>
> speaking against me with lying tongues. They beset me with words of hate. (vv. 2–3)

The hope articulated by the petitioner is that the enemies will in turn be tried by a "wicked" accuser (שט, v. 6) and found guilty. The judgment sought is fairly described as brutal. Psalms 111–18 and the extensive meditation on Torah in Ps 119 and the Songs of Ascents (Pss 120–34) all reflect some wisdom elements including the contrast between the wise and the foolish or the righteous and the wicked (Pss 112:8, 10; 119:53, 61, 95, 98, 110, 119, 139, 155, 157; 127:5). Psalm 119 exhibits some connections to individual complaint psalms. The characterization of the enemies as wicked casts them in contrast to the Torah piety demonstrated by the speaker. In the didactic texts Pss 112 and 119, צר and רשע are used for foes of the righteous (Pss 112:8; 119:139, 157); the enemies oppress those who practice Torah piety. The feminine form of the noun (צרה) is used to describe enemies in Ps 138:7 parallel to איב, though the term could refer to the enmity or oppression itself. The term רשע occurs in Book V nearly as often as צר and איב put together, seventeen times. The term is usually rendered in English as "wicked."

In a recently completed dissertation, Kim Williams Bodenhamer describes the Songs of Ascents and Pss 135–37 appended to that collection in the following way:

> In the shaping of Pss 120–37, we see a movement toward memory. In the final psalm of the group, Psalm 137, YHWH and the people are joined in the task of remembering. For the people, the task is to remember Zion. For YHWH, it is to remember the enemies of Zion. The image of the servant, situated in the household of YHWH, moves from the periphery to the center, from the margins to the place of worship. The height of the

collection is in the remembrance of place, done most effectively through song.[11]

Enemies oppose the move to the center, the place of worship and memory and blessing.

The final Davidic collection (Pss 138–45) includes portrayals of the enemies. Oppressive enemies (איב and רשע) are at hand (Pss 138:7–8; 143:3, 9, 12). Psalm 139 begins with beautiful language of praise but in its last section of petition, the psalm uses צר, איב, and רשע to ask for severe judgment upon the enemies of YHWH who have also become the enemies of the psalmist, who hates the enemies with complete hatred. Psalms 140 and 141 also complain about the wicked. Psalm 143 is an individual complaint in which adversaries crush the life of the petitioner and bring considerable oppression. The psalm moves toward a more hopeful conclusion. The enemies are characterized with open poetic language, again making the text adaptable for use in a variety of life settings.

The Psalter's five-fold concluding doxology also reflects the presence of enemies with "the way of the wicked" in Ps 146:9 and the characterization of YHWH as one who "casts the wicked to the ground" in Ps 147:6.

This look at the enemies depends mostly on language in individual complaint psalms. In Book V it is also important to recognize the presence of ancient Israel's traditional enemies. In Pss 135–37 traditions of exodus, wilderness wandering, and emergence in the land are littered with references to Egypt,[12] Og, Sihon, and the idols of the nations as those who oppose YHWH and the faith community of ancient Israel. The foes of Edom and Babylon are singled out for bone-chilling beatitudes to bring brutal justice upon them. The Songs of Ascents begin with the opposition of Meschech and Kedar, whoever that might be (Ps 120). Of particular note is the conclusion of Ps 149 in which those who are praising YHWH also "have two-edged swords in their hands" to execute judgment on the nations, a troubling reference indeed.

A Context for Book V

One of the recent volumes that brings these things together in helpful ways is Dennis Tucker's *Constructing and Deconstructing Power in Psalms 107–150*.[13] The central claim of the study is that Book V of the Psalter asserts

---

11. Bodenhamer, "Yahweh, Remember!," 174–75.
12. Along with Egypt in Ps 114 of the Egyptian Hallel.
13. Tucker, *Constructing and Deconstructing Power*.

the only reliable power for the ancient reading community of Book V is YHWH the creator. That claim requires a deconstructing of the ideology of the Archaemenid Dynasty that Ahuramazda, the god of earth and heaven, had placed all nations under Cyrus, Cambyses, and Darius. The empire's conquering "secures cosmic order" and thus "joyful participation by the conquered peoples."[14] The benefits of order come to the peoples. Book V of the Psalter asserts that YHWH is the God of heaven and casts the empire as an oppressive power subjugating the community in Jehud following the Babylonian exile. This community is hardly joyfully participating in cosmic order brought by the empire. Tucker thus reads Book V in the context of the Persian Era. The enemies in Book V then become representatives of the empire. Here Tucker follows the scholarly tradition of Birkeland (and Mowinckel) in identifying the enemies as foreign oppressors.[15]

The context of Book V is crucial for this identification of the enemies. Tucker characterizes the book's introductory psalm (Ps 107) as "a didactic meditation on Israel's deliverance out of exile."[16] We will see that the enemy in this text is portrayed as "the hand of צר," that is the power (hand) of Israel's political and military enemies. צר is an inherently political term and so rendering it as "distress," as a number of English translations do is inadequate at best. The oppressive threat of the צר in the empire continues in the first collection of psalms in Book V. Psalm 109, commonly interpreted as an individual complaint and imprecatory psalm, takes on a secondary use of complaint about oppression of a powerless people. Psalm 110 speaks of divine victory over the threatening powers. The Hallel of Pss 111–18 speaks of empires and enemy nations of past and present in negative terms. The Songs of Ascents portray the context of the community in terms of oppression from foreign powers. Psalms 135–37 also recount the oppression of foreign empires and nations. Especially in the imprecatory Psalm 137, the power of empire does not bring the joyous participation in cosmic order by conquered people but rather brings weeping and extreme complaint.

The final Davidic collection of psalms continues to complain of enemies and evildoers against the petitioners. Tucker understands Pss 138 and 144 to contextualize a secondary use of these traditions in terms of the oppression of imperial power. The final Hallel concluding the Psalter

---

14. Ibid., 53.

15. Ibid., 12–15. I need to indicate that I find in Birkeland a kind of "patternism" in which a preconceived notion of enemies from community complaints is applied to individual complaints and the enemies there. I am more inclined to the separation of the portrayal of enemies and evildoers in community psalms and those in individual psalms.

16. Ibid., 59.

continues the emphasis on the deconstruction of imperial power and hope in YHWH only.

This view of the enemies and evildoers in Book V is most helpful in giving a context for understanding their identity and function. The enemies are political enemies in the context of the Persian Empire. I am inclined to agree with this context for Book V. I do not think the enemies and evildoers carry the same identity or function in every psalm in the fifth book, but I think Tucker, following Erich Zenger,[17] has rightly identified the background setting. It is an important piece of the puzzle.

Theological Perspectives

I want to spend the rest of my time considering the issue of these enemies and evildoers from the perspective of theology and hermeneutics. I mention two publications as resources. The first is Aran J. E. Persaud's *Praying the Language of Enmity in the Psalter: A Study of Psalms 110, 119, 129, 137, 139 and 149*. Even the title I find interesting. Persaud, from Ryle Theological College in Ottawa, Canada, writes as a theologian of the church and attempts to deal with the issue that Christians understandably have struggled with the prayer against enemies in the Psalter. They have resisted appropriating these texts which seem to conflict with "more peaceful" sayings in both the Older Testament and in the teachings of Jesus ("Love your enemies") as well as the modern sensibilities of contemporary readers of the Psalms. I have already indicated that I agree with Persaud that the imprecatory elements of the Psalms are not limited to complaint psalms, a view clearly reflected in his choice of texts. All of the psalms treated are in Book V, and so the study is relevant to my concerns. Persaud proceeds with a translation and fairly standard exegesis of each psalm. He then summarizes the treatments of the psalm in Christian theology, including major works from leaders of the Early Church and from Reformers. He then compares this historical theology and the exegesis to see what conclusions he can articulate. I am not enamored with this procedure. While I occasionally find helpful tidbits from pre-modern interpreters, I operate primarily from modern and post-modern bases. At the same time, I find some of Persaud's articulations of the issues to be helpful.

He labels the portrayals of the enemies as the "language" or "grammar" of evil. "Blood and violence, war atrocities such as the killing of little ones, murder, hatred, battlefields, and corpses heaped up are part of this language. Praying the language of enmity is really praying the 'language'

---

17. Zenger, "Der jüdische Psalter," 95–108.

or 'grammar' of evil."[18] Persaud understands the texts on the enemies to be important articulations of evil in the world in prayers that have the underlying purpose of seeking divine justice.[19] These psalms are then examples of ancient theodical texts in the form of protest to God rather than theoretical explanations of the ways of God.[20] This grammar of enmity seems even more relevant in our age of terrorism. This view of the psalmic imprecations as articulations of evil in the world in some ways reminds me of Gerald Sheppard's suggestion that since the enemies are also members of the same community as the petitioners in the psalms, the imprecations serve as a warning to the opponents.[21]

A more familiar and more helpful volume on the issue is Erich Zenger's.[22] He also is of the view that we ought not in a Marcionite way remove or avoid these difficult texts. He says

> We have suppressed in our Christian consciousness the idea that judgment is for the sake of justice, especially for those who are the victims of injustice, and that the purpose of this judgment is to restore everything "as it should be"—even to confront the wicked with their injustice in such a way that they honor justice through their repentance.[23]

A further clue to his approach comes when Zenger characterizes Ps 137 as

> an attempt, in the face of the most profound humiliation and helplessness, to suppress the primitive human lust for violence in one's own heart, by surrendering *everything* to God—a God whose word of judgment is presumed to be so universally just that even those who pray the psalm submit themselves to it.[24]

So both Zenger and Persaud take the imprecatory psalms to be prayers for divine justice and to be prayers that submit the issue to YHWH. Clint McCann goes so far as to say of Ps 109:

> The anger is expressed, but it is expressed in prayer and thereby submitted to God. While it is not explicit, we may assume that the psalmist's submission of anger to God in prayer was sufficient

18. Persaud, *Praying the Language of Enmity*, 193.
19. Ibid., 215.
20. Ibid., 196; see Bellinger, "Psalter as Theodicy Writ Large," 147–60.
21. See Sheppard, "'Enemies' and the Politics of Prayer," 71–73, 81.
22. Zenger, *God of Vengeance?*
23. Ibid., 64.
24. Ibid., 48 (italics original).

(see vv. 21, 27). This angry, honest prayer thus removes the necessity for the psalmist to take actual revenge upon the enemy. It seems that the psalmist honors God's affirmation in Deut 32:35, "Vengeance is mine" (NRSV; see also Psalm 94). Thus this vehement, violent-sounding prayer is, in fact, an act of nonviolence.[25]

Others suggest that serious contemplation of the enemies in the imprecations could well bring the conclusion that we, the reading community, often act as oppressors and representatives of evil empires.[26] Nancy deClaissé-Walford[27] and Joel LeMon[28] provide brief but helpful surveys of the various approaches to the imprecatory psalms that avoid the tendencies effectively to remove them from the church's biblical canon. LeMon suggests that a community is central as a check on the interpretation of these texts as contemporary prayers and scriptural texts. That is an important piece of the puzzle but it also does not solve the matter. LeMon's essay makes clear the risks in praying these psalms in our world with its violence and harsh language. I heartily commend struggling with these texts as canonical Scripture and as part of the church's liturgical tradition. To do so, however, is a risky business.

I draw some conclusions about the imprecatory psalms.

1. Enemies pervade the Psalms and persist in the pilgrimage of faith. Even the instruction to love your enemies suggests that enmity is part of faith.
2. The Psalms' imprecations are in the context of prayer and in particular of the covenant dialogue of faith. In these texts Israel holds YHWH accountable to act as the powerful covenant God on behalf of a powerless community.
3. The context of Book V as an anti-imperial collection suggests that the speakers of these imprecatory psalms come from a context of powerlessness in the face of imperial power.
4. As Book V moves toward the conclusion of the Psalter with an emphasis on praise, complaint is still seriously present, and language of imprecation seems to become even more passionate.
5. As I think about the enemies and evildoers in Book V, it seems to me that the best analogues in our world are hierarchies that powerfully

---

25. McCann, "Book of Psalms," 1127.
26. LeMon, "Saying Amen to Violent Psalms," 101–2.
27. DeClaissé-Walford, "Theology of the Imprecatory Psalms," 77–92.
28. LeMon, "Saying Amen to Violent Psalms," 93–109.

oppress those in great need, whether it be the current American administration or terrorist organizations or other violent and repressive regimes in power around our globe or institutions that use people in oppressive ways.

I believe it important to let these difficult texts stand in all their oddness as part of the Christian canon of Scripture and to struggle responsibly and thoughtfully with them. Still we must remember that prayer and proclamation based on these texts may be heard as words of hate and violence since we live in a time characterized by extreme hate speech and terrorism, the realities these imprecations portray. Congregations that embrace the critical and charitable study of these texts in their historical, literary, and theological contexts may be one of the only contexts to make it possible to emerge from such darkness.[29]

Works Cited

Anderson, George W. "Enemies and Evildoers in the Book of Psalms." *BJRL* 48 (1965) 18–29.
Bellinger, W. H., Jr. *Psalms: A Guide to Studying the Psalter*. 2nd ed. Grand Rapids: Baker Academic, 2012.
———. "The Psalter as Theodicy Writ Large." In *Jewish and Christian Approaches to the Psalms: Conflict and Convergence*, edited by Susan Gillingham, 147–60. Oxford: Oxford University Press, 2013.
Beyerlin, W. *Die Rettung der Bedrängten in den Feindpsalmen der Einzelnen auf institutionelle Zusammenhänge untersucht*. Göttingen: Vandenhoeck & Ruprecht, 1970.
Birkeland, Harris. *The Evildoers in the Book of Psalms*. Olso: Dybwad, 1955.
———. *Die Feinde des Individuums in der israelitischen Psalmenliteratur*. Oslo: Grøndahl & Søn Forlag, 1933.
Bodenhamer, Kim Williams. "'Yahweh, Remember!': Place, Memory, and Ritual in Psalms 120–137." PhD diss., Baylor University, 2017.
DeClaissé-Walford, Nancy L. "The Theology of the Imprecatory Psalms." In *Soundings in the Theology of Psalms: Perspectives and Methods in Contemporary Scholarship*, edited by Rolf A. Jacobson, 77–92. Minneapolis: Fortress, 2011.
Eaton, John H. *Kingship and the Psalms*. SBT 2/32. London: SCM, 1976.
Gunkel, Hermann. *Introduction to the Psalms: The Genres of the Religious Lyric of Israel*. Completed by Joachim Begrich. Translated by James D. Nogalski. MLBS. Macon: Mercer University Press, 1998.
Kraus, Hans-Joachim. *Psalms 1–59: A Continental Commentary*. Translated by Hilton C. Oswald. Minneapolis: Fortress, 1989.
LeMon, Joel M. "Saying Amen to Violent Psalms: Patterns of Prayer, Belief, and Action in the Psalter." In *Soundings in the Theology of Psalms: Perspectives and Methods*

---

29. See especially DeClaissé-Walford, "The Theology of the Imprecatory Psalms."

in Contemporary Scholarship, edited by Rolf A. Jacobson, 93–109. Minneapolis: Fortress, 2011.

McCann, J. Clinton., Jr. "The Book of Psalms." In *NIB*, 4:641–1280.

Mowinckel, S. *Psalmenstudien I. Åwän und die individuellen Klagepsalmen*. Kristiania: Dybwad, 1921.

Persaud, Aran J. E. *Praying the Language of Enmity in the Psalter: A Study of Psalms 110, 119, 129, 137, 139, and 149*. Eugene, OR: Wipf & Stock, 2016.

Schmidt, Hans. *Das Gebet des Angeklagten im Alten Testament*. BZAW 49. Giessen: Töpelmann,1928.

Sheppard, Gerald T. "'Enemies' and the Politics of Prayer in the Book of Psalms." In *The Bible and the Politics of Exegesis: Essays in Honor of Norman K. Gottwald on His Sixty-fifth Birthday*, edited by David Jobling et al., 61–82 Cleveland: Pilgrim, 1991.

Tucker, W. Dennis, Jr. *Constructing and Deconstructing Power in Psalms 107–150*. AIL 19. Atlanta: Society of Biblical Literature, 2014.

Westermann, Claus. *Praise and Lament in the Psalms*. Translated by Keith R. Crim and Richard N. Soulen. Atlanta: John Knox, 1981.

Zenger, Erich. *A God of Vengeance? Understanding the Psalms of Divine Wrath*. Translated by Linda M. Maloney. Louisville: Westminster John Knox, 1996.

———. "Der jüdische Psalter—ein anti-imperiales Buch?" In *Religion und Gesellschaft: Studien zu ihrer Wechselbeziehung in den Kulturen des Antiken Vorderen Orients*, edited by Rainer Albertz, 95–108. Veröffentlichungen des Arbeitskreises zur Erforschung der Religions-und Kulturgeschichte des Antiken Vorderen Orients 1 / AOAT 248. Münster: Ugarit, 1997.

Matthew's "Messianization" of Mark

Lidija Novakovic

Introduction

MATTHEW'S USE OF MARK has received increased attention in contemporary Matthean scholarship. This concern goes back to redaction-critical studies of the Gospel of Matthew, but the main interest has shifted from Matthew's editorial techniques and his particular theology to the overall purpose of Matthew's rewritten version of Mark's narrative. It is possible to distinguish two major interpretations of Matthew's editorial aims. On the one hand, the evangelist could be seen as a fairly conservative redactor whose main purpose was to expand and supplement Mark's narrative with additional information available to him, such as Jesus's sayings and the special Matthean material. On the other hand, Matthew could be seen as a critical editor who wanted to correct and ultimately replace the Markan narrative.

One of the best-known representatives of the first view is Ulrich Luz. He argues that Matthew added a largely untouched Markan narrative to the saying tradition available to his circle and concludes that Matthew's "story renarrates a *given* story. There are no indications in Matthew's Gospel (as has been suggested for Luke) that he intended his new story to replace the Markan Gospel with which, as evidenced here and there, he assumed at least some of his readers to be familiar."[1] A similar assessment of Matthew's purpose can be found in the published dissertation of J. Andrew Doole, which seeks to demonstrate Matthew's continuity with Mark. Doole concedes that Matthew frequently altered his sources, but he nevertheless insists that "[i]t is essential that the evidence gathered from Matthew's additions, omissions,

---

1. Luz, *Studies in Matthew*, 35. See also Davies and Allison, *Matthew*, 1:95–96; Beaton, "How Matthew Writes," 120; O'Leary, *Matthew's Judaization of Mark*, 112.

and amendments be considered only in the broader context of Matthew's loyalty to Mark whose tradition he inherits."[2]

A major proponent of the second view is David C. Sim. In his response to Bauckham's proposal that the evangelists wrote their Gospels for a broad Christian audience rather than for their specific communities,[3] Sim contends that "Matthew and Luke clearly believed that Mark was wrong on a number of significant points, so they radically altered Mark's text in order to conform it to their own very different perspectives."[4] In another article that addresses the question of whether Matthew intended to supplement or to replace his primary sources, Sim argues that Matthew identified "serious failings" in Mark's Gospel, such as "its crude language, short length, offensive features and the fact that Mark was simply inadequate to meet the very different needs of Matthew's own Jewish Christian community towards the end of the first century. . . . Whatever value Matthew placed on Mark, he still viewed it as an inadequate presentation of Jesus' story that required correction, improvement and expansion, and which needed to be updated to meet the needs of his intended readership."[5] Other scholars have expressed similar considerations. Jesper Svartvik alleges that "Matthew not only regarded Mark as *insufficient* and *inadequate*, but also as *inaccurate*. Mark was, according to Matthew, clearly off the mark. . . . Matthew writes his Gospel not only to *insert, enlarge and refine* (as when organizing his material into five speeches), but also to *blot out, diminish and correct* (as when challenging Markan antinomianism)."[6] Matthias Konradt likewise claims that Matthew's rewritten narrative represents a clear critique of the Markan portrayal of Jesus because his redaction is not focused on theological adiaphora but on the aspects "die für Matthäus *Kernthemen* darstellen."[7]

In this essay, I wish to examine Matthew's revisions of the Markan portrayal of Jesus's messianic identity in order to offer support for the view that Matthew wanted to correct Mark's narrative. I will argue that Matthew disagreed with the "unmessianic" character of Mark's portrayal of Jesus's public ministry and sought to amend this deficiency by providing the evidence for Jesus's Davidic messiahship beginning with his birth as "the child who has been born king of the Jews" (Matt 2:2–6) until his crucifixion as "the King of the Jews" (Matt 27:37).

2. Doole, *What Was Mark for Matthew?*, 186.
3. Bauckham, "For Whom Were Gospels Written?" 9–48.
4. Sim, "Gospels for All Christians?" 16.
5. Sim, "Matthew's Use of Mark," 178, 185.
6. Svartvik, "Matthew and Mark," 37 (original emphasis).
7. Konradt, *Studien zum Matthäusevangelim*, 53.

Matthew's "Messianization" of Mark's Portrayal of the Earthly Ministry of Jesus

Most scholars would agree with Eugene Boring that "Matthew writes from the conviction shared by the Christian community then and now that the definitive event in human history is this: God has sent the promised Messiah."[8] What needs to be noted, however, is that Jesus's messiahship is not only the foundational conviction that "lends coherence to the entire narrative"[9] but also its main argument. Matthew does not merely believe that Jesus is the promised Messiah. He also wants to demonstrate it.

Matthew's christological aim stands in tension with our usual reconstructions of christological developments in primitive Christianity. Nils Dahl has repeatedly emphasized that the confession of Jesus as the Messiah is the presupposition of New Testament Christology, not its content. He bases this conclusion on the evidence from Greek-speaking Christian communities, which shows that "within a few years of the crucifixion, the name Christ as applied to Jesus must have been firmly established. This presupposes that Jesus was already designated 'the Messiah' and 'Jesus the Messiah' in the Aramaic-speaking regions. To this extent the Christology of the primitive community from the very first must have been a Messiah-Christology."[10]

Martin Hengel has similarly argued that "the striking pre-eminence of the Christ name (or title) in the letters, that is, outside the Gospels, in which the linguistic usage of the earthly Jesus has left more trace than is commonly recognized, can only be explained if from the beginning—indeed, especially *at the beginning*—it was fundamental for the post-Easter community."[11] Hengel's comment is especially helpful because it makes a distinction between the letters and the Gospels. One should not be surprised, it seems, if the Gospels emphasize Jesus's messianic identity because they belong to the genre of ancient biographies, i.e., their subject is the life of Jesus. But, a closer look at Mark's narrative reveals that this is not what the author of our earliest Gospel has done. Mark, like Paul, puts great emphasis on Jesus's death.[12] Following Martin Kähler's suggestion, the Gospel

---

8. Boring, "Matthew's Narrative Christology," 356 (original emphasis).
9. Davies and Allison, *Matthew*, 3:718.
10. Dahl, *Crucified Messiah and Other Essays*, 25.
11. Hengel, *Studies in Early Christology*, 10 (original emphasis).
12. There is a growing recognition of Paul's influence on Mark in recent Markan studies; see Goulder, "Those Outside (Mk. 4.10–12)," 289–302; Painter, *Mark's Gospel*, 4–6; Telford, *Theology of the Gospel of Mark*, 164–69; Marcus, "Mark—Interpreter of Paul," 473–87; Marcus, *Mark 1–8*, 73–75; Svartvik, "Matthew and Mark," 30–34. For a more cautious view of Paul's possible influence on Mark, see Crossley, "Mark, Paul, and

of Mark is frequently described as "a passion narrative with an extended introduction."[13] Indeed, the centrality of Jesus's death in Mark is undeniable. Moreover, Mark, like Paul, acknowledges "that the proclamation of a crucified Messiah is scandalous and contrary-to-sense because it calls on human beings to see God's eschatological power, life, and glory displayed in a scene of the starkest human weakness, degradation, and death."[14]

One of the most remarkable features of Mark's passion narrative, which expresses the scandalous character of the crucified Messiah, is that it is dominated by royal imagery. Donald Juel has nicely articulated the significance of this aspect of Mark's presentation of Jesus's death:

> [T]he charge against Jesus that he is "the King of the Jews" ... is interesting for several reasons. For one thing, it absolutely dominates the account of Jesus' trial and death.... Jesus is tried, mocked, and executed as King (whether expressed in Jewish terms as "the Christ, the King of Israel," or in Roman terms as "the King of the Jews"). While others are crucified with Jesus, only he is executed as would-be king. The royal imagery is striking, because of its almost complete absence from Jesus' public ministry. Jesus is identified as "Christ" (King) by no one besides Peter and the disciples (8:29). People observing his ministry draw analogies with prophetic figures like Moses or Elijah—not surprisingly, because Jesus' ministry of teaching with authority and displaying "signs and wonders" is precisely what typified prophets like Elijah and would characterize the ministry of the "prophet like Moses" whose return was expected.... Mark's story makes the point, and it is confirmed by a study of Jewish literature: nothing about Jesus' early ministry indicated that he was the promised Messiah, and the climax of his ministry—his death—would have ruled out the possibility for everyone.[15]

I suggest that for Matthew, the "unmessianic" character of Jesus's earthly ministry was probably one of the most troubling features in his Markan source. It seems that he was content with Mark's emphasis on the absurdity of a crucified Messiah because Matthew's presentation of Jesus's trial and death generally follows Mark. What he modifies, however, is the narrative that precedes Jesus's passion and leads to his crucifixion. The story he narrates is no longer a story in which almost no one except Jesus's closest followers recognizes him as

---

the Question of Influences," 10–29.

13. Kähler, *So-Called Historical Jesus*, 80, n. 11.
14. Marcus, "Mark—Interpreter of Paul," 480.
15. Juel, *Gospel of Mark*, 153–54.

the Messiah and in which his messianic identity must be kept secret. Instead, Matthew constructs a narrative which from the very beginning establishes Jesus's messianic credentials and in which multiple characters, even gentiles, recognize him as the Davidic Messiah.

Matthew begins his Gospel with the genealogy of Jesus (1:2–17) and its "enlarged footnote" (1:18–25)[16] that seek to explain how Jesus, whose mother Mary "was found to be with child from the Holy Spirit" (1:18), became "engrafted" into the Davidic lineage. Matthew significantly expanded the number of instances in which Jesus is called the "Son of David." While in Mark this title appears only twice—on the lips of blind Bartimaeus before Jesus's triumphal entry to Jerusalem (Mark 10:46–52) and in the question about David's son (Mark 12:35–37)—the same title occurs ten times in Matthew (1:1; 9:27; 12:23; 15:22; 20:30, 31; 21:9, 14; 22:42, 45). Apart from the infancy narrative in Matt 1 and the dialogue about the Davidic sonship of the Messiah in 22:41–46, all other occurrences of the title "Son of David" are found almost exclusively in the healing contexts (the only exception is 21:1–11). On several occasions, Jesus is either addressed by the messianic title "Son of David" when the sick approach him asking for a cure (Matt 9:27–31; 15:21–28; 20:29–34), or his healings provoke a question concerning his messianic identity: "Can this be the Son of David?" (Matt 12:22–24). In Matt 21:14–16, Jesus's identity as the Son of David is recognized by the children after he healed the blind and the lame in the temple. The citation of Ps 8:3 ("Out of the mouths of infants and nursing babies you have prepared praise for yourself"), which Matthew adds to the episode, unambiguously confirms the validity of the children's conclusion and interprets it as a revelation from God.

Matthew takes pains to demonstrate that Jesus's healing miracles have a messianic character.[17] He achieves this goal not only by adding the title "Son of David" to the healing accounts that he takes over (15:21–28), expands (9:27–31; 20:29–34), or adds to his Markan source (12:22–24; 21:14–16), but also by inserting the phrase "the deeds of the Messiah" (τὰ ἔργα τοῦ χριστοῦ) into the Q-episode about John the Baptist, who heard about Jesus's miracles but could not conclusively perceive their messianic significance (Matt 11:2–6; cf. Luke 7:18–23). John's question, "Are you the one who is to come, or are we to wait for another" (Matt 11:2), which he asks after hearing the reports about Jesus's miracles, confirms what we otherwise know from Second Temple literature: the Messiah was not expected to be a wonderworker. Matthew's insistence to the contrary is intelligible only in light of

---

16. Stendahl, "Quis et Unde?" 61.
17. Cf. Novakovic, *Messiah*, 77–123.

Matthew's messianic reinterpretation of the Jewish Scriptures. Jesus's answer to the question of John the Baptist alludes to several salvific oracles from Isaiah, such as Isa 26:19, 29:18, 35:5–6, and 61:1, to show that they are applicable to Jesus's career and are to be read messianically.[18]

Whereas Matthew regularly supports Jesus's claim to messiahship by scriptural quotations or allusions (8:16–17; 12:15–21),[19] he also wants to explain why most of the Jews remained oblivious to or outright rejected Jesus's messianic claim. One of the answers he gives is that they were willfully and spiritually blind (15:12–14; 23:16–26). This is why blindness is the most frequent illness that Jesus heals in his capacity as the Davidic Messiah (9:27–31; 12:22–24; 20:29–34; 21:14–16).[20] The metaphor of blindness reinforces the plausibility of Matthew's narrative, because the rejection of Jesus by the Jewish leaders, whose scriptural knowledge was generally affirmed, would otherwise have remained enigmatic to the Christian reader/auditor. When one reads/audits Matthew's narrative of Jesus's life, which shows time and again how Jesus's contemporaries remained spiritually blind, the absurdity of Jesus's messianic claim, even as he dies on the cross, disappears. In Matthew's presentation, those who mocked Jesus's royal identity were unknowingly—and deeply ironically—expressing the truth.

Matthew's Argument for Jesus's Messiahship in Its Socio-Religious Context

While Matthew's focus on the messianic character of Jesus's earthly ministry might have been prompted by the unevenness of Mark's narrative, the character of his redaction of Mark is not thereby completely explained. There were other solutions to the tension between the "unmessianic" character of Jesus's ministry and the confession of Jesus as the Messiah, which were available to Christian interpreters. One of the earliest answers is preserved in Rom 1:3–4. In this passage, Paul quotes an early Christian confession that juxtaposes Jesus's Davidic origin with his status as the Son of God by virtue of his resurrection. In modern scholarship, these two lines have usually been understood as an expression of a two-stage Christology—a juxtaposition of Jesus's earthly career as a Davidic Messiah with his heavenly reign as a Son of God. It is also generally assumed that the emphasis in the formula falls on the second stage, that is, on Jesus's status as the Son of God since his resurrection from the dead. Eduard Schweizer

---

18. Cf. Grimm, *Weil ich dich liebe*, 124–36; Novakovic, *Messiah*, 159–83.
19. Novakovic, *Messiah*, 124–51.
20. Cf. Loader, "Son of David," 570–85.

speaks for many when he declares that "the earthly existence of the Son of David has clearly been regarded as the lowly first stage which was fulfilled only by exaltation to the Sonship of God."[21]

This interpretation, however, should be reassessed in light of the text's relationship to Israel's Scripture.[22] Most interpreters agree that the first part of the formula ("who was born of the seed of David according to the flesh") refers to God's promise to David in 2 Sam 7:12, while the second part ("who was appointed Son of God in power according to the spirit of holiness") alludes to Ps 2:7.[23] If, however, Ps 2:7 furnishes the scriptural pattern for Rom 1:4, then the designation "Son of God" functions as a messianic title. This further means that Rom 1:3-4 alludes to two principal elements of God's promise to David in 2 Sam 7:12-16—that God will raise up his seed and that this seed will be a son to God. Davidic descent does not establish someone's royal status but merely functions as a genealogical marker specifying the conditions that any claimant to the Davidic throne must fulfill. Dale Allison helpfully points out that "Jewish kings were not born but made."[24] Within the framework of the promise tradition, a Davidide becomes a king at his enthronement as the rightful Davidic heir. For the earliest Christian interpreters, Jesus's resurrection was the moment at which he was installed to the position of the Son of God and thereby became the Messiah.

The connection between Jesus's exalted post-resurrection status and his messianic identity plays a major role in 1 Cor 15:23-28, where Paul outlines the future that has been put in motion with the resurrection of Jesus. Paul appears to focus here on the period between the resurrection of Jesus and the resurrection of believers. His description of this interim period is replete with royal categories. Paul portrays Jesus, who is in this passage consistently called "Christ" (vv. 20, 22, 23), as the ruler of the temporary messianic kingdom who must reign until he destroys all his enemies. This description of Christ's royal status is based on the assumption that at his resurrection Jesus became the messianic king who has since been reigning in his kingdom.[25] The same assumption underlies the elaborate scriptural

---

21. Schweizer, *Lordship and Discipleship*, 59.

22. Cf. Novakovic, *Raised from the Dead*, 138-45.

23. Cf. Hayes, "Resurrection as Enthronement," 337, 340; Dunn, *Christology in the Making*, 34; Whitsett, "Son of God," 676-78; Lövestam, *Son and Savior*, 47.

24. Allison, *Constructing Jesus*, 289.

25. Hill ("Paul's Understanding of Christ's Kingdom," 317) points out that "Paul understands the kingdom of Christ in I Cor 15:24-28 to be Christ's present, cosmic lordship which he exercises from heaven. It does not await the parousia for its inauguration, it is not a kingdom of this world comparable to those anticipated in *4 Ezra* and *2 Baruch*, but began with the resurrection . . . and the accession of God's throne in heaven

arguments in the programmatic speeches of Peter and Paul in Acts 2:22–36 and 13:16–41, which seek to demonstrate the significance of the resurrection of Jesus for his status as the Messiah.[26]

Matthew appears to be familiar with this interpretive tradition because he ends his Gospel with a description of the risen Jesus who appears to his disciples on the mountain in Galilee and declares, "All authority in heaven and on earth has been given to me" (28:18). Davies and Allison assert that "28.18 implies the same conviction that is expressed in several of the NT Christological hymns, namely, that through the resurrection Jesus is exalted and made Lord of the cosmos" and conclude that "Mt 28.16–20 preserves a primitive enthronement Christology."[27]

If, then, Matthew's Gospel betrays the evangelist's familiarity with the link between Jesus's resurrection and his exalted messianic state, why has he transferred the main argument for Jesus's messianic status to his earthly ministry? I suggest that the main reason for this shift in emphasis lies in the polemic between the Matthean community and formative Judaism. No other claim in Matthew's Gospel is met with such hostility by the Jewish leaders as the acknowledgment, or even a suggestion, of his Davidic messiahship. This motif appears in several episodes in which Jesus is identified as the royal Messiah, and all of them are redactional.[28]

The first instance is the reaction of King Herod and "all Jerusalem" to the news about "the child who has been born king of the Jews," delivered to him by wise men from the East (Matt 2:1–3). While Herod's reaction may be plausible, the reaction of "all Jerusalem" is difficult to explain. The news about the birth of the long-expected Messiah should have caused a joyful rather than hostile response of the Jews residing in Jerusalem.

The next example occurs immediately after the first episode that associates the "Son of David" title with the healing motif (Matt 9:27–34). Jesus's healing of two blind men, who cry for help by calling him "Son of David," is followed by his healing of a demoniac, which provokes, on the one hand, the amazement of the crowds and, on the other hand, the accusation by the Pharisees that Jesus casts out the demons by the ruler of the demons.

A similar sequence of events, with an even stronger emphasis on the link between Jesus's healings and his messianic identity, is found in Matt 12:22–30. Because of Matthew's editorial activity, the story of Jesus's healing

---

by the greater son of David."

26. Novakovic, *Raised from the Dead*, 197–215.

27. Davies and Allison, *Matthew*, 3:683.

28. Cf. Stanton, *Gospel for a New People*, 180–85; Stanton, *Studies in Matthew*, 245–46.

of the blind and mute demoniac (vv. 22–24) functions as an introduction to and a cause of the Beelzebul controversy that follows. In his reply to the accusation that he casts out demons with the help of Beelzebul, the ruler of the demons, Jesus persuasively demonstrates that this charge does not make sense (vv. 25–27). Rather, he exorcises by the Spirit of God, and this is taken as a proof that the kingdom of God has arrived and, by extension, that the Pharisees are the ones operating against God and in line with Beelzebul.

The fourth redactional passage is a small scene in the temple that takes place right after Jesus drove out all who were selling and buying in the temple precincts (Matt 21:14–16). Matthew narrates how the chief priests and the scribes became angry when they heard the children's acknowledgment of Jesus as the Son of David.

Matthew's tendency to relate the recognition of Jesus's messianic identity to the persistent opposition of the Jewish leaders seems to be derived from the polemical context of his own day. His account of the bribe and deception perpetrated by the Jewish leaders, who fabricated the story about the theft of Jesus's body by his disciples (Matt 28:11–15), directly connects his story-world to the circumstances of his own community: "And this story is still told among the Jews to this day" (28:15). Even without such explicit clues, however, the hostility of the Jewish leaders, triggered by the acknowledgment of Jesus's messianic identity, cannot be coincidental. But why is it focused so much on the "Son of David" title? Chapter 17 of *Psalms of Solomon*, written most likely after Pompey's conquest of Jerusalem in 63 BCE, is the only pre-Christian Jewish source as well as the earliest Jewish document that applies the titles "Son of David" and χριστός as a *terminus technicus* (i.e., without a modifier) to the future deliverer of Israel. While Matthew's familiarity with this document cannot be established, numerous parallels between Pss. Sol. 17 and his Gospel suggest that both documents share a common messianic conception.[29] By attributing the messianic title "Son of David" to Jesus, Matthew has "messianized" the Markan "unmessianic" Messiah. This theological move was probably caused by the increased prominence of the "Son of David" title in post-70 Judaism, which is indicated by the frequency of this title in rabbinic literature[30] as well as by the objections concerning the plausibility of the Christian claim about Jesus's messiahship by Matthew's Jewish contemporaries.

Another reason for Matthew's focus on the title "Son of David" could have been the widespread association of this designation with the

---

29. Willitts, "Matthew and *Psalms of Solomon*'s Messianism," 27–50.

30. For example, in *b. Sanh.* 97b–99a the rabbis discuss the conditions of the coming of the Son of David, the time when he will come, the names that he will have, and the length of his rule.

traditions about Solomon and his ability to exorcise demons.[31] The notion of Solomon's exorcistic skills developed out of a growing tradition about his extraordinary wisdom. One of the fullest expressions of the blossoming legends of Solomon's wisdom is preserved in Wis 7:5–22. The *locus classicus* of this tradition about Solomon is found in Josephus's *Antiquities* 8.42–49. This is also the only complete account of a Jewish healer from the Second Temple period who performed an exorcism with the help of the exorcistic technique attributed to Solomon. The technique consisted of two principal elements: a special root prescribed by Solomon placed under a seal of a ring and special incantations composed by Solomon. The task of the first element was to drive a demon out of a possessed person and of the second to prevent the demon from returning back to the victim. The only evidence about the magical properties of the seal-rings like the one mentioned in Josephus's account comes from later documents and artifacts, such as the *Testament of Solomon*, Aramaic magical bowls, the Babylonian Talmud, and the *Sepher Ha-Razim*. For all practical purposes, this type of cure is indistinguishable from magic. We do not know whether such traditions were used by Matthew's Jewish contemporaries to portray Jesus as a magician,[32] but it is certainly noteworthy that Matthew "purified" his portrayal of Jesus as a Davidic healer from all the essential elements found in the traditions about Solomon: there is no direct confrontation of Jesus and a demon, no seal-ring, no secret knowledge of how to exorcise demons, no reference to Solomon's name, and no technical language associated with exorcisms. It also seems that Matthew deliberately wished to dissociate Jesus's miraculous healings from exorcistic connotations. In two episodes in which Jesus is asked to heal a person possessed by a demon in his capacity as the Son of David—Matt 12:22-24 and 15:21-28—the verb ἐκβάλλω has been omitted from the Markan material and has been replaced either with the verb θεραπεύω (Matt 12:22) or with the plea for mercy (Matt 15:22). Also, in Matt 15:28, two Markan references to the actual exit of a demon from the girl have been replaced with Jesus's praise of her mother's faith and the report about the momentous healing.

It seems, then, that the main impulse for the shift of Matthew's argument for Jesus's messiahship toward his earthly ministry came from the outside. Mark's Gospel was not only unable to counteract the objections of Matthew's Jewish contemporaries, but his portrayal of the "unmessianic"

---

31. Cf. Fisher, "Can This Be the Son of David?" 82–97; Lövestam, "Jésus Fils de David," 97–109; Berger, "Die königlichen Messiastraditionen," 1–44; Duling, "Solomon, Exorcism, and the Son of David," 235–52; Charlesworth, "Solomon and Jesus," 125–51; Novakovic, *Messiah*, 96–109.

32. This is one of the accusations against Jesus in rabbinic literature (*b. Sanh.* 107b).

ministry of Jesus may have even intensified them. Even if the actual circumstances in which Matthew rewrote Mark's narrative remain elusive, we can still conclude that his version of Jesus's life sought to remedy the deficiencies of the Markan portrayal of Jesus's earthly ministry by demonstrating the veracity of the Christian claim that Jesus was indeed the promised Davidic Messiah.

Concluding Remarks

I have argued that Matthew not only presumes but also wants to demonstrate to his Christian audience that Jesus is the expected Davidic Messiah. To accomplish this goal, he employs several editorial strategies whose purpose is to authenticate the messianic character of Jesus's earthly ministry: (1) he opens his narrative with Jesus's genealogy to establish Jesus's Davidic origin; (2) he removes the secrecy motif from his Markan source and emphasizes the public character of Jesus's messiahship; (3) he presents Jesus's miracles as his distinctive deeds that either provoke speculations about or disclose his messianic identity; and (4) he alludes to or directly quotes Israel's Scripture to demonstrate the messianic character of Jesus's healings.

Matthew revised Mark's narrative so thoroughly because Mark was not able to meet adequately the needs of the evangelist's Jewish Christian community at the end of the first century. I have offered several reasons for his corrections of Mark: (1) the unevenness of Mark's narrative and its inability to explain Jesus's execution as would-be-king; (2) Jewish objections concerning the plausibility of the Christian claim about Jesus's messiahship; and (3) association of Jesus's healings with exorcistic practices and magic deriving from the traditions about Solomon. While it seems unlikely that Matthew's "messianization" of Mark had apologetic purposes, his rewritten narrative could nonetheless be seen as a witness to an ongoing Jewish-Christian polemic about the identity of Jesus and the character of his ministry.

Works Cited

Allison, Dale C., Jr. *Constructing Jesus: Memory, Imagination, and History*. Grand Rapids: Baker Academic, 2010.

Bauckham, Richard. "For Whom Were the Gospels Written?" In *The Gospels for All Christians: Rethinking the Gospel Audiences*, edited by Richard Bauckham, 9–48. Grand Rapids: Eerdmans, 1998.

Beaton, Richard C. "How Matthew Writes." In *The Written Gospel*, edited by Markus Bockmuehl and Donald A. Hagner, 116–34. Cambridge: Cambridge University Press, 2005.

Berger, Klaus. "Die königlichen Messiastraditionen des Neuen Testaments." *NTS* 20 (1973/74) 1–44.

Boring, M. Eugene. "Matthew's Narrative Christology: Three Stories." *Int* 64 (2010) 356–67.

Charlesworth, James H. "Solomon and Jesus: The Son of David in Ante-Markan Traditions (Mark 10:47)." In *Biblical and Humane*, edited by L. B. Elder et al., 125–51. Atlanta: Scholars Press, 1996.

Crossley, James G. "Mark, Paul, and the Question of Influences." In *Paul and the Gospels: Christologies, Conflicts and Convergences*, edited by Michael F. Bird and Joel Willitts, 10–29. LNTS 411. London: T&T Clark, 2011.

Dahl, Nils A. *The Crucified Messiah and Other Essays*. Minneapolis: Augsburg, 1974.

Davies, W. D., and Dale C. Allison Jr. *A Critical and Exegetical Commentary on the Gospel of Matthew*. 3 vols. ICC. London: T&T Clark, 1988.

Doole, J. Andrew. *What Was Mark for Matthew? An Examination of Matthew's Relationship and Attitude to His Primary Source*. WUNT 2/344. Tübingen: Mohr Siebeck, 2013.

Duling, Dennis C. "Solomon, Exorcism, and the Son of David." *HTR* 68 (1975) 235–52.

Dunn, James D. G. *Christology in the Making: A New Testament Inquiry into the Origins of the Doctrine of Incarnation*. 2nd ed. London: SCM, 1989.

Fisher, Loren R. "Can This Be the Son of David?" In *Jesus and the Historian*, edited by F. T. Trotter, 82–97. Philadelphia: Westminster, 1968.

Goulder, Michael D. "Those Outside (Mk. 4.10–12)." *NovT* 33 (1991) 289–302.

Grimm, Werner. *Weil ich dich liebe: Die Verkündigung Jesu und Deuterojesaja*. ANTJ 1. Bern: Herbert Lang, 1976.

Hayes, John H. "The Resurrection as Enthronement and the Earliest Church Christology." *Int* 22 (1968) 333–45.

Hengel, Martin. *Studies in Early Christology*. Edinburgh: T&T Clark, 1995.

Hill, C. E. "Paul's Understanding of Christ's Kingdom in I Corinthians 15:20–28." *NovT* 30 (1988) 297–320.

Juel, Donald H. *The Gospel of Mark*. Interpreting Biblical Texts. Nashville: Abingdon, 1999.

Kähler, Martin. *The So-Called Historical Jesus and the Historic Biblical Christ*. Philadelphia: Fortress, 1964 (1892).

Konradt, Matthias. *Studien zum Matthäusevangelium*. Edited by Alida Euler. Tübingen: Mohr Siebeck, 2016.

Loader, William R. G. "Son of David, Blindness, Possession, and Duality in Matthew." *CBQ* 44 (1982) 570–85.

Lövestam, Evald. "Die Davidssohnfrage." *SEÅ* 27 (1962) 72–82.

———. "Jésus Fils de David chez les Synoptiques." *ST* 28 (1974) 97–109.

———. *Son and Savior: A Study of Acts 13,32–37. With an Appendix: "Son of God" in the Synoptic Gospels*. Lund: Gleerup, 1961.

Luz, Ulrich. *Studies in Matthew*. Translated by Rosemary Selle. Grand Rapids: Eerdmans, 2005.

Marcus, Joel. *Mark 1–8: A New Translation with Introduction and Commentary*. AB 27. New Haven: Yale University Press, 1999.

———. "Mark—Interpreter of Paul." *NTS* 46 (2000) 473–87.

Novakovic, Lidija. *Messiah, the Healer of the Sick: A Study of Jesus as the Son of David in the Gospel of Matthew*. WUNT 2/170. Tübingen: Mohr Siebeck, 2003.

———. *Raised from the Dead according to Scripture: The Role of Israel's Scripture in the Early Christian Interpretations of Jesus' Resurrection.* Jewish and Christian Texts 12. London: Bloomsbury T&T Clark, 2012.
O'Leary, Anne M. *Matthew's Judaization of Mark: Examined in the Context of the Use of Sources in Graeco-Roman Antiquity.* LNTS 323. London: T&T Clark, 2006.
Painter, John. *Mark's Gospel: Worlds in Conflict.* New Testament Readings. London: Routledge, 1997.
Schweizer, Eduard. *Lordship and Discipleship.* SBT 28. London: SCM, 1960.
Sim, David C. "The Gospels for All Christians? A Response to Richard Bauckham." *JSNT* 84 (2001) 3–27.
———. "Matthew's Use of Mark: Did Matthew Intend to Supplement or to Replace His Primary Source?" *NTS* 57 (2011) 176–92.
Stanton, Graham. *A Gospel for a New People: Studies in Matthew.* Edinburgh: T&T Clark, 1992.
———. *Studies in Matthew and Early Christianity.* Edited by Markus Bockmuehl and David Lincicum. WUNT 309. Tübingen: Mohr Siebeck, 2013.
Stendahl, Krister. "Quis et Unde? An Analysis of Matthew 1–2." In *Judentum, Urchristentum, Kirche: Festschrift für Joachim Jeremias*, edited by Walther Eltester, 94–105. BZNW 26. Berlin: Alfred Töpelmann, 1960.
Svartvik, Jesper. "Matthew and Mark." In *Matthew and His Christian Contemporaries*, edited by David C. Sim and Boris Repschinski, 27–49. LNTS 333. London: T&T Clark, 2008.
Telford, William R. *The Theology of the Gospel of Mark.* Cambridge: Cambridge University Press, 1999.
Whitsett, Christopher G. "Son of God, Seed of David: Paul's Messianic Exegesis in Romans 1:3–4." *JBL* 119 (2000) 661–81.
Willitts, Joel. "Matthew and *Psalms of Solomon*'s Messianism: A Comparative Study in First-Century Messianology." *BBR* 22 (2012) 27–50.

St. Peter's Crisis of Faith at Harvard

The Scarsellino Picture and Matthew 14

Heidi J. Hornik[1]

Ippolito Scarsella (1550–1620), commonly known by his contemporaries and friends as Scarsellino, was a Ferrarese artist, heavily influenced by his Venetian training, who produced Post-Trent religious paintings in the Mannerist style. Considered amongst the "Reformers" in late sixteenth-century Italy, his theological iconography anticipates the Baroque style of the next century. *Christ and Saint Peter at the Sea of Galilee* (fig. 1), the subject of this paper, is located in the Harvard Art Museums in Cambridge.[2] The connoisseurship issues of the painting, including its attribution to Scarsellino, and the dating of the painting will be discussed. This is among the first publications that discuss this painting as a Scarsellino work. Through a comparison with other scenes of walking on water, the form and content of the picture will be discussed using an art historical methodology with a theological bent, attending to the commentaries and doctrinal sources that may have influenced Scarsellino at this time in the history of religious art.

---

1. This paper is the product of a 2017 Visiting Scholar Fellowship in-residence at Harvard University and a Baylor University Research Leave for the spring 2017 semester. I also thank Deans Lee Nordt, Robin Driskell, Kimberly Kellison, and Professor and Chair Mark Anderson for their continued support of my work through research travel and financial support. An Allbritton Grant for Faculty Scholarship 2017–18 provided the funding for the copyright permissions to illustrate the paintings. I am pleased to contribute this essay to a volume honoring my colleague and friend, Naymond Keathley.

2. I express my appreciation to Heather Linton, Division of European and American Art, for making it possible for me to review the curatorial files on this painting at the Harvard Art Museums.

Figure 1: Scarsellino (Ippolito Scarsella) (c. 1550–1620). Christ and Saint Peter at the Sea of Galilee. c. 1585–90. Oil on canvas. 27 ¼ x 45 ¾". Credit: Harvard Art Museums/Fogg Museum, Bequest of Grenville L. Winthrop.

The Artist

The year of Ippolito Scarsella's birth is estimated to be circa 1550 and he died on October 27, 1620.[3] We do know that he was born in Ferrara and his father, a "painter of architecture," was Sigismondo Scarsella (1530–1614).[4] Ippolito's initial training was with his father probably between the ages of 15 and 17. The main primary source for this artist is Girolamo Baruffaldi's *The Lives of the Ferrarese Painters and Sculptors* written between 1697 and

---

3. Novelli, *Scarsellino*, 9. See also Ruggeri, "Scarsellino."
4. Novelli, *Scarsellino*, 9.

1722.[5] Baruffaldi suggests that Ippolito went to Bologna "to study the famous works of that school and especially the miracles by the Carracci."[6] Baruffaldi also claims this occurs before Ippolito turned 17, so sometime between 1565–70. This was impossible as the Carracci were not yet active. If Baruffaldi was correct about Ippolito going to Bologna to study, which is very likely as still today Ferrara is along the main travel passage between Bologna and Venice, then he would have encountered the work of Later Mannerist painters Orazio Samacchini, Lorenzo Sabatini, and Prospero Fontana.[7] After this Bolognese period, Ippolito went to Venice and trained with Paolo Veronese for four years beginning in 1570.[8] His earliest paintings find inspiration from Veronese and a richness of color reminiscent of Titian. Scholars also find stylistic echoes of earlier Ferrarese painters such as Sebastiano Filippi and Giuseppe Mazzuoli.[9]

The Painting—Style, Connoisseurship, Attribution, and Dating

Formerly attributed to Jacopo Tintoretto, *Christ and Saint Peter at the Sea of Galilee* bears many of the hallmarks of sixteenth-century Venetian painting: a rustic outdoor setting, dramatic contrasts of light and dark, rich color, and a loose, gestural style of depicting drapery with "lightning bolt" strokes that index the rapid movements of the brush.[10] The work is oil on canvas and measures 27¼" x 45¾". It depicts the moment that Peter loses faith in his ability to walk on water because he loses focus on Christ. The Sea of Galilee is calm as the storm that raged through the night has ended. The story where Peter walks on water is unique to the Gospel of Matthew. The disciples are in a boat having just endured a storm for most of the previous night, and they see Christ walking on water. Peter asks Jesus to allow him to walk on the water to prove that it is really him. Jesus says, "Come," and Peter walks on water until he loses faith, becomes fearful of what is happening to him, loses his focus on Christ, and starts to sink in the water. Jesus reaches out to him and saves him. Three other disciples react to the event while still in the boat. As dawn breaks on the horizon, light surrounds Christ's head

5. Baruffaldi, *Vite de' pittori*, 2:65–107.
6. Novelli, *Scarsellino*, 9.
7. Ibid.
8. Ruggeri, "Scarsellino."
9. Ibid.
10. "*Christ and Peter at the Sea of Galilee* by Ippolito Scarsellino." Harvard Art Museums, http://www.harvardartmuseums.org/collections/object/230293?position=0.

like an aureole.[11] The expressive gestures and luminous seascape lend the scene an urgent, ecstatic quality.[12]

The unpublished curatorial files of the Harvard Art Museums (combining the Fogg, Sackler, and Busch-Reisinger Museums now in one building designed by Renzo Piano) include secondary sources that attribute the painting to Tintoretto, a follower of Tintoretto, and most recently (and most convincingly) to Scarsellino.[13] Connoisseurship plays a major role in the attribution, Scarsellino, and the dating, circa 1585–90. As is the case with connoisseurship, a painting's provenance (history of ownership/location) and study of who is giving the attribution, or change of attribution in this case, is critical. The bill of sale listed the painting as by Jacopo Tintoretto when it was purchased in 1929 by Grenville L. Winthrop, New York. It was bequeathed to the Fogg Art Museum at Harvard in 1943 and carried the attribution as "Tintoretto (?)." In 1958, the attribution was changed to "sixteenth-century Venetian School" by art historian Millard Meiss.

The painting currently maintains the (re)attribution to Scarsellino in 1968 made by Everett Fahy. He was working at the Fogg Art Museum at Harvard in Cambridge from 1968–70, while completing his Ph.D. there. Fahy received a letter of evaluation from Philip Pouncey of Sotheby & Co (London) dated 8 March 1968 suggesting an attribution to Scarsellino.[14] After the Fogg, Fahy became the Curator-in-Chief of the Metropolitan Museum of Art's European Paintings department in 1970. In 1973, Fahy moved to the Frick Collection where he served as its director for 13 years. He returned to the Met as the first John Pope-Hennessy Chairman of European Paintings, a position he held until 2009. Dr. Fahy, born in 1941, began serving as a consultant for Christie's in 2010.[15] Phillip Pouncey (1910–1990) was another distinguished art historian who worked at the Fitzwilliam, National Gallery of Art in London, the British Museum and became the director of Sotheby's London in 1966. His reattribution of works was so renowned and

11. Ibid.

12. Ibid.

13. As Tintoretto (in chronological order), see Erich von der Bercken and August L. Mayer, *Jacopo Tintoretto*, 1 repr., 6, 141, 197; Tietze, ed., *Masterpieces of European Painting in America*, 98, 314, cat. no. 85, repr. 98; Pallucchini, *La Giovinezza del Tintoretto*, 153; Bernari, *L'opera completa del Tintoretto*, 134, no. C1, repr.; Pallucchini and Rossi, 242, no. A 19. As Follower of Tintoretto and as Scarsellino, see Fredericksen and Zeri, *Census of Pre-Nineteenth-Century Italian Paintings*, 184, 199; Bowron, *European Paintings Before 1900 in the Fogg Art Museum*, 129, repr. no. 692.

14. Letter from Philip Pouncey of Sotheby & Co. London to Everett Fahy, dated March 8, 1968.

15. "The Personal Collection of Dr. Everett Fahy."

respected that an exhibition of solely reattributed paintings was held on his 75th birthday at the British Museum.[16]

Most art historians and connoisseurs consider an attribution agreed upon by Fahy and Pouncey to be a respected and secure attribution. Yet, the only monograph on Scarsellino, written in Italian by Maria Angela Novelli and published in 2008, does not discuss the Harvard picture. Novelli's book functions as a catalogue raisonné (evaluating the attributions of all of the known paintings attributed to a painter).[17] The Harvard painting is not listed in the 301 attributions or 28 former attributions. There are two paintings in Boston at the Museum of Fine Arts also attributed to Scarsellino, *Christ on the Way to Calvary* (fig. 2) and *Saint Demetrius*. Both of these works are included by Novelli and categorized as secure attributions to Scarsellino.[18] Stylistically the *Christ on the Way to Calvary* can be dated to the same period as the Harvard picture. The Venetian color palette recalls the style of Veronese and Sebastiano del Piombo. The texture and technique are quite similar and the use of strong diagonals is present in both pictures. The figure of Christ is the same facial type. The flowing, windblown drapery adds drama and movement to the compositions.

Jonathan Bober, former Curator of the Blanton Museum and now Curator of Prints and Drawings at the National Gallery in Washington, DC, proposed the circa 1575–80 dating and Scarsellino's period in Venice as about that time period. The Ferrarese school is the current listing for Scarsellino.[19] The painting underwent treatment in February 2014 to correct discolored retouchings and glaze back braded areas in the distant landscape. The frame was conserved at the same time. Digital photographs before and after treatment in normal and ultra violet light were taken.[20]

16. "Pouncey, Phillip."
17. Novelli, *Scarsellino*.
18. Ibid., 292; cat. nos. 10 and 11.
19. Scarsellino (Ippolito Scarsella), *Christ and Peter at the Sea of Galilee*.
20. Painting Laboratory Treatment Reports dated February 13, 2014 (painting), March 26, 2014, and July 17, 2014 (frame).

Figure 2: Scarsellino (Ippolito Scarsella) (c. 1550–1620). Christ on the Way to Calvary. c. 1585–90. Oil on canvas. 20 ½ x 17 ¾". Museum of Fine Arts Boston. Credit: M. Theresa B. Hopkins Fund.

Interpretation of the Biblical Narrative and Select Visual Examples

The Jesus walking on water story appears in Matt 14:22–33; Mark 6:45–52; and John 6:15–21, but Peter walking on water is unique to Matt 14: 28–31. Matthew 14 begins with the beheading of St. John the Baptist by Herod and, after hearing this, Jesus flees Herod and goes to the desert where he feeds 5,000 people with five loaves and two fish.

> Immediately he made the disciples get into the boat and go on ahead to the other side, while he dismissed the crowds. And after he had dismissed the crowds, he went up the mountain by himself to pray. When evening came, he was there alone, but by this time the boat, battered by the waves, was far from the land, for the wind was against them. And early in the morning he came walking toward them on the sea. But when the disciples saw him walking on the sea, they were terrified, saying, "It is a ghost!" And they cried out in fear. But immediately Jesus spoke to them and said, "Take heart, it is I; do not be afraid." Peter answered him, "Lord, if it is you, command me to come to you on the water." He said, "Come." So Peter got out of the boat, started walking on the water, and came toward Jesus. But when he noticed the strong wind, he became frightened, and beginning to sink, he cried out, "Lord, save me!" Jesus immediately reached out his hand and caught him, saying to him, "You of little faith, why did you doubt?" When they go into the boat, the wind ceased. And those in the boat worshiped him, saying, "Truly you are the Son of God." (Matt 14:22–33, NRSV)

The visual tradition begins with the lost mosaic, known as the *Navicella* (little ship), located above the entrance arcade that faced the main façade of Old Saint Peter's basilica. It is attributed to Giotto di Bondone, circa 1305–1308.[21] The scene of Matt 14:24–33 was almost completely destroyed when St. Peter's was rebuilt in the seventeenth century but original fragments were incorporated into a new design in 1675 installed in the center of the portico. The story of Christ's walking on water that includes Peter is unique to Matt 14:28–31 and has been associated with a pro-papal context since this mosaic is in the first church of Christendom.

Another very early visual example of the *navicella* theme was by a contemporary of Giotto, Andrea da Firenze (1346–1349). The scene of *Christ and Peter on the Sea of Galilee* by Andrea da Firenze is in the frescoed dome of the Spanish chapel in the Florentine Dominican church of Santa Maria

---

21. Venturi, "La 'Navicella' di Giotto," fig. no. 2, and 50, ill.

Novella (fig. 3). The fresco is part of a larger program in the chapel. It is one of four scenes (Resurrection, Navicella, Ascension, and Pentecost) frescoed in the dome vault. The other objects that continue this tradition that will be included in this discussion are a gold coin depicting *Christ Walking on the Water* (fig. 4) from the Papal State from the time of Pope Alexander VI (1492-1503) and a painting by Alessandro Allori (1535-1607), a contemporary of Scarsellino and a Florentine Mannerist (fig. 5).[22]

Figure 3: Andrea da Firenze (1346-1379). Vault. Pendentive with Saint Peter's Boat. *Fresco (post-restoration 2003-2004). Spanish Chapel, S. Maria Novella, Florence, Italy. Scala / Art Resource, NY.*

Scarsellino was painting just after the conclusion of the Council of Trent. Art from that period is largely a product of the decrees made in the twenty-fifth and final session held on 3-4 December 1563. The decree "On Invocation, Veneration, and Relics of Saints, and on Sacred Images" directed bishops to see to the proper preaching on these subjects. Trent dealt with the veneration of sacred images, a subject that first received solemn church ratification at the Second Council of Nicaea, 787, in reaction to the

22. See "Kirchenstaat: Alexander VI."

violent outburst of iconoclasm in the Eastern Empire.[23] Nicaea had declared that sacred images were legitimate and they were helpful for instruction and devotion. Trent went further by saying they should be free of all "sensual appeal" (*lascivia*), false doctrine, and superstition.[24]

The Council of Trent decreed that sacred images were to be instructive and decorous.[25] It is critical for this study to ask whose written works and commentaries would have been of importance to Scarsellino and to his patrons. The writings of seventeenth-century theological writer Cornelius à Lapide (1567–1637) is a source whose commentary on earlier writers may have value for this interpretation. Cornelius à Lapide was born in Bocholt, Germany and studied humanities and philosophy at Jesuit colleges in Maastricht and Cologne. His theological studies included the University of Douai and Louvain. He entered the Society of Jesus on 11 June 1592, and was ordained a priest on 24 December 1595. Lapide became Professor of Scripture at Louvain in 1596 and, a year later, was also named Professor of Hebrew. In 1616, he was called to Rome by his Jesuit superiors to assume the same positions there.

Lapide's *Great Commentary* incorporates the writings of the Patristic Church Fathers from the second to the fourth centuries. In particular, he commented on the works of Jerome, Saint Hilary, Augustine, and John Chrysostom.[26] The relevant commentary includes Lapide's discussion of verses 28–31. Through a discussion of these literary interpretations, an evaluation of several artistic versions (numismatic and painted) may be studied.

Figure 4: Christ Walking on the Water. *Gold coin of the Papal State with a value of 5 ducats (verso). Time of Pope Alexander VI (1492–1503).*

23. O'Malley, *Trent*, 244.

24. Ibid.

25. For the "Decree of the Council of Trent Concerning Images," see Chemnitz, *Examination of the Council of Trent*, 4:53–54, and exact date cited by Waterworth, *Council of Trent*.

26. For biographical information, see Coulombe, "Foreword," 1:vii–xv.

Gold, diam. 41 mm, weight 16,75 g. Inv. 18232173. Muenzkabinett, Staatliche Museen, Berlin, Germany. Photo Credit: bpk Bildagentur / (Muenzkabinett, Staatliche Museen, Berlin, Germany) / (Lutz Jürgen Lübke) / Art Resource, NY.

"V. 28 And Peter making answer; said: Lord, if it be thou, bid me come to thee upon the waters." Lapide states that Calvin accuses Peter of rashness and folly but that the fathers and commentators give a two-fold answer. Lapide explains, "1. Peter recognised by his voice, gesture, dress and much more by an interior prompting that this was not an apparition, but Christ indeed. When, therefore, Peter says, if it be Thou, it is not the voice of doubt, but of one exulting with joy, desiring, furthermore, to come quickly to Christ, that he might be near to Him who was approaching miraculously on the sea and whom he loved above all things."[27] Scarsellino's interpretation echoes this sentiment when we study the disciples in the boat who seem oblivious to what is happening. They did not get out of the boat and are distant from Jesus. The disciple in the center of the boat is actually pointing in a different direction indicating that his attention is focused on something else. Lapide reminds us that Saint Hilary comments, "In Peter, consider how he goes before the others in faith." The painting reaffirms a positive reading of Peter's action as a leader and is an appropriate pro-papal message for Scarsellino's audience, contemporary Catholics in the 1570s. Further evidence of this story reinforcing the primacy of Peter at this time and, by extension the Papacy, is the papal coin of Alexander VI (1492–1503) depicting *Christ Walking on the Water* (fig. 4). The coin depicts Christ and Peter in the lower right corner of the composition while the boat dominates the field. Christ's body is placed on the edge of the coin and acts as a bridge in the inscription between MODICE and FIDEI. The inscription continues OVARE DUBITASTI. It translates, "Oh you of little faith why did you doubt?" Nine disciples are depicted on the boat on the coin (fig. 4) and in the Andrea da Firenze (fig. 3), unlike the Scarsellino and Allori (fig. 5) paintings, and are actively watching, and reacting, to the event.

27. Lapide, *Great Commentary*, 62.

Figure 5: Alessandro Allori (1535–1607). Saint Peter Walking on Water. Oil on copper, 18 1/2 x 15 3/4". Uffizi, Florence, Italy. Photo Credit: Scala/Ministero per i Beni e le Attività culturali / Art Resource, NY.

Lapide explains the second answer given by the church fathers and commentators: "2. If you insist that the words, *if it be Thou*, are spoken in doubt, then it must be said that by the expression *bid me come to Thee upon the waters*, Peter asked that this command should not merely be given him, but that it should be given with power, in such manner, indeed, that Christ should command him, not only externally but also internally, and that by this command He should infuse such boldness, confidence and security, that he should not doubt that he would walk safely upon the waves, since Christ bade him."[28] Peter is given the confidence to walk towards Christ, and in the Scarsellino Jesus welcomes him with open arms.

"Verse 29. And he said: Come. And Peter going down out of the boat walked upon the water to come to Jesus." Painters very rarely portrayed this verse. Perhaps they felt the drama of the moment was his sinking or that the walking on water should be reserved for Jesus. Lapide offers several explanations as to how it could have happened physically. "This was done in one of three ways. Either Christ, by His divine power, held Peter fast, that he should not sink, as the angel held Habakkuk fast by the hair of his head, and carried him to Babylon (Daniel 14:35). Or else He did not allow Peter's body to be sufficiently heavy to weigh him down and sink him in the waves. Or else He did not concur with the yielding action of the water, but rather made the waters to be firm and solid beneath Peter's feet, like ice or crystal."[29]

"Verse 30. But seeing the wind strong, he was afraid: and when he began to sink, he cried out, saying: Lord, save me." Lapide comments, "The strength of the wind caused Peter to fear: fear caused doubt: doubt gave rise to danger. For the one whom faith bore upon the wave, doubt sank. The cause was Peter's little faith." Lapide's explanation is that Peter had not yet received the power of the Holy Spirit at Pentecost. He believes that Christ permitted this so that Peter could recognize his own weakness and his little faith, and might humble himself, and "ask Christ to increase his faith, that he might become the rock of the Faith, according to the words, *Thou are Peter, and upon this rock I will build My church* (Matt 16:18)."[30] Saint Augustine says, "in Peter walking upon the waters are symbolized those who are strong in faith, but in Peter doubting, those who are weak in faith."[31] Peter, then, becomes an example of strength with a completely human character who becomes stronger after making a mistake.

"Lord save me" is the final statement of Peter in verse 30. Lapide recalls Augustine saying, "That shaking, brethren, was as it were the death of faith. But when he cried out, faith rose again. He could not have walked unless he believed, neither would he have begun to sink unless he had doubted. In Peter, therefore, we must regard the common condition of us all, that if in any temptation the wind is about to capsize and sink us in the waves, we should cry aloud to Christ."[32] Scarsellino chooses to depict the Sea of

28. Ibid., 63.
29. Ibid., 64.
30. Ibid.
31. Ibid.
32. Ibid., 65.

Galilee as calm. Most visual examples of this scene include rough waters. Another Italian Mannerist, Alessandro Allori (fig. 5), paints the rough seas that clearly continue to bounce the boat around. The figures are large and the gestures dramatic. The drapery colors are bright, with Christ wearing a rose-colored gown and a blue mantle as in the Scarsellino. Peter wears a similar shade of deep blue with a golden mantle that expands as the wind blows it outward. The sea remains rough from the storm that battered the boat. In the background, the apostles are visibly terrified, having mistaken Christ on the water for a ghost. The sails are down indicating the storm has passed. Scarsellino's boat also has lowered sails.

Like the Scarsellino, Andrea da Firenze, and the Allori, the moment that is portrayed is when Christ saves Peter and raises him out of the water by the hand. In the Andrea da Firenze and Allori, Peter holds onto Christ's hand with his two hands. The papal coin depicts Peter not yet touching Christ. In all of these visual renditions, Peter looks to be kneeling before Christ.

"V. 31. And immediately Jesus stretching forth his hand took hold of him, and said to him: O thou of little faith, why didst thou doubt?" Lapide concludes, "For two things were here presented to Peter, that is to say, the strength of the wind making him afraid of being drowned, and the voice of Christ instilling confidence and security. But the strength of the wind was more obvious, and, therefore, more powerful than the voice of Christ. For it drew Peter's mind to itself, so that intent on that alone, and not thinking of Christ's promise, he wavered and feared drowning, when he ought to have listened with his full attention to Christ's voice reassuring him, and thus have resisted temptation . . . Strictly speaking there is a lack of confidence in Peter here, originating however in a lack of faith. The same applies to anyone who is tempted by any temptation."[33] Chrysostom parallels how Christ deals with Peter in the same way a mother bird cares for one of her young before it is old enough to fly. He says, "Like as a young bird which, before it is able to fly, falls out of its nest upon the ground, whose mother quickly restores it to the nest, so also at this time did Christ deal with Peter."[34]

Peter has lost focus on Jesus and that is the moment Scarsellino paints. He removes the wind as a contributing element to the falling in the water. Instead, we are to conclude his mind wandered and he became fearful with the realization that he was walking on water and could sink. Jesus, positioned close to shore, grabs Peter with his right hand while his left guides him towards land. Jesus's lower body is positioned towards the shore and is in close proximity to it. Jesus raises Peter out of the water. This swift

33. Ibid.
34. Ibid.

elevation is echoed in Peter's cape extended behind him. Jesus does not rebuke Peter but rather teaches him to trust and have faith in Him. The viewer understands that both Jesus and Peter will soon be safely on land.

Lapide cites Clement of Alexandria and reminds us of Heb 11:1: *Faith is the substance of things to be hoped for.* The papal coin of Pope Alexander VI further emphasizes the power of this story. The inscription "(God) Save Us" is in the center of the coin. As stated above, "Oh you of little faith why did you doubt?" circles the outer portion of the coin with Christ's body along the edge and continuing the inscription as it moves around the coin. The Papacy is reaffirming the necessity of faith and associating it with hope. Scarsellino's *Christ and Saint Peter at the Sea of Galilee* turns one of Peter's lowest moments into one of his highest. He is closer to Christ for coming to him and now touches Christ as he saves him.

Conclusion

Through an assessment of the connoisseurship and stylistic comparisons, a secure attribution to Scarsellino is achieved. The commentary tradition has aided our understanding of the narrative, the historical context, and the importance of defining Peter's moment with Christ on the sea as one of success rather than failure. The message of Scarsellino and other artists discussed here contribute not only to the raising of Peter from the sea but also to the elevation of the Papacy in the eyes of contemporary Christians.

Works Cited

Baruffaldi, Girolamo. *Vite de' pittori e scultori ferraresi*, vol. 2. Ferrara, 1697–1722/R 1844–6.

Bernari, Carlo. *L'opera completa del Tintoretto*. Milan: Rizzoli Editore, 1970.

Bowron, Edgar Peters. *European Paintings before 1900 in the Fogg Art Museum: A Summary Catalogue including Paintings in the Busch-Reisinger Museum*. Cambridge: Harvard University Art Museums, 1990.

Chemnitz, Martin. *Examination of the Council of Trent*. Part 4. St. Louis: Concordia, 1986.

"Christ and Peter at the Sea of Galilee by Ippolito Scarsellino." Harvard Art Museums, http://www.harvardartmuseums.org/collections/object/230293?position=0.

Coulombe, Charles A. "Foreword." In *The Great Commentary of Cornelius à Lapide: The Holy Gospel According to Saint Matthew*, translated by Thomas W. Mossman, 1:vii–xv. Fitzwilliam, NH: Loreto, 2008.

Fredericksen, Burton B., and Federico Zeri. *Census of Pre-Nineteenth-Century Italian Paintings in North American Public Collections*. Cambridge: Harvard University Press, 1972.

"Kirchenstaat: Alexander VI." *Münzkabinett Online Catalogue*, http://ikmk.smb.museum/object?lang=en&id=18232173&view=rs.

Lapide, Cornelius à. *The Great Commentary of Cornelius à Lapide: The Holy Gospel According to Saint Matthew*, translated by Thomas W. Mossman. Fitzwilliam, NH: Loreto, 2008.

Letter from Philip Pouncey of Sotheby & Co. London to Everett Fahy, March 8, 1968. Curatorial File, Harvard Art Museums, Object Number 1943.124, Fogg Art Museum, Harvard University.

Novelli, Maria Angel. *Scarsellino*. Milan: Skira, 2008.

O'Malley, John W. *Trent: What Happened at the Council*. Cambridge: Belknap Press of Harvard University Press, 2013.

Painting Laboratory Treatment Reports dated February 13, 2014 (painting), March 26, 2014, and July 17, 2014 (frame). Curatorial File, Harvard Art Museums, Object Number 1943.124.

Pallucchini, Rodolfo. *La Giovinezza del Tintoretto*. Milan: Edizioni Daria Guarnati, 1950.

Pallucchini, Rodolfo, and Paola Rossi. *Tintoretto: Le opere sacre e profane*. Venice and Milan: Alfieri/Gruppo Editoriale Electa, 1982.

"The Personal Collection of Dr. Everett Fahy." *Christie's*, http://www.christies.com/features/The-Personal-Collection-of-Dr-Everett-Fahy-7712-1.aspx.

"Pouncey, Phillip." *Dictionary of Art Historians*, https://dictionaryofarthistorians.org/pounceyp.htm.

Ruggeri, Ugo. "Scarsellino." *Grove Art Online. Oxford Art Online*. Oxford University Press, http://www.oxfordartonline.com.ezproxy.baylor.edu/subscriber/article/grove/art/T076347.

Scarsellino (Ippolito Scarsella). *Christ and Peter at the Sea of Galilee*. Curatorial File, Harvard Art Museums, Object Number 1943.124.

Tietze, Hans, ed. *Masterpieces of European Painting in America*. New York: Oxford University Press, 1939.

Venturi, Lionello. "La 'Navicella' di Giotto." *L'arte* 25 (1922) 49–69.

von der Bercken, Erich, and August L. Mayer. *Jacopo Tintoretto*. Munich: R. Piper & Co. Verlag, 1923.

Waterworth, James, ed. *The Council of Trent: Canons and Decrees*. Chicago: Christian Symbolic Publication, 1848.

Jewish Purification Practices and the Gospel of John

Frank Wheeler, Sr.[1]

INTERPRETING JESUS WITHIN THE context of his Jewish culture has been a mainstay of Jesus research for several decades.[2] Much of the discussion has focused on the extent of Jesus's observance of Jewish purity laws.[3] The purpose of the present study is more specifically focused on the Gospel of John's portrayal of Jesus[4] within the context of the post-70 struggle of the Jewish community for maintaining identity, faith, purity, and holiness.

In an insightful study of the Jewish festivals in the Gospel of John from the perspective of social memory, Mary Spaulding demonstrates that "those festival practices that could not be continued because of the destruction of the temple became transferred directly onto Jesus and the Spirit" in order to help the readers grasp more fully the significance of Jesus. Spaulding notes that by presenting new understandings of commemorative practices at the former temple, "the Gospel of John represents structures of continuity with the past that provide identity in the present."[5] The present study seeks to

---

1. I appreciate the invitation to honor Dr. Naymond Keathley. His help and guidance as a professor as well as his contribution to both the church and academia are greatly appreciated by myself as well as many others.

2. The literature on Jesus and the Law is vast, but see especially Meier, *Marginal Jew*.

3. Kazen, *Jesus and Purity Halakhah*; Booth, *Jesus and the Laws of Purity*; Fiensy, *Jesus the Galilean*, 147–86; Haber, "Going Up to Jerusalem," 181–206; Magness, *Stone and Dung*, 8, 24–25.

4. To whatever extent Jesus observed the purification practices, it is evident that he focused on internal purity and shared that with others. See further Magness, *Stone and Dung*, 21–25; and Holmen, "Contagious Purity," 199–229, esp. 208–22.

5. Spaulding, *Commemorative Identities*, 143, 164, respectively.

show that the Gospel of John is doing something similar with Jewish purification practices.

In the late Second-Temple era disagreements occurred as to whether the ritual purity laws should be observed only in the temple area, throughout the city of Jerusalem, or throughout the whole of Israel.[6] Different levels of practice may have existed, but evidence is strong for purification practices in both Judea and Galilee during the late Second-Temple era.[7]

Stepped plastered pools for ritual immersion, or *mikva'ot*, have been found in numerous Jewish villages, some near synagogues, some near cemeteries, and a few even in private homes along with stone vessels. Such discoveries suggest a continuing interest in ritual purity after 70 CE. David Amit and Yonatan Adler observe, "We have seen how recent discoveries point to continuity in the use of ritual baths and (to a lesser extent) stone vessels from second temple times throughout the Mishnaic and Talmudic periods."[8] Stuart S. Miller argues that the practices of ritual purity *increased* or *intensified* in everyday life after the destruction of the temple, especially within domestic settings. He states that the vacuum left by the destruction of the temple was not addressed by forming various "sects and groups" but by the lingering desire to maintain purity and holiness. "The holiness of the land and of the people of Israel continued to have meaning after 70 C.E. Once the 'Holy House' (*bet hamiqdash*, i.e., the temple) had been destroyed, the inextricable connection between these residual notions of holiness and the biblically-derived purity laws would have been *more* acutely perceived, leading, after some adjustment, if not to an increase, certainly to an intensifying of ritual purity practices in everyday life and a new emphasis of their centrality in the home."[9]

The continuing interest in purity regulations within the developing post-70 rabbinic tradition is well documented not only in the archaeological record but also in the literary record. Jodi Magness observes that "whereas before 70 debates on halakhic issues divided Jews along sectarian lines, after 70 the rabbis tolerated and preserved different opinions. Most scholars therefore view the rabbinic period as characterized by an

---

6. Magness, *Stone and Dung*, 6; Poirier, "Purity," 247–65, esp. 249, 256–58.

7. Reed, *Archaeology*, 44; Freyne, "Archaeology of Bathing," 117–19.

8. Amit and Adler, "Observance of Ritual Purity," 142. Amit and Adler document the increased archaeological discoveries of *mikva'ot* dating after 70 CE. See Adler's updated numbers in "Decline," 270.

9. Miller, "Stepped Pools," 247. Adler, "Decline," 277, convincingly argues, "As the evidence stands today, both *miqwa'ot* and chalk vessels persisted as widespread phenomena for generations after 70 CE, with no apparent evidence of decline prior to the middle of the second century."

inclusive and pluralistic attitude that contrasts with the period before 70."[10] This early rabbinic inclusiveness has been described by Miller "as a type of 'complex adaptive system' that maintained enough order or structure to amount to 'common Judaism,' but which was sufficiently 'chaotic' to allow for innovation and individuality."[11] Thus, after the destruction of the temple, the struggles of the Jewish people encouraged them to be open to different and new ways of maintaining their identity and faith, though certainly within limits.

Using sociological and anthropological perspectives, Eyal Regev examines the relevant literary and archaeological evidence to explore the rise of purity practices among non-priestly individuals, including but not limited to Pharisees. Regev argues that in their competition with the priests for influence among the people, the Pharisees emphasized "non-priestly purity" in order to show that they too were masters of purity and piety. The Pharisees used bodily purity to gain public influence and religious status which, Regev observes, was the focus of Jesus's criticism.[12] The promotion of purity as propaganda for their cause was "directed toward individuals and their religious needs and perplexity, especially in times of crisis, after the destruction of the second Temple and the Bar-Kokhba revolt."[13] The two decades after the destruction of the Jewish temple would be the time frame of the Gospel of John.[14]

Why would the Fourth Gospel even address the issue of purity if, as most think, its readers were primarily diaspora Jews (either believers or unbelievers)? The answer would be similar to why the Fourth Gospel spends so much time on the temple itself and the Jewish festivals. Diaspora Jews had the same purity concerns as those of Palestine, but their practices no doubt were different. *Mikva'ot* were scarce, if used at all, nor have stone vessels been found in Jewish diaspora settings. The impact of the destruction of the temple on diaspora Jews would have been profound, but they had already worked out ways of maintaining their identity, including their purity,

---

10. Magness, *Stone and Dung*, 182. See also Magness, "Sectarianism."

11. Miller, *Sages and Commoners*, 25–26. Miller qualifies E. P. Sanders's "common Judaism," argued for especially in Sanders, *Judaism*, 214–30.

12. Regev, "Pure Individualism," 201.

13. Ibid., 202. At the beginning of his article Regev discusses how Jews in the diaspora were concerned with individual purity as early as the first half of the second century BCE.

14. For this time frame for the Fourth Gospel see, Kostenberger, "Destruction of the Second Temple." For more on the struggles of Jewish people during this era see Jensen, "Purity and Politics," 25–34.

without the temple.[15] Nevertheless, the Fourth Gospel reaches out to these Jews and Jewish believers in Jesus demonstrating Jesus's fulfillment of the temple and its cultic practices, their festivals, and purity concerns. Furthermore, Romans themselves were well acquainted with the idea of purity and ritual washings. Such practices were widespread throughout the empire.[16]

The Fourth Gospel uses the language of purification: "purification" (2:6; 3:25); "pure" (13:10–11; 15:3); "to purify" (11:55); but our focus will be more on the references to water.[17] Two perspectives that will help shape our discussion are those of Hannah Harrington and Gary Burge. Harrington analyzed parallels between the Gospel of John and several Qumran texts to argue that the Gospel of John uses water symbolism to anticipate the new life available through Jesus and the Holy Spirit, including atonement, revelation, and the eschaton.[18] Burge suggests that most of the references to water in the Gospel of John refer in some manner to the Jewish ritual of water purification practices.[19] I will analyze several passages in John to see how the author engages the discussion among various groups of Jews regarding how to move on as a people of God without the temple while still celebrating the presence of God in their daily lives.

The story of Jesus at the Wedding Feast in John 2 explicitly mentions the Jewish ritual purification regulations in regard to the stone jars holding the water for ritual washing.[20] Since stone did not contract ritual impurity, the large stone jars for purity practices would have provided enough water for the guests to wash their hands and perhaps face and feet. *Mikva'ot*, ritual washing pools, have been found in individual houses not only in Jerusalem but in Galilee as well, specifically Sepphoris. At Cana, excavators have un-

---

15. See Goodman, "Diaspora Reactions"; Tuval, "Doing without the Temple." See further Magness, "Purity," who argues that the absence of *mikva'ot* and stone vessels in the diaspora suggest that Jews of the diaspora followed the practice later formalized in the rabbinic Baraita Boundaries of the Land of Israel (purity practices such as *mikva'ot* and chalk vessels were tied to keeping the land, Israel, holy, and thus were not necessary in the diaspora).

16. See Fantham, "Purification in Ancient Rome"; Ferguson, "Washings for Purification in Greco-Roman Paganism."

17. Water symbolism in John has been analyzed by several people; see Ng, *Water Symbolism in John*; and Jones, *Symbol of Water*. Neither of these studies nor others analyze the Jewish rituals of purification in relationship to John as a whole. Only Burge, "Revisiting," and Harrington, "Purification," have investigated the use of Jewish purification rites throughout the Gospel of John.

18. Harrington, "Purification," 137.

19. Burge, "Revisiting," 131.

20. Keener, *Gospel of John*, 1:509–10; Burge, "Revisiting," 131; Reed, "Stone Vessels and Gospel Texts," 379–401.

covered more than ten *mikva'ot*, but none seem to be household *mikva'ot*.²¹ A full washing in a *mikva'ot* would have been the expected practice, but the host had only provided the jars of water for washing.²² John identifies the act of turning the water into wine as Jesus's first "sign" but adds another level of understanding to Jesus's work that he and others only later realized—the implications for purity practices. For the moment, John indicated that the disciples and Jesus's mother and brothers see Jesus's "glory" through this sign and believe in him. Later, however, John realized something greater was here and paired this sign with the clearing/cleansing of the temple. By putting the Cana sign and the clearing of the temple back to back, John may be suggesting that through Jesus there is now a new way that one may find the level of purity necessary to approach the presence of God. There is a new way to be made clean—a new way to atone for sin—a new way to come into the presence of God. Gary Burge has observed, "This opening scene immediately alerts the reader that the work of Jesus now has implications for ritual instruments of Judaism."²³

Reference to being born of water and spirit in Jesus's conversation with Nicodemus (3:5) could hardly be Christian baptism, but more likely the Jewish practice of ritual purification. The addition of spirit might suggest a distinction between the regular Jewish ritual purification rites and that of John the Baptist. In fact, the reference in 3:25 to a discussion about purification between John's disciples and another Jew perhaps suggests that John the Baptist's disciples saw his baptism as a ritual purification and they were wondering how it compared not only to normal Jewish purification rites but also to that of Jesus. John the Baptist's response implies that he viewed the baptism of Jesus as superior. Combining the reference to the spirit along with water in 3:5 with the discussion in 3:25 suggests that the author of the Fourth Gospel sees John the Baptist's baptism as superior to the Jewish purification rites and Jesus's baptism as superior to that of John the Baptist.²⁴

In John 4:10 Jesus offers "living water" to a woman who has come to draw water from Jacob's well at the foot of Mt. Gerizim. "Living water," in contrast to the water in the well, would likely refer to fresh, running water. Such water was required by the Law for purification of severe impurities (Lev 15:13), as well as to fill the *mikva'ot* used for ritual purification throughout

---

21. Charlesworth and Aviam, "Reconstructing First-Century Galilee," 133.
22. Keener, *Gospel of John*, 1:510.
23. Burge, "Revisiting," 131.
24. Keener, *Gospel of John*, 1:549, sees the "born of water" in 3:5 as Jewish proselyte baptism.

Galilee and Judea.[25] Numerous references to "living water" are found in the Old Testament, referring to water for ritual purposes and metaphorical uses indicating spiritual blessings from God himself and the temple (Lev 14:5, 50–52; 15:13; Jer 2:13; 17:13; Isa 44:2–3; Zech 14:8).[26] It is the "living water" that provides the cleansing people need in order to approach the presence of God, which Jesus indicates will at some point no longer be in the temple on Mt. Gerizim, at which the Samaritans worship, or at the temple in Jerusalem where the Jews worship, but rather through Jesus himself (John 4:21–24). Keener notes that "this passage thus continues the water motif of the Gospel, which contrasts ritual waters (not always negative but always comparatively impotent) with what Jesus brings (1:33; 2:6; 3:5, 22)."[27]

Jesus's healing at the pools of Bethesda and Siloam continues the idea of Jesus's bringing new healing and purification. Both pools were viewed as places of purification.[28] Archaeologists have studied both pools extensively and realize that the nature of the pools and their close proximity to the temple were such that people used them for ritual cleansing before approaching the temple area. The pools of Bethesda[29] were considered by many to be a place of healing. At the pools of Bethesda Jesus's ability to heal/purify without the water shows that his ability to heal and to purify is more powerful than the healing or purifying associated with the pools. As the man was healed he was also made clean and thus able to function within society once again as a whole person.

On the last day of the Festival of Tabernacles, Jesus promised "rivers of living water" to those who would believe in him (7:37–39). As noted earlier, the phrase "living water" was used to describe the water required for purification purposes in the Old Testament as well as the water used for the *mikva'ot*. The phrase also described God and the spirit of God (Jer 2:13; 17:13; Isa 44:2–3).[30] The water rituals of Judaism "illustrate rejuvenation and

---

25. Harrington, "Purification," 123, notes, "the rabbis view only water that has issued directly from God—that is, from rain, a natural pool, or a stream—as effective for ritual purification."

26. See further Lawrence, *Washing in Water*, 132.

27. Keener, *Gospel of John*, 1:604.

28. von Wahlde, "Pools of Bethesda"; von Wahlde, "Pool of Siloam"; Burge, "Revisiting," 123–33.

29. The pools of Bethesda were actually a complex of two primary pools in the first century CE and six smaller pools later in the second century. For further descriptions of the area see von Wahlde, "Pools of Bethesda"; von Wahlde, "Puzzling Pool of Bethesda." Also see Gibson, "Pool of Bethesda."

30. Harrington, "Purification," 123.

renewal.... To be sure, only the Spirit of God can bring true renewal, but the water ritual anticipates and illustrates that gift (cf. John 7:37–39)."[31]

Obviously, by the time the Fourth Gospel was written the Festival of Tabernacles was celebrated very differently because the temple no longer existed. The morning water ceremony and the evening light ceremony could no longer be practiced—both required the temple. Ritually clean water, "living water," was drawn each morning from the pool of Siloam and poured into a basin before the altar at the temple and in the evening tall torches were lit in the temple courtyard. Yet, it is those very rituals of the past that John addresses. John shows how one may now "give them a purpose and meaning that requires no physical Temple.... Jewish Christ-followers needed to know how they should understand these vital memory associations with their own past.... Because the Temple-centered rituals of the feast have been transformed by Johannine Christology, the festival itself would take on new symbolic meaning as well; it now would also be understood in light of that Christology."[32] The water drawn from the pool of Siloam was a symbol of God providing water for those in the wilderness wanderings as well as the rains for the annual crops. It was also often viewed as representing the Spirit of God.[33] Spaulding notes that following the discussion in John 6 on Moses and the Exodus wanderings, "It would take little prompting for a reader who has just experienced a lengthy discourse on manna from heaven to 'hear' water flowing from the rock." Furthermore, "Jesus is again presenting himself as the presence and provision of God among his people."[34] Miller agrees with this idea noting: "It is no wonder then that the Gospel of John has Jesus proclaim that he is a conduit of 'living water' on the Festival of Booths."[35] In light of the pool of Siloam being used as a large *mikveh*, John may very well be presenting Jesus as the one through whom God works to purify and replenish his people, i.e., the living water is Jesus himself through whom the Spirit will be given (John 7:39).

As mentioned earlier, the pool of Siloam was considered to be a pool for ritual cleansing. It was near the temple and was used for ritual cleansing during the large festivals in which thousands would need to wash in a *mikveh* before approaching the temple. In John 9, Jesus sent a blind man to wash in the Pool of Siloam. It was appropriate that Jesus would send the blind man to Siloam, because it was a pool for ritual cleansing. The blind

31. Ibid., 124.
32. Spaulding, *Commemorative Identities*, 160.
33. Keener, *Gospel of John*, 1:724.
34. Spaulding, *Commemorative Identities*, 130, 131, respectively.
35. Miller, *At the Intersection of Texts and Material Finds*, 139.

were considered perpetually unclean ritually, since they were not able to see unclean things in order to avoid them.[36] This meant they were never able to enter the temple area. Since the water flowed from the Gihon spring through Hezekiah's tunnel into the Pool of Siloam, and from there out into the Kidron Valley, the water would have been considered ritually clean, known as "living water." Normally, people came there for ritual washing, but Jesus sent the man there to be physically healed, something neither the man nor anyone else would have expected. The blind man was both healed and made clean as he washed in the ritually clean waters of Siloam. Throughout the remainder of chapter nine, the man, now purified, grows in his belief and understanding of Jesus's identity in the midst of confrontations with the Jewish authorities. The man is an example of one made pure by Jesus who also strengthens the man's faith and courage to deal with the struggles of being a believer. There is power in the purity Jesus provides. No doubt John's readers would have been encouraged by such a thought.

Two other possible allusions to the idea of purification are found in the Passover meal. As Jesus began to wash the disciples' feet, Peter refused to allow it. When Jesus told Peter that he could not be a part of him unless he washed his feet, Peter then asked Jesus to wash his hands and his head along with his feet. Jesus's response (13:10) suggests that they had already made the necessary preparations for the meal by performing the ritual purification rites of washing,[37] likely in a *mikveh*. Washing of the feet upon arrival at the location for the meal would have been expected, whether for the Passover meal or not, but for the Passover meal it would have had the greater significance of a ritual washing. The notion of Jesus ritually washing their feet for purity purposes would not have gone unnoticed by John's readers. Jesus is the one who now makes us clean. Jerome Neyrey notes that the language of purification suggests more is present than an act of hospitality. He concludes that the ritual washing of Peter's feet was for the purpose of transforming his role among the disciples. Furthermore, the washing of the other disciples' feet was a confirmation of their role, which should be repeated among themselves.[38] Once again, the Fourth Gospel is presenting Jesus as purifying his followers.

Another passage perhaps of significance is John 15:3 where Jesus tells the disciples, "You have already been cleansed by the word that I have spoken to you." The context of this statement is the traditional analogy of the vine and the vine-dresser used numerous times in the Old Testament with

---

36. von Wahlde, "Pool of Siloam," 173.
37. Keener, *Gospel of John*, 2:909.
38. Neyrey, "Footwashing in John 13:6–11," in *Gospel of John*, 356–76.

reference to the relationship between Israel and God (Ps 80:8–16; Isa 27:2–6; Jer 2:31; Ezek 15:2–6; etc.). In talking about the need for the disciples to remain "in him" (15:3), Jesus says they had already been made clean/pure. His word, his teachings, his perspective have purified them. The analogy of pruning the vines and remaining connected focuses on relationship; being purified by Jesus's teachings also has to do with relationship.

In her study of "Purification in the Fourth Gospel in Light of Qumran," Harrington argues that the residents of Qumran most likely required ritual washing before study of the Torah, thus purifying themselves in anticipation for revelation of the word of God. In parallel fashion, the Fourth Gospel proposes that spiritual truth purifies—but unique to the Fourth Gospel, "'Word,' 'Truth,' and 'Living Water' are all personified by Jesus himself, who is expected to purify believers. . . . It is a basic thesis of the Fourth Gospel that the disciples of Jesus are pure because of their acceptance of Jesus's teachings."[39]

In addition to these passages' individual implications, there appears to be a progression of thought dealing with purity throughout the Gospel of John. The first and most direct reference to Jewish purification practices is the mention of the stone jars with water for the wedding guests to purify themselves at the wedding in chapter two. Normally, a full immersion in a *mikveh* would have been expected, but the lesser washing of hands, face, and/or feet is implied. Jesus's replacing the water with wine presents a new purification. In his conversation with Nicodemus in chapter three, Jesus mentioned being born of water and spirit. Within the context of a Jewish conversation the water would have been understood as a ritual cleansing, though the term "born anew" confused Nicodemus. The discussion between followers of John the Baptist and a Jew, later in chapter three, suggests that the water of "water and spirit" was the ritual cleansing. The "spirit" of "water and spirit" clearly adds a dimension to the ritual cleansing that only later does the reader realize should be defined more specifically as Jesus himself. The addition of "spirit" begins the progression toward a more complete purification that also includes forgiveness. The "living water" that Jesus provides, mentioned in the conversation with the woman at the well in chapter four, describes the waters of ritual purification and suggests that Jesus, who is identified as a prophet, the Messiah, and Savior of the World, provides the Spirit and eternal life. One who partakes of the living water needs neither the temple at Gerizim or Jerusalem. In chapter five an invalid is healed directly by Jesus rather than by the waters of healing which were also seen as waters of purification. Jesus both heals and purifies the man,

---

39. Harrington, "Purification," 133–34.

giving him a new life. While at the Festival of Tabernacles, Jesus declares that he has the "living water." The water used for the morning ceremonies each day came from the pool of Siloam, which was pure since it was used as a *mikveh*, having "living water" running through it. The statement in 7:39 specifies that Jesus is giving the Spirit along with the "living water," or purification. The blind man in chapter nine is both healed and made clean by Jesus at the pool of Siloam and thus finds new life. The disciples had no doubt already washed themselves in a *mikveh* before the meal in chapter thirteen, but Jesus cleanses them further with the washing of their feet, and appoints them to a new role in his kingdom. Later in the meal, Jesus indicated that they had been made clean by his word—his teachings (15:3). No water was necessary for this cleansing; Jesus's word itself had cleansed them. This would be the most powerful cleansing so far. Yet, as Jesus died the reference to water and blood coming from his side (19:34) is the most complete reference to purification in John. While the water would refer to purification for his followers,[40] the blood refers to forgiveness for his followers. Clearly, this would be the most intense fulfillment of the Jewish purification that John has been attributing to Jesus. The ritual purification through water can ultimately lead to moral purification through the blood of the Son. Though some of this may be speculative, it does lead the reader to the realization that Jesus can heal and purify without the traditional waters of Judaism; his own words can heal and purify; he can forgive sin without the temple. All of this points to the christological focus of the book—belief in Jesus as the Messiah brings new Life (20:30–31).

As we have seen, numerous issues were at play after the destruction of the temple: the role of synagogues, the festivals, leadership (would the priests or Pharisees be more influential), how to cope with the loss of the temple, its sacrifices, and even the presence of God. It is precisely this post-70 milieu that Miller suggested "allowed for innovation and individuality,"[41] and which the Fourth Gospel engages according to Magness and Regev. John presents Jesus as the Messiah from God who now fulfills the purposes of the temple sacrifices, festivals, etc., but also the means for purification, i.e., experiencing the presence of God. The Fourth Gospel charts a new way toward purity and holiness for its readers. This new way does not reject the idea of purity, rather it demonstrates that purity/holiness can no longer be established in relationship to the temple and its rituals. The way to find purity/holiness is through belief in Jesus as the Messiah who brought new life. Those in the diaspora had already worked out a way to maintain purity and those in Israel were

---

40. See Burge, "Revisiting," 132.
41. Miller, *Sages and Commoners*, 26.

struggling to do the same, religious leaders as well as common folk. John knows their struggles and speaks to them, giving them a new Way, a new Life, and a new purity. Providing a continuity with the past provides a new identity for the present.[42] In the aftermath of the destruction of the temple everything associated with the temple and Jewish identity, including purity practices, had to be rethought. John is doing exactly that—presenting Jesus as the way to maintain identity, faith, purity, and holiness.

Works Cited

Adler, Yonatan. "The Decline of Jewish Ritual Purity Observance in Roman Palaestina: An Archaeological Perspective on Chronology and Historical Context." In *Expressions of Cult in the Southern Levant in the Greco-Roman Period*, edited by Oren Tal and Zeev Weiss, 269–84. Turnhout, Belgium: Brepols, 2017.

Amit, David, and Yonatan Adler. "The Observance of Ritual Purity after 70 C.E.—A Reevaluation of the Evidence in Light of Recent Archaeological Discoveries." In *"Follow the Wise": Studies in Jewish History and Culture in Honor of Lee I. Levine*, edited by Zeev Weiss et al., 121–43. Winona Lake, IN: Eisenbrauns, 2010.

Booth, Roger P. *Jesus and the Laws of Purity: Tradition History and Legal History in Mark 7*. Sheffield: Sheffield Academic, 1986.

Burge, Gary M. "Revisiting the Johannine Water Motif: Jesus, Ritual Cleansing, and Two Purification Pools in Jerusalem." In *New Testament Theology in Light of the Church's Mission: Essays in Honor of I. Howard Marshall*, edited by Jon C. Laansma et al., 123–34. Eugene, OR: Cascade, 2011.

Charlesworth, James H., and Mordechai Aviam. "Reconstructing First-Century Galilee: Reflections on Ten Major Problems." In *Jesus Research: New Methodologies and Perceptions*, edited by James H. Charlesworth, 103–37. Grand Rapids: Eerdmans, 2014.

Fantham, Elaine. "Purification in Ancient Rome." In *Rome, Pollution, and Propriety*, edited by Mark Bradley, 59–66. Cambridge: Cambridge University Press, 2012.

Ferguson, Everett "Washings for Purification in Greco-Roman Paganism." In *Baptism in the Early Church: History, Theology, and Liturgy in the First Five Centuries*, 25–37. Grand Rapids: Eerdmans, 2009.

Fiensy, David A. *Jesus the Galilean: Soundings in a First Century Life*. Piscataway, NJ: Gorgias, 2007.

Freyne, Sean. "The Archaeology of Bathing: Religious and Cultural Aspects of First Century Palestine." In *A City Set on a Hill: Essays in Honor of James F. Strange*, edited by Daniel A. Warner and Donald D. Binder, 98–127. Mountain Home, AR: Borderstone, 2014.

Gibson, S. "The Pool of Bethesda in Jerusalem and Jewish Purification Practices of the Second Temple Period." *Proche Orient-Chretien* 55 (2005) 270–93.

Goodman, Martin. "Diaspora Reactions to the Destruction of the Temple." In *Jews and Christians: The Parting of the Ways A.D. 70 to 135*, edited by James D. G. Dunn, 27–38. Grand Rapids: Eerdmans, 1992.

---

42. Spaulding, *Commemorative Identities*, 164.

Haber, Susan. "Going Up to Jerusalem: Purity, Pilgrimage, and the Historical Jesus." In *"They Shall Purify Themselves": Essays on Purity in Early Judaism*, edited by Adele Reinhartz, 181–206. Atlanta: Society of Biblical Literature, 2008.

Harrington, Hannah. "Purification in the Fourth Gospel in Light of Qumran." In *John, Qumran, and the Dead Sea Scrolls: Sixty Years of Discovery and Debate*, edited by Mary L. Coloe and Tom Thatcher, 117–38. Atlanta: Society of Biblical Literature, 2011.

Holmen, Tom. "A Contagious Purity: Jesus' Inverse Strategy for Eschatological Cleanliness." In *Jesus Research: An International Perspective*, edited by James H. Charlesworth with Petr Pokorny, 199–229. Grand Rapids: Eerdmans, 2009.

Jensen, Morten Horning. "Purity and Politics in Herod Antipas's Galilee: The Case for Religious Motivation." *JSHJ* 11 (2013) 3–34.

Jones, Larry Paul. *The Symbol of Water in the Gospel of John*. Sheffield: Sheffield Academic Press, 1997.

Kazen, Thomas. *Jesus and Purity Halakhah: Was Jesus Indifferent to Impurity?* Stockholm: Almqvist & Wiksell, 2002.

Keener, Craig S. *The Gospel of John*. 2 vols. Peabody, MA: Hendrickson, 2003.

Kostenberger, Andreas J. "The Destruction of the Second Temple and the Composition of the Fourth Gospel." *Trinity Journal* 26 (2005) 205–42.

Lawrence, Jonathan D. *Washing in Water: Trajectories of Ritual Bathing in the Hebrew Bible and Second Temple Literature*. Atlanta: Society of Biblical Literature, 2006.

Magness, Jodi. "Purity Observance among Diaspora Jews in the Roman World." *Archaeology and Text* 1 (2017) 39–65. https://archaeology-text.cas2.lehigh.edu/.

———. "Sectarianism Before and After 70 CE." In *Was 70 CE a Watershed in Jewish History? On Jews and Judaism Before and After the Destruction of the Second Temple*, edited by Daniel R. Schwartz and Zeev Weiss, 69–89. Boston: Brill, 2012.

———. *Stone and Dung, Oil and Spit: Jewish Daily Life in the Time of Jesus*. Grand Rapids: Eerdmans, 2011.

Meier, John P. *A Marginal Jew, Rethinking the Historical Jesus*. Vol. 4, *Law and Love*. New Haven: Yale University Press, 2009.

Miller, Stuart S. *At the Intersection of Texts and Material Finds: Stepped Pools, Stone Vessels, and Ritual Purity among the Jews of Roman Galilee*. Göttingen: Vandenhoeck & Ruprecht, 2015.

———. *Sages and Commoners in Late Antique 'Eretz Israel: A Philological Inquiry into Local Traditions in Talmudic Yerushalmi*. Tübingen: Mohr Siebeck, 2006.

———. "Stepped Pools, Stone Vessels, and Other Identity Markers of 'Complex Common Judaism.'" *JSJ* 41 (2010) 214–43.

Neyrey, Jerome H. *The Gospel of John in Cultural and Rhetorical Perspective*. Grand Rapids: Eerdmans, 2009.

Ng, Wai-Yee. *Water Symbolism in John: An Eschatological Perspective*. New York: Peter Lang, 2001.

Poirier, John C. "Purity beyond the Temple in the Second Temple Era." *JBL* 122 (2003) 247–65.

Reed, Jonathan. *Archaeology and the Galilean Jesus: A Re-Examination of the Evidence*. Harrisburg, PA: Trinity Press International, 2000.

———. "Stone Vessels and Gospel Texts: Purity and Socio-Economics in John 2." In *Zeichen aus Text und Stein: Studien auf dem Weg zu einer Archaologie des Neuen*

Testaments, edited by Stefan Alkier and Jurgen Zangenberg, 379–401. Tübingen: Francke, 2003.

Regev, Eyal. "Pure Individualism: The Idea of Non-Priestly Purity in Ancient Judaism." *JSJ* 31 (2000) 177–202.

Sanders, E. P. *Judaism: Practice and Belief*. London: SCM, 1992.

Spaulding, Mary B. *Commemorative Identities: Jewish Social Memory and the Johannine Feast of Booths*. New York: T&T Clark, 2009.

Tuval, Michael. "Doing Without the Temple: Paradigms in Judaic Literature of the Diaspora." In *Was 70 CE a Watershed in Jewish History: On Jews and Judaism Before and After the Destruction of the Second Temple*, edited by Daniel R. Schwartz and Zeev Weiss, 181–239. Leiden: Brill, 2012.

von Wahlde, Urban C. "The Pools of Bethesda and the Healing in John 5: A Reappraisal of Research and of the Johannine Text." *RB* 116 (2009) 111–35.

———. "The Pool of Siloam: The Importance of the New Discoveries for Our Understanding of Ritual Immersion in Late Second Temple Judaism and the Gospel of John." In *John, Jesus, and History*. Vol. 2, *Aspects of Historicity in the Fourth Gospel*, edited by Paul N. Anderson et al., 155–73. Atlanta: Society of Biblical Literature, 2009.

———. "The Puzzling Pool of Bethesda, Where Jesus Healed the Crippled Man." *BAR* 37 (2011) 40–47, 65.

The Knowledge of God

Prophetic Vision and Johannine Theme

R. Alan Culpepper

"But the earth will be filled with the knowledge of the glory of the Lord, as the waters cover the sea." (Hab 2:14)[1]

This essay has a deep, personal taproot. It reaches back to my love and admiration for my father, Hugo H. Culpepper, and his influence on my theological convictions. In the back of his Bible he wrote the words of Hab 2:14. The verse expresses his understanding of the biblical basis for missions and the nature of salvation. In June 1979, my father delivered an address at a conference sponsored by the Education Commission of the Southern Baptist Convention in Galveston, Texas. This address, entitled "The Rationale for Missions," which is the best summary of his mature theology of missions, ends with a reference to Habakkuk:

> When the gracious love of God is present in the human heart, the only appropriate response is radical humility. With a spirit of profound gratitude to God, our deepest desire is that he may come to be known experientially, as he is by nature, in his own character. He is truth; he is ultimate reality. To know him is to glorify him. That is the rationale—the underlying reason—for missions.

---

1. This essay is a token of gratitude for the years of friendship and collegiality with Naymond Keathley, mentor, friend, teacher, scholar, and churchman. His decades of teaching, service, and mentoring students at Baylor University and at Seventh and James Baptist Church will bear fruit for generations to come. In him we have seen "the knowledge of the glory of the Lord."

Scripture quotations come from the NRSV unless otherwise indicated.

The earth *will* be filled
With the *knowledge* of the *glory* of the Lord,
As the waters cover the sea.[2]

The image and language of this verse continue to intrigue and challenge. The virtual universality of religion across human cultures and generations is eloquent testimony to the native sense of human beings that there must be a God and to the human quest to know God.[3] But what does it mean to "know God," and how has this goal shaped the Christian faith?

These questions are much too broad for a single essay, so the following pages will simply highlight the role of knowing God in key passages in the prophets in the Hebrew scriptures and the Gospel of John in the New Testament. Still, these reflections will have to be cursory and exploratory.

1. The Knowledge of God in the Prophets

The saying in Hab 2:14 occurs with only minor variations in Num 14:21 and Isa 11:9, suggesting that it was a traditional formulation that may date back to the pre-exilic period. In Numbers, it is an oath formula as the Lord declares to Moses that, "as I live, and as all the earth shall be filled with the glory of the Lord," none of those who tested him in the wilderness and did not obey his voice would see the land God promised to their ancestors. In Isaiah, where it "sounds like a liturgical refrain,"[4] it closes an oracle announcing the eschatological restoration of paradise. The coming of an ideal king from the house of Jesse, the father of David, will bring a period of righteousness, peace, and harmony to Israel. Wolves and lambs, leopards and kids, calves and lions, cows and bears, nursing children and asps, weaned children and adders will live together in harmony, and the stronger will not hurt the weaker, "for the earth will be full of the knowledge of the Lord as the waters cover the sea" (Isa 11:9). Whereas Habakkuk emphasizes the coming judgment and the establishment of God's righteousness on earth, Isaiah characterizes the time of fulfillment that will follow the establishment of righteousness as a return to the peaceful paradise, but "this change will

---

2. Culpepper, *Eternity as a Sunrise*, 328; see also 334. I revised and republished "The Rationale for Missions" as a co-authored essay in *On Mission with God*, 21–34.

3. Contrary to the charge that God is merely the projection of a human sense of need and longing (Nietzsche, Feuerbach) or an inter-subjective reality that enabled humans to organize and control ever larger communities (so, recently, Harari, *Homo Deus*, esp. 181–90), the universality of the quest for God is itself evidence of a Creator who has given human beings both the capacity and the need to live in fellowship with their Creator.

4. Clements, *Isaiah 1–39*, 124.

take place only because, and not until, the land is full of the knowledge of God, and when all exercise righteousness under the guidance of the one who alone is righteous."[5]

In Habakkuk, the saying occurs in a series of five woe oracles (see "alas" in Hab 2:6, 9, 12, 15, and 19) that has the character of a parody of a Hebrew funeral song or dirge, a "dirge over the doomed tyrant":[6]

> Unfortunately the song he records is a little premature. The tyrant isn't yet dead. . . . But God has authorized them to celebrate the tyrant's death ahead of time, and that was his way of reasserting that it is He, and no one else, who rules the world.[7]

These five oracles are directed against "the proud" (Hab 2:4) and record "a vision for the appointed time" (Hab 2:3). In the third oracle, which ends with 2:14, those who "build a town by bloodshed" (2:12) will be punished when "the knowledge of the glory of the Lord" fills the earth—a reference to the coming day of the Lord. This verse appears to be intrusive in the context of the woes, and may have been added by a later commentator who saw that "the ultimate aim of God's purpose is no less than a different world, filled with the knowledge of God's 'glory', in which his universal presence is recognized."[8] As in Numbers, so here, this traditional pronouncement retains its character as an oath: " . . . it is the oath of Yahweh himself that *the earth shall be filled with the knowledge of the glory of Yahweh* that guarantees the vanity and futility of all efforts to the contrary."[9] Habakkuk is distinctive in the combination of *knowledge* with *glory*. The oath inspires optimism as it looks forward to the time when the knowledge of God will be carried to the corners of the globe, and Habakkuk looks forward to the time when the knowledge of God's glory will spread throughout the world, to all humanity, and to the whole of creation:

> Elsewhere in the covenant Scriptures a filling with God's glory is associated particularly with the tabernacle or temple as the place of God's dwelling on earth (Exod. 40:34-35; 1 K. 8:10-11; Ezek. 10:3; cf. Hag. 2:7). But now the splendors emanating from the presence of God shall fill the entirety of creation.[10]

---

5. Kaiser, *Isaiah 1–12*, 161.
6. Szeles, *Wrath and Mercy*, 35; cf. Gowan, *Triumph of Faith in Habakkuk*, 59.
7. Gowan, *Triumph of Faith in Habakkuk*, 62.
8. Mason, *Zephaniah*, 91-92; cf. Andersen, *Habakkuk*, 242; Szeles, *Wrath and Mercy*, 40.
9. Robertson, *Books of Nahum, Habakkuk, and Zephaniah*, 197.
10. Ibid., 198.

The emphasis on the knowledge of God in these verses is developed more fully in significant passages related to covenant renewal or the establishment of a new covenant. Ezekiel 34 ends with the promise that is echoed in the discourse on the Good Shepherd in John 10:

> They shall know that I, the Lord their God, am with them, and that they, the house of Israel, are my people, says the Lord God. You are my sheep, the sheep of my pasture, and I am your God, says the Lord God. (Ezek 34:30–31)

This refrain, "you/they shall know that I am the Lord," is repeated throughout Ezekiel but especially following Ezek 34 (cf. 35:4, 9, 12, 15; 36:1, 38; 37:6, 13, 14; 39:28). Furthermore, the nations "shall know that I am the Lord" (36:23; 38:23; 39:6, 7) and that "I the Lord sanctify Israel" (37:28). Similarly, Jeremiah's promise of a new covenant with the house of Israel ends with the affirmation,

> And I will be their God, and they shall be my people. No longer shall they teach one another, or say to each other, 'Know the Lord,' for they shall all know me, from the least to the greatest, says the Lord. (Jer 31:33–34)[11]

The importance of "knowing the Lord" and the "knowledge of God" in these passages, which are foundational for the interpretation of the new covenant in the New Testament, and the Gospel of John especially, prompts us to look further at the Hebrew understanding of what it means to know God.

For the prophets, the basic problem was that the people did not know God but they ought to:[12]

> The ox knows its owner,
> and the donkey its master's crib;
> But Israel does not know,
> my people do not understand. (Isa 1:3)

On the other hand, God knows Israel (Amos 3:2; Hos 5:3), and each individual person:

> O Lord, you have searched me and known me.
> You know when I sit down and when I rise up;
> You discern my thoughts from far away. (Ps 139:1–2; cf. Jer 1:5)

---

11. This paragraph also appears in my "The Ethics of the Shepherd."
12. Dodd, *Interpretation*, 157; Thompson, *God*, 102.

Accordingly, we are to "know" God because God created us with the capacity to do so and because God calls us into relationship with him. Knowing God, therefore, means being conscious of being known by God.[13]

Knowledge of God in the Hebrew scriptures involves perception, righteousness, and faithfulness in a covenant relationship. God is perceived in the creation (Ps 19:1; 97:6), in revelatory historical events (Exod 7:5, 17; 8:10; 9:14; 14:18), and in the Lord's declarative word ("I am the Lord"; Exod 6:7; 20:2; Isa 42:8; 43:15; passim).[14] The exodus experience is foundational. Moses reminds the Israelites in a "recognition statement"[15] that their eyes had seen the great work of the Lord; "To you it was shown so that you would acknowledge that the Lord is God; there is no other besides him" (Deut 4:35). They are to "keep his statutes and his commandments" (Deut 4:40). Knowledge of God is therefore an important element of the covenant relationship. Summing up the characteristics of the Old Testament covenant relationship, Sherri Brown said, "the flourishing of this knowledge of God made possible through the dynamic of daily living in covenantal obedience breathes life into the relationship between God and his people."[16]

Botterweck observed that in the prophets, "the knowledge of the Lord" appears primarily in oracles of judgment and salvation oracles (as in the verses from Jeremiah and Ezekiel above): "the presence or absence of *da'at* [knowledge] is crucial for the salvation of society as a whole."[17] Specifically, the forgiveness of sins and purity of heart make such knowledge of God, indeed, "intimate communion with God," possible.[18] Such knowledge is not detached, propositional, or objective information. It arises from experience and moves toward acknowledgment and confession. As Bultmann characterized it, "It is thus respectful and obedient acknowledgment of the power and grace and demand of God."[19] The Hebrew concept of knowing, which consists in "*experience* of the object in its relation to the subject," as Dodd summarized it, is therefore qualitatively different from the Greek concept, which "conceives of the process of knowing as analogous to seeing . . . externalizes the object of knowledge, *contemplates* (θεωρεῖ) it from a distance, and endeavours to ascertain its essential qualities."[20] Drawing

---

13. Dodd, *Interpretation*, 160–61.
14. Cf. Botterweck, "יָדַע," 471.
15. Ibid.
16. Brown, *Gift upon Gift*, 67.
17. Botterweck, "יָדַע," 476, 477.
18. Ibid., 477.
19. Bultmann, "γινώσκω," 698.
20. Dodd, *Interpretation*, 151–52.

on the Hebrew concept, which is foundational for the biblical understanding, Marianne Meye Thompson put it this way: "so knowledge of God is not contemplation of but communion with God."[21] Furthermore, if for the Greek knowledge is analogous to seeing, for the Hebrew it is more akin to hearing.[22] Words do not have meanings that they carry into every context, however. Rather, their usage must be determined within each context. In Hellenistic, Jewish writings, including New Testament writings, natively Hebrew concepts may be expressed in Greek terms,[23] so one must construct the sense from each writing and each context.

The revelation of the Lord to Israel, however, was part of a larger design. Solomon's prayer at the dedication of the temple points toward the knowledge of God among all the peoples of the earth. At the dedication of the temple, where the glory of the Lord dwelt among his people, Solomon prayed also for the foreigner who would pray toward the temple, "then hear in heaven your dwelling place, and according to all that the foreigner calls to you, so that all the peoples of the earth may hear your name and fear you, as do your people Israel" (1 Kgs 8:43), "so that all the peoples of the earth may know that the Lord is God" (1 Kgs 8:60).

This brief survey exposes something of the character of the knowledge that is evoked by the majestic refrain in Hab 2:14 and its parallel occurrences. It expresses the hope of the coming of the day of the Lord, when the entire earth and all people will acknowledge and confess the sovereignty of God, know and conform to God's divine will, and live faithfully, maintaining justice, peace, and righteousness.

2. The Knowledge of God in the Gospel of John

Linking the reference to "the knowledge of the glory of the Lord" in Hab 2:14 to the Gospel of John may seem, at first, to be making a connection where there is none. After all, neither Hab 2:14 nor Isa 11:9 is quoted in John (or anywhere else in the New Testament), and the Gospel of John never uses the noun "knowledge." Nevertheless, the theme of Hab 2:14, the knowledge of God, runs deep in the Gospel, and δόξα (glory) occurs

---

21. Thompson, *God*, 143.

22. Bultmann, "γινώσκω," developed this analogy, and Thompson, *God*, 104–17, qualified and added nuance to it.

23. See Hengel, *Judaism and Hellenism*, 1:107, "When foreign—in this case Greek—conceptions were transferred into the language of the Jews, they were considerably altered.... It is often difficult to say whether a particular idea is developed on a line consistent with Jewish thought or whether alien influences are present."

23 times in John—more frequently than in any other book of the New Testament. While it is true that "glory" in John is more typically seen or beheld than known (1:14; 2:11; 11:40; 12:41; 17:24), seeing and knowing are closely related.

The Terms for Knowing

Before the Johannine development of this theme can be explored, its theological matrix and linguistic expressions in John need to be recognized. Taking the latter first, we find that while the noun γνῶσις (knowledge) does not appear in John, neither does the noun πίστις (faith). John and 1 John prefer verbs over nouns and use two verbs for knowing: γινώσκειν and εἰδέναι.[24]

	John	1 John
knowledge (γνῶσις)	0	0
to know (γινώσκειν)	56	25
to know (εἰδέναι)	85	15

It was once thought that the two verbs for knowing carried different meanings in John, that γινώσκειν refers to the experiential acquisition of knowledge, while εἰδέναι refers to immediate certitude.[25] After examining the patterns of usage in the Gospel and the variability of other terms in John, Raymond Brown modified this assessment, concluding that "John may tend to use one verb in one way and the other verb in another way, but it is really a question of emphasis and not of sharp distinction."[26] John Painter's assessment is similar:

> The two verbs translated "know" are used as equivalents as they are in the Septuagint, the Greek version of the Old Testament. John's preference for εἰδέναι occurs in narrative passages. The two verbs are used almost the same number of times in discourse passages, thirty-five or thirty-six times each.[27]

There has also been a shift in the prevailing view of the relationship between John's use of the terms for knowing and Gnosticism. Bultmann

---

24. Painter, *John*, 86; cf. Brown, *Gospel according to John*, 514, and for further analysis of the patterns of usages of these terms, Gaffney, "Believing and Knowing," esp. 216–28.

25. de la Potterie, "*Oida* et *ginôskô*."

26. Brown, *Gospel according to John*, 514; see also Gaffney, "Believing and Knowing," 228.

27. Painter, *John*, 86.

claimed that the Johannine concept of knowing "is paradoxically building on the γινώσκειν of Hellenistic Gnosticism."[28] Heinrich Seesemann was even more categorical, asserting, "Only in the Fourth Gospel can one say with certainty that Gnostic usage has intruded into εἰδέναι."[29] Others assumed that John's avoidance of the noun γνῶσις (knowledge) was a deliberate move to disassociate the Gospel from Gnosticism, a view that Painter finds "absurd."[30] It is more likely that gnostic teachers in the second century were attracted to John because of its use of the terminology for knowing than that it was either influenced by Gnosticism or sought to refute it. Indeed, Charles Hill has recently argued that gnostic use of John was never widespread, and therefore there was no need for anyone in the early church to "rescue this Gospel from gnostic hands."[31]

In John, knowing God is inextricably bound up with a cluster of other themes that give the Johannine understanding of this prophetic theme its distinctive sense. In order to set it in its theological matrix in John, we will need to explore these related themes: Jesus's relationship to the Father, abiding in love, eternal life, believing and obeying, and the mission to the world.

Jesus's Relationship to the Father

Moving to the theological matrix of the theme of knowing in the Gospel of John, we may observe that Jesus's relationship to the Father exerts a controlling influence in the Gospel's development of what it means to know God. The incarnation makes knowledge of God possible. In spite of the spate of recent literature on creation imagery in the Gospel,[32] John does not speak of direct knowledge of God through contemplation on the creation: "He was in the world, and the world came into being through him; yet the world did not know him" (1:10). Nevertheless, for those who will see, commonplace elements (bread, water, wine) point to God's sovereignty as creator, exercised by Jesus the incarnate Logos.[33] To be sure, "Moses and the prophets" also bear witness to Jesus (John 1:45; 5:39), but knowledge of God is mediated uniquely through Jesus, who makes God known (1:18).[34]

28. Bultmann, "γινώσκω," 712.
29. Seesemann, "οἶδα," 118.
30. Painter, *John*, 86.
31. Hill, *Johannine Corpus*, 280, 474.
32. See Culpepper, "Creation Ethics," esp. n. 23.
33. See Koester, *Symbolism*, 2; and Thompson, *God*, 136–40.
34. My father quipped: "Verbalization of the gospel is not enough. We must make the gospel incarnate. Even God could not find a better way."

Those who reject Jesus do not know the Father (7:28; 8:19). If they knew Jesus, they would know the Father (14:8–9). John explores the nature of belief and the reasons why some do not believe (1:10; 3:11). To know Jesus, one must know where he is from and where he was going, his "whence" and "whither." Some cannot believe because they do not know where he was from (1:46; 6:42; 7:27–28; 8:14; 9:29–30). Others stumble over his exaltation and return to the Father (14:5, 12, 28; 16:5, 10). To understand his messianic identity, one must know that he came from the Father and returned to the Father (16:28). Some do not believe because they love their own life (12:25), or the praise of others (5:44; 12:43), more than the praise of God. Others do not believe because they love darkness rather than light—their works are evil (3:19). Still others refuse to see; saying they see, they remain blind (9:39–41).[35]

Jesus's knowledge of God is inherent in his unique relationship to the Father. Jesus is sent by the Father and does the work of the Father (4:34). Jesus abides in the Father and the Father in him (10:38; 17:21); the two are one (10:30; 17:22). Jesus's relationship to the Father is therefore not the model for the believer; it is unique. Because of this relationship, however, the Son is uniquely able to make the Father known, thereby addressing the problem of the prophets, namely, that the people do not know God (7:28; 8:55). The one who has "seen" Jesus, who has "beheld his glory" (1:14), has seen the Father who sent him (12:45; 14:9). Therefore, Thomas's confession at the end of John 20, "my Lord and my God," represents the fulfillment of Jesus's mission to make God known (1:18).

As the one sent by the Father, Jesus mediates the knowledge of God to those who receive him, who believe in his name (1:12). As Bultmann famously said, "Jesus as the Revealer of God reveals nothing but that he is the Revealer,"[36] but that is not entirely true.[37] Jesus reveals God's love for the world (3:16).[38] Jesus reveals God's sustaining (even bountiful) providence, symbolized in the provision of bountiful wine, abundant bread and fish, and the miraculous catch of 153 large fish. Jesus reveals his relationship to God as Son with the Father (e.g., 5:19; 10:30; 14:9–10, 24; 17:21) and the nature of the life that God gives to those who believe in Jesus and thereby enter into the communion with God that he makes possible (15:4–6; 17:3, 20–26).

35. Painter, *John*, 73. On the issue of God's calling, choosing, and drawing people to faith, see Bultmann, *Theology of the New Testament*, 2:21, and Culpepper, "Inclusivism and Exclusivism in the Fourth Gospel," 95–97.

36. Bultmann, *Theology of the New Testament*, 2:66.

37. Cf. Thompson, *God*, 141.

38. Moloney, *Love in the Gospel of John*, establishes the centrality of this theme in the Gospel.

Abiding in Love

Akiba insightfully saw that both the divine gift and the knowledge of the gift are expressions of God's love:

> He [Akiba] used to say: Beloved is man for he was created in the image [of God]; still greater was the love in that it was made known to him that he was created in the image of God, as it is written, *For in the image of God made he man* [Gen 9:6]. Beloved are Israel for they were called children of God; still greater was the love in that it was made known to them that they were called children of God, as it is written, *Ye are the children of the Lord your God* [Deut 14:1]. . . . (*m. 'Abot* 3:15)[39]

In light of the Johannine understanding of the connection between love and the knowledge of God, we might add that humanity was created with the capacity to know God and still greater was the love in that the means to the knowledge of God was made known in Jesus. Love is both the basis for knowledge of God and an essential quality of eternal life: "Whoever does not love does not know God, for God is love" (1 John 4:8). The Father sent the Son to bring knowledge of God to humankind because of God's love for the world—for every human person (3:16). By means of what he did as well as what he said, Jesus revealed the Father's divine love.[40] He revealed the inclusiveness of God's love by reaching out to people regardless of background, ethnicity, or status—male and female, Jew and Samaritan, blind beggar and Roman prefect.[41] Finally, through his death, which John characterizes as his exaltation, his being "lifted up," Jesus would draw all people to himself (12:32).

Eternal Life

Conceptually, eternal life is closely related to believing and knowing in John. On the one hand, one who believes/knows enters into eternal life; on the other hand, the defining quality of eternal life is knowing God.[42] Life in the distinctive Johannine sense of eternal life comes through knowledge of God because God is the creator and sustainer of life (1:4; 5:21). John therefore defines the essence of eternal life as knowing God through Jesus (17:3). As

---

39. Danby, *Mishnah*, 452.
40. See Moloney, *Love in the Gospel of John*, xi.
41. Culpepper, "Inclusivism and Exclusivism," 90–95.
42. Cf. Gaffney's discussion in "Believing and Knowing," 237–38.

the background for this verse, Dodd insightfully engaged Hos 6:2–3, "on the third day he will raise us up, that we may live before him. Let us know, let us press on to know the Lord." Dodd commented:

> Whatever may have been the precise meaning of Hosea's original Hebrew, there is no doubt that to a Greek reader this meant: "we shall rise (from the dead) and live in His presence, and have knowledge; we shall press forward to know the Lord." To know the Lord is to live before him, that is, to have eternal life . . .[43]

This knowledge of God is also related to the mutual indwelling that comes through believing.[44] The Father and Son, who give life, abide in those who believe (14:23; 17:21, 24). Perhaps the best summation of the connection between knowing God and experiencing eternal life comes at the end of 1 John, where the elder writes: "And we know that the Son of God has come and has given us understanding so that we may know him who is true; and we are in him who is true, in his Son Jesus Christ. He is the true God and eternal life" (1 John 5:20). Eternal life, for John, is therefore an integral part of what it means to have faith, to believe. It is both a present reality for the one who lives in such communion with God through Jesus (11:25–27) and a reality yet to be fully realized (6:39, 40, 44, 54; 11:26; 14:3). First John asserts the future fulfillment in terms of seeing God: "What we do know is this: when he is revealed, we will be like him, for we will see him as he is" (1 John 3:2).

Believing and Obeying

Believing and knowing are closely related in Johannine thought. Believing is the means by which one receives the knowledge of God. It is significant, therefore, that in the Johannine equivalent to Peter's confession at Caesarea Philippi in the Synoptic Gospels, Peter confesses, "We have come to *believe and know* that you are the Holy One of God" (6:69). Believing has a cognitive as well as a volitional dimension. The disciples at least profess to know Jesus's messianic identity and commit themselves to him. Later, Jesus extends the same invitation to those who did not believe in him: "*believe* the works, *so that you may know* and understand that the Father is in me and I am in the Father" (10:38). In 1 John believing and knowing also occur

---

43. Dodd, *Interpretation*, 163.

44. Ibid., 169: "γνῶσις is awareness of a relation of mutual indwelling of God and man." The Johannine understanding of abiding and mutual indwelling in 1 John was explored thoroughly by Malatesta, *Interiority and Covenant*.

together but in reverse order: "So *we have known* and *believe* the love that God has for us" (1 John 4:16).

Knowing and believing are expressed in the life of the believer in worship and obedience. The blind man who had received his sight confesses, "'Lord, I believe.' And he worshiped him" (9:38). Just as Jesus knows the Father and keeps his word (8:55), so those who believe in him should keep his commandments (14:15, 21, 23, 24). Indeed, keeping his commandments became a test of whether one "knew" Jesus: "Now by this we may be sure that we know him, if we obey his commandments" (1 John 2:3). At the same time, those who keep his commandments, especially the love command and the mission he gives them, will abide in his love (15:10). Throughout, the Johannine formulas and images are relational. The Son who knows the Father and abides in him does the Father's work (4:34), calls the disciples to believe in him, and sends them to gather fruit "for eternal life, so that sower and reaper may rejoice together" (4:36).

The Mission to the World

Jesus also called his disciples to the mission of fruit gathering (4:38; 17:18; 20:21), consecrated them with the Holy Spirit (20:22), and sent them to bear witness to the world. Central to that mission is declaring the knowledge of God that comes through Jesus so that all might be drawn into the life that comes through communion with God. And here John comes close to the hope expressed in Hab 2:14, that the knowledge of the glory of the Lord might fill the earth, "as the waters cover the sea." The Johannine Jesus alludes to the universal scope of this mission by saying that he had "other sheep that do not belong to this fold" (10:16), "children of God" who are scattered abroad (11:52), so when the Greeks came asking to "see" Jesus it was a sign to him that the hour of his death had come. He would need to die and be buried, like a seed falling into the ground that dies to itself so it might bear "much fruit" (12:24). Before he died, Jesus enacted the meaning of his death by washing the disciples' feet and giving them the "new command," that they love one another as he loved them (13:1–20, 34–35). He prayed for the disciples and those who would believe because of their testimony, that they might be one, as he and the Father are one (17:20–26). It is certainly no coincidence that Jesus's last words before he goes out to be arrested are "I made your name known to them, and I will make it known, so that the love with which you have loved me may be in them, and I in them" (17:26). Appropriately, when Jesus's hour came, the inscription on the cross was written in three languages so that all might read it (19:20), and his tunic, which was woven "from above" (ἄνωθεν), was untorn, just as later the net full of 153 large fish, which Peter brought to Jesus, was untorn (21:10–11). How appropriate, in light of our verse from Habakkuk, that, having told the story of the one who brought the knowledge of God to the world, John ends his story at the sea!

3. Conclusion

Both the prophetic problem—the people do not know God but they ought to—and the prophetic vision—"the knowledge of the glory of the Lord will fill the earth"—shape John's understanding of the incarnation. God is mysterious, unknowable to human beings, search as we may to know God. Because God is personal, it took the incarnation of the divine Logos in Jesus to enable human beings to know God. The one who was sent by God, who spoke the words of God, did the work of God, and was God has revealed the Father. Through faith in him, which involves believing, love, keeping his commandments, and entering into the work of bearing witness and gathering fruit, we share in the life of God, eternal life. Albert Schweitzer's dramatic and personal conclusion to *The Quest of the Historical Jesus* still rings true:

> And to those who obey Him, whether they be wise or simple, He will reveal Himself in the toils, the conflicts, the sufferings which they shall pass through in His fellowship, and as an ineffable mystery, they shall learn in their own experience Who He is.[45]

We are able to know God in a personal, experiential sense because God knows us. The insight reached above goes to the heart of the mystery: knowing God means being conscious of being known by God. Adopting the image of a shepherd and his sheep, Jesus said, "I am the good shepherd. I know my own and my own know me . . . . My sheep hear my voice. I know them, and they follow me" (10:3, 14, 27). Jesus knew Nathanael before Philip called him (1:48), the Samaritan woman reported, "he told me everything I have ever done" (4:39), he knew Judas would betray him (6:70–71; 13:27), and the Johannine narrator also tells us that Jesus knew, literally, "what is in each person" (2:23).

Even after Peter denied Jesus three times in the high priest's courtyard, saying, as Mark records his words, "I do not know this man you are talking about" (14:71), the risen Lord accepted Peter's three professions of love and

---

45. Schweitzer, *Quest of the Historical Jesus*, 403.

commissioned Peter, "feed my sheep." John Claypool imagines that in later years Peter would get a far-off look in his eyes and muse,

> Someday I'll stand in the judgment hall of God and, in that moment he will do for me what I failed to do for him in his hour of greatest need. There will come to my ears the sound of my best friend's voice saying, "Yes, I do know him, Father, he is one of us."[46]

And if Peter did say something like this, it was because he had learned in his own experience "Who He is."

Works Cited

Andersen, Francis I. *Habakkuk*. AB 25. New York: Doubleday, 2001.
Botterweck, G. Johannes. "יָדַע." In *TDOT* 5:448–81. Edited by G. Johannes Botterweck and Helmer Ringgren. Translated by David E. Green. Grand Rapids: Eerdmans, 1986.
Brown, Raymond E. *The Gospel according to John, I–XII*. AB 29. Garden City, NY: Doubleday, 1966.
Brown, Sherri. *Gift upon Gift: Covenant through Word in the Gospel of John*. Princeton Theological Monograph Series. Eugene, OR: Pickwick, 2010.
Bultmann, Rudolf. "γινώσκω." In *TDNT* 1:689–719. Edited by Gerhard Kittel. Translated by Geoffrey W. Bromiley. Grand Rapids: Eerdmans, 1964.
———. *Theology of the New Testament*. Translated by Kendrick Grobel. 2 vols. New York: Charles Scribner's Sons, 1951–55.
Claypool, John R. *The First to Follow: The Apostles of Jesus*. Edited by Ann Wilkinson Claypool. Harrisburg: Morehouse, 2008.
Clements, R. E. *Isaiah 1–39*. NCB. Grand Rapids: Eerdmans, 1980.
Culpepper, Hugo H., and R. Alan Culpepper. "The Rationale for Missions." In *On Mission with God: Free and Faithful Baptists in the Twenty-First Century*, edited by Pamela R. Durso and William O'Brien, 21–34. Atlanta: Baptist History and Heritage Society, 2011.
Culpepper, R. Alan. "The Creation Ethics of the Gospel of John." In *Johannine Ethics: The Moral World of the Gospel and Epistles of John*, edited by Christopher W. Skinner and Sherri Brown, 67–90. Minneapolis: Fortress, 2017.
———. *Eternity as a Sunrise: The Life of Hugo H. Culpepper*. Macon: Mercer University Press, 2002.
———. "The Ethics of the Shepherd." In *Biblical Ethics and Application: Purview, Validity, and Relevance of Biblical Texts in Ethical Discourse: Essays in Honor of Jan G. van der Watt*, edited by Ruben Zimmermann and Stephan Joubert, 139–62. Kontexte und Normen neutestamentlicher Ethik [Contexts and Norms of New Testament Ethics] 9. WUNT 384. Tübingen: Mohr Siebeck, 2017.

---

46. Claypool, *First to Follow*, 36.

———. "Inclusivism and Exclusivism in the Fourth Gospel." In *Word, Theology, and Community in John*, edited by John Painter, R. Alan Culpepper, and Fernando F. Segovia, 85–108. St. Louis: Chalice, 2002.

Danby, Herbert, trans. *The Mishnah*. Oxford: Oxford University Press, 1933.

de la Potterie, Ignace. "*Oida* et *ginôskô*, les deux modes de la connaissance dans le quatrième évangile." *Bib* 40 (1959) 709–25.

Dodd, C. H. *The Interpretation of the Fourth Gospel*. Cambridge: Cambridge University Press, 1953.

Gaffney, James. "Believing and Knowing in the Fourth Gospel." *TS* 26 (1965) 215–41.

Gowan, Donald E. *The Triumph of Faith in Habakkuk*. Atlanta: John Knox, 1976.

Harari, Yuval N. *Homo Deus: A Brief History of Tomorrow*. London: Harvill Secker, 2016.

Hengel, Martin. *Judaism and Hellenism*. Translated by John Bowden. 2 vols. Philadelphia: Fortress, 1974.

Hill, Charles E. *The Johannine Corpus in the Early Church*. Oxford: Oxford University Press, 2004.

Kaiser, Otto. *Isaiah 1–12: A Commentary*. OTL. Philadelphia: Westminster, 1972.

Koester, Craig R. *Symbolism in the Fourth Gospel: Meaning, Mystery, Community*. 2nd ed. Minneapolis: Fortress, 2003.

Malatesta, Edward. *Interiority and Covenant: A Study of εἶναι ἐν and μένειν ἐν in the First Letter of Saint John*. AB 69. Rome: Biblical Institute, 1978.

Mason, Rex. *Zephaniah, Habakkuk, Joel*. OTG. Sheffield: JSOT, 1994.

Moloney, Francis J. *Love in the Gospel of John: An Exegetical, Theological, and Literary Study*. Grand Rapids: Baker Academic, 2013.

Painter, John. *John: Witness and Theologian*. 3rd ed. Australia: Beacon Hill, 1986.

Robertson, O. Palmer. *The Books of Nahum, Habakkuk, and Zephaniah*. NICOT. Grand Rapids: Eerdmans, 1990.

Seesemann, Heinrich. "οἶδα." In *TDNT* 5:116–19. Edited by Gerhard Friedrich. Translated by Geoffrey W. Bromiley. Grand Rapids: Eerdmans, 1967.

Schweitzer, *The Quest of the Historical Jesus: A Critical Study of Its Progress from Reimarus to Wrede*. Translated by W. Montgomery. New York: Macmillan, 1950.

Szeles, Maria Eszenyei. *Wrath and Mercy: A Commentary on the Books of Habakkuk and Zephaniah*. Translated by George A. F. Knight. ITC. Grand Rapids: Eerdmans, 1987.

Thompson, Marianne Meye. *The God of the Gospel of John*. Grand Rapids: Eerdmans, 2001.

Romans 6:1–14

The Case for a Chiastic Q&A

Rudolph D. Gonzalez

Introduction

THE MOST CURSORY READING of the major commentaries on Romans 6 shows that there is no structural consensus. While some consider 6:1–14 a unit, others see a break at v. 11 with vv. 12–14 as transitional or incorporated with vv. 15–23.[1] And there is more, for some link Romans 6 back to chapters 5 and/or 3, raising the issue whether Paul digresses to treat questions raised earlier.[2] As we might expect, the way structure is perceived drives theological interpretation. Thus, for example, while both C. H. Talbert and J. D. G. Dunn see vv. 1–14 (or vv. 1–11) as focusing on death to sin, J. A. Fitzmyer sees vv. 1–11 as discussing death to sin and life under grace with these verses constituting "the main discussion of baptism by Paul."[3] In his analysis, T. R. Schreiner maintains that vv. 2–14 focus on the power of grace to break the

---

1. Those who take 6:1–14 as a unit include: Cranfield, *Romans*; Deibler, *Semantic and Structural Analysis*; Denney, "St. Paul's Epistle"; Kruse, *Paul's Letter*; Moo, *Epistle to the Romans*; Morris, *Epistle to the Romans*; Nygren, *Commentary on Romans*; Sanday and Headlam, *Epistle to the Romans*; Schreiner, *Romans*; and Talbert, *Romans*. Those who see 6:1–11 as a unit include: Barth, *Epistle to the Romans*; Dunn, *Romans 1–8*; Fitzmyer, *Romans*; Käsemann, *Commentary on Romans*; Kaye, *Argument of Romans*; Murray, *Epistle to the Romans*. Additionally, both NA28 and UBS5 place a paragraph break at 6:12. However, UBS5 begins another paragraph at 6:15.

2. So, for example, Cranfield, *Epistle to the Romans,* 1:296; Kaye, *Argument of Romans,* 23; Morris, *Epistle to the Romans,* 244; Fitzmyer, *Romans,* 429. Jeremias, "Chiasmus in Den Paulusbriefen," 145–56. Jeremias argues for Rom 6 picking up unresolved issues going back to chapter 3:1, 31.

3. Talbert, *Romans,* 159; Dunn, *Romans,* 302–3; Fitzmyer, *Romans,* 430.

dominion of sin.[4] Others could be included, but it becomes evident that the theological concepts of sin, grace, death, law, flesh, and baptism are nuanced *ad infinitum*, driving most structural decisions, with no clear-cut winner.

Is there a solution to this impasse? Here we suggest one is possible by proposing that Rom 6:1–14 is chiastic. This is not entirely new, for Hendrikus Boers and Sang-Hoon Kim have proffered detailed chiastic proposals, but neither extends its properties beyond v. 11, and we can see why.[5] Most apropos literature sees *chiasmus* as consisting of approximate parallel panels,[6] and both Boers and Kim are committed to this form.[7] But, is there room for creative deviation? Here we contend that Paul, no literary pedestrian, designed Romans 6:1–14 with chiastic properties somewhat analogous to a Q&A scenario.[8]

Romans 6:1–14: A Chiasm Built on Questions and Answers

As we begin, we do so against a preponderance of scholars who take 6:1b as putting forth the only real question Paul addresses. A review of major commentaries shows that despite vv. 2, 3 being composed of two interrogatives, these tend to be read as declarative statements.[9] And even Boers and Kim either leave the questions outside the limits of their chiastic proposal or treat them as continuous statements.[10] But, does this do justice to the interrogatives as such?

In recent times speech act theorists have educated us as to the nature of "authentic" and "non-authentic" questions and to the persuasive strategies

---

4. Schreiner, *Romans*, 298–99.

5. Boers, "Structure and Meaning," 675–82. Boers limits the chiasm to 6:4c–11, leaving vv. 1–4b and vv. 12–14 outside. Kim, "Triple Chiastic Structures," builds his chiasm on 6:1–11.

6. Lund, *Chiasmus in the New Testament*, uses "panel" when referring to the two individual halves of the structure and the central unit. Though other terms are used, "panel" will be used exclusively throughout this essay.

7. Note Boers, "Structure and Meaning," parallels B/B' and C/C'; Kim, "Triple Chiastic Structures," parallels A/A', B/B', and C/C'.

8. We do not argue that the modern Q&A pattern dates to antiquity. The characterization is only suggestive.

9. All commentaries reviewed see 6:1b as the only actual question, with vv. 2–3 incorporated into vv. 2–11 (see Dunn, *Romans*, 305–6) or into vv. 2–14 (see Schreiner, *Romans*, 299; Witherington, *Paul's Letter*, 155).

10. Boers, "Structure and Meaning," 676; Kim, "Triple Chiastic Structures," 9.

employed in the latter.[11] Thus, while authentic questions expect to be answered, non-authentic questions are rather veiled statements, conveying emotion, or emphasis, seeking some response act. This is important to keep in mind for the interpretation of this passage may depend on how the questions in vv. 1–3 are understood. In our analysis, the question in v. 1a, Τί οὖν ἐροῦμεν, is rhetorical, non-authentic, setting the reader up for a new theme.[12] And the rhetorical emphasis continues for the questions at v. 1b and v. 2b; both have absurd, non-authentic indicators.[13] Yet, despite its break from the rule of politeness, the question in v. 3 concerns knowledge of baptism and is arguably answerable. Generally, it is reasonable to see that persuasive strategies are at play, yet the interrogatives are not merely stated for their rhetorical force.[14] Ernst Käsemann notes that Paul does not use rhetoric simply for adornment, but rather as "a means of substantive argument."[15] Additionally, A. H. Snyman has noted that the progressive lengthening of questions, as ours do, can also draw attention to the substance the writer is wanting to communicate.[16] As we hope to show, despite their rhetorical features, questions A, B, and C are answered. Romans 6:1–14 reveals two panels consisting of three question and answer parallels radiating out from a central panel as configured below:

Τί οὖν ἐροῦμεν; (v. 1a) [17]

A: ἐπιμένωμεν τῇ ἁμαρτίᾳ, ἵνα ἡ χάρις πλεονάσῃ; (v. 1b)

B: μὴ γένοιτο. (v. 2a) οἵτινες ἀπεθάνομεν τῇ ἁμαρτίᾳ, πῶς ἔτι ζήσομεν ἐν αὐτῇ; (v. 2b)

11. See Verster, "Implications of Non-Authentic Questions," 142–61.

12. Ibid., 148. Per Verster, the question in v. 1a can be classified as a "rational-argumentative question" as it is too non-specific to expect a response. It is rather an appeal meant to draw the receiver's attention to a new theme.

13. Ibid., 147. The questions in vv. 1b and 2b can be seen as non-authentic, emphatic rhetorical questions, intent on making a statement. The absurdity of the questions in v. 1b, "sinning to increase grace," and v. 2, "dying to sin, yet still living in it," is clarified by the question in v. 3, making sense of the previous absurdity. Verster sees μὴ γένοιτο as a strong indicator of emotion.

14. For example, the absurdity of question A (v. 1b) takes on a more substantive note when we consider that Paul is picking up on an authentic question in 3:7, raising the same issue, albeit in a different form, at 6:15.

15. Käsemann, *Commentary on Romans*, 293.

16. Snyman, "Style and the Rhetorical Situation," 224, 228. Per Snyman, the progressive lengthening of questions is used to strengthen adherence to Paul's teaching and not simply for rhetorical effect. The questions in 6:1–3 expand as follows: v. 1a, 3 words; v. 1b, 7 words; v. 2b, 9 words; v. 3, 13 words. Progression is used again at 8:31–39.

17. Textual variants for 6:1–14 are negligible with respect to chiasticity.

C: ἢ ἀγνοεῖτε ὅτι, ὅσοι ἐβαπτίσθημεν εἰς Χριστὸν Ἰησοῦν, εἰς τὸν θάνατον αὐτοῦ ἐβαπτίσθημεν; (v. 3)

> D: συνετάφημεν οὖν αὐτῷ διὰ τοῦ βαπτίσματος εἰς τὸν θάνατον, ἵνα ὥσπερ ἠγέρτη Χριστὸς ἐκ νεκρῶν διὰ τῆς δόξης τοῦ πατρός, ὡς καὶ ἡμεῖς ἐν καινότητι ζωῆς περιπατήσωμεν. εἰ γὰρ σύμφυτοι γεγόναμεν τῷ ὁμοιώματι τοῦ θανάτου αὐτοῦ, ἀλλὰ καὶ τῆς ἀναστάσεως ἐσόμεθα· (vv. 4–5)

C': τοῦτο γινώσκοντες ὅτι ὁ παλαιὸς ἡμῶν ἄνθρωπος συνεσταυρώθη, ἵνα καταργηθῇ τὸ σῶμα τῆς ἁμαρτίας, τοῦ μηκέτι δουλεύειν ἡμᾶς τῇ ἁμαρτίᾳ· ὁ γὰρ ἀποθανὼν δεδικαίωται ἀπὸ τῆς ἁμαρτίας. εἰ δὲ ἀπεθάνομεν σὺν Χριστῷ, πιστεύομεν ὅτι καὶ συζήσομεν αὐτῷ, εἰδότες ὅτι Χριστὸς ἐγερθεὶς ἐκ νεκρῶν οὐκέτι ἀποθνήσκει, θάνατος αὐτοῦ οὐκέτι κυριεύει. ὃ γὰρ ἀπέθανεν, τῇ ἁμαρτίᾳ ἀπέθανεν ἐφάπαξ. ὃ δὲ ζῇ, ζῇ τῷ θεῷ. (vv. 6–10)

B': οὕτως καὶ ὑμεῖς λογίζεσθε ἑαυτοὺς εἶναι νεκροὺς μὲν τῇ ἁμαρτίᾳ ζῶντας δὲ τῷ θεῷ ἐν Χριστῷ Ἰησοῦ (v. 11)

A': Μὴ οὖν βασιλευέτω ἡ ἁμαρτία ἐν τῷ θνητῷ ὑμῶν σώματι εἰς τὸ ὑπακούειν ταῖς ἐπιθυμίαις αὐτοῦ, μηδὲ παριστάνετε τὰ μέλη ὑμῶν ὅπλα ἀδικίας τῇ ἁμαρτίᾳ, ἀλλὰ παραστήσατε ἑαυτοὺς τῷ θεῷ ὡσεὶ ἐκ νεκρῶν ζῶντας καὶ τὰ μέλη ὑμῶν ὅπλα δικαιοσύνεις τῷ θεῷ. ἁμαρτία γὰρ ὑμῶν οὐ κυριεύσει· οὐ γὰρ ἐστε ὑπὸ νόμον ἀλλὰ ὑπὸ χάριν. (vv. 12–14)

Τί οὖν; (v. 15a)

Ten Criteria for Evaluating Chiasticity

Of course, one could charge that this chiasm is in the eye of the beholder, so it behooves us to test the merits of this proposal, by applying the most objective and accepted chiasmus criteria.[18]

---

18. The sources for the following ten criteria are Thomson, "Matters of Background" in *Chiasmus in the Pauline Letters*; Welch, "Criteria for Identifying"; and Smith, "Criteria for Identifying Chiasm." The criteria of Density and Reduplication, while not formally treated, are addressed throughout the essay. The criterion of Aesthetics requires its own treatment and is beyond the purview of this study. On Aesthetics see Talbert, "Artistry and Theology," 341–66.

Objectivity

Does 6:1–14 stand out as a chiasm? Admittedly, its chiastic properties are not readily apparent.[19] Yet, this may be in part due to a *received* definition, which dictates that all chiasms are built on statements of roughly parallel length. However, as C.A. Smith notes, "chiasms of design are more likely to occur in works by authors with a demonstrable affinity for the chiastic form."[20] In this regard, J. W. Welch has listed a number of verifiable chiasms in Paul's uncontested letters, and thirty specifically in Romans.[21] The criterion of objectivity alone does not prove that 6:1–14 is chiastic, but it does keep open the possibility. If Paul is capable of using midrash, diatribe, and early hymn and catechetical traditions to couch his message, chiasmus, prolific in Hellenistic and Hebrew literature, was certainly at his disposal.[22]

Boundaries

Romans 6:1–14 fits within the category Ian H. Thomson identifies as an intermediate chiasm.[23] Note that at 6:1a our chiasm is prefaced by Τί οὖν ἐροῦμεν, while v. 15a introduces Τί οὖν, setting its limits. Within the text, the two "grace" phrases (vv. 1b, 14b), the first with a nominative χάρις, the latter with an accusative χάριν, function as a fitting *Inclusio*.[24]

---

19. Talbert, a proponent of NT chiasm, fails to note its presence (*Romans*, 159–83). Ellis proposes an overarching chiastic structure of Romans (*Seven Pauline Letters*, 203–5), but does not note 6:1–14 as a chiasm (see 200–264).

20. Smith, "Criteria for Identifying Chiasm," 304.

21. Ibid., 309. Smith cites Welch, *Chiasmus Bibliography*, 175. Welch identifies the following numbers of verifiable chiasms in the undisputed Pauline corpus: 63 in 1 Corinthians, 9 in 2 Corinthians, 16 in Galatians, 6 in 1 Thessalonians, and 1 in Philemon.

22. See Lund, *Chiasmus in the New Testament*, 9–29; Thomson, "Classical and Semitic Background of Chiasmus," in *Chiasmus in the Pauline Letters*, 14–18; "Paul and the Cultural Context of Chiasmus," in *Chiasmus in the Pauline Letters*, 18–22. See also Porter and Olbricht, eds., *The Rhetorical Analysis of Scripture*.

23. Thomson, "Classical and Semitic Background of Chiasmus," in *Chiasmus in the Pauline Letters*, 23.

24. For the purpose of this essay, *Inclusio* is understood to be a literary device in rhetorical studies used to bracket a theme or a concept at both the beginning and at the end of a text. *Inclusio* generally employs a word or a phrase intended to introduce the theme and also signal its closure.

Length

For Thomson, intermediate chiasms allow for theological development. Smith agrees, ruling out aesthetics and rhetoric as primary motivations for longer chiasms and seeing them rather as conveyors of semantic intent.[25] Since a central panel also factors in chiasms with semantic function, 6:1–14 is long enough to support a critical theological message, which we will duly note under the criteria of *Centrality, Climax,* and *Return.*[26]

Dominance

This criterion seeks to discover the degree to which the parallels in both panels exhibit common dominant language and themes proving chiasticity. Note the three pairings.

C (v. 3) and C' (vv. 6–10)

Question C asks, ἢ ἀγνοεῖτε . . . , eliciting information, albeit in an impolite manner, and C' answers accordingly with the demonstrative τοῦτο reacting to the negative question.[27] Taking on C, parallel C' asserts that believers do in fact know some things. First, believers know (γινώσκοντες) that the old man has been crucified with Christ so that they might no longer be slaves to sin (v. 6). Additionally, in v. 9, C' asserts that believers also know (εἰδότες) of Christ's crucifixion and resurrection (vv. 9–10).[28] If one should inquire on what ground believers can base such knowledge, both participles γινώσκοντες and εἰδότες have a causal function,[29] saying in effect, "we know these things 'because' we have experienced and hope for such things," pointing back to vv. 4–5.[30]

---

25. Smith, "Criteria for Identifying Chiasm," 272.

26. Ibid., 280.

27. Deibler, *Semantic and Structural Analysis,* 142. For Deibler, the cataphorical function of τοῦτο is so pronounced it introduces a new idea with no logical relationship to v. 5.

28. Cranfield, *Epistle to the Romans,* 1:313. We agree with Canfield that εἰδότες should be preceded by a colon at v. 8, as γινώσκοντες is at v. 5, thus meaning, "and we know," and introducing yet another consideration.

29. See Wallace, *Greek Grammar,* 631; Rogers, *New Linguistic and Exegetical Key,* 327.

30. Dunn, *Romans,* 322. Additionally, the causal participles weaken the argument that Paul is introducing knowledge unbeknownst to his readers by making the ground of knowledge their shared experience "in Christ" (vv. 4–5).

Structurally, Smith observes that some chiasms will have *nested mini-chiasms* embedded in the parallels.[31] In this regard note how both C and C' can be configured along chiastic lines:

Parallel C	Parallel C'
a: have been baptized (v. 3a)	a: crucified with Christ, freed from sin (vv. 6–7)
b: into Christ Jesus (v. 3b)	b: if we have died to sin (v. 8a)
b': into his death (v. 3c)	b': we believe we will live with him (v. 8b)
a': have been baptized (v. 3d)	a': Christ, freed from death, serves God (v. 9–10)

These nested chiasms make our case compelling in light of the surplus knowledge C' offers. [32]

B (v. 2) and B' (v. 11)

This parallel focuses on a mental exercise. Following C/C', which is assumed as factual, B basically asks readers to ponder, to think. Knowing they have died to sin (C'), the question πῶς ἔτι ζήσομεν ἐν αὐτῇ follows inferentially. Thus, B' takes question B as authentic, cautioning readers to λογίζεσθε themselves dead to sin, but alive to God in Christ.[33] While there is a difference of opinion whether λογίζομαι means "to take stock," "to regard," "to think of oneself," or "to judge," [34] each possible meaning emphasizes an act of reasoning.[35] The chiastic relationship is strong.

A (v. 1b) and A' (vv. 12–14)

Concerning A', S. Levinsohn notes that with the use of οὖν Paul goes from thought to action.[36] And indeed A' responds to the absurdity of continuing to

---

31. Smith, "Criteria for Identifying Chiasm," 122–25.

32. Jewett, *Romans*, 392. Jewett also makes note of this chiasm.

33. Heidland, "λογίζομαι, λογίζμος," 288. Λογίζεσθε implies that actions should conform to the act of thought.

34. See Käsemann, *Commentary on Romans*, 170–71.

35. Paul uses λογίζομαι eight times in Rom 4. Abraham was "reckoned" righteous consistently on the basis of a mental activity: *he believed* (v. 3, 5, 9, 11, 19–22). Note that λογίζεσθε is the first use of the imperative in Romans. See Morris, *Epistle to the Romans*, 256; Schreiner, *Romans*, 322.

36. Levinsohn, *Discourse Features*, 16.

sin to πλεονάσῃ grace (A). It does so by calling for a number of imperatival prohibitions and encouragements. In vv. 12–13a, Μὴ . . . μηδέ challenges readers to reign in bodily ἐπιθυμίαις not surrendering their bodies to serve as ὅπλα ἀδικίας. The adversative ἀλλά (v.13b) introduces the opposite, to present τὰ μέλη ὑμῶν ὅπλα δικαιοσύνεις. The imperatives (παριστάνετε and παραστήσατε) preceded by μηδέ challenge readers both to cease sinning, and to begin ongoing moral actions.[37]

Mavericks

What about μὴ γένοιτο in parallel B v. 2a? Here we contend that far from being extraneous to the chiastic structure, this negation expresses a heightened sense of outrage,[38] the effects of which are manifested in several directions. First, it is a fitting visceral rhetorical response to question A. Second, as such, it provides the ground for the menacing ἢ ἀγνοεῖτε of C (v.3) and third, it anticipates the strong Μὴ . . . μηδὲ imperatives in A'.

Centrality

One criterion which strengthens chiasticity is a central panel.[39] In our target text, vv. 4–5 function as D, the pivotal element. At first blush, one could see vv. 4–10 as one continuous whole, for language of death/dying (vv. 4, 7), life/living (vv. 4b, 8, 10), and raised/ resurrection (vv. 4c, 5, 9a) would seem to unite these verses. But to do so would come at the cost of missing a vital distinction. In our analysis, vv. 4–5 relate to an experience per se,[40] while vv. 6–10 describe a person's telling of it. Thus, in panel D, Paul evokes the believer's experience of being united with Christ through baptism, resulting in "newness of life" (v. 4), also sharing in the ὁμοιώματι of his death with hope to share in the likeness (implied) of his resurrection (v. 5).[41] Ben Witherington rightly notes that the conditional statement in v.

---

37. Wallace sees these two imperatives as ingressive progressives (*Greek Grammar*, 720–21).

38. There are fourteen usages of μὴ γένοιτο in Paul's undisputed epistles: Rom 3:4, 6, 31; 6:2, 15; 7:7, 13; 9:14; 11:1, 11; 1 Cor 6:15; Gal 2:17; 3:21; 6:14.

39. Smith, "Criteria for Identifying Chiasm," 290.

40. Barrett, *Epistle to the Romans*, 124; Dodd, *Epistle of Paul*, 87; Dunn, *Romans*, 313–14; Fitzmyer, *Romans*, 434–35; Käsemann, *Commentary on Romans*, 168–69; Morris, *Epistle to the Romans*, 248; Moo, *Epistle to the Romans*, 361–71; Schreiner, *Romans*, 312; Sanday and Headlam, *Epistle to the Romans*, 162–63.

41. Schreiner sees vv. 6–10 as a restatement of vv. 3–5, failing to take note of the

5 "is in the form of a real or genuine condition, not merely hypothetical."[42] Few note the demarcation line between vv. 4–5 and vv. 6–10,[43] but it is the difference between the ground of the Christian life and further theological reflection on that ground.[44]

Beginnings

Under this criterion, the beginnings of the corresponding parallels should be crisp, relating logically to the questions they address. In our case, C' is not an independent sentence, but continues from v. 5. The demonstrative τοῦτο, however, ameliorates this issue through its cataphorical function, shifting the reader forward to a new line of thought, vv. 6–10.[45] With respect to B', οὕτως καὶ is comparative connecting back to v. 10. While v. 11 is a new sentence, its connectivity to C' (v. 10) suggests a direct bond between knowledge of Christian truth and one's contemplation of it. In parallel A', the postpositive οὖν is a definite grammatical indicator of a new thought. On balance, the beginnings of parallels A', B', and C' support chiasticity, albeit each in its own way, which is to say, there is no recurrent form. Rather, beginning with v. 4, the central and lower panels flow dialogically, guided not by a rigid structure, imposed by the diatribe per se, but rather by Paul's adaptation of this form to fit his own aims and purposes.[46]

Climax

A review of Romans 1:18—8:39 shows that apart from 4:24–25, there is no mention of Christ's resurrection prior to 6:5;[47] following this, resurrection

---

shift from experience (vv. 4–5) to after-the-fact knowledge of the experience (vv. 6–10) (*Romans*, 315).

42. Witherington, *Paul's Letter*, 158–59. V. 5 is a first class, true to fact, condition. So also v. 8.

43. Moo does take note of this vital shift (*Epistle to the Romans*, 372).

44. Wedderburn, *Baptism and Resurrection*, 49–50.

45. Levinsohn, *Discourse Features*, 9; Deibler, *Semantic and Structural Analysis*, 142. Deibler, drawing from other NT examples of τοῦτο γινώσκοντες (cf. Luke 12:39; 2 Pet 1:20; 3:3) and ἐν τούτῳ in the Johannine corpus, sees this dative prepositional phrase as decidedly cataphorical, introducing a new basis with no logical relationship to the previous v. 5.

46. Stowers, "Diatribe," 75. Stowers notes that the diatribe has no "typical structure," varying considerably from author to author.

47. Schreiner notes the complete absence of any discussion of the resurrection prior to this point in Paul's exposition (*Romans*, 311–12). Paul does mention the resurrection

references abound.[48] This suggests that "union with Christ in death and resurrection" (however interpreted) is the theme which dominates D, and which most likely serves as the interpretive lens for Rom 6:1–14.[49] This view is further supported by J. Beekman's critical insights concerning chiasms. Beekman observes that in uneven chiasms, as is the case in this proposal, "the center tends to be the place of prominence."[50]

Return

Does our proposed structure close the chiastic circle? In our estimation it does, for central panel D gives prominence to a believer's present union with Christ in death and their future hope for resurrection. Experience D makes knowledge of experience C/C' and personal reflection B/B' possible, providing the ground for A/A', the imperatival call to moral action. As such, the central panel with its ineluctable progression radiates out from experience, to knowledge, to mental ascent, to moral action, becoming the message by which subsequent references to a believer's union with Christ in death, in life, and in future resurrection may be interpreted.

Balance

In assessing the proposal, we note that all three parallels have some words and concepts in common. Nevertheless, every parallel has unique verbiage. Thus, for example, while C speaks of "baptism," C' uses the concepts of "crucifixion" and "slavery," among others. On the other hand, Parallel B' calls on readers "to reckon." Finally, while A speaks of "increase," A' uses language of "forbiddance," of "bodily lusts," of "instruments of unrighteousness," and "of righteousness." While this list is partial, it does force us to ask whether such lexical imbalance eliminates 6:1–14 as a chiasm. Applying Smith's formula for macro-variance yields a variance of about 72 percent, undermining

---

at 1:4. Within 1:18—8:39, it is treated substantively only at 6:1–14.

48. Romans 7:4; 8:11, 29, 34. On πρότοκος in 8:29, see Rom 1:4 (also Col 1:18) where it is used metaphorically in reference to Jesus's resurrection from the dead.

49. Boers's proposal sees v. 6d ("so that we might no longer be enslaved to sin") as the pivotal passage, dealing only with the first two questions (vv. 1–2). Kim's proposal, which sees v. 6 as the center is dubious, for it gives prominence to what is essentially the continuation of background information, relevant to v. 5. Both Boers and Kim build their chiasms on vv. 1–11, shifting the focus of this text away from resurrection. See Boers, "Structure and Meaning," 679; Kim, "Triple Chiastic Structures," 9.

50. Beekman, Callow, and Kopesec, *Semantic Structure*, 120.

all possibility of this being a design chiasm.[51] While C. H. Talbert shows that ancient writers eschewed near perfect symmetry,[52] Smith is not keen on extending license to chiasms unless "a compelling reason can be given for the lack of symmetry."[53] Thus, to be totally objective, it is the criterion of *Balance* as currently defined which stands as the strongest case against our proposal. Yet it seems incontrovertible that the organizing principle of Romans 6:1–14 is chiastic, putting into question whether this criterion can be applied as settled law.

Conclusion

Whether this proposal is inducted into the hall of chiasms remains to be seen. If it has any merit, it should spur interest in investigating other similar structures in the Pauline corpus[54] and perhaps elsewhere in the New Testament. Its validity would call for a reevaluation of *Balance* criteria.

With respect to structural issues, this proposal strengthens the unity of vv. 1–14 thereby refuting both Boer's and Kim's chiastic arrangements, and indeed challenging any construct that separates out the questions in vv. 2–3, or cuts out the imperatival vv. 12–14.[55]

Among the issues to be addressed would be to ascertain how its concentric message fits within Romans 1:18—8:39. Is this passage a watershed text separating 1:18—5:21 from 6:15—8:39, and if so, how so and why? Can this passage still be viewed as digressing back to previous chapters, is it forward leaning in light of central panel D and the resurrection themes moving forward in Romans, or does it have a bi-directional purpose?

Difficult structural issues can often lead to what I call interpretive stalemate, or we can make progress—perhaps—by approaching the challenge in a fresh way.

---

51. Smith, "Criteria for Identifying Chiasm," 190. The raw word count is 29 words in the upper panel and 134 in the lower panel, for a macro-variance of 29/134, or 72 percent.

52. Talbert, *Literary Patterns*, 78.

53. Smith, "Criteria for Identifying Chiasm," 191.

54. Paul's epistles reveal the following interrogatives: 74 in Rom, 97 in 1 Cor, 23 in 2 Cor, 19 in Gal, 1 in Phil, 1 in Col, 3 in 1 Thess, and none in 2 Thess or Phlm. See Kaye, *Argument of Romans*, 14–23. Kaye discusses rhetorical questions.

55. This proposal does not make any explicit or implicit claims about the structure of Rom 6:15–23 other than to note that Τί οὖν (v. 15a) would seem to be a non-authentic rhetorical interrogative, introducing a new theme.

Works Cited

Barrett, C. K. *The Epistle to the Romans*. HNTC. New York: Harper & Row, 1957.
Barth, Karl. *The Epistle to the Romans*. Translated by Edwyn C. Hoskyns. 6th ed. Oxford: Oxford University Press, 1968.
Beekman, John. "Analyzing and Translating the Questions of the New Testament." In *Notes on Translation*, 44:3–21. Dallas: Wickliffe Bible Translators International, 1972.
Beekman, John, and J. Callow. *Translating the Word of God*. Grand Rapids: Zondervan, 1974.
Beekman, John, J. Callow, and M. Kopesec. *The Semantic Structure of Written Communication*. 5th ed. Dallas: Summer Institute of Linguistics, 1981.
Boers, Hendrikus. "The Structure and Meaning of Romans 6:1–14." *CBQ* 63 (2001) 664–82.
Breck, John. "Biblical Chiasmus: Exploring Structure for Meaning." *BTB* 17 (1987) 70–74.
Bruce, F. F. *The Letter of Paul to the Romans*. TNTC. Grand Rapids: Eerdmans, 1994.
Chomsky, Noam. *Language and the Mind*. New York: Harcourt Brace Jovanovich, 1972.
Clark, David J. "Criteria for Identifying Chiasmus." *LB* 35 (1975) 63–72.
Cranfield, C. E. B. *The Epistle to the Romans*. 2 vols. ICC. Edinburgh: T&T Clark, 1975.
Deibler, Ellis W. *A Semantic and Structural Analysis of Romans*. Dallas: Summer Institute of Linguistics, 1998.
Denney, James. "St. Paul's Epistle to the Romans." In *The Expositor's Greek Testament*, edited by W. Robertson Nicoll, 2:555–725. London: Hodder and Stoughton, 1903. Reprint, Grand Rapids: Eerdmans, 1961.
Dodd, C. H. *The Epistle of Paul to the Romans*. MNTC. New York: Harper, 1932.
Dunn, James, D. G. *Romans 1–8*. WBC. Dallas: Word, 1988.
Ellis, Peter F. *Seven Pauline Letters*. Collegeville, MN: Liturgical, 1984.
Faab, Nigel. *Language and Literary Structure*. Cambridge: Cambridge University Press, 2002.
Fitzmyer, Joseph A. *Romans*. AB 33. New York: Doubleday, 1992.
Godet, Frédéric L. *Commentary on Romans*. Kregel Classic Reprint Library. Grand Rapids: Kregel, 1977.
Goody, Esther N. "Questions and Politeness: Strategies in Social Interaction." Cambridge Papers in Social Anthropology, no. 8. Cambridge: Cambridge University Press, 1978.
Green, Joel B., ed. *Hearing the New Testament: Strategies for Interpretation*. Grand Rapids: Eerdmans, 1995.
Heidland, H. W. "λογίζομαι, λογίζμος." In *TDNT* 4:284–92.
Jeremias, Joachim. "Chiasmus in den Paulusbriefen." *ZNW* 49 (1958) 145–56.
Jewett, Robert. *Romans: A Commentary on the Book of Romans*. Hermeneia. Minneapolis: Fortress, 2006.
Käsemann, Ernst. *Commentary on Romans*. Translated by Geoffrey W. Bromiley. Grand Rapids: Eerdmans, 1980.
Kaye, Bruce N. *The Argument of Romans with Special Reference to Chapter 6*. Austin, TX: Schola Press, 1979.
Kim, Sang-Hoon. "Triple Chiastic Structures in Romans 6." Paper presented at the International Conference of the Society of Biblical Literature. Tartu, Estonia, 2010.

Kruse, Collin G. *Paul's Letter to the Romans*. PNTC. Grand Rapids: Eerdmans, 2012.
Levinsohn, Stephen H. *Discourse Features of New Testament Greek: A Coursebook on the Information Structure of New Testament Greek*. 2nd ed. Dallas: SIL International, 2000.
Longman, Tremper. *Literary Approaches to Biblical Interpretation*. Grand Rapids: Academie, 1987.
Lund, Nils W. *Chiasmus in the New Testament: A Study in the Form and Function of Chiastic Structures*. Peabody: Hendrickson, 1992.
Mann, Ronald E. "The Value of Chiasm for New Testament Interpretation." *BSac* 141 (1984) 146–57.
Moo, Douglas J. *The Epistle to the Romans*. NICNT. Grand Rapids: Eerdmans, 1996.
Morris, Leon. *The Epistle to the Romans*. Grand Rapids: Eerdmans, 1988.
Mounce, Robert H. *Romans*. NAC. Nashville: Broadman & Holman, 1995.
Murray, John. *The Epistle to the Romans*. Reprint, Grand Rapids: Eerdmans, 1984.
Nygren, Anders. *Commentary on Romans*. Translated by Carl C. Rasmussen. Philadelphia: Muhlenberg, 1949.
Porter, Stanley E., and Thomas H. Olbricht, eds. *Rhetoric and the New Testament: Essays from the 1992 Heidelberg Conference*. JSNTSup 90. Sheffield: Sheffield Academic, 1993.
———. *The Rhetorical Analysis of Scripture: Essays from the 1995 London Conference*. JSNTSup 146. Sheffield: Sheffield Academic, 1997.
Rogers, C. L., III. *The New Linguistic and Exegetical Key to the Greek New Testament*. Grand Rapids: Zondervan, 1998.
Sanday, William, and Arthur C. Headlam. *The Epistle to the Romans*. ICC. 5th ed. Edinburgh: T&T Clark, 1901.
Schreiner, Thomas R. *Romans*. BECNT. Grand Rapids: Baker, 1998.
Smith, C. A. "Criteria for Identifying Chiasm of Design in New Testament Literature." PhD diss., University of Bristol, 2009.
Snyman, A. H. "Style and the Rhetorical Situation of Romans 8.31–39." *NTS* 34 (1988) 218–31.
Stowers, Stanley K. "Diatribe." In *ABD* 2:190–93.
———. "The Diatribe." In *Greco-Roman Literature and the New Testament*, edited by D. E. Aune, 71–83. SBLSBS 21. Atlanta: Scholars, 1988.
———. *The Diatribe and Paul's Letter to the Romans*. SBLDS 57. Chico, CA: Scholars, 1981.
Talbert, Charles H. "Artistry and Theology: An Analysis of the Architecture of Jn 1:19—5:47." *CBQ* 32 (1970) 341–66.
———. *Literary Patterns, Theological Themes and the Genre of Luke–Acts*. Atlanta: SBL & Scholars, 1974.
———. *Romans*. SHBC. Macon: Smyth & Helwys, 2002.
Thomson, Ian H. *Chiasmus in the Pauline Letters*. Sheffield: Sheffield Academic, 1995.
Verster, P. "The Implications of Non-Authentic Questions in Galatians." In *Exploring New Rhetorical Approaches to Galatians*, edited by D. F. Tolmie, 142–61. Acta Theologica Supplementum 9. Bloemfontein: University of the Free State, 2007.
———. "Die Implikasies van Stellings as Kategorie van Nie-Egte Vrae in Romeine." *AcT* 1 (2001) 198–214.
———. "Nie-egte vrae in die Romeinbrief: 'n Taalhandelingsperspektief." MA diss., Bloemfontein, University of the Free State, 2000.

Vorster, J. N. "The Context of the Letter to the Romans: A Critique on the Present State of Research." *Neot* 28 (1994) 127–45.

Wallace, Daniel B. *Greek Grammar Beyond the Basics: An Exegetical Syntax of the New Testament*. Grand Rapids: Zondervan, 1996.

Watson, D. F. "Diatribe." In *Dictionary of Paul and His Letters*, edited by G. E. Hawthorne and R. P. Martin, 213–14. Downers Grove, IL: Intervarsity, 1993.

Wedderburn, A. J. M. *Baptism and Resurrection: Studies in Pauline Theology Against Its Graeco-Roman Background*. Tübingen: Mohr Siebeck, 1987.

Welch, John W., and Daniel B. McKinley, eds. *Chiasmus Bibliography*. Provo, UT: Research, 1999.

———. "Criteria for Identifying and Evaluating the Presence of Chiasmus." Provo, UT: Research, 1999.

Witherington, Ben. *Paul's Letter to the Romans: A Socio-Rhetorical Commentary*. Grand Rapids: Eerdmans, 2004.

Slave and Free

Ideal Ideologies in Vesuvian Villas and in Galatians 3:28

BRUCE W. LONGENECKER

IN THE GRECO-ROMAN WORLD, relational dynamics were marked by a thousand shades of status. Never a simple thing, one's social status was always highly layered, with any number of factors contributing to it in any given moment. For instance, when the town magistrates of Pompeii dedicated a prominent burial site to the public priestess Mamia, they might have invited as part of their procession to the burial site another one of the town's female benefactors, Eumachia, who had donated a huge building to enhance Pompeii's forum.[1] It is very unlikely, however, that any simple male artisan (say, the one whose entrepreneurial efforts were based in one of Pompeii's little workshops at 6.17.22) would have been invited to participate in the procession. On the other hand, when it came time to vote in local elections, it was the free (or freed) male artisan whom the magistrates allowed to cast a vote in Pompeii's forum; Eumachia was not entitled to vote because she was a woman.

These hypothetical examples illustrate how a single status differential (in this case, gendered sexuality) had different levels of impact in different social contexts. Other identity indicators would also have been thrown into the mix of status calculation (e.g., ethnic origin, citizenship, personal

---

1. This hypothetical situation builds on what we know of Mamia and Eumachia, both female benefactors of the Augustan age. We do not know which of them died first. I postulate that it was Mamia, since Eumachia's tomb is post-Augustan, suggesting that she thrived in the Augustan period and died in the post-Augustan period. We know that the civic magistrates dedicated a burial place for Mamia, residing just beyond Pompeii's Herculaneum Gate (at HGW04, with the tomb inscription being *CIL* 10.998).

liberty, wealth, occupation, age, public office, public honors, family heritage). Consequently, negotiating status in the Greco-Roman world would have involved calculating degrees of status in something like a complex three-dimensional matrix. In any situation, each person would have been exceedingly conscious of his or her place within that matrix in relation to others. Participants in any given situation were probably doing status computations simultaneously, taking into account all the status variables that determined their social standing in relation to everyone else.

If social relationality within the Greco-Roman world was determined by that ever-present matrix of status, one of the most fundamental factors of that matrix was the distinction between the slave on the one hand and, on the other hand, the free or freed person. On the part of the matrix that pertained to slavery, freedom was treasured in contrast to slavery in (almost) every instance.[2]

Of course, since the matrix of status was multi-dimensional, there was no simple guarantee that life would inevitably be better for a free person than for someone in servitude. Free people were often exposed to certain kinds of economic vulnerability that were not shared by slaves (who had other forms of economic vulnerability). Poor artisans, for instance, often struggled just to get by in their small workshops, selling their products in private businesses that left them vulnerable to twists and turns of fate; by contrast, although a slave within a household might have owned virtually nothing, he/she would have derived some benefits from the overarching security of the household in which he/she was embedded. There may not have been much difference between the free artisan and the household slave in terms of their personal economic reserves, but in terms of their long-term prospects, in some instances the household slave may have had more security than the free artisan.

A similar complication in the ideal dichotomization between slavery and freedom is that freedom was not always of the same order. Among those who were free, an important distinction was made between (1) those who were born in freedom and (2) those who were born into slavery but were later granted freedom. These freed persons shared some privileges with the freeborn, such as the right to vote, but also shared some aspects of life that applied to slaves, such as being ineligible to hold public office. These gradients within the category "free" (much like the gradients within slavery itself,

---

2. One rare exception is when people found it necessary to sell themselves into slavery to clear their personal debt by the proceeds of the sale. Even in that instance, however, slavery was not the ideal.

with some slaves in much better situations than others) were part and parcel of the matrix of status that had to be negotiated at every turn of life.³

Figure 1: A fresco depicting diners who have gathered for a dinner party, as a young slave holding pitchers of wine waits to assist them (from Pompeii 5.2.4; MANN 120031; all photos are used by permission of the Special Superintendency for Archaeological Heritage of Pompeii, Herculaneum, and Stabiae, and reproduction or duplication of these images is prohibited by the Superintendency)

In ideal terms, however, with all else being equal, freedom was prized above slavery in the Greco-Roman world. This aspect of status is

---

3. There were, of course, permutations of slavery, with some forms of slavery being far more socially advantageous than others. This essay is not the place for a full taxonomy of servile relationality on display in the Vesuvian towns. For further consideration of this issue, see Longenecker, "Household and Slaves," in *In Stone and Story*.

vividly displayed within two first-century villas about a mile to the north of Pompeii—identified simply as Oplontis Villa A and Oplontis Villa B. The archaeological remains of these Vesuvian villas contain important clues regarding a prominent relational ideology within the Greco-Roman world. Outlining a few aspects of these Vesuvian villas will help to foster some preliminary observations about relationality between slave and free within early Christian discourse. Along the way, we will see two ideologies of relationality that differed in their orientations. Moreover, we will also notice how they acted as idealized principles for the regulation of social interactions, even if the *telos* of those principles may not have been completely realizable in concrete situations.

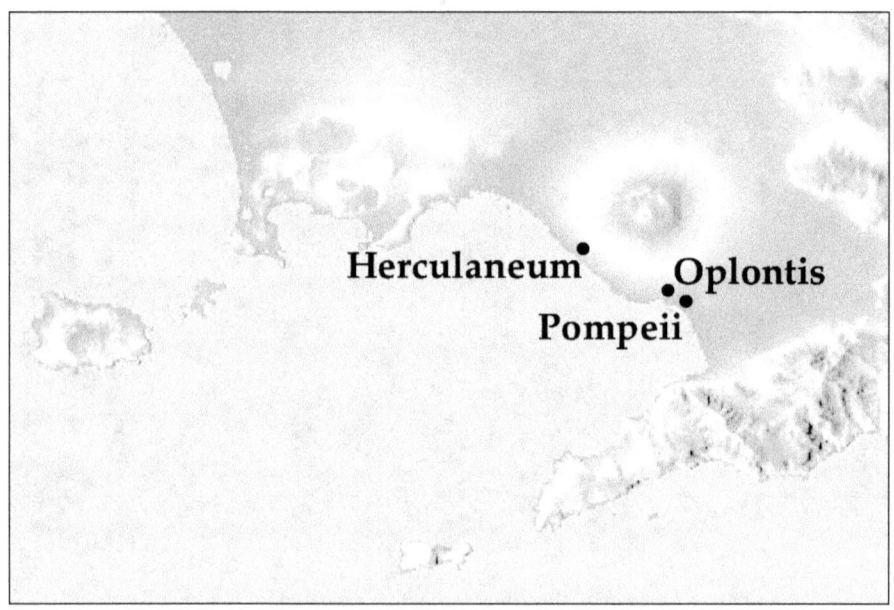

Figure 2: The location of Oplontis on the road between Pompeii and Herculaneum, situated between Mount Vesuvius and the Mediterranean Sea

Status and Space in Oplontis Villa A

Covered by volcanic material in the eruption of Mount Vesuvius in 79 CE, Oplontis Villa A was originally a simple agricultural villa that later underwent significant rounds of expansion. By the mid-first century, it had come to reflect grandeur and opulence far beyond anything we generally see among the Vesuvian material remains—except in other exceptional Vesuvian villas of the elite. Its massive swimming pool alone would have been built to enhance festivities among the elite of Roman society, representing the villa's palatial ethos for the pursuit of *otium*—an environment conducive to physical recreation, emotional refreshment, and intellectual reflection, and an environment where culture and nature intertwined in refreshing ways.[4]

Figure 3: A section of Oplontis Villa A, seen from the back; the opposite side sat at the coast overlooking the Mediterranean Sea; much of the villa falls beyond this picture or remains covered by Vesuvian ash

The villa is often referred to as "the Villa of Poppaea," referencing the second wife of emperor Nero from 62–65. Poppaea was known to have owned a property in this area, and her extended family had a notable presence in Pompeii, just down the road. However, unless new evidence comes to light (the villa is only half excavated at present, with the rest still buried under volcanic pumice and modern buildings), it is best to be agnostic as to whether this villa had ever been owned by the woman with whom emperor Nero was so infatuated.[5] One thing is clear. This is the kind of villa that only someone

4. See especially D'Arms, "Ville rustiche"; Bergman, "Art and Nature."
5. For further discussion on the possibility of a Poppaean connection to the villa, see Longenecker, "Empress, the Goddess, and the Earthquake," 71–72.

with access to enormous amounts of money could afford. This villa, then, must have been a base for someone high in the echelons of Roman power. It would have catered to someone of considerable social prestige, who would have used it to entertain elite guests for days at a time.

Slaves would have been essential to the running of the villa, and in relatively high number. Moreover, on those occasions when guests arrived for a few days of rest and relaxation, the number of slaves would have increased exponentially, as the owner's slaves (who knew the premises well) mixed with slaves of the invited guests (who would not have known the premises previously). We should probably imagine significant numbers of slaves servicing the villa when the opulent owners and their guests were in residence.[6]

During times of their residency in the villa, some of Rome's elite would have gathered to enjoy *otium*, serviced in their enjoyment by the slaves that catered to them. This was not simply the mixing of free and slave, but of the massively rich and powerful on the one hand and their retinues of slaves on the other. It would have been eminently clear who belonged to each of the two categories. Everything from their clothing, their speech, and their manner of presenting themselves would have marked them out. In this way, the Oplontis Villa A is ancient space devoid of the various contingencies that complicate the otherwise binary contrast of "slave" and "free." In the case of Oplontis Villa A, the adjective "free" would have corresponded in almost all instances to enormous wealth—a rare correspondence that differentiated Oplontis Villa A from most other contexts. If we could visit a bakery down the road in Pompeii, for instance, we might struggle at first glance to differentiate the baker from his slaves working alongside him in the oven room. Similarly, in Pompeii's fullery of Stephanus (at 1.6.7), it might at times have been difficult to differentiate Stephanus's son from Stephanus's slaves, as they worked to clean the garments of their customers. By contrast, the Oplontis Villa A is essentially space in which virtually pure social identities of "slave" and "free" would have existed in stark contrast, space in which a more ideal differentiation of slave identity and free identity could hardly be imagined. There would have been a few free workers or artisans or merchants showing up occasionally for one purpose or another, of course, but for the most part, this was a villa comprised of the elite and their slave entourages. Within the Oplontis Villa A, the social contrasts could hardly have been more plainly evident.

---

6. The villa was undergoing renovation at the time of the eruption, so the elite owner and his entourage would not have been in residence to experience that horror within the villa.

If the stark contrast between "free" and "servile" was readily apparent in Villa A, we might imagine that there was little need to demarcate those obvious status differences within that villa. In fact, however, just the opposite seems to have been the case. Having entered the world of the super-rich where there was virtually no one else in residence except those in servitude, it was possible (and evidently important) to demarcate social differences in a fashion that was not as easily done in the more ordinary contexts of everyday life that we find in Pompeii and Herculaneum.

The demarcation of social differences was embedded within the villa's walls—in what might be called the villa's "decoration code." The villa displays some of the most ornate and superior frescoes of the ancient world (offering some of the best examples from the Vesuvian remains of what archaeologists and art historians have labeled "second style," "third style," and "fourth style" art). Notably, its breath-taking frescoes are all situated in prime locations, adorning the spaces set aside for the elite owner and his or her guests.

Figure 4: Two of the many beautiful frescoes that decorate the spaces dedicated to the elite in Oplontis Villa A (painted on flat walls but with 3-D effects suggesting columns, moldings, lintels, ledges, niches, even a peacock; right photo shows a second-style fresco, left photo [depicting Hercules] shows a third-style fresco)

There is, however, another kind of decoration manifested on the walls of certain sectors within the villa. This kind of decor features a "zebra stripe" pattern, comprising parallel stripes of black and white, painted along any angle but often diagonally (see figure 5).

Figure 5: An example of the "zebra stripe" decor of the Oplontis Villa A

What explains the placement of these different kinds of frescoes? The best interpretation is that these stripes marked out the expected working spaces or traffic routes for the workers within the villa.[7] Parts of the villa were decorated in "zebra stripes," and these tend to appear in the "lowliest" sectors of the villa—narrow and dark passageways, small cubicles, and back service rooms. They are also highly concentrated in the central hub of the villa (especially the original peristyle), with the exquisite spaces for the elite running around the outer band of the villa, where the ornate frescoes predominate. Evidently, then, zebra stripes were painted on walls where slaves carried out duties to service the smooth running of the villa. These were not spaces where the elite would normally want to be seen. Instead, they were

---

7. See, for instance, Wallace-Hadrill, *Houses and Society*, 39–44; Foss, "Kitchens and Dining Rooms," 139; Balch, "Rich Pompeian Houses," 38; Osiek and Balch, *Families in the New Testament*, 29–30, n. 114 with fig. 8. Most recently, Joshel ("Geographies of Slave Containment") places this view in larger textual and archaeological contexts. The alternative interpretation is that these stripes were solely intended to imitate marble without any social function (e.g., de Carolis, *Gods and Heroes*, 6; Lessing and Varone, *Pompeii*, 76; most recently Cline, "Imitation vs. Reality"). This seems unlikely, since many of these frescoes would have to be judged inferior in their quality of artisanship—precisely the kind of impression that the villa's owner would have been intent to avoid. Moreover, some zebra stripes appear in places wholly out of keeping with marble adornment (i.e., ceiling slabs and wrapped around columns).

spaces demarcating service areas, where slaves would have congregated in concentrated numbers.

It would not be wholly accurate to say that the zebra stripes demarcate "slave space." Zebra stripes are found in various other settings in the Vesuvian towns, and when the full register of zebra stripes is considered, it would seem that they identify service areas or, in a few instances, common areas.[8] But in the Oplontis Villa A (where the social differences are so extreme without much middle ground), to say that they demarcate the "service area" is virtually the same as saying "servile area" or "slave area."[9] There would have been the odd exception to that rule, of course, but those exceptions would have been relatively few. These "common" service areas, then, were places that elite visitors might best avoid, since there were much better areas dedicated to their pursuit of *otium*, separated from the hustle and bustle of the service areas populated primarily by slaves.

In a few parts of the villa, however, the two styles appear together on the same wall. For instance, the large corridor through the center of the villa is comprised of zebra stripes from the base of the walls up to approximately six feet, above which a standard pattern typical of elite sections of the villa begins, carried up to the top of the high walls (see figure 6). This corridor had a utilitarian purpose in ensuring the smooth running of the villa, since it provided quick access from the heart of the villa (service space) to several of the villa's outer extremities set aside for the elite to enjoy. This corridor clearly needed to be accessed by slaves. But the pleasing frescoes that enhance the top of the walls tell us that the corridor was also deemed useful for elite passage. This makes perfect sense, since the corridor connected some of the outer extremities of the villa to the latrine area (which itself was based in the service section at the heart of the villa), and since the corridor allowed covered access from the beautiful colonnaded gardens to the *hospitum* area without the need to pass outside—a useful path at those

8. For instance, the complex of Julia Felix (2.4), the Stabian Baths (7.1.8), the Marine Gate (where civic slaves were probably on duty), and the exterior seats at Casa dell'Ara Laterizia in Herculaneum (where it may signal inferior status rather than slave status).

9. The zebra stripe phenomenon within Oplontis Villa A was used in relation to various kinds of service space, probably including an upper bedroom area connected to the zebra-striped peristyle. Evidently the manager of the villa, even if he were a slave, was not expected to sleep in the central corridor (on one of the platforms?) or around the peristyle, as other slaves might well have done. Whether slave or free, the household manager was an important authority figure within the villa, since he ensured the smooth running of the villa in all circumstances, regardless of whether the elite owner was in residence. It was important to signal to (other) slaves that he had preeminent authority over them, and a separate bedroom area for him would have served that purpose, even if it was also characterized by zebra-strip décor. For a helpful scenario of this kind, see Matt 24:45–47.

times of extreme heat or torrential rain. In other words, this corridor had the potential to be shared space, and the wall decor reflected that fact. The zebra stripes on the bottom reflected the slave orientation of the service corridor (being positioned low on the wall for the lowly), while the attractive frescoes above the zebra stripes were there to ensure the elite that they were welcome to pass through the corridor on the understanding that they might need to share the space with the servile occupants of the villa.[10]

Figure 6: A corridor with zebra stripe decor at the bottom, and decor suitable to the elite displayed above

All this made good sense for a villa of this kind. When important guests arrived at the villa, they would have brought an entourage of their own slaves, who would not have known the layout and ethos of the villa. Quite simply, the zebra stripes catered to that common eventuality, increasing the chances that the elite guests were not unduly offended by slaves wandering without direction throughout the villa. Of course, an elite master might choose to have a slave by his or her side at times, but that would be different to slaves uninvitedly wandering into space where they did not belong.

10. One or two other places in the villa share this dual register phenomenon. In each case, it is easy to see how the space needed to be recognizable as shared space, of differing concentration levels.

In short, the decor of Oplontis Villa A served an important function in terms of the traffic flow within the villa, so that all the residents, both service providers (predominantly slaves) and elite, could gauge where they were within the house—in accordance with the matrix of Greco-Roman status. The villa's wealthy visitors and their slaves could easily read the "signs" regarding the use of space throughout the villa.[11]

Beyond Villa A

Variations on this theme are on display elsewhere in the Vesuvian material remains, of course, although in less extreme form. In the House of the Tragic Poet (at 6.8.5), for instance, the grand dining room is adorned with wonderful visuals of mythological scenes; the adjoining room is the kitchen where a slave served the household in a room bare of all decorative accoutrements. Much the same is evident in the House of the Lovers (at 1.10.11), where the rooms used for entertaining guests were adorned with attractive frescoes and floor patterns while the rooms used as service rooms had no floor patterns and were crudely painted.

Other variations are also visible in other features of Vesuvian architecture. In some Vesuvian houses, for instance, a passageway appears next to the *tablinum* (originally intended as the office and reception room of the householder), permitting slaves to pass from one section of the house to another without having to pass through the space of the householder and his guests or clients (as in the House of Menander at 1.10.4, the House of the Tragic Poet at 6.8.5, and the House of the Black Salon in Herculaneum; see figure 7). These passageways could have been used by non-slaves as well, of course, but slaves were clearly expected to "know their place" within the architectural design of the house, and these passageways were ideal for that purpose, allowing them access to different parts of the house without intruding on the important relationships being orchestrated by the free members of the household.

---

11. Another way of saying all this is simply that, when taking fresco cues as traffic signals, a person would walk through some parts of the villa along a slightly different route when following slave cues than when following elite cues.

Figure 7: A nineteenth-century artist's impression of the interior of the House of the Tragic Poet (now in relative disrepair), showing a slave emerging from the service corridor without interrupting the householder in the triclinium/office (from Gell, Pompeiana, *in the public domain)*

Yet another variation of demarcating slave space is visible in the grand House of Menander (1.10.4). There, the service areas of the slaves are at the periphery of the residence and accessed only through long narrow corridors. Similar attempts to separate the slaves' service quarter from the opulence of the main house are evident in other remarkable houses too, such as the House of the Faun (6.12.2) and the House of the Vettii (6.15.1).

The Vesuvian towns offer numerous examples of this sort of thing. The residents of the Vesuvian towns were familiar with strategies that reinforced the social differences between slave and free and demarcated their use of space within residences. As noted already, at times the free would have needed to pass through spaces dedicated primarily to the service of the household. When they did go into such spaces, however, it was clear to all that their status was somewhat incongruous with their presence in those spaces. The same is true in instances where slaves needed to service the free in the spaces where the free were placed most naturally within a residence. In those instances, the incongruity of the slave's status and his/her spatial presence would have been evident to all parties. And the more opulent the residence, the more these incongruities were on display.

More could be said about the differentiation of space according to social status within the realia of the Vesuvian towns. We have seen enough, however, to recognize that a consciousness of the vastly different social worth of servile and free status was often deeply embedded within the decor and/or architecture of Greco-Roman residences.

If people lived with a consciousness of this deeply entrenched social differentiation, at times they also died fully aware of that differentiation. Only three hundred meters away from Villa A lay another villa, Villa B (sometimes referred to as the Villa of Lucius Crassius Tertius), which operated primarily as a storage and distribution center for wine and other goods. In this working villa, fifty-four skeletons were found in a ground-floor room. Perhaps these people were waiting for the worst to end, or were hoping for a maritime rescue from the dangers of the angry mountain behind them. But instead of being rescued, they died together when the first of six deadly pyroclastic flows sped down the mountain and destroyed any life it touched.[12]

What is interesting about the unfortunate deaths of these people is how they had assembled themselves in the room that would turn out to be their final abode. The arrangement of their skeletons suggest that these fifty-four people were exceedingly conscious of their social differences even as death was imminent. People who carried nothing of value (or nothing that survived the pyroclastic flows, at least) had huddled together toward the rear of the room. They were separated from another group of people huddled together toward the entrance of the room. Those people carried possessions of considerable wealth—coins and jewelry indicating this group to have comprised elite men and women. For instance, one of the women in this group (who was eight months pregnant) wore a necklace of gold and emerald, together with pearl earrings—jewelry that is thought to be "the single most costly jewelry find that's ever been made on the Roman Bay of Naples."[13] People of such elite status would not have been resident in this busy working villa.[14] This elite woman and her companions must have sought the strategic setting of Villa B when seeking rescue from the eruption. But in their assemblage within their final resting place, they adopted patterns of separation that coincided with the ideology of slave and free embedded in the frescoed walls of Villa A.

---

12. Despite their proximity to Pompeii, the Oplontis villas were decimated by the first pyroclastic flow from Vesuvius, whereas Pompeii itself was untouched until the third flow (which only reached its walls), and then by the fourth, fifth, and sixth (which completely penetrated the town).

13. Barbara Kellum, quoted in Lerose, "Ancient Class Distinctions."

14. Neither were they from Villa A, which (as noted in n. 6 above) was in the process of renovation at the time of the eruption, to the extent that the elite would have resided elsewhere.

Comparing Ideologies

We have seen an ideology of slave and free advertised on the walls of Oplontis Villa A (and beyond). By the mid-first century, that villa had become an exceptional residence in the Vesuvian region. Like a few other opulent villas dotted around Mount Vesuvius, it served selected members of the elite, fostering their interests in the pursuit and pleasures of *otium*. The villa was well suited for that purpose, being removed from the ordinary hustle and bustle of the busy nearby towns, and providing a stress-free environment conducive to the enhancement of physical exercise, relaxing social exchange, and reflective contemplation. Within that virtually ideal situation, an ideology was advertised within the villa's decor—an ideology that reinforced a blatant distinction between slave and free, and intimated a starkly stratified code of relationality between those two groups. In less opulent settings, an ideology of this kind would not have resulted in such practical measures of differentiation. For instance, a spatial demarcation such as the one apparent in Villa A would never have been practical in the operating of bakeries and fulleries in Pompeii. In those contexts, space was far more permeable, with the intermixing of slave and free being a given. The ideal environment of Villa A enabled this ideology to be translatable into a consciousness of space-usage that matched the idealized worldview of highly differentiated social status between slave and free.[15]

There were a hundred and one permutations in how slave and free related in the Greco-Roman world. Different contexts and different personalities meant that the character of relationality between slave and free was negotiated anew in each instance according to particular situations. Villa A allows us into one context where the common ideology differentiating slave and free could be enacted in a virtually ideal form. And Villa B shows us how the same ideology could affect their identities beyond the everyday moments and include even the moment of death.

It is in this context that Paul's words in Gal 3:28 are intriguingly suggestive: "There is neither Jew nor Greek, neither slave nor free, no 'male and female,' for in Christ Jesus all of you are one." Scholars have often suggested that this was part of a creed of constitutional identity that was spoken in the context of early Christian baptismal celebrations. But whether or not that is true, these words nonetheless articulate a vision of corporate unity in which a single form of identity (that is, being "in Christ Jesus") makes other forms of deeply entrenched identities inconsequential by comparison. In that way, they advertise a different ideology of slave and free to the ideology

---

15. This is true also of most other contexts in which the zebra stripes appear within the Vesuvian remains—such as those listed in n. 8 above.

evidenced within Oplontis's Villa A and Villa B. The simple phrase "neither slave nor free . . . for all of you are one" seems almost intentionally to run against the grain of the common ideology of slave and free that permeated the Greco-Roman world—an ideology that regulated so much of life and death in the Oplontis villas.

Figure 8: A fresco of diners getting ready to leave a dinner party, with three slaves attending them; a young child puts on the shoe of the man at the far left, who is being served a goblet of wine from another slave in the middle of the painting, while another slave assists a man who has had too much to drink at the lower right (from Pompeii 5.2.4; MANN 120029)

Nonetheless, very much like the ideology evidenced in the Oplontis villas, Gal 3:28 is an idealized ideology, being fully practicable only in ideal conditions—perhaps even something that slips beyond the grasp of human organization. There is a double-sidedness to this issue. On the one hand, the literature of early Christianity often evidences discourse that moves in the direction of this ideal. On the other hand, early Jesus-followers were not experts in teasing out practical patterns of novel relationality between slave and free within Christian groups. Their texts occasionally testify to the difficulty of implementing ideal ideologies in concrete situations, and at times the ideal is far from view (for instance, in 1 Pet 2:18–23). Nonetheless, some early Christians leaned some way into the ideal ideology of Gal 3:28. That exercise of relational creativity was given legitimation by the fact that they were "in Christ Jesus." At times, that awareness opened possibilities of relational innovation within early communities of Jesus-devotion in the Greco-Roman world.[16] For some people of the first century, this might well have been an attractive feature of what apostolic figures were calling "good news."

Works Cited

D'Arms, J. H. "Ville rustiche e vile do optimum." In *Pompei 79: raccolta di studi per il decimonono centario dell'eruzione vesuviana*, edited by F. Sevilla, 65–86. Naples: G. Macchiaroli, 1984.

Balch, David L. "Rich Pompeian Houses, Shops for Rent, and the Huge Apartment Building as Typical Spaces for Pauline House Churches." *JSNT* 27 (2004) 27–46.

Bergman, Bettina. "Art and Nature in the Villa at Oplontis." In *Pompeian Brothels, Pompeii's Ancient History, Mirrors and Mysteries, Art and Nature at Oplontis, & The Herculaneum 'Basilica'*, edited by T. McGinn, P. Carafa, N. de Grummond, B. Bergmann, and T. Najbjerg, 47–61. Journal of Roman Archaeology Supplementary Series 47. Portsmouth, RI: Journal of Roman Archaeology, 2002.

de Carolis, Ernesto. *Gods and Heroes in Pompeii*. Los Angeles: J. Paul Getty Museum, 2001.

Cline, Lea. "Imitation vs. Reality: Zebra Stripe Paintings and Imitation Marble in the Late Fourth Style at Oplontis." In *Actes du XIe Colloqie de l'Association Internationale pour la Peinture Murale Antique*, edited by Norbert Zimmermann, 565–70. Vienna: Österreichische Akademie der Wissenschaften, 2014.

Foss, Pedar W. "Kitchens and Dining Rooms at Pompeii: The Spatial and Social Relationship of Cooking to Eating in the Roman Household." PhD diss., University of Michigan, 1994.

Gell, William. *Pompeiana*. 3rd ed. Vol. 2. London: Bohn, 1852.

Joshel, Sandra R. "Geographies of Slave Containment and Movement." In *Roman Slavery and Roman Material Culture, The Sixth E. T. Salmon Conference in Roman Studies*, edited by Michele George, 99–128. Toronto: University of Toronto, 2013.

Lerose, Robert. "Ancient Class Distinctions Displayed in Rome Exhibit." *Christian Science Monitor*, May 9, 2017. https://www.csmonitor.com/the-culture/arts/2017/0509/ancient-class-distinctions-displayed-in-rome-exhibit.

Lessing, Erich, and Antonio Varone. *Pompeii*. Paris: Éditions Pierre Terrail, 1995.

Longenecker, Bruce W. "The Empress, the Goddess, and the Earthquake: Atmospheric Conditions Pertaining to Jesus-Devotion in Pompeii." In *Early Christianity in Pompeian Light: People, Texts, Situations*, edited by Bruce W. Longenecker, 59–92. Minneapolis: Fortress, 2016.

---

16. For further discussion of early Christian approaches to slavery, see Longenecker, "Household and Slaves," in *In Stone and Story*.

———. *In Stone and Story: A Pompeian Introduction to the Greco-Roman Setting of Early Christianity.* Forthcoming.

Osiek, Carolyn, and David L. Balch. *Families in the New Testament World: Households and House Churches.* Louisville: Westminster John Knox, 1997.

Wallace-Hadrill, Andrew. *Houses and Society in Pompeii and Herculaneum.* Princeton: Princeton University Press, 1994.

The Ideal King in Hebrews
The Exemplary and Empowering Rule of the Son of God[1]

Jason A. Whitlark

Though Jesus is never called "king" in Hebrews, the related titles of "son of God" and "great shepherd of the sheep,"[2] the description of his heavenly enthronement,[3] his comparison with Melchizedek (king of Salem), the fact that he rules over an unending βασιλεία,[4] and his identification with Davidic messianic hopes,[5] all unmistakably point to Jesus as a king of cos-

---

1. I would like to thank Michael Martin, Julien Smith, and the editors of this volume who read earlier versions of this essay and offered helpful feedback. I am also honored to contribute to a Festschrift in celebration of Naymond Keathley's career as a scholar and teacher.

2. From the Jewish Scriptures, the title "son of God" was associated with God's choice of the king from the line of David. Cf. 2 Sam 7:14; Ps 2:7. The title was also commonly associated with the Roman emperor. For further discussion on the emperor as the son of God see Mowery, "Son of God," 100–110; Peppard, *Son of God*, 31–49. The king as shepherd was a common metaphor in the ancient world. See, e.g., Homer, *Il.* 2.75–109; *Od.* 3.156; Xenophon, *Cyr.* 8.2.14; Epictetus, *Diatr.* 3.22.35; Dio Chrysostom, *Or.* 1.12–13; 2.6; 3.41; 4.45; Philo, *Ios.* 1.2; *Legat.* 1.44; *Mos.* 1.60. The Messiah was also the shepherd of God's people (Ezek 34:23–24; Mic 5:2–4; *Pss. Sol.* 17:21–40).

3. The whole catena of Scripture in Heb 1:5–14 is a celebration of the enthronement of the Son in the world to come (not his incarnation or Parousia), which concludes with Ps 110:1 where God invites the Son to sit at his right hand until all his enemies are subjected to him. For further discussion see Martin and Whitlark, "Encomiastic Topics," 427–29; Jipp, "Son's Entrance," 557–75; Barnard, *Mysticism of Hebrews*, 144–70, 217–42, esp. 237–42.

4. Cf. Heb 12:28; 1:8.

5. Many of the Psalms quoted in Heb 1:5–14 can be associated with David or the Davidic ruler. Cf. Motyer, "Psalm Quotations of Hebrews," 13–22. Furthermore, the

mic proportions who has inherited all things and to whom all things will be subjected (cf. 1:2, 13; 2:5–9). In the ancient Mediterranean world during the classical, Hellenistic, and imperial periods there was a rich and robust interest in the topic of the ideal king or ruler.[6] This study asks in what ways Hebrews's depiction of Jesus as "king" participates in the discourse about the ideal king. The primary focus of this study will center upon the depictions of the ideal king who, as "living law," is an example to his subjects and whose transformative presence empowers the virtuous lives of those under his rule. These aspects of kingship especially address the need of members of the audience of Hebrews to persevere in their confession and loyalty to God and his king, Jesus.

The Discourse on Ideal Kingship in the Ancient Mediterranean World

After surveying the literature on ideal kingship from Xenophon (ca. 428–357 BCE) to Suetonius (ca. 70–130 CE), Julien Smith lists some common elements associated with the ideal king. He is "preeminent in virtue, a benefactor, a 'living law,' the vicegerent of the gods, and the one who establishes divine harmony on earth."[7] Additionally, the ideal king is commonly presented as a priest.[8] Because of the limited aims of this study, I will give primary attention, as mentioned above, to the king or ruler as "living law" and as a transformative presence or vision for those under his rule.

---

author of Hebrews knows of the tradition of Jesus's descent from Judah (Heb 7:14).

6. See Walbank, "Monarchies," 7:75–81.

7. Smith, *Christ the Ideal King*, 87. Much of the discussion of ideal kingship in this essay is indebted to Smith's excellent and thorough survey of the materials on kingship from the ancient Mediterranean world. See also the succinct surveys by Jipp, *Christ is King*, 16–42; Walbank, "Monarchies," 81–84.

8. Cf. Diotogenes, *On Kingship* (Stob. 4.7.61); Moses in Philo, *Mos.* 2.5; Roman emperors as *pontifex maximus*, among whose titulature, P.M. is ubiquitously found on coin legends. From the Flavian period (69–96 CE), there are coins with the legend PONTIF. MAXIM. and Vespasian seated holding a branch and a scepter (*RIC* 2:23 no. 83). See also the inscriptions from *Opuscula Archeologica* 6 (1950) 85,46 (Titus: [ἀρχιερεὺ]ς [μ]έ[γιστος]) and I.Eph. 3409 (Augustus containing both Latin and Greek titles: [pont]ifex [maximus] . . . ἀρχιερεὺς μέγιστος). For a concise discussion of the *pontifex maximus* and the importance and development of the priestly role of the emperor during the Flavian period see, Rüpke, "Starting Sacrifice," 114–22.

The Ideal King as "Living Law"

The ideal king in the ancient Mediterranean world was a worthy example for his subjects to imitate since he embodied in himself all necessary virtue and conduct. First, we will consider relevant texts from the Greco-Roman context. Xenophon notes that a good ruler, like Cyrus, internalizes the law in order to supply an example for his subjects to follow (*Cyr.* 8.1.21). Consequently, as Xenophon observes, "By setting such an example, Cyrus secured at court great correctness of conduct" (*Cyr.* 8.1.33 [Miller, LCL]). In the opening address to Alexander, Anaximenes of Lampsacus in *Rhetorica ad Alexandrum* similarly states that the ruler needs "to know that the greatest part of mankind regulate their conduct either by the law or by your life and principle (βιός καὶ λόγος); therefore you must make every effort to excel all Greeks and foreigners, in order that those who occupy themselves in these pursuits may by means of the elements of virtue draw a fair copy therefrom" (1420b [Rackham, LCL]).

The king who internalizes law, even divine law, and whose life then serves as a model for his subjects to imitate also finds its expression among the Neopythagorean philosophers, Diotogenes, Ecphantus, and Archytas, in the notion of the king as one who is "living law" (νόμος ἔμψυχος) or as one who is possessed of indwelling *logos*.[9] According to Ecphantus, though the king is made of the same stuff/body as his subjects, he is specially created by God to represent him because the king's virtue is from God. This is because the divine *logos* indwells the king making him a model for his subjects (Stob. 4.7.64). According to Diotogenes, the king is most just (δικαιότατος) and is thus a "living law" (νόμος ἔμψυχος) to his subjects (Stob. 4.7.61). Likewise, Archytas states that "laws are of two kinds, the animate law which is the king (ἔμψυχος βασιλεύς) and the inanimate, written law" (Stob. 4.1.135 [Goodenough, 59]).

The king as "living law" is also picked up in the first- and second-century CE discourses of the Roman imperial period. Musonius Rufus, a Stoic (ca. 30–102 CE), refers to the ideal ruler as the νόμος ἔμψυχος and thus one who truly imitates Zeus in his rule (cf. 64.10–15).[10] Similarly, Plutarch

---

9. Greek texts of these philosophers can be found in Wachsmuth and Hense, *Ioannis Stobaei Anthologium*. Citations include reference to Stobaeus. English translations are found in Guthrie, *Pythagorean Sourcebook and Library,* and Goodenough, "Political Philosophy," 55–102. These Neopythagorean fragments have been dated from the third century BCE to the first and second centuries CE. See the discussion of dating in Smith, *Christ the Ideal King*, 36–37, n. 59. Smith notes that the Neopythagorean revivals in the first century BCE and first century CE make this period a likely one for the composition of these treatises.

10. Smith, *Christ the Ideal King*, 61, n. 157. Greek text and translation found in Lutz,

states, "Who shall rule the ruler? The Law . . . not law written outside him in books or on wooden tablets or the like, but reason (λόγος) endowed with life (ἔμψυχος) within him, always abiding with him and watching over him and never leaving his soul without its leadership" (*Pric. iner.* 780C [Fowler, LCL]). As the ruler "by his virtue forms himself into the likeness of God," he then is "the image of God (εἰκὼν θεοῦ) who orders all things (πάντα)" (780F [Fowler, LCL]).

Pliny in his panegyric to Trajan declares that Trajan has been chosen by Jupiter (cf. 1.3, 5) and imitates Jupiter in his rule over the Empire (cf. 80.5).[11] Moreover, Trajan is a model to be imitated by those under his rule. "[W]e are reaching the point when we shall all conform with the ways of a single man. . . . You need only continue as you are, Caesar, and the principle of your conduct will have the same effective power as a censorship. Indeed the emperor's life *is* a censorship, and a perpetual one; this is what guides and directs us, for example is what we need more than command" (45.5–6 [Radice, LCL], emphasis original).[12] By stating that the emperor's life is a censorship, Pliny reflects something of the concept of the ruler as "living law" to his subjects to whom they can look as a model of a virtuous life.

Second, Jewish texts during the Hellenistic and imperial periods portray the ideal king as "living law" or one who is indwelled by divine wisdom and thus serves as a model or an example to imitate. The ideal Israelite king who internalized God's law and led the people in covenant faithfulness was already a feature in the Deuteronomist's legislation on kingship (cf. Deut 17:18–20). In Wis 6:1–11, the failure of kings is recounted because they lacked God's wisdom. They have need of wisdom to rule justly (v. 21). "Solomon" then prays for "the wisdom that sits by [God's] throne" so that wisdom may "labor at my side . . . then my works will be acceptable and I shall judge your people justly (δικαίως) and shall be worthy of the throne of my father" (9:4, 10–12 [NRSV]). Indwelling wisdom, which passes into holy souls (cf. 7:27), enables the king to rule in harmony with God and his created order. Such representation of wisdom shares similarities with the divine *logos* that indwells the king in Ecphantus's account. Similarly, Tacitus recounts that the

---

"M. Rufus," 61–67.

11. Similarly, Dio states that the king receives the scepter from Zeus to shepherd his people (cf. *Or.* 1.12–13), and, in imitation of Zeus, he rules with justice (δικαίως) because he keeps his eyes upon Zeus (cf. *Or.* 1.44–45). Cf. Callimachus, *Hymn. Jov.* 68–85.

12. The Roman office of censor, in part, oversaw public morality. On Roman censors see Dionysius of Halicarnassus, *Ant.* 10.13.1; Plutarch, *Cat. Maj.* 16:1–3; Valerius Maximus 2.9. These texts address the following fives aspects of a Roman's private life with which censorship was concerned: private house, marriage, obedience of children, alcoholism, and religion. This list is derived from Paschke, "*cura morum*," 105–19.

"monarch is the incarnation of wisdom" (*Dia.* 41).[13] Finally, Philo of Alexandria portrays Moses as God's chosen ideal king, who will inherit the cosmos and lead the people. As such, Moses is God's νόμος ἔμψυχος (*Mos.* 1.162; 2.4). Thus, Moses, as God's "living law," is the perfect appearance of virtue and a model to be imitated by the people (cf. *Mos.* 1.158–59).

In sum, Goodenough concludes that the monarch, as an example or νόμος ἔμψυχος, is "the vivid representation to men of *the* law, that will of the gods to which all local and state law must conform. He seems to have this unique quality by virtue of his office, at the same time that he has it by the virtue of his own moral character, which itself must be νόμιμος, that is, in accordance with the higher law."[14]

The Transformative Presence of the Ideal King

The ideal king, as "living law," serves more than just as a virtuous example for his subjects. His very presence has a powerful transformative effect on the lives of those under his rule. We can trace this idea in Xenophon, the Neopythagoreans, Philo, Plutarch, and Dio Chrysostom. For instance, Xenophon has Ischomachus compare aptitude for governing to managing all forms of business. Concerning the transformative presence of the master in the workplace, Ischomachus states that such a presence emulates something of the nature of ideal kingship. He says, "But if at the sight of him they stir themselves and a spirit of determination, rivalry, and eagerness to excel falls on every workman, then, I should say: this man has a touch of kingly nature in him" (*Oec.* 21.10 [Merchant and Todd, LCL]). Thus, the analogy by Ischomachus assumes that the presence of the ideal king cultivates virtuous inner dispositions among his subjects.[15]

Among the Neopythagoreans, Ecphantus describes the ideal king's nature as radiant because of his virtue:

> Thus, royalty is explained in the fact that by its divine character and excessive brilliance it is hard to behold, except for those who have a legitimate claim . . . he who stands in it must be pure and radiant (διαυγέστατον) in nature, so that he may not tarnish its exceeding brightness by his own blemishes. (Stob. 4.7.64 [Goodenough, 77])

---

13. Cf. Sthenidas in Stob. 4.7.63: "Indeed he who is king and wise will be a lawful imitator and servant of God" (Goodenough, "Political Philosophy," 74).

14. Goodenough, "Political Philosophy," 61 (emphasis original). Quoted by Smith, *Christ the Ideal King*, 45. See also, Chesnut, "Ruler and the Logos," 1310–32.

15. Cf. Smith, *Christ the Ideal King*, 27.

This radiant and virtuous presence brings transformation as a result of the indwelling *logos* in the king. Ecphantus writes:

> This king alone is capable of putting this good into human nature so that by imitation of him, their Better, they will follow in the way they should go. But his *logos*, if it is accepted, strengthens those who have been corrupted by evil nurture as if by drink, and who have fallen into forgetfulness ... the *logos*, associating with man, restores what has been lost by sin. (Stob. 4.7.65 [Goodenough, 89])

Diotogenes is even more emphatic about the radiant presence of the king bringing about transformation in those who behold him. As in Ecphantus, the ideal king has divine majesty imprinted upon him (Stob. 4.7.62). Thus, "a good king should be able to turn (τρέπεν) those who behold his radiance (τῶν ποταυγασμένων/προσαυγασμένων), no less than the sound of a flute and harmony attract those that hear them" (Stob. 4.7.62).[16] Smith notes that τρέπεν means to turn and conveys a sense of repentance or change of heart. He cites 4 Macc 7:3 where the term is used for not committing apostasy. Thus those who behold the king's radiant majesty and virtue are "turned" to a life of virtue.[17] Similarly, Goodenough concludes from his analysis of Diotogenes that "the virtues, the propriety, and the excellent character of the king have the effect of drawing into inner harmony the character of men who only gaze upon him."[18]

As we have seen, for Philo, Moses, as God's king, is the model of virtue to be imitated by the people. Elsewhere, Philo writes about the powerful effect of the presence of such models on those who would constantly look to them:

> For to gaze continuously upon noble models imprints their likeness in souls which are not entirely hardened and stony. And therefore those who would imitate these examples of good living so marvelous in their loveliness, are bidden not to despair of changing for the better or of a restoration to the land of wisdom and virtue from the spiritual dispersion which vice has wrought. (*Praem.* 114–15 [Colson, LCL][19]

The kingly presence of Moses, then, brings about virtue in those who constantly behold him.

---

16. My translation adapts Guthrie's (223).
17. Smith, *Christ the Ideal King*, 42.
18. Goodenough, "Political Philosophy," 75.
19. Cf. Philo, *Mos.* 1.161.

Plutarch takes up a similar perspective in his discussion of the Roman king, Numa. Plutarch writes that Numa "kept his life free from every taint of vice" (*Num.* 20.6 [Perrin, LCL]). Plutarch then goes on to discuss the power of Numa's virtuous presence among the people to bring about transformation:

> But when they see with their own eyes a conspicuous and shining example of virtue in the life of their ruler, they will on their own accord walk in wisdom's ways ... He is most a king who can inculcate (δυνάμενος ἐνεργάσασθαι) such a life and such a disposition in his subjects. (*Num.* 20.7–8 [Perrin, LCL])

Thus, Numa is more than an example, as an ideal king he energizes or implants the desire of virtue within his subjects.[20] Dio, as well, in his third oration on kingship writes that the king's

> justice gives of itself to the unjust, and his courage is able not only to save the less valiant, but even to fire them with greater courage ... This, it seems to me, is exactly Homer's view as well; for, after speaking of the ideal king, he concludes by saying, "And virtuous the people beneath him."[21] (*Or.* 3.8–9 [Cohoon, LCL])

In conclusion, ideal kings were especially considered to be powerful *exempla* as "living law" and as peculiarly indwelt by *logos* or wisdom. As such, ideal kings inculcated virtue in their subjects by the king's very presence among them. In the next section, we will turn to Hebrews and examine how Jesus is possibly depicted as an ideal king who, as "living law," is a transformative presence among his followers who are particularly in need of perseverance and faithfulness.

Jesus, the Ideal King in Hebrews

Jesus's kingship in Hebrews appears to share in this widespread ancient Mediterranean discourse on ideal kingship in several ways. (1) Jesus is God's vicegerent who is chosen to sit at God's right hand and rule on God's behalf (cf. 1:3, 5, 13).[22] (2) Jesus is also a king who loves righteousness (δικαιοσύνη,

---

20. Cf. Smith, *Christ the Ideal King*, 76.

21. Cf. *Od.* 19.114.

22. Hebrews 1:5 quotes Ps 2:7 to indicate God's choice of Jesus as God's kingly representative. In Ps 2:8, the nations, even the whole earth, are given to the newly enthroned Davidic ruler as his inheritance. In discussing Moses's kingship, Philo describes him as the one to whom God gave the cosmos and the one who inherits the whole world (*Mos.* 1.155–57). For further discussion see Smith, *Christ the Ideal King*, 92–96; Fears, "Cult

1:9). He is preeminently "the righteous one (ὁ δίκαιος)" who lives by faith/ with faithfulness (cf. 11:38). No attribute might be more important in the discussion of ideal kingship than that the king is righteous and rules with righteousness.[23] (3) Jesus is a victorious peace-bringer of eschatological abundance who defeats his enemy (the devil) and leads his people into the world to come where they will be crowned with glory and honor and will be given rest (cf. 2:5–18; 4:10). Likewise, victory and peace are elements of ideal kingship that were especially central to Augustan and Flavian propaganda.[24] (4) Like Diotogenes's king, Philo's Moses, and the Roman emperors, Jesus also takes up the office of the great high priest who represents his people to God (cf. 2:17; 4:14).[25] It is of particular interest that the author identifies the priest-king Melchizedek to whose priestly order Jesus belongs as a "*king* of righteousness" and a "*king* of peace." In view of these brief observations, it would seem that ideal kingship is an apropos category by which to consider the presentation of Jesus in Hebrews. Again, what is of particular interest in this study is whether, in the portrayal of Jesus as the ideal king, the audience of Hebrews would also have heard or experienced King Jesus as "living law" and a transformative presence in the community.

King Jesus as "Living Law"

Although the author of Hebrews never identifies Jesus as νόμος ἔμψυχος, there are, however, two ways in which this idea is present in Hebrews. First, when Jesus takes up his earthly life (i.e., enters the cosmos) only to present his indestructible life before God after his death on the cross, the words of Ps 40:6–8 are attributed to Jesus in which he declares, "Behold, I have come … to do your will, O' God" (Heb 10:7).[26] In fact, Jesus so perfectly does God's will, that he can be said to be "without sin" (Heb 4:15), just as Numa

---

of Jupiter," 86. Cf. Koester, *Hebrews*, 78–79.

23. Cf. Musonius Rufus 60.21—62.9; Plutarch, *Pric. iner.* 781B–C; Dio, *Or.* 1.12–13, 44–45.

24. Cf. Smith, *Christ the Ideal King*, 67, who identifies the motifs of virtue and of peace or a golden age as central elements of the discourse on kingship in the Flavian period. For further discussion of Jesus as the bringer of victorious peace and the one who leads the community to God's eschatological place of rest see, Whitlark, "God of Peace," 155–78.

25. Cf. n. 8 above.

26. The quotation and explanation of Ps 40:6–8 likely points to the offering of Jesus's body as a postmortem presentation of his resurrected body (i.e., indestructible life, Heb 7:16) in heaven. For further discussion of this point see Moffitt, *Atonement*, 238–47. Though the offering of Jesus's body is postmortem, the whole of Jesus's life is in view in Heb 10:5–10 (cf. ibid., 255).

was "free from every taint of vice" according to Plutarch. How is Jesus able to do God's will so completely? Of particular interest, is the remainder of the unquoted words from Ps 40:8, in which the psalmist goes on to declare, "your law is within my heart." It is difficult to say why the author did not include the remainder of the quote from Ps 40:8. Perhaps, it was for stylistic reasons. Karen Jobes notes that the authorial manipulation of the quotation from the Psalm in Heb 10:7 preserves assonance at the ending of clauses (μοῦ and σοῦ) which would be disrupted by including the remainder of the unquoted material.[27] Further, Luke Timothy Johnson notes several underlying thematic parallels from Ps 40 in Hebrews beyond the quotation from Ps 40:6–8a in Heb 10:5–7.[28] Most importantly, the idea of the indwelling law, suggested by the latter part of Psalm 40:8, certainly echoes the author's emphasis on the new covenant promise in Jeremiah where the law will be written on the hearts and minds of the people (cf. Heb 8:10; 10:16). This notion befits the author's portrayal of Jesus as God's new-covenant priest (and king), although the specific reference to the law being in the heart from Ps 40:8 is not quoted. Jesus's perfect obedience to God is indicative of the fact that God's law is within him, and, thus, characterizes him as the ideal king. This portrayal of Jesus then shares similarities with Xenophon's depiction of Cyrus or the Deuteronomist's account of the ideal Israelite king; namely, the ideal king is one who has internalized the divine law.

Second, Jesus is a king who has been indwelt by divine wisdom similar to Ecphantus's recounting of the divine *logos* that resides uniquely in the ideal king. In the opening exordium (Heb 1:1–4), scholars have noted the potential relationship of Jewish wisdom-*logos* speculation to the Son.[29] Like wisdom, the ages are made through the Son, he is the radiance (ἀπαύγασμα) of God's glory, and he sits at God's right hand. These descriptions suggest correlations with the Wisdom of Solomon, where wisdom is "the fashioner of all things" (7:22), where wisdom is "the radiance (ἀπαύγασμα) of eternal light" (7:26), and where wisdom "sits by [God's] throne" (9:4). Such identification of the Son with the functions of God's wisdom possibly reflects what Goodenough notes in Hellenistic kingship discourse where divine attributes may be interchanged with human rulers so that what is said of deity can be said of the king. The potential allusions to the Wisdom of Solomon also recall a context, as previously noted, where the king ("Solomon") prays to be indwelt by God's wisdom. By implication, then, the Son is that king who has received God's wisdom. If the king is possessed of divine *logos* or

27. Jobes, "Rhetorical Achievement," 391.
28. Johnson, *Hebrews*, 250–51.
29. E.g., Thompson, *Hebrews*, 33–34; Hurst, "Christology," 161–62.

wisdom or, as Tacitus affirmed, the monarch may even be considered the incarnation of Wisdom itself, then such a king could also be understood as νόμος ἔμψυχος or a model/pattern for his people.[30] The royal, exalted depiction of the Son in the opening exordium then is one that includes the Son as God's king who has been indwelt by or who incarnates God's wisdom and is thus a "living law" who reveals God's purposes for humanity and the pattern of life that the community is to follow (e.g., Heb 2:5–13).

Consequently, like the ideal king who has internalized the law or is indwelt by divine wisdom, Jesus in Hebrews is the supreme and worthy example for his people to imitate. It is fitting that Jesus concludes the *exempla* of faith(fulness) that begins with the community in Heb 10:32–39 and continues with the past elders of faith(fulness) in Heb 11:1–40. In Heb 12:1–3, Jesus is the one who endured (ὑπομένω) the shameful death of crucifixion and opposition by sinners for the "joy that was set before him." Jesus is thus the "beginning and end" or "author and perfecter" of faith for those who acknowledge him as king.[31]

Faithful endurance is chief among the virtues that the community is to imitate in Jesus if they wish to inherit, like Jesus, the promise of God: "for you have need of endurance (ὑπομονή) so that after doing the will of God you will receive the promise" (Heb 10:36). In fact, enduring (ὑπομένω) suffering is part of God's fatherly education that brings about the peaceable fruit of righteousness in those who have been trained by it (Heb 12:4–11). The ideal king, as Xenophon writes, "ought to surpass those under his rule ... in ... willingly undergoing toil" (*Cyr.* 1.6.8 [Miller, LCL]). Xenophon writes, elsewhere, that the king must endure hunger, thirst, cold, sleeplessness (all these toils) willingly (*Mem.* 2.1.17) and then quotes Hesiod, "But before Virtue the gods immortal have put sweat" (*Mem.* 2.1.20 [Merchant and Todd, LCL]). It is an education through suffering that leads to the necessary virtue of endurance. Suffering and hardship were the standard curriculum of divine education in the ancient world. It was the type of education of the ideal king, even "sons of Zeus."[32] Just as the community is undergoing its divine education and is in need of endurance, Jesus, the ideal king, has already successfully completed his education by the Father, where he "learned obedience from what he suffered (ἔμαθεν ἀφ' ὧν ἔπαθεν τὴν ὑποκοήν)" (Heb 5:8).[33]

---

30. Goodenough, *By Light*, 161–62.
31. Cf. Easter, *Faith and the Faithfulness of Jesus*.
32. Cf. Dio, *Or.* 4.27–31. For further discussion see Whitlark, "Cosmology," 125.
33. Cf. Martin and Whitlark, "Encomiastic Topics," 430–34.

King Jesus as a Transformative Presence

Jesus, however, is more than a kingly example. He is the "source of eternal salvation to all who obey him" (Heb 5:9). In bringing about this salvation, Jesus is the mediator of the new covenant (cf. Heb 7:22; 8:6; 9:15; 12:24). As previously mentioned, in this covenant, God's laws are written on the hearts and minds of the people (cf. 8:10; 10:16). They in effect will become "living law" like their king, who "will not have laws written outside in books" but will be ruled by the law within (Plutarch, *Princ. iner.* 780C [Fowler, LCL]).[34] Jesus, thus, as an ideal ruler, transforms the audience by his inauguration of the new covenant through his priestly ministry.[35]

There also is some indication that Jesus, as the ideal king, brings about persevering endurance in his followers, in part, through his kingly presence among the worshipping community. The audience of Hebrews would have possibly heard or experienced the transformative kingly presence of Jesus in at least three ways.

First, the author uses language in the exordium (Heb 1:1–4) that points to the transformative vision and presence of Jesus, the king. Jesus's cosmic kingship is emphasized in the exordium through such statements that declares he is "the heir of all things" (1:2), he "bears all things" (1:3), and he is the one who "sits at the right hand of the majesty on high" (1:3). What is particularly interesting is the description of Jesus as the "radiance of God's glory (ἀπαύγασμα τῆς δόξης)" and "the imprint of God's nature (χαρακτήρ τῆς ὑποστάσεως)" (1:3).[36] We have already seen that Diotogenes describes the ideal king as one who has the imprint of the divine majesty upon him. Moreover, it is "beholding his radiant nature (τῶν ποταυγασμένων/ προσαυγασμένων)" that, as Diotogenes states, is able to turn the king's subjects to lives of virtue. Ecphantus also describes the ideal king as "radiant (διαυγέστατον) in nature." Wisdom is even said to have kingly radiance

---

34. Cf. Goodenough, "Political Philosophy," 91, who states that the goal of all Greek ethical thinking was "to live spontaneously by divine law and dispense with the seriatim compulsion and injustice of the written codes."

35. See my chapter, "Fidelity and New Covenant Enablement in Hebrews," in Talbert and Whitlark, *Getting "Saved,"* 72–91.

36. Χαρακτήρ (a *hapax legomenon* in the New Testament, only occurring in Heb 1:3) could be used to refer to the impression of an image, especially on a coin. Imperial coins often had the image of the emperor imprinted on them. The phrase εἰκών τοῦ θεοῦ, which could refer to the king as the ruling representative of God, might also bear some relationship to χαρακτήρ τῆς ὑποστάσεως. In alluding to Gen 1:26, *1 Clem.* 33:4 relates χαρακτήρ and εἰκών though they are not identical (τῆς ἑαυτοῦ εἰκόνος χαρακτῆρα). In Matt 22:20, εἰκών is used to refer to the image of Caesar on a coin. See also Wilckens, "χαρακτήρ," 418–23.

(ἀπαύγασμα) because it is the image of God's goodness and sits by God's throne (Wis 7:26; 9:4, 10). When the author of Hebrews describes Jesus as the ἀπαύγασμα τῆς δόξης and even the imprint of God's nature within a context that presents Jesus as king, we recognize that such ideas and terminology evoke the discourse of the transformative presence of the ideal king. Jesus is the radiant king whose saving presence is a "revelation of deity" to those who behold him.[37]

Second, in the first syncrisis (Heb 1:5–14), the author seems to mediate the awesome kingly presence of Jesus to the community in his ecphrastic narration of Jesus's comparison to angels.[38] The comparison is set within the context of Jesus's heavenly enthronement to God's right hand. The detailed comparison between Jesus and angels follows a systematic encomiastic topical progression that is chronologically ordered (origins, birth, pursuits, death, and events beyond death). It begins with the choice by God (origins) to exalt Jesus as the Son, the cosmic king. Jesus then enters into the world (birth) as God's chosen king where he is enthroned and promised the eschatological subjugation of his enemies (events beyond death).[39] The experience of Jesus's enthronement within this syncrisis is vividly related, in part, by the description of Jesus's entry that includes God's direct address to the Son with the words of Scripture. Moreover, the description is amplified by his comparison to angels. Additionally, in 1:5 the author shifts from direct address by God to the Son to God speaking of the Son in the third person, as though the community itself with the angels (who are addressed in 1:6) is present at the Son's royal ascension to the throne.[40] Such ecphrastic narration functions to invite participation by the audience.[41] The audience is transported into the heavenly realm to overhear and behold God's installation of Jesus as his cosmic ruler.

As some have pointed out, the ecphrasis or ἐνάργεια in the description of Jesus's enthronement might point to a communal, mystical experience of "seeing" the enthroned king. Elsewhere, the encouragement to approach God's throne (cf. Heb 4:16) where Jesus sits at his right hand (cf. Heb 8:1) may

---

37. Cf. Goodenough, "Political Philosophy," 98.

38. A key quality of ecphrasis was ἐνάργεια or vividness, which was especially appropriate to narration in general and the *narratio* of a speech in particular. Cf. Ps.-Hermogenes, *Prog.* 22–23; Quintilian, *Inst.* 4.2.63–64; 6.2.32; Apsines, *Rhet.* 10.32.

39. Cf. Martin and Whitlark, "Encomiastic Topics," 427–29.

40. Cf. Mackie, "Heavenly Mysticism," 96. Mackie notes that, in line with the advice of rhetorical theorists, the author of Hebrews does not describe everything in his account of Jesus's heavenly enthronement but leaves room for the audience's imaginations to fill the gaps (105, n. 74).

41. Cf. Webb, *Ekphrasis*, 7–9.

as well evoke this experience of the transformative presence of God through his king in the worshipping community.[42] Such a powerful vision of a radiant king would have been understood to have transformative effect on those who shared such a vision. Such a transformative vision might be implied in Heb 11:27 where Moses was one who "endured because he saw him who is invisible." Moses's vision may have entailed a vision of the eschatological hope of God's people embodied in Jesus as the enthroned Son since God's faithful will share in Jesus's kingly rule in the world to come. Similarly, Xenophon has Socrates relate that the one who toils or endures suffering willingly "is comforted by hope" (*Mem.* 2.1.18 [Merchant and Todd, LCL]).

Third, the author summons members of his audience to consider Jesus's kingly example of endurance. In Heb 12:2, the author uses visual language to exhort members of his audience to "fix their eyes (ἀφοράω) on Jesus, the author and perfecter of faith."[43] In particular, they are to consider his contest of endurance in going through the shameful death of crucifixion as well as the outcome of such unwavering endurance. In 4 Macc 17:10, ἀφοράω is used to relate a type of intense consideration of God that overcomes torture even unto death. Thus, as in 4:16, the exhortation to look continually to the king and his virtue of endurance would have been understood to have a transformative effect on the community from the perspective of the discourse on ideal kingship.

Conclusion

In Hebrews, Jesus is *the* ideal king. He is God's chosen ruler and in him is embodied God's law, and specifically the endurance and faithfulness to God that inherits the promise of God. Certainly, his royal priestly role, modeled after Melchizedek as priest-king, inaugurates the new covenant and effects the forgiveness of sins, purification of the conscience, and the necessary enablement to empower the faithfulness of his beleaguered community of followers. The approach to God's throne where grace and mercy are found is only possible through the new covenant ministry of Jesus as the great high priest. In this approach, the audience also experiences the transformative presence of God through Jesus as king at God's right hand. In view of the discourse of ideal kingship, Jesus is "living law" whose royal, radiant nature and presence in the worshipping community transforms and enables his followers to undergo the same educational curriculum of suffering and to

---

42. Cf. Mackie, "Heavenly Mysticism," 77–117, esp. 87–99 and 104–6.
43. Cf. ibid., 104.

bring forth the same faithful endurance he exhibited in his life upon earth.⁴⁴ Such a ruler is fitting and meets the needs of the community who are also becoming "living law" and rulers in the world to come, like their king.

Works Cited

Barnard, Jody A. *They Mysticism of Hebrews*. WUNT 2/331. Tübingen: Mohr Siebeck, 2012.
Carradice, I., and T. Buttrey, eds. *Roman Imperial Coinage, vol. II, part 1. AD 69–96: Vespasian to Domitian*. 2nd ed. 10 vols. London: Spink, 2007.
Chesnut, Glenn F. "The Ruler and the Logos in Neopythagorean, Middle Platonic, and Late Stoic Political Philosophy." *ANRW* 16 (1978) 1310–32.
Easter, Matthew C. *Faith and the Faithfulness of Jesus in Hebrews*. SNTSMS 160. New York: Cambridge University Press, 2014.
Fears, J. Rufus. "The Cult of Jupiter and Roman Imperial Ideology." *ANRW* 17 (1981) 3–141.
Goodenough, Erwin R. *By Light, Light: The Mystical Gospel of Hellenistic Judaism*. Amsterdam: Philo, 1969.
———. "Political Philosophy of Hellenistic Kingship." *YCS* 1 (1928) 55–102.
Guthrie, Kenneth S. *The Pythagorean Sourcebook and Library: An Anthology of Ancient Writings Which Relate to Pythagoras and Pythagorean Philosophy*. Edited by David R. Fideler. Grand Rapids: Phanes, 1987.
Hurst, L. D. "The Christology of Hebrews 1 and 2." In *The Glory of Christ in the New Testament: Studies in Christology in Memory of George Bradford Caird*, edited by L. D. Hurst et al., 151–64. Oxford: Clarendon, 1987.
Jipp, Joshua W. *Christ is King: Paul's Royal Ideology*. Minneapolis: Fortress, 2015.
———. "The Son's Entrance into the Heavenly World: The Soteriological Necessity of the Scriptural Catena in Hebrews 1.5–14." *NTS* 56 (2010) 557–75.
Jobes, Karen. "Rhetorical Achievement in the Hebrews 10 'Misquote' of Psalm 40." *Bib* 72 (1991) 387–96.
Johnson, Luke Timothy. *Hebrews: A Commentary*. NTL. Louisville: Westminster John Knox, 2006.
Koester, Craig R. *Hebrews: A New Translation with Introduction and Commentary*. AB 36. New York: Doubleday, 2001.
Lutz, Cora E. "M. Rufus, 'The Roman Socrates.'" *YCS* 10 (1947) 3–147.
Mackie, Scott D. "Heavenly Mysticism in the Epistle to the Hebrews." *JTS* 62 (2011) 77–117.
Martin, Michael W., and Jason A. Whitlark. "The Encomiastic Topics of Syncrisis as the Key to the Structure and Argument of Hebrews." *NTS* 57 (2011) 415–39.
Moffitt, David M. *Atonement and the Logic of Resurrection in the Epistle to the Hebrews*. NovTSup 141. Leiden: Brill, 2011.
Motyer, Stephen. "The Psalm Quotations of Hebrews 1: A Hermeneutic-Free Zone?" *TynBul* 50 (1999) 3–22.

---

44. For the type of suffering and pressures from the imperial pagan society the audience of Hebrews living in Rome faced, see Whitlark, *Resisting Empire*.

Mowery, Robert. "Son of God in Roman Imperial Titles and Matthew." *Bib* 82 (2002) 100–110.

Paschke, Boris A. "The *cura morum* of the Roman Censors as Historical Background for the Bishop and Deacon Lists of the Pastoral Epistles." *ZNW* 98 (2007) 105–19.

Peppard, Michael. *Son of God in the Roman World: Divine Sonship in Its Social and Political Context*. New York: Oxford University Press, 2011.

Rüpke, Jörg. "Starting Sacrifice in the Beyond: Flavian Innovations in the Concept of Priesthood and Their Reflections in the Treatise 'to the Hebrews.'" In *Hebrews in Contexts*, edited by Gabriella Gelardini and Harold W. Attridge, 109–32. AJEC 91. Leiden: Brill, 2016.

Smith, Julien. *Christ the Ideal King*. WUNT 2/313. Tübingen: Mohr Siebeck, 2011.

Talbert, Charles H. and Jason A. Whitlark. *Getting "Saved": The Whole Story of Salvation in the New Testament*. Grand Rapids: Eerdmans, 2011.

Thompson, James W. *Hebrews*. PCNT. Grand Rapids: Baker 2008.

Wachsmuth, Curtius, and Otto Hense, eds. and trans. *Ioannis Stobaei Anthologium*. 5 vols. Berlin: Weidmann, 1884–1912.

Walbank, F. W. "Monarchies and Monarchic Ideas." In *The Hellenistic World*. Vol. 7, *The Cambridge Ancient History*, edited by F. W. Walbank et al., 62–100. Cambridge: Cambridge University Press, 1984.

Webb, Ruth. *Ekphrasis, Imagination and Persuasion in Ancient Rhetorical Theory and Practice*. Surrey: Ashgate, 2009.

Whitlark, Jason A. "Cosmology and the Perfection of Humanity in Hebrews." In *Interpretation and the Claims of the Text: Resourcing New Testament Theology*, edited by Jason A. Whitlark et al., 155–78. Waco: Baylor University Press, 2014.

———. "The God of Peace and His Victorious King: Hebrews 13:20–21 in Its Roman Imperial Context." In *Hebrews in Contexts*, edited by Gabriella Gelardini and Harold W. Attridge, 155–78. AJEC 91. Leiden: Brill, 2016.

———. *Resisting Empire: Rethinking the Purpose of the Letter to "the Hebrews."* LNTS 484. London: T&T Clark, 2014.

Wilckens, Ulrich. "χαρακτήρ." In *TDNT* 9:418–23. Edited by G. Kittel and G. Friedrich. Translated by Geoffrey W. Bromiley. Grand Rapids: Eerdmans, 1974.

II. Interpreting Luke and Acts

Luke, Metalepsis, and the Deuteronomistic History

James M. Kennedy[1]

The following study looks at Luke's Gospel through the lens of metalepsis to suggest that Luke is not simply alluding to the LXX, but that the gospel he produces is, in effect if not by intent, the continuation of and the fulfillment of the Deuteronomistic History in the LXX. Certainly Luke used more from the LXX than the Deuteronomistic History, but the salient point of this essay is the Deuteronomistic History was especially important. Much of the work that explores Luke's relationship with the LXX deals with the book of Acts. Thomas Römer and Jean-Daniel Macchi read Luke within the rubric of the Deuteronomistic traditions but focus their attention on Acts.[2] They interpret Acts as a text of theodicy similar to the Deuteronomistic History. Römer and Macchi point, for instance, to the similarity between the end of the book of Acts and the Deuteronomistic History. The latter ends with Jerusalem in ruins, but adds that Evil-merodach, king of Babylon, grants King Jehoiachin special privileges involving release from prison, a place at the king's table, and an allowance for the rest of Jehoiachin's life (2 Kgs 25:27–30). Acts ends with Paul in a privileged position of proclaiming for two years the kingdom of God without hindrance (Acts 28:30–31). Both histories have open endings. Although Römer and Macchi employ the ter-

---

1. Author's note: In my undergraduate days, both my wife and I benefited greatly from Naymond Keathley's teaching and scholarship. Indeed, Dr. Keathley's course on Luke was one of the courses my wife and I took in our college years. For the past thirty-one years, it has been my fortunate lot to be his colleague at Baylor University. It is an honor and privilege to present this paper to him on the publication of a well-deserved Festschrift. All errors and infelicities in this article are my own.

2. Römer and Macchi, "Luke," 182.

minology of influence without seeking to flesh out the details of how Luke cites the Deuteronomistic material, they have, in my view, begun a metaleptic reading of Acts in relation to the Deuteronomistic History. Although they certainly make a substantial case for reading Acts as carrying forward the Deuteronomistic agenda, what of the Gospel?

Metalepsis is a trope that allows readers to analyze allusions from an older and therefore distant text, with the aim of illuminating the meanings of a target text. It involves movement from one narrative to another, allowing condensed meanings to proliferate along a line of allusions that culminate in the target text.[3] The impact is to qualify a target text as deriving its meanings, in part, from the older string of texts by way of allusion.

On the one hand, metalepsis beckons readers to find out more about the original context from which the allusion in the target text draws.[4] On the other hand, it raises the issue of how allusion to the older texts sharpens or enhances the interpretation of the target text. If text A draws from text B, the allusions from text B likely will enrich the interpretation of text A. Text B is not necessarily the source of text A, but the allusive nature of text A to text B reveals meaning in text A. A causal relationship or an intermediate substitution of terms that readers infer may be the basis of the meaning.[5]

Text A may so extensively draw on the narrative world of text B that the former begins to appear in some way as an extension of the latter. David Herman and Gerard Genette depict metalepsis as a trope that transgresses boundaries.[6] It violates the ontological borders of texts. Metalepsis links texts to the degree that two or more texts may respond to the previous text(s) as in some sense continuous with them or at least as expressing in various ways thematic sympathies. Metalepsis focuses the inherent literary quality of intertextuality from simple allusion to hermeneutic signification.

Scholars of Luke's Gospel seem to have reached a consensus that Luke is well familiar with the LXX.[7] It is likely, furthermore, that beyond familiarity with the LXX as a whole, Luke places the story of Jesus within Israel's biblical history.[8] This paper suggests that the evangelist, consciously or not, portrays the story of Jesus as continuing and fulfilling the Deuteronomistic History by a process of metalepsis or transumption. It is not simply that

3. McFadden, "Metalepsis or Transumption," 862–63.
4. Brown and Hays, "Deep and Subtle Unity."
5. "Sylva Rhetoricae," http://rhetoric.byu.edu/.
6. Herman, "Toward a Formal Description"; Genette, *Narrative Discourse*, 234–35.
7. Kümmel, *Introduction*, 135; Pervo, "Israel's Heritage," 130. See as well Muraoka, "Luke and the Septuagint," 13–15; Brodie, "Departure for Jerusalem," 96; Brodie, "Luke 7,36–50," 457–85.
8. Fitzmyer, *Gospel According to Luke*, 9.

Luke copies or imitates the LXX, but that he places his story in continuity with the Deuteronomistic History. This is not to suggest that Luke ignores the rest of the LXX. Luke grounds his story of Jesus in metaleptic compressions or expansions of various themes from the Deuteronomistic History. The suggested effect is that the evangelist casts the gospel he writes, consciously or not, as the answer to the tragedy of Israel and Judah's fall that 2 Kgs 17 and 25 describe.

Whether or not one reads the end of the Deuteronomistic History as hopeless or as hinting at a future for Israel, it still implies the question, "what next?" An interpretation of hopelessness, which is Noth's reading,[9] suggests the writer lived at the time of Jehoiachin's release from prison. For the historian, that is all there is to record. The ending of his history presents, therefore, a truly existential crisis. If the Babylonian king's gracious treatment of Jehoiachin suggests an end open to new possibilities, as von Rad avers,[10] the reader may suppose that David's descendants have, at least, some significance for the future. The problem with the hopeful ending is that according to the Deuteronomistic History, Yahweh had decreed a full end to Judah (2 Kgs 21:14). When the Lord forsakes "the remnant of my heritage" (ἀπώσομαι τὸ ὑπόλειμμα τῆς κληρονομίας μου [2 Kgs 21:14]), certainly the terrible determination cannot exclude the Davidic covenant of 2 Sam 7. Not even the reforms that Josiah brings about can persuade God to relent. By way of a momentary forward glance, Luke's Gospel will address God's apparent relentless rage in the songs of the birth narratives of John and Jesus.

Although Thomas L. Brodie does not use the term metalepsis in his studies of Luke's use of the prophets Elijah and Elisha, in my view, his studies present a development that leads to metaleptic analysis of Luke in relation to the Elijah/Elisha narratives. These narratives have no corresponding significance for the Chronicler's history. A connection between Luke's Gospel and the Deuteronomistic History seems all the more likely. Brodie employs the terminology of rhetorical imitation or *imitatio* to survey the evidence of how the new author, Luke, stakes out the stories of the old characters, Elijah and Elisha, to characterize Jesus's prophetic persona.[11] Brodie sees *imitatio* as exercising a range of techniques, the most

---

9. Noth, *Deuteronomistic History*, 98

10. von Rad, "Deuteronomic Theology," 220–21.

11. Brodie, "Luke 7,36–50," 462. He does not, however, do so with the aim of exploring the Gospel's specific relationship with the wider Deuteronomistic History.

basic of which are contraction (or abbreviation) and expansion. Another technique is that of fusing and dividing.[12]

Metalepsis, or transumption, is a composite trope by which a writer develops themes from other literary productions and releases or expands their meaning into his or her own work, thus overriding the ontological boundaries between the works. It is composite because it operates in conceptual fields of tropes of meaning such as intertextuality, metonymy, and metaphor.[13] This is not to assert that intertextuality, metonymy, and metaphor are examples of metalepsis. They do not necessarily compel the reader to consult the source expression of a theme to uncover the theme's occurrence in the subsequent text. Brodie interprets *imitatio* in Luke as illuminating the older text. Metalepsis, however, works to engage the older text as a way that illumines the new text. [14]

Whatever its source, the birth narrative of John the Baptizer breathes the air of the Deuteronomistic History. The appearance of the angel of the Lord is significant in light of references to it in the announcement of Samson's birth (Judg 13:3–21). Only once in the Deuteronomistic History does the angel of the Lord announce the birth of a child, namely, Samson. As in the story of Zechariah and Elizabeth, the angel's appearance links to a barren woman and promises progeny. The fact that Gabriel tells Zechariah that his son must not drink wine or strong drink adds a further associative dimension between the narratives. Samson also must never indulge in wine or strong drink (Judg 13:2–7).

Furthermore, Elizabeth's statement expressing her release from the disgrace of being barren (Luke 1:25) reminds Luke's readers of the disgrace Hannah bore (1 Sam 1:6–7) and of the joy she experiences at finally bearing a child. Hannah depicts the birth of her first born as a mockery to those who once mocked her. She declares, "I make wide my mouth over my enemies" (ἐπλατύνθη ἐπὶ ἐχθροὺς τὸ στόμα μου [1 Sam 2:1]).

Gabriel's declaration to Mary concerning her son's destiny seems tailor-made to speak to the issue of the ending of the Deuteronomistic History. David's descendants will continue and one of them will be the Messiah. The focus of Mary's song in Luke 1:46–55 is the fulfillment of the Davidic covenant through the conception of the Messiah.[15] In terms that draw attention to 2 Sam 7:9, 13, 14, 16, Gabriel announces, "He will be great, and will be called the Son of the Most High, and the Lord God will give to

---

12. Ibid., 462.
13. McFadden, "Metalepsis or Transumption," 862–63.
14. Brodie, "Departure for Jerusalem," 102.
15. Brown, *Birth*, 360.

him the throne of his ancestor David" (Luke 1:32-33). Fitzmyer charts the comparisons:[16]

2 Sam 7:9, "a great name"	Luke 1:32, "he will be great"
2 Sam 7:13, "the throne of his kingdom"	Luke 1:32, "throne of his father David"
2 Sam 7:14, "he will be my son"	Luke 1:32, "Son of the Most High"
2 Sam 7:16, "your house and your kingdom"	Luke 1:33, "king over the house of Jacob forever"

At least since 1901, scholars have viewed Hannah's song in 1 Sam 2:1-10 as a model for the Magnificat in Luke 2:46-55.[17] The point here is not systematically to compare the two songs, but to advance the case that Luke carries forward a major moment (Hannah's song) in 1 Samuel to characterize Mary's rejoicing. The parallelism between Hannah and Mary also involves both mothers taking their sons to holy places for dedication to God. Mary takes Jesus to Jerusalem (Luke 2:22-40) whereas Hannah takes Samuel to the temple in Shiloh (1 Sam 1:21-28). Mary and Hannah are, so to speak, sisters of faith in the same story of redemption.

Still, behind the promise of Mary's son stands the dreadful divine declaration of 2 Kgs 21:14, which the narrative reinforces in 23:26-27. If readers can take Luke's Gospel as in some sense continuing the Deuteronomistic History, they must take into account the Lord's final judgment of total disaster. It lies between the Deuteronomistic History and Luke like the proverbial dead whale. Surely, a scholar such as Luke would have been aware of the proclamation of doom.

Luke's answer is not to take on 2 Kgs 21:14 directly, but to undermine it by emphasizing God's grace and mercy. In part, the songs of Mary, Zechariah, and Simeon, indeed, the birth narratives of John and Jesus as a whole, mitigate the divine rage by emphasizing God's mercy. In the Magnificat, Mary rejoices in what God has done for her personally (Luke 1: 46-49). In verses 50-55, she exalts God's mercy by celebrating the fall of the powerful and the divine uplifting of the lowly. The Lord does this because of mercy (ἔλεος, 1:50) on those who fear him. Even more revealing is the phraseology of verse 54: ἀντελάβετο Ἰσραὴλ παιδὸς αὐτοῦ, μνησθῆναι ἐλέους, "He has helped Israel his child, remembering mercy." The phrase μνησθῆναι ἐλέους, "remembering mercy," is significant. The word ἔλεος certainly can mean mercy but in the language of late Judaism, it may bear an eschatological

---

16. Fitzmyer, *Gospel According to Luke*, 338.

17. Plummer, *Critical and Exegetical Commentary*, 300. See also Fitzmyer, *Gospel According to Luke*, 359; Brown, *Birth*, 357.

connotation.[18] The Messianic age is dawning precisely because God has laid aside anger and is now acting to bring Israel's history to its true end.

Luke's story of the widow's son at Nain (7:11–17) is more than an allusion to prophetic resuscitation narratives from the LXX. Allusion indeed, but there is more at work and it is that "more" that calls for our attention. Luke is careful to construct his story to recall 1 Kgs 17. In 1 Kgs 17:10, Elijah comes as far as the gate of the city (εἰς τὸν πυλῶνα τῆς πόλεως) where he meets a widow gathering sticks. Luke 7:12 portrays Jesus as coming near the city gate (ὡς δὲ ἤγγισεν τῇ πύλῃ τῆς πόλεως) where he encounters a funeral procession. A widow's son has died, thus leaving her grieving and bereft of material support. Although the widow of Zarephath's son has not yet died, death permeates the atmosphere as the widow explains to Elijah that she is gathering sticks to make a final loaf of bread and then die. Approaching the gate is a hint that Luke's story works, in part, with 1 Kgs 17.

In 1 Kgs 17:8–24, as a famine grips the land, Elijah asks the widow of Zarephath for water, which she soon delivers. When Elijah asks for a morsel of bread, the woman points out that she has only a little flour and oil. Elijah replies, "take courage" (θάρσει), and then continues to give her instructions that culminate with a divine promise of abundance. Similarly, Jesus tells the bereft widow, "do not weep" (μή κλαῖε). Jesus's consolation to the widow mirrors Elijah's comment, θάρσει. Elijah's attempt to resuscitate the widow's son takes time, effort, and prayer and the Lord rewards him by restoring life to the boy. Luke's story compresses Elijah's elaborate and sustained efforts to resuscitate the widow's son by portraying Jesus as simply touching the bier and speaking four words, Νεανίσκε, σοὶ λέγω, ἐγέρθητι, "young man, I say to you, rise!" In 1 Kgs 17:22, when the widow's son revives, "he cries out" (ἀνεβόησεν τὸ παιδάριον). In Luke's story, the young man sits up and begins to speak, καὶ ἤρξατο λαλεῖν, whereupon Luke tells his reader, "and he gave him to his mother" (καὶ ἔδωκεν αὐτὸν τῇ μητρὶ αὐτοῦ). Significantly, in Luke, Jesus does the same thing Elijah does after the resuscitation: καὶ ἔδωκεν αὐτὸν τῇ μητρὶ αὐτοῦ (1 Kgs 17:23).

According to Fitzmyer, the crowd's identification of Jesus as a great prophet and the allusion to the Elijah story (7:15–16) suffice to show that Luke uses this incident to cast Jesus in the role of *Elias redivivus*.[19] However, the crowd also exclaims, "God has looked favorably (ἐπεσκέψατο) upon his people" (7:16). Interestingly, Luke uses the same verb to depict God's attention toward the people as the historian uses to tell readers that "the Lord

---

18. Bultmann, "ἔλεος," 2:481. See Wis 3:9; 4:15; 2 Macc 2:7; 7:29; Pss. Sol. 8:34; 17:51; 18:6.

19. Fitzmyer, *Gospel According to Luke*, 656.

took note (ἐπεσκέψατο) of Hannah" (1 Sam 2:19). The widow of Zarephath responds by confessing Elijah to be a man of God and then declares, "the word of the Lord is truly in your mouth" (ῥῆμα κυρίου ἐν στόματί σου ἀληθινόν [1Kgs 17:24]). Luke's readers miss a significant point if they forget to take into consideration the widow's confession that God's word is truly in the prophet's mouth. The widow's confession is conceptually necessary if Luke's readers are to see the significance of the crowd's confession regarding the widow of Nain's experience. The word of God in Jesus's mouth is true. Metaleptically, the widow of Zarephath confesses that Jesus is a man of God. Yet, Jesus is more than a prophet; he is, as Luke 7:13 tells readers, "the Lord" (ὁ κύριος). This is the first occurrence in Luke of κύριος in third person narrative referring to Jesus. That Luke so depicts Jesus as he is coming near the gate where he will meet the stark reality of death is significant. Jesus, a prophet indeed, is also the Lord of life.[20] Prophets and kings of Israel and Judah failed in various ways relative to their offices to prevent the catastrophes of 722 and 587 BCE. Jesus the Messiah will bring a new beginning.

Perhaps one of the most telling texts that link Luke's Jesus to the Deuteronomistic History is Luke 4:25–30. Here is Luke's first reference to both Elijah and Elisha. Luke's Gospel more closely associates itself with the Deuteronomistic History in this brief pericope. Significantly, apart from extra-canonical references to these two prophets, in the LXX the bulk of their stories occurs in 1 and 2 Kings. Interestingly, Elisha does not occur in the Chronicles, whereas Elijah occurs once (2 Chr 21:12). The narratives about Elijah and Elisha in 1 and 2 Kgs speak in favor of associating, not simply the LXX as a whole with Luke's portrayal of Jesus, but specifically the Deuteronomistic History. Raymond Brown observes that Jesus himself compares his actions to Elijah and Elisha.[21]

Fitzmyer observes that although Luke clearly portrays Jesus as setting out for Jerusalem, a problem that rises is that Jesus eventually seems not to be en route at all.[22] The result, he avers, is that Luke's readers lose sight of the fact that Jesus is on a journey. Whether or not such is the case with Luke's readers, the travel narrative is one of the ways Luke prepares readers for Jesus's ἔξοδος.[23] Furthermore, the Lucan travel account (Luke 9:51–19:28) provides Luke's readers with an expansive literary compilation that conveys Jesus's teachings, parables, legal and wisdom sayings, and miracle stories.[24]

---

20. Garland, *Luke*, 303.
21. Brown, "Jesus and Elisha," 85–104.
22. Fitzmyer, *Gospel According to Luke*, 824.
23. Ibid., 826.
24. Ibid., 825.

It begins with a brief pericope that recalls Elijah.[25] On the way to Jerusalem, Jesus and his followers go through a Samaritan village (Luke 9:51–56). The Samaritans do not welcome him because he has set out for Jerusalem. James and John are indignant and ask Jesus if they should call down fire from heaven, thus recalling Elijah's fiery response in 2 Kgs 1. Several manuscripts add "as Elijah did." Instead, Jesus turns and rebukes them as they make their way to another village. Jesus's nonviolence sets him apart from Elijah and Elisha and draws on Jewish traditions that advocate a perspective of God as willing to withhold punishment out of divine mercy.[26]

The narrative about the Shunamite woman (2 Kgs 4:8–37) combines two type scenes. First, there is the annunciation of the birth of a child (2 Kgs 4:8–18). Second, there is the prophetic resuscitation of the dead child (2 Kgs 4:18b–37). Metaleptically, both provide theological substance that Luke works into his narrative by way of the story of Zechariah and Elizabeth as well as the story of Jairus's daughter. After Elijah tells her that she shall have a son, the Shunamite widow says to Elisha, κύριέ μου μὴ διαψεύσῃ τὴν δούλην σου, "my sir, do not deceive your servant" (2 Kgs 4:16). Similarly, when Gabriel tells Zechariah that Elizabeth will have a son (Luke 1:13–17), the priest says, "how shall I know this? For I am elderly and my wife has advanced in her days" (κατὰ τί γνώσομαι τοῦτο; ἐγὼ γάρ εἰμι πρεσβύτης καὶ ἡ γυνή μου προβεβηκυῖα ἐν ταῖς ἡμέραις αὐτῆς). After her son dies, the Shunamite woman makes her way to Elisha where she "takes hold of his feet" (ἐπελάβετο τῶν ποδῶν αὐτοῦ, 2 Kgs 4:27). Similarly, Jairus falls at Jesus's feet (καὶ πεσὼν παρὰ τοὺς πόδας [τοῦ] Ἰησοῦ) (Luke 8:41). That the Shunamite woman takes hold of Elisha's feet suggests that Luke has transposed the act to fit Jairus's encounter with Jesus. It is not simply a case of Luke using Mark as a source. Luke alludes to the Shunamite woman. The fact that both stories involve resuscitations from death tells against Luke simply using Mark as a source for this detail.

The feeding narrative in Luke 9:10–17 recalls 2 Kgs 4:42–44 where Elisha presides over the feeding of a hundred men with a small amount of food. Just as Elisha tells his servant to give his food to the hundred to let them eat (2 Kgs 4:42), Jesus similarly commands his disciples to give the multitudes something to eat (Luke 9:13). Elisha's servant and Jesus's disciples express doubt about how such a small amount of food can feed such a large crowd. Both narratives also note that there were leftovers. The linking of the two

---

25. Hultgren, "Apostolic Church's Influence," 199.
26. Allison, "Rejecting Violent Judgment," 459–78.

stories seems clear. Luke is alluding to 2 Kgs 2:42, and thus continues his narrative by portraying Jesus as a prophet. [27]

In Luke 9:51–56, Jesus sets out for Jerusalem as the time of his assumption (ἀνάλημψις) draws near. The word ἀνάλημψις occurs only here in the New Testament and more likely refers to Jesus's assumption into heaven than to his crucifixion.[28] It also suggests an allusion to Elijah's ascent into heaven in 1 Kgs 2:11 where the historian tells readers "and Elijah was taken up in a storm wind into heaven" (καὶ ἀνελήμφθη Ηλιου ἐν συσσεισμῷ ὡς εἰς τὸν οὐρανόν). The verb ἀνελήμφθη coalesces a metaleptic associative gesture between 2 Kings and Luke.

Whoever Theophilus was, it behooved him to have read the Deuteronomistic History together with his reading of Luke's Gospel and the book of Acts. Whatever my own readers may conclude, I will take my own advice to Theophilus as a challenge of interpretation.

Works Cited

Allison, Dale C., Jr. "Rejecting Violent Judgment: Luke 9:52–56 and Its Relatives." *JBL* 121 (2002) 459–78.
Brodie, Thomas L. "The Departure for Jerusalem (Luke 9,51–56) as a Rhetorical Imitation of Elijah's Departure for the Jordan (2 Kgs 1,1–2,6)." *Bib* 70 (1989) 96–109.
———. "Luke 7,36–50 as an Internalization of 2 Kings 4,1–37: A Study in Luke's Use of Rhetorical Imitation." *Bib* 64 (1983) 457–85.
Brown, Garrett, and Richard B. Hays. "The Deep and Subtle Unity of the Bible." *Books and Culture*, November/December 2016. http://www.booksandculture.com/articles/2016/novdec/deep-and-subtle-unity-of-bible.html.
Brown, Raymond E. *The Birth of the Messiah: A Commentary on the Infancy Narratives in Matthew and Luke*. Garden City, NY: Image, 1979.
———. "Jesus and Elisha." *Perspective* 12 (1971) 85–104.
Bultmann, Rudolph. "ἔλεος." In *TDNT* 2:477–87. Edited by Gerhard Kittel. Translated by Geoffrey W. Bromiley. Grand Rapids: Eerdmans, 1964.
Fitzmyer, Joseph A. *The Gospel According to Luke*. AB 28. Garden City, NY: Doubleday, 1981.
Ferguson, Russell, et al., eds. *Discourses: Conversations in Postmodern Art and Culture*. New York: New Museum of Contemporary Art, 1990.
Garland, David. *Luke*. ZECNT. Edited by Clinton E. Arnold. Grand Rapids: Zondervan, 2011.
Gennette, Gérard. *Narrative Discourse: An Essay in Method*. Translated by Jane E. Lewin. Ithaca, NY: Cornell University Press, 1980.

---

27. Fitzmyer, *Gospel According to Luke*, 766, does not read the feeding account in Luke 9 as drawing on the feeding story in Mark 6.

28. Ibid., 878.

Herman, David. "Toward a Formal Description of Narrative Metalepsis." *JLS* 26 (1997) 132–52.

Huddelston, Jonathan. "What Would Elijah and Elisha Do? Internarrativity in Luke's Story of Jesus." *JTI* 5 (2011) 265–82.

Hultgren, Stephen. "The Apostolic Church's Influence on the Order of the Sayings in the Double Tradition, Part II: Luke's Travel Narrative." *ZNW* 100 (2009) 199–222.

Kümmel, Werner G. *Introduction to the New Testament*. Rev. ed. Translated by Howard Clark Kee. New York: Abingdon, 1975.

McFadden, Kevin. "Metalepsis or Transumption." In *The Princeton Encyclopedia of Poetry and Poetics*, edited by Roland Greene et al., 862–63. 4th ed. Princeton: Princeton University Press, 2012.

Miscall, Peter. "Isaiah: New Heavens, New Earth, New Book." In *Reading Between Texts: Intertextuality and the Hebrew Bible*, edited by Danna Nolan Fewell, 41–56. Louisville: Westminster John Knox, 1992.

Muraoka, Takamitsu. "Luke and the Septuagint." *NovT* 54 (2012) 13–15.

Noth, Martin. *The Deuteronomistic History*. JSOTSup 15. Translated by Jane Doull et al. Sheffield: University of Sheffield, 1981.

Parsons, Mikeal C., and Richard I. Pervo. *Rethinking the Unity of Luke and Acts*. Minneapolis: Fortress, 1993.

Plummer, Alfred. *A Critical and Exegetical Commentary on the Gospel According to S. Luke*. ICC. Edinburgh: T&T Clark, 1901.

Pervo, Richard. "Israel's Heritage and Claims upon the Genre(s) of Luke and Acts." In *Jesus and the Heritage of Israel: Luke's Narrative Claim upon Israel's Legacy*, edited by David P. Moessner, 127–43. Harrisburg, PA: Trinity Press International, 1999.

Römer, Thomas, and Jean-Daniel Macchi. "Luke, Disciple of the Deuteronomistic School." In *Luke's Literary Achievement: Collected Essays*, edited by C. M. Tuckett, 178–87. Sheffield: Sheffield Academic Press, 1995.

von Rad, Gerhard. "The Deuteronomic Theology of History in *I* and *II Kings*." In *The Problem of the Hexateuch and Other Essays*, 205–31. Translated by E. W. Trueman Dicken. London: SCM, 1984.

"Filled with the Spirit"

Improvisational Speech in Acts 4:5–31

WILLIAM D. SHIELL

IMPROVISATION WAS ONE OF the most effective forms of delivery in the ancient world. Instead of relying on a rehearsed manuscript, orators chose to speak extemporaneously to convey their authenticity, express admiration for their audiences, connect to their listeners, or silence a judge. For the educated elites, improvisation was the "crown" of rhetorical education (Quintilian, *Inst.* 10.7.1).

Over the last century in biblical research, the study of improvisation has been dormant.[1] Recently, Kevin Vanhoozer and Samuel Wells have introduced improvisation as a theological method. They claim that Christian communities can use improvisation to help them discern moral judgments. Vanhoozer suggests that improvisation is a form of biblical φρόνησις or practical wisdom, designed to help communities who fear God act appropriately.[2] Similarly, Wells suggests that improvisation is not primarily about words but is a "process of corporate discernment and embodiment central to the mission and worship of the church."[3]

From the perspective of the ancient world and early Christianity, improvisation is precisely about oral delivery in public addresses. While adaptable for contemporary moral discernment in churches, the ancient world rarely used improvisation for decision-making in communities. Rather, improvisational speakers communicated spontaneously at the right place at the right time to an audience. Orators knew that they would need to leave

---

1. The most recent thorough analysis of improvisational speech was published in 1914: Brown, *Extemporary Speech in Antiquity*.

2. Vanhoozer, *Drama of Doctrine*, 336–37.

3. Wells, *Improvisation*, 18.

behind a manuscript and rely on their knowledge of the subject to convince and connect to their audiences.

Early Christian speakers were no different than their ancient counterparts. Because improvisation was such an effective form of communication in the ancient world, we can expect that early Christians did the same. The New Testament suggests that believers prepared to speak spontaneously. In a seminar on First Peter, Naymond Keathley first helped me understand 1 Pet 3:15 in this way. The defense that early Christians offered arose not from a rehearsed script but flowed naturally from someone who had "sanctified Christ in their hearts." First Peter instructs those who are suffering for their faith to be prepared to make a defense gently and reverently (1 Pet 3:15). Jesus expresses similar sentiments in Matt 10:20, Luke 12:11–12, and Luke 21:15 when preparing disciples for trials. Jesus teaches disciples not to be anxious because the Spirit would teach them the words to speak in the moment (Matt 10:20; Luke 12:12). Jesus encourages disciples to endure suffering by relying on him when speaking before kings and governors because he would give them a "mouth and wisdom that none of their adversaries would be able to withstand or contradict" (Luke 21:15).

The ancient rhetorical conventions of improvisation can help us understand how early Christians communicated in emergencies so effectively. In this essay, we study how speakers improvised in Greco-Roman, Jewish, and early Christian settings. We then turn to the most likely examples of improvisation in the New Testament: two speeches in Acts 4 where apostles and their companions are "filled with the Spirit" and speak boldly. One is delivered by Peter and John, the other by a community in prayer. We will learn that speaking extemporaneously gives the apostles and their audiences the confidence to speak at trial, an authentic connection to those they address, and endurance to face opponents.

Improvisation in the Ancient World

Orators and philosophers from the fourth century BCE to the fourth century CE discussed improvisation. The word comes from a Latin phrase and a Greek word: *extempore facere* and αὐτοσχεδιάζω, both meaning to "act on the spur of the moment." In practice, improvisational speech was a prepared, unrehearsed, and unscripted address or a response delivered in an emergency, on trial, or at a public festival.[4] As such, even trained extemporaneous speakers were often anxious because of the sudden, unplanned nature of the speech. Most orators learned improvisation in rhetorical schools by

---

4. Barton, "Signification of 'Extempore Speech,'" 238.

practicing declamation, memorized topics designed to be used for a variety of occasions to spread propaganda for the emperor or to entertain at festivals (Seneca, *Contr.* 4.*praef*.7; 7.*praef*.2).[5] Much to the chagrin of rhetorical teachers, many others possessed the natural ability to speak extemporaneously without training and were very effective communicators. Quintilian worried that if "barbarians and slaves" could improvise there would be no need for the rhetorical schools (*Inst.* 2.11.7; cf. Philostratus, *Lives* 577.7).[6]

Settings

Improvisation typically occurred at trial. Quintilian noted that there were times when, on short notice, an orator was called upon to plead a case for a friend. He wrote, "For there are countless occasions when the sudden necessity may be imposed upon him of speaking without preparation before the magistrates or in a trial which comes on unexpectedly" (*Inst.* 10.7.2 [Butler]). Speakers were encouraged to prepare for spontaneous moments when they might be called upon to address various topics or to respond to questions and interruptions in a defense.[7]

Emperors could invite orators to improvise on a topic, usually to spread propaganda (Philostratus, *Lives* 530). At public festivals, audiences gave speakers topics to address on the spot. In a speech at a festival in the Theater of Agrippa, the audience chose a topic for Alexander. Philostratus wrote, "After pausing for a brief space he sprang from his seat with a look of gladness on his face, like one who brings good news to those who shall listen to what he has to tell them" (*Lives* 572). In the middle of his speech, Herodes arrived, and Alexander adapted his speech and asked Herodes if he would like him to continue the same topic. Philostratus continued, "For the sentiments he had so brilliantly expressed before Herodes came he now recast in his presence, but with such different words and different rhythms, that those who were hearing them for the second time could not feel that he was repeating himself" (*Lives* 572).

Conventions

Speakers improvised using a variety of methods. Preparation began long before the trial or public address. Trained orators built a storehouse of images

---

5. Bonner, *Roman Declamation*, 49.
6. Holcomb, "Crown of All Our Study," 58.
7. Barton, "Signification of 'Extempore Speech,'" 238.

and epigrams in their memories that could fit most situations (Quintilian, *Inst.* 2.11.4; 11.2.46–47).

When called upon, most orators spoke immediately; but some asked for one night to prepare (Philostratus, *Lives* 583). They spoke individually or in pairs. The partner prompted the speaker at transitions and calmed his emotions. For instance, Haterius spoke extemporaneously (and quickly) with a freedman. According to Seneca, "He seemed to charge downhill rather than run. He was full of ideas as well as words. He would say the same thing as often as you liked and for as long as you liked with different figures and development on every occasion. He could be controlled but not exhausted" (Seneca, *Contr.* 4.*praef.*7 [Winterbottom, LCL]).

In delivery, orators treated an improvisational speech like a journey on a long road. They imagined the destination and thought of the various steps along the way as they spoke. They arranged the parts of the speech while uttering what was immediately on their minds (Quintilian, *Inst.* 10.7.16). Consequently, extemporaneous speeches contained fewer arguments than scripted ones. The orators expressed their views in a flexible style with unpolished words at a quick pace. They memorized common words, images, and epigrams and adapted their content to the audience (Alcidamas, *On Sophists* 3, 18–19). The images evoked passion from the audience, and the epigrams persuaded and delighted the audience (Philostratus, *Lives* 573).

For instance, Albucius "spoke in a swift onrush, yet with premeditation." His epigrams "were simple, open, bringing no hidden or unexpected point with them, merely resonant and brilliant. He was effective at rousing emotion . . . He never agonized over how to say things, merely over what to say. He had the gift of developing a topic to the extent he desired; and so he himself used to say, in order to illustrate his lack of hesitation in the choice of words. When my mind has taken hold of something, the words come eagerly flocking round" (Seneca, *Contr.* 7.*praef.*3).

Benefits

Extemporaneous speeches changed the speaker and affected the audience. Most orators were highly anxious and afraid to fail in these situations. Speaking improvisationally channeled their fears, inspired the audience, and silenced their opponents.

First, the delivery of the speech helped the speaker overcome his fears and increase his confidence and boldness. Those who could only deliver written speeches panicked when having to speak extemporaneously. Those who could speak extemporaneously had a free readiness of wit and flexibility and spoke the way people like (Alcidamas, *On Sophists* 16). Extemporaneous speakers were motivated by the fear of failure, the expectation of praise, and the crowd of listeners (Qunitilian, *Inst.* 10.1.17). They treated speeches like a soldier mustering an army. According to Quintilian, "For the sheer necessity of speaking thrusts forward and forces out our laboring thought, and the desire to win approbation kindles and fosters our efforts" (*Inst.* 10.7.17 [Butler]). The speaker received intense pleasure in the process, overcame his anxieties, and developed increased confidence in his topic and abilities. The more one practiced extemporized speeches, the better one became at delivering them (*Inst.* 10.7.17). By speaking extemporaneously, the speaker improved his memory and mental flexibility (Alcidamas, *On Sophists* 34).

For instance, when describing extemporaneous speech, Tacitus's interlocutor Aper said:

> If he produces a speech carefully worked out and rehearsed, there is a certain gravity and lasting quality not only in his manner of speaking but in his satisfaction; if he presents a novel and fresh oration not without some nervousness, his very lack of confidence adorns the outcome and produces greater pleasure. But there is particular pleasure in boldness (*audacio*) and rashness that are extempore, for the products of genius, as of the earth, give greater pleasure when they spring up of their own accord, though others are sown and worked over for a long time. (Tacitus, *Dial.* 6 [Benario])

Secondly, extemporaneous speech benefited defendants and audiences in their "hour of need." The speaker shortened the length of the speech depending on the needs of the audience and countered unexpected arguments made in a courtroom by a prosecutor. "The speech spoken straight from the heart on the spur of the moment has a soul in it and is alive and follows upon events and is like those real bodies" (Alcidamas, *On Sophists* 10, 23, 26, 28 [Muir]). They made good use of critical moments without worrying about particular words.

These speeches gained goodwill and admiration from the audience and overcame their accusers' resentment. Scripted speeches could "fill the minds of their hearers with distrust and resentment," but spontaneous speeches were more authentic and trustworthy (Alcidamas, *On Sophists* 12, 34). The audiences connected with the speaker's anxiety in the moment and admired their willingness to address them without a script. Judges assumed speakers were not trying to "outwit" them because the orator lacked time to plan a crafty argument. In the moment, they thought that the gods inspired such a performance (Quintilian, *Inst.* 11.2.46–47).

Quintilian observed, "When this occurred, the old orators, such as Cicero, used to say that some god had inspired the orator. But the reason is obvious. For profound emotion and vivid imagination sweep on with unbroken force, whereas, if retarded by the slowness of the pen, they are liable to grow cold, and if put off for the moment, may never return" (*Inst.* 10.7.14 [Butler]; see also Cicero, *Arch.* 17–18; Philostratus, *Lives* 503–13).[8]

In summary, extemporary speech was a common form of delivery at trials and festivals. With no more than a night to prepare, trained and untrained speakers defended themselves and persuaded audiences. They fed off the anxiety of the moment and the size of the crowds. They expected surprise questions and interruptions. They overcame their fears by improvising frequently. Using epigrams and images, they spoke individually and in pairs quickly and effectively. Their approach persuaded their audience and engendered a sense of trust and authenticity from otherwise skeptical judges.

Jewish and Early Christian Improvisation

The Greek and Latin words for improvisational speech do not occur in the LXX or early Christian literature. The characteristics of these speeches observed in Greco-Roman settings do occur occasionally. In the Hebrew Bible, individuals pray freely to God unscripted. In early Christian literature, individuals are encouraged to be prepared to speak at trial, and congregational leaders are permitted to lead corporate prayer at their discretion.

Prayer in Jewish Settings

Individual and corporate prayers in the Hebrew Bible suggest that persons could pray to God in a variety of ways, especially improvisationally, whether or not in an emergency. According to Moshe Greenberg, they "arise immediately and naturally from life" whether making petition, interceding, confessing sin, or expressing gratitude.[9] While scripted prayers were permitted from the Psalms, humans, whether Jewish or pagan, could also talk to God personally as if talking to another human being. The petitioner could bless, confess, and request things from God extemporaneously. Although the

---

8. Holcomb, "Crown of All Our Study," 58. Also see Polemo's speech at the dedication of the temple of Zeus and Aristides's speech before Marcus (Philostratus, *Lives* 530–32, 583)

9. Greenberg, *Biblical Prose Prayer*, 36.

prayers contain similar structures, the wording varies from person to person and circumstance to circumstance.[10]

For instance, in the Hebrew Bible and LXX, individuals offered petitionary prayers following a three-fold pattern: address, petition, and motivation. They adapted the content to the circumstances of the prayer. As Moshe Greenberg notes, "In the motivation, the pray-er appeals to a common value, some identity of interest between him and God, some ground on which he can expect God's sympathy and a demonstration of solidarity."[11]

For example, in Isa 37:16–20, facing a threat from Sennacherib, Hezekiah prays a three-part prayer for deliverance: address, petition, and motivation.

> Address: "O LORD of hosts, God of Israel, who are enthroned above the cherubim, you are God, you alone, of all the kingdoms of the earth; you have made heaven and earth. Incline your ear, O LORD, and hear; open your eyes, O LORD, and see; hear all the words of Sennacherib, which he has sent to mock the living God. Truly, O LORD, the kings of Assyria have laid waste all the nations and their lands, and have hurled their gods into the fire, though they were no gods, but the work of human hands—wood and stone—and so they were destroyed."
>
> Petition: "So now, O LORD our God, save us from his hand,"
>
> Motivation: "so that all the kingdoms of the earth may know that you alone are the LORD." (NRSV)

This freely spoken prayer is indicative of many prayers that were improvised by Jewish and gentile persons in Jewish literature. Even pagans in Jonah 1:14 pray in a similar form when seeking deliverance in an emergency.[12] Rather than being an exception to a larger rule of scripted speech, Greenberg suggests that these numerous prayers in the Hebrew Bible and LXX are part of the fabric of ancient and middle Judaism. These individualized prayers extended to synagogue patterns into the fourth century CE.

We cannot say with certainty what the rules were for synagogue prayers in the first century. We do know worshipers used a variety of benedictions, petitions, and intercessions in the literature from Qumran to the rabbinic texts.[13] In reciting synagogue prayers into the fourth century CE, Jewish worshipers were encouraged not to repeat the same formula of the

---

10. Ibid., 20.
11. Ibid., 11.
12. Ibid., 14.
13. Bouley, *From Freedom to Formula*, 33.

prayer each time and were given permission to improvise their prayers especially when someone else had already recited another prayer in the synagogue. They were also encouraged to compose their own benedictions while praying.[14]

Speeches and Worship in Early Christian Settings

We have already mentioned the examples from the New Testament that reference extemporaneous speech at trials. Most sermons were delivered this way, and early Christians used improvisation in worship, prayer, and on trial. Bishops extemporized prayers through the fourth century.[15]

During trials, early Christians relied on the Spirit to provide the words and Jesus to provide discretion to defend themselves. As noted in the introduction, four times in the Synoptics, Jesus warns his disciples that they will face trials. First Peter 3:14–15 echoes the same instructions. They are not to rehearse speeches or worry. Instead they "sanctify Christ in their hearts."

In Luke 12, the Holy Spirit will teach them what to say. They are not to "worry about how you are to defend yourselves or what you are to say, for the Holy Spirit will teach you at that very hour what you ought to say" (Luke 12:12).

In Luke 21 they are to "lay up therefore in your hearts not to prepare a defense" because Jesus himself will give them a "mouth and wisdom" (21:13, 15). At trials, the Spirit supplies the words, and Jesus supplies the gift of prudence. Jesus teaches disciples what to say and when to say it. Just as God spoke through Moses and Aaron before Pharaoh, Jesus speaks through the disciples. Jesus wants the disciples to endure the trial, giving the opponents nothing to contradict.[16]

In worship, most assume that the Psalms functioned as some sort of script. Paul, however, instructs the audience in Eph 5:19 to speak psalms to one another prior to singing. By implication, the congregation would improvise the psalms spoken.

Other Christian texts indicate that bishops and individuals speak freely based on their abilities. In the *Didache*, the bishop permits prophets to pray thanksgiving prayers at the end of the eucharist "as they will" (Did. 10.7).[17] In Justin Martyr's description of the eucharist, the prayers offered are given "at length" with no indication of a script or a timeframe. The presiding min-

---

14. Heinemann, *Prayer in the Talmud*, 46, 51. See b. Ber. 21a; 29b.
15. Bradshaw and Phillips, *Apostolic Tradition*, 70.
16. Shiell, "Will Give You a Mouth and Wisdom," 616.
17. Bouley, *From Freedom to Formula*, 151.

ister would also offer prayers and thanksgivings "according to his ability" (*1 Apol.* 67). According to Bouley, the prayer depended on the additional power or δύναμις of the bishop beyond whatever set form was given to the service.[18] When praying for the emperor, Tertullian says that Christians do not use a prayer prompter because they "pray from the heart" (*Apol.* 30.4).[19]

In the *Apostolic Constitutions,* Hippolytus encourages bishops in the third century to improvise:

> It is not at all necessary for him to repeat these words that we said before, as if recited by rote giving thanks to God, but according to each one's ability he shall pray. If, on the one hand, he has ability to pray sufficiently with a prayer that is honorable, then it is good. But if, on the other hand, he prays and recites a prayer briefly, [let] no one hinder him, only let him pray being sound in orthodoxy. (Apos. Con. 9.3–5 [Bradshaw-Phillips])

Hippolytus instructed the bishop to follow a structure that likely included a prayer of thanksgiving, mention of the creation, doxology, crucifixion, resurrection, ascension, and the words of institution.[20]

Like most preachers in the early churches, Augustine preached extemporaneously. He encouraged speakers who lacked formal training in eloquence to search the scriptures for wisdom and assistance when speaking wisely (*Doct. chr.* 5.7–8). Drawing on Luke 12, he argued that prior to preaching, the minister should pray before speaking and rely on the Holy Spirit to speak through him (*Doct. chr.* 4.15.32).

Summary

Although not widely attested, improvisation was a part of individual Jewish prayer and early Christian speeches and gatherings. There were several characteristics worth noting. In worship, prayers, and benedictions, speakers could deviate from the Psalms. The audience spoke psalms to one another, and leaders improvised sections of the liturgy not out of exigency but personal ability.

Early Christian trial instructions appear to follow the conventions of Greco-Roman courts. The speakers are intentionally unrehearsed and unafraid in emergencies. The anxiety that would normally surface in such improvisational moments is allayed because they have prepared by

---

18. Ibid., 113.
19. Hanson, "Liberty of the Bishop," 173.
20. Ibid., 176; Bouley, *From Freedom to Formula,* 129.

"sanctifying Christ in their hearts." They rely on divine empowerment and are able to speak freely when summoned. The Spirit supplies the words, and Jesus the discretion.

Reading the Speeches in Acts 4:5–31 as Extemporaneous Speech

Given that improvisational speaking was a prominent form of delivery in ancient religious and public settings, and that Christians spoke freely in their gatherings, it seems likely that many of the speeches in Acts can be interpreted improvisationally. Of the twenty-five speeches in Acts, twenty are spoken by apostles and one by a congregation. Of these, the apostles address an audience on short notice at least fourteen times. Even though the words for improvisation are not used in the New Testament, the most likely signals for extemporaneous speech are the phrase "filled with the spirit," signaling divine presence, and "boldness," signaling the confidence of an improvisational speaker. Both are prominent themes in Acts and occur together in Acts 4:5–31. The first part of the scene is a trial (4:5–22), the second a corporate prayer gathering (4:23–31). Both reflect the conventions of extemporaneous speech.

Speech at Trial

After they heal a lame man in Acts 3, Peter and John continue preaching in the temple courts and are arrested for preaching the resurrection of Jesus. "The elders of Israel" summon Peter, John, and presumably the healed man to appear at trial the next morning (Acts 4:5, 14).[21]

From the elders' perspective, there is already opportunity for Peter and John to improvise their speech. What do they do with the lame man when they speak on trial? Is he a co-defendant or a witness to the resurrection? As Alcidamas noted, their spur of the moment speech helps the healed man "in his hour of need" (*On Sophists* 23). Peter and John speak on his and their behalf.

The rulers summon the defendants to a trial to respond to their charges. They ask an ambiguous question that Peter has not prepared for, "By what power or by what name did you do this?" (Acts 4:7). To what does *this* refer? Are they arrested for healing a man, or preaching, or both? The sudden charge, the imprecision of the question, and the lack of preparation

---

21. Mundhenk, "Invisible Man," 204–5.

on the part of the apostles give Peter and John a chance to improvise using the Holy Spirit as a guide.

Peter is "filled with the Holy Spirit," a sign of divine presence on the apostle as well as a fulfillment of Jesus's promises in Luke 12:11–12.[22] In this case, we would expect the Holy Spirit to give Peter the words to say. We would also anticipate a reaction of silence from the accusers.

His opening *captatio benevolentiae* employs a phrase unique to the New Testament, "elders of Israel." An improvised speech would use varying forms of address respectfully. Peter seeks to gain their good will and reframe the question. He asks if they are charged with benefaction toward a crippled man (4:8–12). On behalf of Jesus, the apostles have provided wholeness to the lame man and he has responded by pledging loyalty to Jesus.[23] If so, Peter wants to present a concise version of the same case to the elders that he gave at Pentecost (2:21–25). We would expect that improvisation would follow familiar topics and expand or summarize the theme in varying ways, much like a declamation.

In verses 9–11, he uses alliteration to draw their attention to a synecdoche defining who or what this power is. The rhetorical conventions indicate that Peter spoke quickly, just as Seneca suggested, in a "flurry of words."

> Verse 9: ἐν τίνι οὗτος ("with what or by whom, this man")
>
> Verse 10: ἐν τούτῳ οὗτος ("by this, this man")
>
> Verse 11: οὗτός ἐστιν ὁ λίθος ("this is the stone")

The phrase in verse 9 "with what" or "by whom" is ambiguous. Peter could be referring to the name of Jesus ("with what") or Jesus himself ("by whom") when referencing the healing.[24] In other words, he asks, "If we are being charged with this, what is 'this' you accuse us of?" Verse 10 answers the question and literally says, "whom God raised from the dead, by this this [man] stands before you whole." We can imagine that according to Luke's account the healed man actually stands with Peter and John. If so, we can anticipate a gesture from Peter toward the man, "this man stands before you whole." By implication, he would be in the midst of the council as a co-defendant.[25] In the moment, Peter says that God is behind the apostles' preaching, the man's healing, Jesus's resurrection, and Jesus himself.

---

22. "Filled with Spirit" is a popular theme in Luke and Acts. See Luke 1:15, 41, 67; 4:1; Acts 2:4; 4:31; 6:3, 5; 7:55; 9:17; 13:9.

23. Parsons, *Acts*, 63.

24. Parsons and Culy, *Acts of the Apostles*, 66.

25. Mundhenk, "Invisible Man," 204.

Verse 11 clarifies who and what this is. He defines "this" as a stone (referring to Jesus of Nazareth). Peter invokes the architectural imagery of a large house under construction. The elders of Israel have rejected the cornerstone predicted in Ps 118 that God has now vindicated.

The council responds with the same kind of response we would expect by a judge from an improvisational speech at court (Acts 4:13). They comment on their boldness (παρρησίαν), very similar to the boldness that would be expected of an extemporaneous speech in antiquity (Tacitus, *Dial.* 6).[26]

They remark that the accused have "been with" Jesus but they lack the formal training they would expect of those who could speak so freely and knowledgably. Like the orators with natural abilities in Quintilian's day, they have learned their ability to defend themselves outside the conventional education process. The elders already knew they followed Jesus; now they realize that they have learned from him how to defend themselves.[27] The presence of the healed man forces them to remain silent. They are unable to contradict the defendants, just as Jesus predicted in Luke 21:15.

They call a recess to confer among themselves. When they return to order them not to speak and teach in Jesus's name, John speaks with Peter. John functions like a prompter to Peter's speech. Just as Haterius improvised with a prompter, and as Aaron stood with Moses, so John reminds Peter what to say (Seneca, *Contr.* 4.praef.7). He was the wisdom for Peter's mouth and assisted Peter to have "sudden necessity" in this emergency (Quintilian, *Inst.* 10.7.2).

They invoke an epigram, popularized by Socrates in Greek philosophy and also common among Hellenistic Jews: "We must obey God rather than men" (Plato, *Apol.* 29D–E).[28] The miraculous healing of the lame man, and his subsequent appearance with Peter and John, silences the opponents.[29] Like the epigrams used in improvisational speech in Seneca and Alexander, they conclude the trial on a powerful note.

Prayer with Others

After being released, Peter and John leave the trial to return to "their own," and by implication, to embolden their friends who await the outcome of the

---

26. The term παρρησίαν and its cognates are popular terms in Acts: for the noun, see 2:29; 4:13, 29, 31; 28:31; for the verb, see 9:27, 28; 13:46; 14:3; 18:26; 19:28; 26:26.

27. Bock, *Acts*, 196.

28. Also see 1 Clem 14:1; 2 Clem 4:4; Josephus, *Ant.* 17.6.3; 18.8.2; 2 Macc 7:2; 4 Macc 5:16–21.

29. Alexander, "Acts of the Apostles," 31.

trial (Acts 4:23). The people respond by praying extemporaneously.[30] This prayer is loosely based on Hezekiah's prayer in Isa 37 and echoes Ps 2:1–2 and is the only account in the New Testament of group prayer. The prayer follows the three-fold pattern of both deliberative prayer in the ancient world and Jewish petitionary improvisational prayer from the Hebrew Bible. Peter's speech points the elders to the power, name, and person behind the healing of the lame man. Now the petitioners receive Peter's report and focus their attention on the hand of God at work carrying out God's plan.

Even though Luke is known for crafting speeches to carry out his purposes, we should not dismiss the possibility that Luke could record an improvisational prayer scene. The petitioners ask for the ability to speak; we expect Luke's audience would certainly recognize this scene as an unscripted prayer scene.[31]

The petitioners follow the three-part pattern of prayer illustrated by Hezekiah's prayer in Isa 37: address (Acts 4:24–28), petition (4:29), and motivation (4:30). A leader could have led the gathering while the group prayed "together." They address God respectfully and directly in a *captatio beneveloentiae*, reminding God of the way God communicated through David in the Psalms. Verse 24 can be rendered, "Sovereign Lord, you, the one who made heaven and earth and everything in them." Verse 25 is a *testimonia* from Ps 2:1–2 LXX. This citation has an unusual word order. The verse could be a form of early Christian *pesher*, similar to those from Qumran. A psalm is cited, and the community gives its interpretation.[32] The setting, however, is a community at prayer, not study. As Paul indicates in Eph 5:19, they are to speak psalms to one another. The awkward syntax suggests we should read this verse aloud and imagine how many voices speaking simultaneously would be heard praying. The word order emphasizes God's speech and can be rendered:

> [You] through the mouth of our father David your child-servant *said*, "Why did the Gentiles rage, and the peoples plot vain things? The kings of the earth took their stand and the rulers have gathered together against the Lord and against his Messiah." (4:25–26)[33]

Their address raises two issues, one about the speakers and the other about the nature of the opposition. Their question suggests that as the Holy Spirit

---

30. Gaventa, *Acts*, 95.
31. Hamm, "Acts 4:23–31," 231.
32. Ibid., 229; Johnson, *Acts*, 94.
33. Ibid., 85.

spoke through his child-servant David through Ps 2 and child-servant Jesus, the Spirit also speaks through Peter and John. They also ask why so many people oppose the Lord and his Anointed ones, whether David from Ps 2 or Jesus as the new David, and now the apostles Peter and John. According to verse 28, the hand of God is at work. Instead of indicting the Jewish elders for rejecting Jesus, their address reveals an ironic and providential twist to the story. Herod, Pontius Pilate, the gentiles, and the "peoples" of Israel "gather together" against Jesus, but their conspiracies are part of an overall design. Paradoxically by plotting against Jesus, and rejecting him at trial, they exalt him as savior.

With these questions in mind, the companions transition from address to petition, "and now." They use an ambiguous phrase "their decisions" to signal the kind of threats that have led up to this moment (v. 29). The phrase suggests that the decisions of the elders of Israel fall in a long line of conspiracies mentioned in verses 24–28 that activate God's plan. As such, Peter and John follow the footsteps of David and Jesus who speak boldly in the face of opposition. The petitioners now position themselves as slaves willing to do the same. They want to deliver bold messages on behalf of their master (Acts 4:29). The companions want nothing less than the same reaction from the opponents and desire the same power the apostles had. God's hand has worked through the apostles to heal a lame man, and Peter and John were allowed to stand trial and speak improvisationally/boldly. The companions now ask for God to empower them as servants with the same bold speech that the apostles had and that Jesus promised (Acts 4:29). Just as Jesus is God's anointed servant, the apostles and their companions are too. They recognize that any arrests and/or prosecutions function the way Jesus and the apostles' trials do. Their unexpected speeches accomplish God's plan.

Verse 30 reveals their motive. While they continue to speak boldly, they hope for God to perform signs and wonders in Jesus's name. In Isaiah 37, Hezekiah prays for God to act so that God will be recognized as the only God. The apostles claim that Jesus is now revealed as savior. The companions pray for God to perform ongoing signs and wonders of healing in Jesus's name so that they can continue to speak boldly. God is responsible for signs and wonders; they are responsible for speaking.[34] In response to their prayer, the earth shakes. They are filled in the same way with the Holy Spirit, and they are able to speak boldly and extemporaneously to each other. By placing this extemporaneous prayer scene here, Luke is previewing what

---

34. Witherington, *Acts*, 204.

the gathered believers were doing and experiencing in Jerusalem in Acts 4:32–35.[35]

In Isa 37, Hezekiah prays for deliverance so that the people will know that God is God alone. The believers in Acts 4 hear Peter's report and realize that just as the rulers conspired against Jesus, now they are trying to assemble against the early believers. The incidents with the rulers become a source not of intimidation but inspiration. They view the healing, arrest, and release as a sign of God's handiwork.

They anticipate there are more conspiracies to come and signs to be performed. They want their response to be the same as Peter and John's. They want to have the same boldness (παρρησία) that Peter and John expressed in order for God to perform the same kind of signs and wonders that happened with Peter and John.

To summarize, the apostles and the companions speak improvisationally at trial and at prayer. They are "filled with the Spirit" and speak with a bold confidence that signals their abilities as improvisational speakers and God's divine empowerment. With only one night to prepare, Peter and John respond to the interrogation of the elders of Israel by calling upon the audience to trust in the power and person behind their message. The apostles have not learned their ability to speak through conventional means. Unlike other untrained orators with natural talents, their abilities come supernaturally and reflect the Spirit's presence in their lives. Peter and John work together to communicate the message forthrightly.

The gathered companions desire the same ability. They see the conspiracies against Jesus and the apostles as part of the plan for God to succeed. To press the architectural metaphor from Peter's speech, they see God as the designer of a household that has survived an attempted sabotage. Any attempts to conspire against the architect only strengthen the power of the house. Those who are with Peter and John are also with Jesus and desire to be bold servants bearing a confident message so that God can continue to heal and save people.

Conclusion

While useful as a means to help contemporary communities make moral judgments, early Christians more likely employed improvisation in the same way that ancient speakers did. They spoke in emergencies when summoned to testify for Jesus or prayed from the heart individually and corporately. As

---

35. Hamm, "Acts 4:23–31," 233.

they did, they connected to their listeners by showing them respect, silenced their accusers at trial, and endured to the end.

Peter and John's experience and its subsequent transmission to their gathered companions encourage Luke's audience and equip them with the confidence needed to prepare for emergency situations. They can follow their example and trust that the Spirit will be present with them at trial. One does not need to attend a rhetorical school or be with Jesus alone. By listening to the apostles' message and praying accordingly, the early Christian communities prepared for the Spirit to supply the words needed and for Jesus to supply the necessary wisdom. Each time they spoke unrehearsed, their confidence would grow, God's hand would continue to perform signs and wonders, opponents were silenced, and the believers endured the trial. Like the apostles, their bold, confident speech demonstrated that they were "filled with the Spirit."

Works Cited

Alexander, Loveday. "The Acts of the Apostles as an Apologetic Text." In *Apologetics in the Roman Empire: Pagans, Jews, and Christians*, edited by Mark Edwards, Martin Goodman, and Simon Price, 15–44. Oxford: Oxford University Press, 1999.

Barton, Fred. "The Signification of 'Extempore Speech'; in English and American Rhetorics." *Quarterly Journal of Speech* 27 (1941) 237–50.

Benario, Herbert W., trans. *Agricola, Germany, and Dialogue on Orators*. Rev. ed. Norman, OK: University of Oklahoma Press, 1991.

Bock, Darrell L. *Acts*. BECNT. Grand Rapids: Baker Academic, 2007.

Bonner, S. F. *Roman Declamation in the Late Republic and Early Empire*. Berkeley: University of California Press, 1949.

Bouley, Allan. *From Freedom to Formula: The Evolution of the Eucharistic Prayer from Oral Improvisation to Written Texts*. Studies in Christian Antiquity 21. Washington, DC: Catholic University of America Press, 1981.

Bradshaw, Paul, and L. Edward Phillips. *The Apostolic Tradition: A Commentary*. Edited by Harold W. Attridge. Hermeneia. Minneapolis: Augsburg Fortress, 2002.

Brown, Hazel Louise. *Extemporary Speech in Antiquity*. Menasha, WI: Collegiate Press, 1914.

Gaventa, Beverly Roberts. *The Acts of the Apostles*. ANTC. Nashville: Abingdon, 2003.

Greenberg, Moshe. *Biblical Prose Prayer as a Window to the Popular Religion of Ancient Israel*. Taubman Lectures in Jewish Studies 6. Berkeley: University of California Press, 1983.

Hamm, Dennis. "Acts 4:23–31—A Neglected Biblical Paradigm of Christian Worship (Especially in Troubled Times)." *Worship* 77 (2004) 225–37.

Hanson, R. P. C. "The Liberty of the Bishop to Improvise Prayer in the Eucharist." *VC* 15 (1961) 173–76.

Heinemann, Joseph. *Prayer in the Talmud: Forms and Patterns*. Edited by E. L. Ehrlich. Studia Judaica Forschungen zur Wissenschaft des Judentums 9. New York: Walter de Gruyter, 1977.

Holcomb, Chris. "'The Crown of All Our Study': Improvisation in Quintilian's Instiutio Oratorio." *RSQ* 31 (2001) 53–72.

Johnson, Luke Timothy. *Acts*. SP 5. Collegeville, MN: Liturgical, 1992.

Muir, J. V., ed. *Alcidamas: The Works & Fragments*. London: Bristol Classical Press (Duckworth), 2001.

Mundhenk, Norm. "The Invisible Man (Acts 4:9–10)." *Bible Translator* 57 (2006) 203–6.

Parsons, Mikeal. *Acts*. PCNT. Grand Rapids: Baker Academic, 2008.

Parsons, Mikeal, and Martin Culy. *The Acts of the Apostles: A Handbook on the Greek Text*. Waco: Baylor University Press, 2003.

Quintilian. *The Institutio Oratoria of Quintilian*. Translated by H. E. Butler. LCL. Cambridge: Harvard University Press, 1992.

Shiell, William D. "'I Will Give You a Mouth and Wisdom': Prudent Speech in Luke 21:15." *RevExp* 112 (2015) 609–17.

Van Hoozer, Kevin. *The Drama of Doctrine: A Canonical Linguistic Approach to Christian Theology*. Louisville: Westminster John Knox, 2005.

Wells, Samuel. *Improvisation: The Drama of Christian Ethics*. Grand Rapids: Brazos, 2006.

Witherington, Ben. *The Acts of the Apostles: A Socio-Rhetorical Commentary*. Grand Rapids: Eerdmans, 1993.

The Ethiopian Eunuch Unhindered
Embodied Rhetoric in Acts 8

Mikeal C. Parsons

Introduction

THIS ESSAY EXAMINES THE story of Acts 8:26–40, particularly the stated physical condition of the Ethiopian eunuch, in light of the τόπος of "bodily goods" associated with the ancient rhetorical tradition.[1] In his discussion of the preliminary exercise on "encomium and invective," Theon attests the arrangement of attributes of a person by the three traditional goods of Greek philosophy—i.e., goods of the mind, goods of the body, and goods external to the person.[2] These τόποι were not invented by proponents of Hellenistic education but rather were borrowed from the culture generally, classical Greek literature specifically, and classical Greek encomion especially, where they regularly are featured, sometimes by name. The τόποι reflected long-established, culture-specific ways of apprehending the human personality. We may think of them as an ancient Mediterranean anatomy of honorable personhood, born of an honor and shame culture.

---

1. Naymond H. Keathley has been a valued colleague and friend for over three decades. It is no exaggeration to claim that without his lending vocal and written support for me—a largely untested and new PhD at the time—I would not have been elected to the faculty at Baylor University. His support over the ensuing years has been unfailing, and I am delighted to contribute this essay to a volume honoring his life and work among us. An earlier version of this paper was presented to the Adult Forum at Old Cambridge Baptist Church in Cambridge, Massachusetts, in March 2017. Gratitude is expressed to the Rev. Dr. Cody Sanders for that invitation and to the OCBC congregation for their hospitality during my research leave at Harvard Divinity School during the spring semester, 2017.

2. The remaining three theorists (Ps.-Hermogenes, Aphthonius, and Nicolaus) commend a chronological ordering of τόποι more reflective of actual composition.

They frequently reflect, too, the values of the aristocratic classes responsible for ancient Mediterranean culture, literature, and education. Certain qualities generally exclusive to these classes—coming from the right places, the right ancestry, the right families, receiving a quality education, having inherited wealth or power, attaining positions of power or esteem, living to an old age—were institutionalized in Hellenistic education as marks of honor—and their absence, by implication, as marks of shame. Though the τόποι lists vary greatly from one theorist to the next, there is nonetheless a good deal of agreement among them.[3]

Ps.-Hermogenes's exercise, because it provides helpful, concrete illustrations of the τόποι, offers the modern reader an excellent introduction:

> Encomiastic topics are (the subject's) national origin, such as Greek, city, such as Athenian, family, such as Alcmaeonid. You will mention also any marvelous occurrences at birth, for example, from dreams or signs or things like that. After this, nurture; for example, in the case of Achilles, that he was nurtured on lions' marrow and by Cheiron; then upbringing, how he was trained or how educated. Of course, the nature of mind and body will be examined and each of these divided into several qualities. You will say about his body that it was beautiful, large, swift, strong; about his mind that it was just, temperate, wise, brave. After this you will draw on his pursuits; for example, what sort of life he led: Was he a philosopher or an orator or a general? Most important are deeds; for deeds are included among pursuits; for example, having chosen a soldier's life, what did he accomplish in it? As for externals, they include relatives, friends, possessions, servants, luck, and the like. Moreover, from the topic of time comes how long he lived, much or little. Each provides the starting point of encomia; for you will praise one who had long life because of that fact and one who did not in that "he had no share of the diseases of old age." Further, from the manner of his death (for example,) how he died fighting for his country; and if there was anything unusual about it, as in the case of Callimachus, because his corpse remained standing. And you will praise him because of who killed him, for example, that Achilles died at the hand of the god Apollo. You will examine also events after death: if they held games in his honor, as for Patroclus (*Iliad* 23); if there was an oracle about his bones, as with Orestes; if he had famous children, as did Neoptolemus. The best source of argument in encomia is derived

---

3. The previous two paragraphs are taken from Martin and Parsons, *Ancient Rhetoric and the New Testament*.

from comparisons, which you will utilize as the occasion may suggest. (*Prog.* 15–17)[4]

The Τόπος of Bodily Goods in Theory

My concern in this essay is with the τόπος of bodily goods. Reference to bodily goods was a stock feature in the rhetorical repertoire of antiquity. Theon specifies the goods of the body to include "health, strength, and acuteness of sense" (*Prog.* 110). Cicero, likewise, lists the attributes of a person to be used in a confirmation. With regard to "bodily goods," he asserts "we take into consideration such advantages and disadvantages as are given to mind and body by nature, as, for example: whether one is strong or weak, tall or short, handsome or ugly, swift or slow; whether bright or dull" (*Inv.* 1.35 [Hubbell, LCL]; see also Cicero, *Part. or.* 74–75; Quintilian, *Inst.* 3.7.10–18; *Rhet. Her.* 3.6.10–11).[5]

The authors of the progymnasmata all made use of the τόπος of bodily goods in their discussion of narrative, encomium and invective, and syncrisis (Theon, *Prog.* 109–15; Ps.-Hermogenes, *Prog.* 14–20; Aphthonius, *Prog.* 35–44; Nicolaus, *Prog.* 47–63). The passage from Ps.-Hermogenes above gives an example of how reference to bodily goods could serve an encomiastic description ("You will say about his body that it was beautiful, large, swift, strong").

In terms of the appeal to bodily goods in an invective, we may cite an example from Libanius, writing in the fourth century CE, who demonstrates the stability of the τόπος in terms of how bodily goods might be used to characterize an individual negatively. In his invective against Philip of Macedon (382–336 BCE) he writes: "he was also the sort of man physically whom anyone seeing would consider an evil omen—limping, with one eye knocked out, and maimed in many of his limbs" ("Invective 3: Philip," *Prog.* 12 [Gibson]).

---

4. Unless noted otherwise, all translations from the progymnasmata are taken from Kennedy, *Progymnasmata*.

5. In *Inv.* 1.2.127–8, Cicero refers to this list and states that these same attributes are to be used for encomion, only his summation differs in some respects and is arranged by the three goods.

The Τόπος of Bodily Goods in Practice

Beyond and in conjunction with what is said about bodily goods in the rhetorical tradition theory, we find ample evidence of the use of this τόπος in practice among ancient compositions.[6] Of course, slavish correspondence to these rhetorical conventions should not be expected. As D. A. Russell and N. G. Wilson observe: "Even in this very banal and conventionalized branch of literature, the relation between teaching and practice is less close than is sometimes thought."[7]

We find the τόπος of bodily goods in both Greco-Roman non-fiction and fiction. In Tacitus's *Life of Julius Agricola*, we read:[8]

Nature	Body	"Should posterity desire to learn his mere appearance, he was well-proportioned rather than imposing. There was no violence in his face; its dominant expression was benign."
	Mind	"You could easily credit him with goodness, and be glad to think him great."
Age		"As for the man himself, though snatched away in the mid-career of his prime, he lived to a ripe old age measured by renown. The true blessings of life which lie in character he had fulfilled."
Fortune		"What more could fortune have added to one who had been consul and had worn the decorations of triumph. He did not boast of excessive riches but was possessed of an ample fortune. With daughter and wife surviving him, he may even pass for happy to have escaped what was to come with his position unimpaired, his reputation brilliant, his friends and kin safe." (44.2–3 [Hutton/Warmington, LCL]; emphasis added)

In his biography of the youthful Constantine, Eusebius compares the young emperor to his contemporaries via the τόποι of body and mind and under multiple sub-τόποι belonging to each:

6. Numerous other examples could be marshalled; see Martin and Parsons, *Ancient Rhetoric and the New Testament*.

7. Russell and Wilson, *Menander Rhetor*, xviii–xix. Russell and Wilson go on to state that the rhetorical guides to composition "are of course meant as hints, not as models to be copied out, though doubtless the indifferent student will have treated them as just that. And if we look at any respectable epideictic piece—say the *Panathenaicus* or a monody or hymns of Aristides—it is clear that the writer's sophistication and sensitivity to the particular circumstances (*kairos*) is of far greater importance in the successful execution of the commission than the application of rules and formulas. Every ancient rhetor knew this, even if some of his pupils never grasped it" (xix).

8. On *Agricola*, see Warmington, "Introduction," 1:3–24.

Body	Beauty	For no one was comparable to him for grace and beauty of person,
	Size	or height of stature
	Strength	and he so far surpassed his compeers in personal strength as to be a terror to them.
Mind		He was, however, even more conspicuous for the excellence of his mental qualities than for his superior physical endowments;
	Judgment	being gifted in the first place with a sound judgment,
	Training	and having also reaped the advantages of a liberal education.
	Intelligence	He was also distinguished in no ordinary degree by natural intelligence
	Wisdom	and divinely imparted wisdom. (1.19 [*NPNF* 2/1:487–88]; emphasis added)

The use of these conventional τόποι as building blocks is also reflected in fictional narrative. In Xenophon's *An Ephesian Tale*, the writer introduces his main character, Habrocomes, in laudatory terms via a highly conventional encomiastic template:[9]

Origin	City	Among the most influential citizens of Ephesus
	Father	was a man called Lycomedes. He
	Mother	and his wife, Themisto, who also belonged to the city, had a son
Name		Habrocomes;
Body		his good looks were phenomenal,
	Comparison	and neither in Ionia nor anywhere else had there ever been anything
		like them. This Habrocomes grew more handsome every day;
Mind		and his mental qualities developed along with his physical ones.

---

9. For an introduction to *An Ephesian Tale*, see Reardon, *Collected Ancient Greek Novels*, 125–28; and on ancient Greek novels generally, 1–16.

Training	For he acquired culture of all kinds and practiced a variety of arts; he trained in hunting, riding, and fighting under arms. (*An Ephesian Tale* 1.1 [Anderson, LCL]; emphasis added)

The *Aesop Romance*, a novel devoted to the great fabulist, Aesop, begins with appeal to conventional τόποι:

Origin		Ammorius, a town in Phrygia (though some say he is Thracian, others Samian) (1)
Nature	Body	"... his Person deformed, to the highest degree: Flat-nos'd, hunch-
		back'd, blobber-lipp'd; a long misshapen Head; his Body crooked all over" (1)
	Mind	"Excellency of Mind" (1)
Age		"As to the age he lived in ... it was when Croesus governed Lydia." Discussion ensues. (1)
Fortune		"It was Aesop's Fortune to be sent to Ephesus, in company with other slaves to be sold." (2)
Action and Speech		Stories about Aesop, along with his fables and sayings (3–18)
Death		his arrest, trial (falsely accused), and execution (thrown headlong from a rock down a precipice). (19 [Stern]; emphasis added)

In Jewish historiography, one may cite a number of texts from Josephus's writings to demonstrate his knowledge of the conventional τόποι of encomium.[10] In *The Jewish War*, Josephus's account of Sabinus, the first man to surrender after Titus's speech, may be arranged in accordance with the τόποι it takes up:

Name	[there] was one named Sabinus,
Origin	a native of Syria,
Deeds	who showed himself both in might of hand
Virtue	and in spirit the bravest of men;

---

10. See Neyrey, "Josephus' *Vita*," 177–206; see also Martin, "Progymnastic Topic Lists," 18–41.

Body	*Yet anyone seeing him before that day and judging from his outward appearance would not have taken him even for a common soldier. His skin was black, his flesh shrunk and emaciated*
Mind	but within that slender frame, far too strait for its native prowess, there dwelt an heroic soul. (*War* 6.54–57 [Thackeray, LCL]; emphasis added)

These last two examples from the *Aesop Romance* and Josephus are of particular interest in light of the story in Acts 8 because the bodily goods of both Aesop and Sabinus are described in ways that one might expect of an invective, yet both accounts intend to praise the persons described *despite* their physical appearance. Aesop is the famed slave-turned-storyteller and Sabinus is the first to rise to Titus's summons to scale the wall (though ultimately he suffers an untimely end; see *War* 6.62–67). The theorists had advised just this course of action in an encomium if the content of the τόποι were not favorable to the person. Theon, for example, urges that if the person "has none of the previously mentioned goods, one should say that he was not brought low by his misfortunes ... For virtue shines brightest in misfortunes" (*Prog.* 111).

The Ethiopian Eunuch and Embodied Rhetoric

In the story in Acts 8:26–40, Luke appeals to conventional τόποι in his description of the unnamed person Philip encounters on a deserted road from Jerusalem to Gaza.[11] In just two verses, we learn the following information about Philip's interlocutor:

Origin	Now there was a man, an Ethiopian
Body	*a eunuch,*
Position	a court official of the Candace, queen of the Ethiopians, in charge of her entire treasury.
Deeds	He had come to Jerusalem to worship and was returning home; seated in his chariot, he was reading the prophet Isaiah. (8:27–28; emphasis added)

---

11. For Luke, the story is not really "about" a eunuch (regardless of how the story may have functioned in its pre-Lukan form). Rather, in Acts the story serves to highlight the role of God's Spirit in providing divine guidance in the spread of the gospel from Jerusalem to the "end of the earth." Still, it is instructive to examine the ways in which Luke presents the key characters in light of ancient compositional practices.

Of these τόποι, Luke clearly presents goods of the body as most important. Only once is the person referred to as a "court official" and once as an "Ethiopian,"[12] but five times he is called "the eunuch" in this narrative (8:27, 34, 36, 38, 39). How does this τόπος of bodily goods function in this narrative? That is, how were eunuchs perceived in antiquity?[13]

Eunuchs in antiquity "belonged to the most despised and derided group of men."[14] This claim would certainly find support in the writings of Polemo, author of one of the extant Physiognomic handbooks.[15] Polemo notes that a certain kind of eye is reflective of a lack of sexual control. He goes on to claim, "This nature is in the eyes of men who are not like the other men, like the eunuch who is not a [castrated] eunuch but who was born without testicles.... eunuchs are an evil people, and in them is greed and an assembly of various (evil) qualities" (1.162F).[16] This was true despite

---

12. "Ethiopian" is also mentioned in reference to the Candace, queen of the Ethiopians. Space does not allow us to pursue this τόπος, but the eunuch's national origins are, indeed, of crucial importance to the narrative and especially to the subsequent history of interpretation. As Craig Keener has rightly observed: "'Black' complexion was the most common defining feature of Ethiopians in ancient Mediterranean literature" (Acts, 2:1560). See, e.g., Homer, Od. 19.244-48; Herodotus 2.29-32; 3.17-24; 4.183, 197; Seneca, Naturales Questiones 4A.218; Jer 13:23; Petronius, Sat. 102; Lucian, Indictment 6; Lucian, Patriot 4; Heliodorus, Aeth. 4.8; Hippolytus of Rome, Haer. 4.6; cf. Juvenal, Sat. 6.600. The groundbreaking work in this area was Snowden's Blacks in Antiquity. For other studies on the significance of Ethiopia in antiquity and its impact on understanding that this first gentile convert in Acts 8 was a person of color, see, inter alia, Martin, "Chamberlain's Journey," 105-35, and Byron, Symbolic Blackness and Ethnic Difference. This fact has been largely ignored in both academic Eurocentric scholarship and white, evangelical Christianity.

13. See especially Kuefler, Manly Eunuch.

14. Spencer, "Ethiopian Eunuch and His Bible," 156.

15. The relevant passage is found in Foerster's edition of Polemo, 1.160-64 (Foerster, Scriptores Physiognomonici Graeci et Latini). The "physiognomic consciousness" (outer physical appearances reflect inner moral character) was pervasive in antiquity and fueled these kind of invectives against those perceived to be physically "defective" by dominant cultural standards; see Evans, Physiognomics in the Ancient World. I have previously explored Acts 8 in light of this physiognomic consciousness in Body and Character, 123-41.

16. Polemo is evidently thinking of one eunuch in particular. He says, "I do not know if I have seen any of this description [congenital eunuch] except for one man. He was from a land called Celtas" (1.160F; for the translation of the Arabic see Swain, Seeing the Face). This person is Polemo's archenemy, the sophist philosopher Favorinus, a congenital eunuch philosopher who lived at the end of the first century-mid second century CE. Philostratus says that Favorinus "used to speak in oracular riddles about the three paradoxes of his life: he was a Gaul who spoke Greek, a eunuch who was prosecuted for adultery, a man who had quarreled with the emperor and was still alive" (Lives, 489). On Polemo and Favorinus, see Gleason, Making Men, 131-58.

the various ways in which one might become or be made to be a eunuch.[17] One of Herodotus's characters, Hermotimus, a eunuch, took revenge on the man who had castrated him and sold him as a slave into the court of Xerxes, calling the activity "the wickedest trade on earth" (8.104–6). Elsewhere, Lucian of Samosata tells of a supposed eunuch vying for a chair of philosophy in Athens. His assumed status as a eunuch (he claimed to be a eunuch to avoid charges of adultery) led to an invective by one of his opponents who claimed that it was "an ill-omened, ill-met sight if on first leaving home in the morning, one should set eyes on any such person [a eunuch]." Eunuchs, he claimed, "ought to be excluded . . . not simply from all that but even from temples and holy-water bowls and all the places of public assembly" (*Eunuch.*, 6–11).

This attitude was also prevalent among Greek-speaking Jews of the first century as well. Josephus wrote: "Shun eunuchs and flee all dealings with those who have deprived themselves of their virility and of those fruits of generation, which God has given to men for the increase of our race; expel them even as infanticides who withal have destroyed the means of procreation" (*Ant.* 4.290–91).

Why were eunuchs thus demonized and ostracized in antiquity? In part, the answer lies in their ambiguous sexual identity, according to the strict binary understanding of sexuality in antiquity. To quote Lucian again, a eunuch "was an ambiguous sort of creature like a crow, which cannot be reckoned either with doves or with ravens"; he was "neither man nor woman but something composite, hybrid and monstrous, alien to human nature" (*Eunuch.*, 6–11). Josephus comments along similar lines: "For plainly it is by reason of the effeminacy of their soul that they changed the sex of their body also. And so with all that would be deemed a monstrosity by the beholders" (*Ant.* 4.291). Likewise, Philo of Alexandria claims that eunuchs were "men who belie their sex and are affected with effemination, who debase the currency of nature and violate it by assuming the passions

---

17. How were eunuchs "made"? The Matthean Jesus sums up the conventional understanding: "For there are eunuchs who have been so from birth, and there are eunuchs who have been made eunuchs by others, and there are eunuchs who have made themselves eunuchs for the sake of the kingdom of heaven" (Matt 19:12). Aristotle recognizes that some were born eunuch (*Gen. an.* 2.7.25). Some were castrated by others, often slave traders who intended to sell the eunuchs to royal courts (Herodotus 8.104–6). A common, and perhaps mistaken view, was that eunuchs could be trusted to occupy the traditional "female space" of the palace without fear of sexual misconduct (see Chariton, *Chaer.* 5.9; but cf. Martial, *Ep.* 3.81). Finally, some engaged in self-castration, often for religious purposes (so the *galli*, devotees of the goddess Cybele; see Roller, "Ideology of the Eunuch Priest," 118–35; perhaps also Origen? Cf. Eusebius, *Ecc. Hist.* 6.8; see Cheney, *Brief History of Castration*, 188–94).

and the outward form of licentious women" (*Spec. Laws* 1.324–25). In a culture where honor was gender-based, to be sexually ambiguous was to blur clear-cut gender roles and expectations and thus to bring shame upon oneself and one's community.[18]

Further, in Jewish thought, eunuchs, by belonging neither to the cultural expectations of male nor female, had violated purity codes.[19] Like amphibians who lived in two worlds but belonged to neither, eunuchs were considered unclean (see Lev 11). In addition, the physical body was thought to mirror the corporate social body, so a physical body that was damaged or mutilated had the potential of defiling the social body.[20]

This was especially true in Judaism where the physically defective, like eunuchs, were presumably forbidden full participation with the temple cultus: "No one whose testicles are crushed or whose penis is cut off shall be admitted to the assembly of the Lord" (Deut 23:1).[21] The Ethiopian eunuch, as Scott Spencer has noted, "embodied impurity as much as he exhibited shame. His ambiguous sexual identity ('neither male nor female') denied him a distinctive place on the purity map of the social body, even as his defective genital anatomy depicted his polluted map of the physical body."[22]

---

18. On the gender binary in antiquity, see Gleason, *Making Men*, 161; Burke, *Queering the Ethiopian Eunuch*, 67–94.

19. See Spencer, "Ethiopian Eunuch and His Bible," 158–59. Also Spencer, *Portrait of Philip*, 168–72.

20. See Neyrey, "Symbolic Universe of Luke-Acts," 278–85.

21. Beverly Gaventa observes: "Although the remark has prompted some interpreters to conclude that he must be a proselyte to Judaism, Gentiles were permitted entrance to the outer court of the Jerusalem temple (Josephus, *J.W.* 2.409–16). . . . Thus, worshiping in Jerusalem . . . does not necessarily imply his [the eunuch's] conversion to Judaism" (*Acts of the Apostles*, 142).

22. Spencer, "Ethiopian Eunuch and His Bible," 159. In terms of the τόπος of pursuits or occupation, the eunuch is described as one who was a court official in charge of the treasury for the Candace, Queen of the Ethiopians (8:27b). While, in a vacuum, this descriptor might be viewed as positive or at least neutral given the fact that the eunuch's access to power and wealth was dependent on his ambiguous status as a eunuch, there is little here to overturn the negative characterization of the eunuch. In fact, Brittany Wilson has argued convincingly that the eunuch's access to wealth (he is in charge of the queen's entire treasury; he commands a large chariot and travels in a foreign country; he possesses a copy of the Isaiah scroll) "also suggests his unmanliness since elite authors frequently connected effeminacy with both extravagance and 'distant' nations'" (*Unmanly Men*, 133). Luke had earlier made the connection between luxury and effeminacy in the Third Gospel: "But what did you come out to see? A person clothed in soft (*malakos*) robes? Behold! Those in expensive clothing and living in luxury are in palaces" (7:25; cf. Wilson, *Unmanly Men*, 134–35). As Dale B. Martin has observed: "The word *malakos* refers to the entire ancient complex of the devaluation of the feminine" (*Sex and the Single Savior*, 47).

The Ethiopian eunuch was thus a despised, liminal figure who transgressed the sexual, ethnic, and social binary boundaries of the ancient Roman world, which perpetuated a kind of "Roman Privilege" under the "Put Rome first" banner (Roman, not barbarian; male, not female; free, not slave; wealthy, not poor). Sean Burke writes that the Ethiopian eunuch "queers" ancient identity categories of race, sexuality, and social status by disclosing that such identities "are constructed and contingent rather than fixed or natural."[23] Yet Luke presents a positive outcome to the story; the eunuch requests baptism, and Philip complies. The negative perception of his physical body is overturned, and he is granted admission to the community,[24] though the praise of this act is not as full-throated as one might have hoped.

Hindering the Eunuch: A Brief Afterlife

The history of interpretation of Acts 8 reveals various attempts to mute the radical nature of the story. The dominant interpretation ignores the Ethiopian's social status, ethnicity, and, downplays sexual identity (or denies it altogether). *Social status*: Some view the eunuch as a rich official (Basil, *On Baptism* 6) and not as someone whose access to wealth depended on his status as a eunuch, if not an exploited slave. *Ethnicity*: Some view the eunuch as a Jew (Pontius, *Life of St. Cyprian* 3) or a proselyte (Jerome, *Letters* 53.5), thus dulling the edge of a story that portrays a reviled eunuch as the first gentile convert to the Way. Others, who acknowledge that this Ethiopian was a gentile, understand the reference to "eunuch" as a reference to one who has remained celibate (see Athenagoras, *A Plea for the Christians* 33.3; Clement of Alexandria, *Strom.* 3.1) or to refer to a term for a royal official (in LXX Gen 39:1, Potiphar is called a *eunochos* of the Pharaoh). In this regard, John Calvin's comments are revealing. Noting that Luke refers to the eunuch as a man (an ἀνήρ, the Greek term for sexualized male identity, and not ἄνθρωπος, the term for generic humanity), Calvin is forced to conclude that the term "eunuch" refers to a royal official, since surely he could not be called a "man" and also at the same time be a physical "eunuch"![25]

---

23. Burke, *Queering the Ethiopian Eunuch*, 298.

24. As happened also in the examples of Aesop and Sabinus cited above. Despite the negative description of bodily goods (and national origin and socioeconomic status), which were part of the tradition Luke inherited and thus unavoidable, Luke contends that those descriptors do not, in fact, hinder the eunuch's acceptance into God's family (see Parsons, *Body and Character*, 139–41).

25. Calvin says: "He calleth him a man, who he saith shortly after was an eunuch; but because kings and queens in the East were wont to appoint eunuchs over their weighty affairs, thereby it came to pass that lords of great power were called generally

Copyists of Acts were also uncomfortable with the fact that the eunuch receives baptism simply by querying Philip, "Look, here is water. What prevents (hinders) me from being baptized?" (Acts 8:36). So what will later be identified as Acts 8:37 was added to the text in the Western tradition and adopted by Byzantine manuscripts (and thus found its way into the tradition of English translations of which KJV was premier). But Acts 8:37 is missing from the best manuscripts of Acts: "And Philip said, 'If you believe with all your heart, you may.' And he replied, 'I believe that Jesus Christ is the Son of God'" (Acts 8:37). Thus, in the manuscript tradition, the eunuch was not baptized without having first made a christologically appropriate confession. Very little about this text fits conventional expectations!

Domestication of the story, however, is not limited to its later interpreters. The story certainly does not fit Luke's overall scheme. Craig Keener notes: "Luke runs against the grain of his own focus (from Jerusalem to Rome) to point out that the first Gentile convert was an honorable official from Africa."[26] The conversion of the Ethiopian eunuch is presented as an isolated incident. The Ethiopian eunuch is baptized, yes, but not into any particular community. According to early tradition, the eunuch returns home to become Ethiopia's first missionary in spreading the gospel (see Irenaeus, *Haer.* 3.12.8, 4.23.2; Cyril of Jerusalem, *Lecture* 17.25; Ephrem the Syrian, *Seven Hymns on the Faith* 3.2; Eusebius, *Ecc. Hist.* 2.1.13). As Beverly Gaventa astutely notes: "Tradition may be more Lukan than Luke at this point."[27]

For Luke, however, the overall narration of the expansion of early Christianity into the non-Jewish, gentile world pivots on the conversion of Cornelius by Peter (Acts 10–11) and not the conversion of the eunuch by Philip. This tension has led to a number of solutions, some more ingenious than others. C. K. Barrett, among others, resorts to source criticism to solve the conundrum: "Probably we must be content to take the story as a piece of tradition about Philip which Luke placed here not because it fitted into his scheme of Christian expansion but because this was the point at which he was dealing with Philip."[28] Others seek a resolution by reverting to the ancient view that the eunuch was a Jew, or at least a proselyte, on the grounds

---

eunuchs, whereas, notwithstanding, they were men" (Calvin, *Commentary on Acts,* 8:27). On the ways in which Acts 8 challenges traditional notions of masculinity in antiquity, see Wilson, *Unmanly Men,* 135–36.

26. Keener, *Acts,* 1541. Note even here that Keener refers to "an honorable official from Africa," omitting what was ostensibly the most offensive aspect of the first convert's profile: he was a despised eunuch.

27. Gaventa, "Review of *Body and Character,*" 321.

28. Barrett, *Critical and Exegetical Commentary,* 1:426. This solution can be traced as far back as Dibelius, *Studies in the Acts.*

that Luke would not have created this kind of tension within his own narrative.[29] Still others contrast the Ethiopian eunuch's conversion (a private event to show that God's Spirit is leading apostles) with Cornelius's (a public event approved by Jerusalem church).[30]

Perhaps, though, the simplest solution is the most obvious one. Luke is not comfortable with the story he has inherited, yet feels obliged to include it in the narrative. But he relegates the story of the conversion of the Ethiopian eunuch to a place of minor or at best diminished significance for the larger story he narrates.[31] After all, it is more "acceptable" to recognize publicly as the first gentile convert (15:6–14), one Cornelius, a retired Roman centurion, a devout man who fears God (10:2a), who generously gave alms to the Jewish people and prayed constantly (10:2b) and who is well spoken of by the whole Jewish nation (10:22). Cornelius is simply a more respectable, even desirable, first convert than a eunuch, whose bodily goods are defective by dominant cultural standards, whose sexual identity is dangerously ambiguous, whose conversion takes place in isolation, and who does not even make a proper confession of faith![32]

A Concluding Hermeneutical Remark

As I write these words, I am mindful of the debates in churches and the larger American culture about the place in church and society of members of the LGBTQ community. In my opinion, there is no simple one-to-one

---

29. E.g., Haenchen, *Acts of the Apostles*, 314.

30. E.g., Spencer, *Portrait of Philip*, 186–87. Elsewhere, I have also suggested the two stories serve different functions (see Parsons, *Body and Character*, 123). The story of the Ethiopian eunuch is the last of four stories in Luke and Acts that underscores the inclusivity of the Christian community as a fulfilment of the Abrahamic covenant that God's chosen people will be a blessing to the nations (Gen 12). Cornelius's conversion is part of Luke's story of expansion. While I do still think Acts 8 functions in this way, I, along with a host of others, have underestimated the tension that remains between the two stories.

31. This proposal is similar to Wilson's solution (who does not explicitly appeal to a pre-Lukan source): "The eunuch may appear to be a Gentile within Acts 8 itself and a Jew within the larger Acts narrative, but either way, he overlaps with both these ethnic categories and that is precisely the point" (*Unmanly Men*, 117). The space occupied by the eunuch in Wilson's construal may be more liminal than even Wilson allows and, in my opinion, renders her argument that Luke presents the eunuch as a "model convert" unconvincing (137–40).

32. Like the eunuch, Paul is also characterized negatively prior to his conversion in Acts 9. He was "breathing threats and murder against the disciples of the Lord" (9:1). But unlike the eunuch, Paul is integrated into the Christian community at Damascus, despite misgivings on the part of Ananias.

correspondence between the Ethiopian eunuch and a modern person's sexual orientation; we have no idea what the eunuch's sexual orientation may have been. It is unlikely he, or any other ancient, would have understood that distinction. Nor can one easily translate the eunuch's experience in antiquity with the struggles of the transgendered person seeking to establish autonomous sexual identity. In many cases, after all, eunuchs were forcibly castrated and had no choice in the matter whatsoever.

Nonetheless, a great deal of modern anxiety over sexual identity is rooted, in part, in the deep-seated male-female sexual binary of our larger culture that is also reflected in the ancient concern over the sexual ambiguity of eunuch.[33] "They" are neither male nor female; "they" are neither fish nor fowl; and hence, "they" are dangerous because they challenge the traditionally rigid distinction between male and female. The story of the Ethiopian eunuch has yet to play the role in discussions of sexual identity and church membership that it deserves. The eunuch did not say, "Look, here is water! What hinders me from using the bathroom here along with others?" No, his question was much more radical: "Look, here is water! What hinders me from being baptized?" Philip had the courage by his actions to say, "Nothing hinders you," and he baptized the eunuch. Luke, whatever his misgivings may have been, had the courage to preserve the story for posterity, and perhaps for such a time as ours when the implications of such an action can be puzzled out sociologically and theologically. Will we have the courage to follow those implications through to their logical conclusion? "Look, here is water . . ."

Works Cited

Barrett, C. K. *A Critical and Exegetical Commentary on the Acts of the Apostles*. 2 vols. ICC. Edinburgh: T&T Clark, 1994.

Burke, Sean D. *Queering the Ethiopian Eunuch: Strategies of Ambiguity in Acts*. Minneapolis: Fortress, 2013.

Byron, Gay L. *Symbolic Blackness and Ethnic Difference in Early Christian Literature*. London: Routledge, 2002.

Calvin, John. *Commentary on Acts*. Edited by Henry Beveridge. Translated by Christopher Fetherstone. Christian Classics Ethereal Library. https://www.ccel.org/ccel/calvin/calcom36.html.

Cheney, Victor T. *A Brief History of Castration*. Bloomington, IN: Authorhouse, 2006.

Dibelius, Martin. *Studies in the Acts of the Apostles*. Edited by H. Greeven. Translated by M. Ling. London: SCM, 1956.

Evans, Elizabeth C. *Physiognomics in the Ancient World*. Philadelphia: American Philosophical Society, 1969.

---

33. The most recent and hateful expression of this view is found in the so-called "Nashville Statement" (https://cbmw.org/nashville-statement/).

Foerster, Richard, ed. *Scriptores Physiognomonici Graeci et Latini*. 2 vols. Leipzig: Teubner, 1893.
Gaventa, Beverly R. *The Acts of the Apostles*. Nashville: Abingdon, 2003.
———. "Review of *Body and Character in Luke and Acts*, by Mikeal C. Parsons." *PRSt* 35 (2008) 319–22.
Gleason, Maud W. *Making Men: Sophists and Self-Presentation in Ancient Rome*. Princeton: Princeton University Press, 1995.
Haenchen, Ernst. *The Acts of the Apostles*. Translated by Bernard Noble and Gerald Shinn. Oxford: Blackwell, 1971.
Keener, Craig. *Acts: An Exegetical Commentary*. 4 vols. Grand Rapids: Baker, 2013.
Kennedy, George A. *Progymnasmata: Greek Textbooks of Prose Composition and Rhetoric*. Atlanta: Society of Biblical Literature, 2003.
Kuefler, Mathew. *The Manly Eunuch: Masculinity, Gender Ambiguity, and Christian Ideology in Late Antiquity*. Chicago: University of Chicago Press, 2001.
Martin, Clarice. "A Chamberlain's Journey and the Challenge of Interpretation for Liberation." *Semeia* 47 (1989) 105–35.
Martin, Dale B. *Sex and the Single Savior: Gender and Sexuality in Biblical Interpretation*. Louisville: Westminster John Knox, 2006.
Martin, Michael W. "Progymnastic Topic Lists: A Compositional Template for Luke and Other *Bioi*." *NTS* 54 (2008) 18–41.
Martin, Michael W., and Mikeal C. Parsons. *Ancient Rhetoric and the New Testament: A Primer on the Preliminary Exercises*. Waco: Baylor University Press, forthcoming.
Neyrey, Jerome H. "Josephus' *Vita* and the Encomium: A Native Model of Personality." *JSJ* 25 (1994) 177–206.
———. "The Symbolic Universe of Luke-Acts: 'They Turn the World Upside Down.'" In *The Social World of Luke-Acts: Models for Interpretation*, edited by Jerome H. Neyrey, 278–85. Peabody, MA: Hendrickson, 1991.
Parsons, Mikeal C. *Body and Character in Luke and Acts: The Subversion of Physiognomy in Early Christianity*. Waco: Baylor University Press, 2011.
Reardon, B. P., ed. *Collected Ancient Greek Novels*. Berkeley: University of California Press, 2008.
Roller, Lynn E. "The Ideology of the Eunuch Priest." In *Gender and the Body in the Ancient Mediterranean*, edited by M. Wyke, 118–35. Oxford: Blackwell, 1998.
Russell, D. A., and N. G. Wilson, eds. *Menander Rhetor*. Oxford: Clarendon, 1981.
Snowden, Frank M., Jr. *Blacks in Antiquity: Ethiopians in the Greco-Roman Experience*. Cambridge: Harvard University Press, 1970.
Spencer, F. Scott. "The Ethiopian Eunuch and His Bible: A Social Science Analysis." *BTB* 22 (1992) 155–65.
———. *The Portrait of Philip in Acts: A Study of Roles and Relations*. JSNTSup 67. Sheffield: JSOT, 1992.
Stern, Simon, ed. *The Life and Fables of Aesop, A Selection from the Version of Sir Roger L'Estrange*. New York: Taplinger, 1970.
Swain, Simon. *Seeing the Face, Seeing the Soul: Polemon's Physiognomy from Classical Antiquity to Medieval Islam*. New York: Oxford University Press, 2007.
Warmington, E. H. "Introduction." In *Tacitus*, 1:3–24. LCL 35. Cambridge: Harvard University Press, 2006.
Wilson, Brittany E. *Unmanly Men: Refigurations of Masculinity in Luke-Acts*. Oxford: Oxford University Press, 2015.

Recalling the Mount of Olives

Sleeping and Praying in Acts 12:1–17

Andrew E. Arterbury

Peter's miraculous release from prison in Acts 12:1–17 has evoked numerous scholarly discussions. Some, like I. Howard Marshall, question whether Acts 12:1–17 adds anything of substance to the book of Acts.[1] Others, like Robert Wall, argue that Acts 12:1–17 provides a pivotal transition in the narrative of Acts by offering a proper ending to Peter's ministry and the age of the apostles as well as a proper beginning for their successors, namely James, Paul, and those engaged in the gentile mission. In essence, Wall argues that Acts 12 bridges the "apostolic" and "postapostolic" periods within the book.[2]

Many exegetes point out that Acts 12:1–17 is one of three miraculous releases from prison in Acts including Acts 5:17–21 and 16:16–40. These three passages share many elements in common among themselves as well as with a variety of Greco-Roman and Jewish stories about miraculous prison escapes in antiquity.[3] Others focus on typological parallels between the events of the Exodus, a later Jewish tradition about Moses's miraculous release from Pharaoh's prison, and Peter's divine rescue and release from Agrippa's confinement in Acts 12.[4] Finally, many exegetes point to a christological typology in Acts 12:1–17 that consists of a series of parallels between Jesus's passion narrative in Luke 22–24 and Peter's imprisonment in Acts 12:1–17. This last discussion provides the starting point for this chapter.

---

1. Marshall, *Acts*, 218.
2. Wall, "Successors," 628–43.
3. See, e.g., Barrett, *Acts*, 1:571, 580–82.
4. See, e.g., Radl, "Befreiung," 81–96; and Tannehill, *Narrative Unity*, 2:153–55.

Comparing Acts 12:1–17 to Luke 22:47—24:53

To illustrate this connection between Jesus's passion and Acts 12, scholars point to both contextual and linguistic commonalities between these two units, though they typically begin their comparison with Jesus's arrest in Luke 22:47 and conclude with his ascension.[5] Some of the most commonly cited intersections between Luke 22–24 and Acts 12 are as follows: First, both Jesus and Peter are arrested (συλλαμβάνω—Luke 22:54; Acts 12:3) and handed over (παραδίδωμι—Luke 23:25; Acts 12:4) to soldiers or guards by a Roman-appointed ruler at the same time of the year. For instance, the Feast of Unleavened Bread (Luke 22:1, 7) and a Passover meal (Luke 22:1, 7, 8, 11, 13, 15) provide the setting for Jesus's last meal with his disciples. That same night, Jesus is arrested (Luke 22:47–53) and subsequently tried before an assembly of Jewish elders, Pilate, and Herod Antipas (Luke 22:66—23:17). Similarly, Herod Agrippa I arrests Peter during the Festival of Unleavened Bread and delays dealing with him until after Passover is complete in Acts 12:3–4.[6] The story then resumes in Acts 12:6 on the night before Agrippa plans to bring Peter out before the people with the intention of beheading him, just as Pilate did prior to Jesus's crucifixion (Luke 23:13).[7]

Second, some envision Peter's imprisonment and miraculous release as a mirror image of Jesus's death and resurrection. For instance, Dennis Horton contends that Peter's sleep depicts an analogous state to that of Jesus's death.[8] Similarly, when Richard Pervo compares Peter's experiences in Acts 12:1–23 with Jesus's experiences in Luke 22–24, he argues that "the narrative is a symbolic portrayal of Peter's 'passion,' 'resurrection,' and vindication."[9] Third, angels play a prominent role in both texts. Two angels proclaim Jesus's resurrection in Luke 24:3–7, and an angel of the Lord releases Peter from prison in Acts 12.[10]

Fourth, others note that the apostles fail to believe the report of the women about Jesus's resurrection in Luke 24:8–12, and the church that meets in Mary's home does not initially believe the young woman who announces that Peter is at the door in Acts 12:13–17. Fifth, upon

---

5. See, e.g., Wall, "Successors," 634–42; Tannehill, *Narrative Unity*, 2:152; and Witherington, *Acts*, 382.

6. Fitzmyer, *Acts*, 487. Fitzmyer notes that though the Feast of Unleavened Bread and the Passover are technically two separate feasts, by the first century the title "Passover" frequently referred to the entire eight-day celebration.

7. Parsons, *Acts*, 173.

8. Horton, *Death and Resurrection*, 41–45.

9. Pervo, *Acts*, 302.

10. See, e.g., ibid., 309.

seeing the resurrected Jesus, his disciples initially think he is a ghost in Luke 24:36-43; similarly, the church initially concludes that the young woman who answered the door must have seen Peter's guardian angel in Acts 12:15. Finally, after explaining his role as Messiah and instructing the disciples, Jesus ascends into heaven in Luke 24:44-53. Likewise, Peter describes to his fellow believers how the Lord rescued him from prison, instructs the church to tell the story to James and the believers, and then departs Jerusalem in Acts 12:17.[11]

Based upon these types of contextual and linguistic intersections between Luke 22:47—24:53 and Acts 12:1-17, many argue that the author (presumably Luke) crafted his narration of Acts 12:1-17 in order to create a typological effect. Almost certainly Luke's first readers and listeners would have noticed these commonalities; and apparently, Luke believed that recalling portions of the Lukan passion narrative would benefit those who contemplated the conclusion of Peter's ministry in Acts 12. The question remains, however, "How exactly did Luke hope his readers would mentally and theologically process the contextual and linguistic intersections between Luke 22-24 and Acts 12:1-17?"

As briefly illustrated above, many claim that Luke's typological focus in Acts 12:1-17 revolves around a comparison between Jesus and Peter. This line of argumentation generally contends that Luke crafted a meaningful comparison between Jesus's arrest, death, resurrection, and ascension in Luke 22:47—24:53 and Peter's arrest, imprisonment, release, and departure from Jerusalem in Acts 12:1-17 in order to demonstrate that Peter faithfully carries on Jesus's ministry and legacy.[12]

Yet, despite the broad comparison between Jesus in Luke and his disciples in Acts[13] and despite the undeniable similarities between Luke 22-24 and Acts 12, the typological comparisons between Jesus and Peter lack specificity and cannot be pressed very far in this particular instance. In fact, Jesus and Peter play very different roles in these two texts.[14] Even though Luke portrays Jesus as being noticeably more passive in his passion narrative than John does, Luke nevertheless depicts Jesus as being far more active in Luke 22-24 than Peter is in Acts 12:1-17. For example, Jesus or-

---

11. See, e.g., Johnson, *Acts*, 219.

12. See, e.g., ibid.

13. For a larger discussion about how Jesus's disciples in Acts faithfully succeed the Lukan Jesus in both words and deeds, see Talbert, *Literary Patterns*, 16-18, 96-99.

14. Alter, *Art of Biblical Narrative*, 74-75. When comparing type scenes, Alter suggests that one should look for both similarities and differences between seemingly parallel passages. In this case, the dramatic differences point us away from a straightforward comparison between Jesus and Peter.

ganizes and leads the Last Supper (Luke 22:1–23), settles a dispute among his disciples (Luke 22:24–27), encourages and warns his disciples (Luke 22:28–38), prays while facing his impending death (Luke 22:39–46), directs much of the action during his arrest (Luke 22:47–53), strategically elects when to speak and when to remain silent during his cross examinations (Luke 22:63—23:12), speaks to the weeping women on his way to the cross (Luke 23:26–31), prays that the Father would forgive his persecutors (Luke 23:34), assures a criminal on the cross next to him (Luke 22:39–43), prays to release his spirit to the Father (22:44–49), and instructs and encourages his disciples on three occasions after his resurrection (Luke 24:13–53). In short, Jesus remains alert, fully engaged, and prayerful throughout Luke's passion narrative.

Peter, on the other hand, is almost entirely passive in Acts 12:1–17.[15] He is asleep on the evening before his death. The angel of the Lord must strike (πατάσσω) his side and lift him up in order to rouse him from his sleep. Even then, Peter does not believe the angel's presence is real. He thinks he is dreaming. Consequently, the angel of the Lord must instruct Peter about even the simplest of actions. The angel commands Peter to get up, get dressed, put on your sandals, and follow. Peter does not escape; he is released. The Lord's angel does all of the work. Peter does not even realize what is happening until after the prison break is complete and he is out of harm's way.

Furthermore, beyond this general observation that Jesus is active and alert whereas Peter is surprisingly passive, there are also stark differences between the specific activities of prayer and sleep. When comparing who prays and who sleeps in Luke 22–24 and Acts 12, we notice that Jesus and Peter's actions diverge greatly. Jesus prays that the Father might remove the cup of suffering in Luke 22:39–46; he prays that the Father would forgive his persecutors in Luke 23:34; and he prays to release his spirit to the Father in Luke 22:46. In addition, while on the Mount of Olives, Jesus instructs his disciples to pray that they "may not come into the time of trial" in Luke 22:40. Then, after Jesus finds Peter and the disciples sleeping, he rouses them and instructs them a second time to "get up and pray that you may not come into the time of trial" (Luke 22:45–46). In essence, in Luke's passion narrative, Jesus teaches his disciples that a proper response to trials and temptations must include prayer, a theme which the Lukan Jesus firmly establishes in his final public comments known as the little apocalypse (Luke 21:5–38). In fact, in Luke 21:34–36, Jesus associates the activity of prayer with staying alert or awake. Vigilant prayer will provide Jesus's disciples

---

15. Krodel, *Acts*, 214; and Parsons, *Acts*, 175.

with the necessary strength they need to survive the trials and temptations that precede the arrival of the Son of Man.

Conversely, in Acts 12:1–17, even though he seems to be aware of the mortal danger he is facing (12:11), Peter does not pray nor talk about prayer like Jesus did in the Lukan passion narrative. Instead, unlike Jesus, Peter sleeps on the night before his presumed death (Acts 12:6, 12). As a result, the angel of the Lord strikes Peter in the side and lifts him up (Acts 12:7). Notably, the word, "strike" (πατάσσω) frequently connotes divine judgment as we see later in the same chapter when the angel of the Lord strikes (πατάσσω) and kills Herod Agrippa I (Acts 12:23; cf. Acts 7:24; Isa 2:10, 19, 21 LXX; 2 Macc 15:30).[16] Even as the angel leads him out of the prison, Peter cannot discern that the Lord's intervention is real (Acts 12:9). Instead, his sleep has so dulled his senses that he believes he is dreaming until after he has completely exited the prison.

The traditional comparison between Jesus and Peter that begins with Jesus's arrest in Luke 22:47 becomes even more disjointed when we consider the role of the angels and the young women in the two narratives. For instance, the two angels in Luke 24:1–12 announce to the women at the tomb that Jesus has already risen. These angels testify about a past event. Luke does not indicate that they aid Jesus in any way. In Acts 12:1–17, however, divine rescue is accomplished exclusively by the angel of the Lord. Furthermore, the angel does not stay around to announce God's deliverance of Peter to the church. Rather, Peter is the one who testifies about the Lord's rescue to the church in Mary's house. In short, the angels do not perform the same type of actions in Luke 24:1–12 and Acts 12:1–17.

In addition, in Luke 24:1–12, a group of women are informed by the angels that Jesus is risen, but the disciples fail to believe their report. In Acts 12:13–15, there is no group of women. Rather, there is a servant girl (παιδίσκη), who informs the church that Peter is at the door even though her announcement is met with disbelief. So, there is a similar dynamic of disbelief in both texts, but there are significant differences between those proclaiming the shocking news—multiple older women versus one young girl. Of course, there is a servant girl (παιδίσκη) in Luke's passion narrative who recognizes Peter's appearance. Yet when she questions him in front of his foes, he denies that he even knows Jesus (Luke 22:56–57). Conversely, in Acts 12, when the servant girl recognizes Peter's voice, she reports his presence to the members of the church. After they invite him in, Peter verifies, rather than denies, the work of the Lord.

---

16. Keener, *Acts*, 2:1885. Keener refers to πατάσσω as a "harsh term" and notes that "these are the only two verses in the NT where an angel 'strikes' . . ."

In sum, while there are significant commonalities between the Lukan Jesus and his followers throughout Acts and while significant commonalities exist between the Lukan passion narrative and Peter's release from prison in Acts 12:1–17, it is far from clear that Luke is guiding his readers to engage in a typological comparison between Jesus and Peter in Acts 12:1–17. A comparison between Jesus and Peter reveals as many dissimilarities as similarities. As a result, perhaps Luke's first readers were more inclined to read Acts 12:1–17, recall Jesus's passion narrative, and work with a set of even more obvious comparisons between the two texts—Peter's sleep in Luke and in Acts; the prayers of Jesus in Luke and the prayers of the church in Acts; and angelic assistance in Luke 22:43 and Acts 12:6–10.

Comparing Acts 12:1–17 to Luke 22:39–46

Most scholars who pay attention to the parallels between Luke 22–24 and Acts 12 pay little if any attention to the time that Jesus and his disciples spent on the Mount of Olives in Luke 22:39–46. As noted earlier, scholars primarily compare Luke's passion narrative and Acts 12 beginning with Jesus's arrest in Luke 22:47. Perhaps this lacuna is due to the scholarly tendency to conclude that 22:43–44 were not original to Luke's Gospel.[17] Recently, though, Claire Clivaz and Lincoln Blumell have compiled sound arguments for the authenticity of Luke 22:43–44. Clivaz contends that Alexandrian gnostics interpreted Luke 22:43–44 to mean that Jesus was wrestling or fighting against the Demiurge, and therefore proto-orthodox Alexandrian Christians in the second century CE expunged these verses to guard against heresy. As a result, the Egyptian textual tradition of Luke's Gospel moved forward without Luke 22:43–44.[18] Similarly, Blumell points out that recent assessments of MS 0171 date the parchment fragment to "the late second or early third century—one of only a handful of New Testament fragments assigned to this early period." As a result, "our earliest extant piece of manuscript evidence for Luke 22 attests vv. 43–44!"[19] In addition, he argues that it is far more likely that Luke 22:43–44 were "excised from some early manuscripts of Luke prior to the end of the third century for apologetic reasons," rather than added at a later time.[20]

---

17. See, e.g., Westcott and Hort, *New Testament*, Appendix 64–67; and Ehrman and Plunkett, "Angel," 401–16.
18. Clivaz, *L'ange*, 603–7.
19. Blumell, "Luke 22:43–44," 5–7.
20. Ibid., 1.

In short, the recent work of both Clivaz and Blumell provide noteworthy arguments for the authenticity of Luke 22:43-44.

Yet, even beyond the question of originality, no one debates that Luke 22:43-44 appear in a handful of significant, early manuscripts of Luke's Gospel.[21] As a result, many of the earliest readers of Acts associated these verses with Luke's Gospel regardless of whether the original author crafted them or not. For instance, Justin Martyr references the tradition found in Luke 22:43-44 in his *Dialogue with Trypho* (103.8) in the middle of the second century, perhaps not long after Acts began to circulate. In addition, Irenaeus, Hippolytus, Eusebius, Didymus, and Jerome all read these verses in conjunction with Luke 22:39-46.[22] Consequently, a fresh examination of Acts 12:1-17 in light of Luke 22:39-46, including Luke 22:43-44, is warranted.

In fact, if we allow Luke 22:39-46 to enter the conversation more fully, we shall see some striking intersections with Acts 12:1-17. Rather than crisscrossing comparisons between Jesus in Luke and Peter in Acts, I contend that in Acts 12:1-17 the author is primarily highlighting a more straightforward comparison between the events of Luke 22:39-46 and Acts 12:1-17, particularly in regard to the topics of sleep, prayer, and angelic intervention. By focusing upon these more straightforward parallels from Luke 22:39-46 (sleep, prayer, and angels), we will maintain more lucidity when reading Acts 12:1-17 and the theological payoff will perhaps become more self-evident and more fruitful.

Comparing Peter's Sleep with Peter's Sleep

The numerous contextual and linguistic intersections between Luke 22 and Acts 12 suggest that Luke is inviting his readers to compare the portrait of Peter at the end of Jesus's ministry with the portrait of Peter at the end of his own ministry. First, as discussed above, all of the events found in Luke 22:7-65 take place on the same night as the Passover meal. Similarly, Herod Agrippa I arrests Peter during the course of the eight-day Festival of Unleavened Bread (Acts 12:3), and the angel of the Lord releases Peter during the night after Passover has concluded (Acts 12:6). Thus, both the "Gethsemane" event (Luke 22:39-46) and Peter's miraculous release from prison (Acts 12:1-17) take place at night during the same time of the year. Second, during the Passover meal, when Jesus predicts the trials that will soon come

---

21. E.g., see discussions in Fitzmyer, *Gospel According to Luke*, 1443-44; and Bock, *Luke*, 2:1763-64.

22. Fitzmyer, *Gospel According to Luke*, 1443.

upon Peter and the other disciples in Luke 22:31 (cf. Luke 21:5–38), Peter vows that he is ready to go with Jesus to prison (φυλακή) and to death (Luke 22:33). Perhaps a decade later, in Acts 12:1–4 when Herod Agrippa I begins to persecute the apostles, we learn that Agrippa I throws Peter into prison (φυλακή) with the intent to kill him.

Third, after arriving at the Mount of Olives in Luke 22:40, Jesus begins by instructing his disciples to pray that they might not enter into trials (or temptations), which Jesus had just predicted in 22:31 (cf. 21:5–38) and for which he prepares his disciples in 22:32–38. Notably, only Luke records Jesus instructing the disciples to pray as soon as they arrive on the Mount of Olives in 22:39. Jesus then withdraws and is praying as he considers his own impending suffering and death (22:41–44). Yet, the disciples fall asleep (κοιμάω). They are unable to stay awake and pray as Jesus instructed. Consequently, Jesus wakes them by commanding them to get up (ἀνίστημι) and pray (22:45–46).

Similarly, in Acts 12:6 Peter falls into a deep sleep (κοιμάω) on the night before his own death.[23] Ironically, prior to the arrival of the angel of the Lord who instructs Peter to get up (ἀνίστημι), the prison guards and the church meeting in Mary's home appear to be vigilant and alert at the same time that Peter is sleeping. Unlike Jesus on the night of his impending death (Luke 22:39–46), in contradiction to Jesus's instructions about praying in the midst of trials in Luke 21:34–38, 22:40, and 22:46, and unlike Paul and Silas when they are imprisoned in Acts 16:25, Peter is sleeping.[24]

---

23. Pervo, *Acts*, 303.

24. Sleep is metaphorically associated with irresponsibility and negligence in Luke and Acts. The primary exception to this motif is found in the Stilling of the Storm in Luke 8:22–25 when Jesus sleeps in the boat. Even then, in Mark, the disciples who accompany Jesus voice their own belief that Jesus himself is indeed irresponsible and negligent as he sleeps amid the storm (Mk 4:38). It remains unclear whether the disciples in Luke 8:24 hold that same opinion.

Regardless, throughout Luke and Acts, the author(s) distinguishes between the divine power of Jesus and the vulnerability of his disciples. While reading Luke 8:22–25, one quickly realizes that Jesus can sleep in a sea-tossed boat precisely because he possesses the sovereign power of God to control the wind and the waves (Parsons, *Luke*, 137–39). Neither seen nor unseen forces overpower him. Instead, Luke depicts Jesus as both attuned to the Lord's will and more powerful than any adversary (cf. Luke 4:1–13). Jesus, however, exhorts his disciples to avoid sleep and remain vigilant precisely because they are not always aligned with God's salvation history and because they do not possess the divine sovereignty that enables them to resist the principalities and powers on their own (e.g., Luke 21:34–36; 22:31–34, 39–46).

In essence, the context in Luke 8:22–25 reveals that Jesus's sleep carries no negative connotations. Instead, Jesus's sleep enables Jesus's disciples and Luke's readers to grasp Jesus's divine identity and sovereign power more fully. Conversely, the context of Peter's sleep in Acts 12:7–9 reveals that Peter is unprepared for the Lord's intervention. Unlike

Furthermore, despite previously being rescued from prison by an angel of the Lord at midnight in Acts 5:17–20, here Peter is overwhelmingly inactive and inattentive in a prison at midnight. He sleeps at a time when everyone else in the story is exceedingly active and alert. As a result, Peter's failure to stay awake and pray on the night before his beheading in Acts 12 recalls images of the disciples (and Peter) failing to stay awake, pray, and bear witness on the night before Jesus's death in Luke 22:39–46.

At the end of Jesus's biography, Luke leaves us with a conflicted portrait of Peter. Peter courageously vows obedience and loyalty regardless of the circumstances (22:33) and he alone follows Jesus to the high priest's house (22:54); yet Peter also fails to stay awake, pray, or confess that he knows Jesus (22:39–46, 54–62). Similarly, at the end of the Petrine section in Acts, Luke again leaves us with a mixed image of Peter. Peter has been a faithful servant and bold witness to Jesus from the beginning of Acts. In fact, it is precisely his faithfulness and bold leadership that have landed him in prison, yet even now Luke's readers can see that Peter is not beyond a potentially tragic misstep.

Of course, Luke has chronicled Peter's ongoing maturation as a follower of Jesus in the wake of Jesus's ascension, the arrival of the Holy Spirit, and the growth of the church in Acts 1–12. As a result, the mixed depiction of Peter in Acts 12:1–17 is vastly more positive than the mixed depiction of Peter in Luke 22. Whereas in Luke 22, Peter's weaknesses temporarily outweigh his strengths; in Acts, Peter's strengths clearly outweigh his weakness. He does not pray on the night before his death as Jesus did, but after the angel strikes (πατάσσω) him and wakes him and after Peter comes to himself (12:11; cf. Luke 15:17), Peter quickly reunites with the church, testifies to the work of the Lord in the presence of a servant girl, and instructs the church about how to proceed in his absence. In fact, whereas Peter's successes are dwarfed by his failures in Jesus's passion narrative, in Acts 12:1–17 Peter's momentary misstep is dwarfed by his faithfulness. By showing that Peter is still capable of imperfections, Luke provides his readers with a cautionary warning while simultaneously accentuating Peter's growth and maturation since the last time we saw Peter make this same mistake.

Comparing Jesus's Prayer with the Church's Prayer

Luke depicts the believers in Acts 12 in an exceedingly positive light. Peter may have fallen asleep at the wrong time, but the church that meets in

---

Jesus in the boat in Luke 8:22–25, Peter in Acts 12:1–17 cannot understand nor carry out the Lord's will without divine assistance.

Mary's house has been praying earnestly (ἐκτενῶς) for Peter since his arrest (Acts 12:5), just as Jesus prayed earnestly (ἐκτενῶς) on the Mount of Olives in Luke 22:44. In particular, they are awake and praying in the middle of the night on the evening before Peter's scheduled death (Acts 12:7). Shockingly, in Acts 12, Peter appears to be the only believer in Jerusalem who is asleep. Unlike Peter's fellow disciples in Luke 22:39–46, the believers in Acts 12 are doing the very thing that Jesus instructed his disciples to do when he faced his own impending death—pray.

In part, the consequences of Peter's misstep are minor and temporary because the church is praying. The collective faithfulness of the church appears to strengthen and aid the individual faithfulness of Peter, even if the church that meets in Mary's house likewise needs to grow in their belief that God will actually answer their prayers. In essence, the church in Acts 12 are the ones who are carrying on the ministry of Jesus. They pray for Peter just as Jesus did in Luke 22:32 and perhaps in Luke 22:44 as well. This contrast between the disciples' weakness in Luke 22 and the believers' faithfulness in Acts 12 illustrates significant growth and transformation within the church.

Comparing Angelic Assistance in Luke 22 and Acts 12

First, it is not possible to separate the work and aims of angels from the work and aims of God. Clearly within Luke's writings, angels function as representatives of the divine. For example, when Peter reflects on his assistance from the angel who freed him from prison in Acts 12:11, 17, he attributes the rescue to "the Lord" in both instances. Additionally, Luke identifies the angel in Luke 23:43 as "an angel from heaven," which implies that the angel speaks for and represents God in heaven. Similarly, the angel in Acts 12:7–11 is identified as "an angel of the Lord," which implies that the angel speaks for and represents either God and/or Jesus (e.g., Acts 4:33; 7:59; 8:16; 9:5).

Second, divine intervention by means of an angel provides another readily noticeable similarity between the Mount of Olives passage in Luke 22:39–46 and Peter's miraculous rescue from prison in Acts 12:1–17. In Luke 22:43–44, an angel (ἄγγελος) from heaven assists Jesus on the night before his death by strengthening him while he prays (22:43). Relying upon additional strength from heaven, Jesus then prays even more earnestly (22:44). In essence, an angel from heaven appears on the night before Jesus's execution and supplies him with divine strength to pray and fight even more strenuously against "the power of darkness" (22:53).[25]

---

25. Arterbury, "Battle," 37–51.

Likewise, we see an angel (ἄγγελος) of the Lord appear and strengthen Peter on the night before his scheduled execution in Acts 12:7–10. The angel of the Lord performs all of the actions that Peter is unable to accomplish on his own including rousing, lifting, dressing, and guiding Peter. In addition, the angel apparently causes sleep to fall upon the guards while opening the prison's interior doors as well as the outer iron gate.[26] Eventually, Peter realizes that the Lord has rescued him through angelic assistance (Acts 12:11, 17). Shortly thereafter, in Acts 12, Peter does not deny his allegiance to the Lord when he encounters a servant girl as he did in Luke's passion narrative. Rather, the angelic intervention has strengthened Peter, who in turn now acknowledges his identity and persists until he gains entrance into the church's gathering (Acts 12:16)—actions that Peter would not have performed had he remained asleep.

Furthermore, by waking, raising, dressing, and guiding Peter out of prison, the angel also strengthens the church that meets in Mary's house. Like Jesus, the church was already praying earnestly (ἐκτενῶς) even before the angel appeared (Acts 12:5). As a result, they exhibit faithfulness in their prayers, but their faith that God will answer those prayers wanes. Ironically, they fail to believe that Peter is at the door at the same moment that they are praying for him (Acts 12:12–15). By releasing Peter, the angel has likewise aided the church. Once Peter enters the house, the believers are amazed, encouraged by the report, and commissioned to strengthen the Christians in Jerusalem in the wake of Peter's absence by relaying Peter's testimony.

In essence, the angels' presence in both Luke 22:39–46 and Acts 12:1–17 makes it clear to Luke's readers that the Lord was wide awake and present with both Jesus and Peter (as well as the church) on the last night (presumably) of their lives. In both texts, the divine (God and/or Jesus) works to protect and rescue Jesus's followers, and, in particular, Peter (see Luke 22:31–34). In both texts, the Lord commands Peter to get up off the ground and to wake up to the presence and work of the divine work in his midst. Furthermore, in both texts, Peter is enabled by God and/or Jesus to strengthen the "brothers" (ἀδελφός) or believers after coming to himself and regaining his footing (Luke 22:31–34; Acts 12:17).

Conclusion

Based on the numerous similarities between Luke's passion narrative and Peter's miraculous release from prison in Acts 12:1–17, it appears that Luke hoped his readers would recall the end of Luke's Gospel while reading about

---

26. Keener, *Acts*, 2:1885.

the end of Peter's ministry in Acts. Traditionally, scholars have sought to compare Peter's arrest, imprisonment, release, and departure with Jesus's arrest, crucifixion, resurrection, and ascension despite the fact that Peter is extremely passive in Acts 12 whereas Jesus is strikingly engaged and active in Luke 22–24. Including Luke 22:43–44 in the discussion, however, allows another possibility to move to the forefront. The easiest and clearest comparisons between Luke's passion narrative and Acts 12 begin with the Mount of Olives imagery in Luke 22:39–46 and highlight Peter's sleep, angelic intervention, and the midnight prayers of Jesus and the church

These more straightforward comparisons also carry with them important theological payoffs. First, Luke demonstrates for his readers that, though not perfectly transformed, Peter and his fellow disciples have matured considerably since that night on the Mount of Olives. Even though Peter yields to a familiar misstep by falling asleep rather than praying in his time of trial, Luke demonstrates for his readers that Peter's minor misstep is not a fatal flaw as we see with Herod Agrippa I in Acts 12:23. Rather, the angel of the Lord's harsh, though brief, correction is all it takes to realign Peter with God's salvation history.

Similarly, Luke shows the maturation of the other disciples as well. The church at the end of the apostolic age avoids sleep and prays unlike the disciples on the Mount of Olives; yet, they too are taught an important lesson about praying with anticipation. As a result, both Peter and the church are mutually strengthened by one another and by the intervention of the angel of the Lord. Collectively, Peter and the church now walk a much more faithful path. The church prays when Peter cannot, and Peter now testifies rather than denies the Lord's work, which in turn strengthens the faith of the church who prays.

Finally, Luke reminds his readers that God, through the work of angels, is present and desires to aid his servants during the midst of trials and tribulations regardless of whether they live or die. God and God's purposes have not changed. The same God that was at work in and through Jesus continues to be at work to the very end of Peter's ministry. In the end, Luke invites his readers to recall the Mount of Olives while reading Acts 12:1–17. Even after the arrival of the Holy Spirit, Peter and the church must guard against sleep and they must remember to pray in times of trial while knowing that God works in conjunction with those prayers.

Works Cited

Alter, Robert. *The Art of Biblical Narrative.* Revised and updated. New York: Basic, 2011.

Arterbury, Andrew E. "The Battle on the Mount of Olives: Reading Luke 22:39-46 in Its Literary Context." In *Texts and Contexts: Gospels and Pauline Studies and Sermons in Honor of David E. Garland,* edited by Todd D. Still, 37-51. Waco: Baylor University Press, 2017.

Barrett, C. K. *The Acts of the Apostles.* Vol. 1, *Preliminary Introduction and Commentary on Acts I–XIV.* ICC. Edinburgh: T&T Clark, 1994.

Blumell, Lincoln H. "Luke 22:43-44: An Anti-Docetic Interpolation or an Apologetic Omission?" *TC: A Journal of Biblical Textual Criticism* 19 (2014) 1-35.

Bock, Darrell L. *Luke.* Vol. 2, *9:51—24:53.* BECNT. Grand Rapids: Baker Academic, 1996.

Clivaz, Claire. *L'Ange et la sueur de sang: Lc 22,43-44.* Leuven: Peeters, 2010.

Ehrman, Bart D., and Mark A. Plunkett. "The Angel and the Agony: The Textual Problem of Luke 22:43-44." *CBQ* 45 (1983) 401-16.

Fitzmyer, Joseph A. *The Acts of the Apostles.* AB 31. New York: Doubleday, 1998.

———. *The Gospel According to Luke X–XXIV.* AB 28A. New York: Doubleday, 1985.

Horton, Dennis J. *Death and Resurrection: The Shape and Function of a Literary Motif in the Book of Acts.* Eugene, OR: Pickwick, 2009.

Johnson, Luke Timothy. *The Acts of the Apostles.* SP 5. Collegeville, MN: Liturgical, 1992.

Keener, Craig S. *Acts: An Exegetical Commentary.* Vol. 2, *3:1—14:28.* Grand Rapids: Baker Academic, 2013.

Krodel, Gerhard A. *Acts.* ACNT. Minneapolis: Augsburg, 1986.

Marshall, I. Howard. *Acts: An Introduction and Commentary.* TNTC 5. 1980. Reprint, Downers Grove, IL: InterVarsity, 2008.

Parsons, Mikeal C. *Acts.* PCNT. Grand Rapids: Baker Academic, 2008.

———. *Luke.* PCNT. Grand Rapids: Baker Academic, 2015.

Pervo, Richard I. *Acts: A Commentary.* Hermeneia. Minneapolis: Fortress, 2009.

Radl, W. "Befreiung aus dem Gefängnis: Die Darstellung eines biblischen Grundthemas in Apg 12." *BZ* 27 (1983) 81-96.

Talbert, Charles H. *Literary Patterns, Theological Themes, and the Genre of Luke-Acts.* SBLMS 20. Missoula, MT: Scholars, 1974.

Tannehill, Robert C. *The Narrative Unity of Luke-Acts: A Literary Interpretation.* 2 vols. Minneapolis: Fortress, 1990.

Wall, Robert W. "Successors to 'the Twelve' According to Acts 12:1-17." *CBQ* 53 (1991) 628-43.

Westcott, Brooke Foss, and Fenton John Anthony Hort. *The New Testament in the Original Greek [2,] Introduction [and] Appendix.* Cambridge: Macmillan, 1881.

Witherington, Ben, III. *The Acts of the Apostles: A Socio-Rhetorical Commentary.* Grand Rapids: Eerdmans, 1998.

Dream-Visions in the Plot of Acts[1]

Derek S. Dodson

THE STUDY OF VISIONS and dreams in the book of Acts has for the most part focused on their literary form and/or their function as divine communications.[2] Both analyses are quite helpful and contribute greatly to my own reading of dreams and visions in Acts. Little attention, however, has been given to the role of dreams and visions as a contributing literary device to the narrative of Acts. This paper seeks to demonstrate that visions and dreams occur at pivotal moments in the plot of Acts, particularly the beginning, middle, and end.[3] This attention to beginning, middle, and end is not based on a strict, structural outline, but it is concerned with the basic plot, or storyline, of Acts.[4]

It is important, then, to begin with an articulation of the storyline of Acts. The following is a sampling offered by commentators. Richard Pervo states, ". . . Acts is *not* the story of the early church, but an account of the victorious progress of the gospel from Jerusalem to Rome," with an emphasis

---

1. This essay originated as a paper presented at the Southwest Commission on Religious Studies, Irving, Texas, March 5, 2011. I am happy to include it in this volume that so appropriately honors my teacher and now colleague, Naymond Keathley.

2. For a review of scholarship on dream-visions in Acts (and Luke), see Miller, *Convinced*, 81–90.

3. On the one hand, attention to the beginning, middle, and end of Acts is a self-imposed restriction given the space limit of this essay, for dreams and visions are found throughout Acts (see Miller, *Convinced*). But on the other hand, the beginning, middle, and end of narratives have been understood to be critical points of a plot (see the helpful discussion of literary theory in Tate, *Biblical Interpretation*, 102–18).

4. Though issues of beginning, middle, and end for Acts will be addressed below, see also Pervo, *Mystery of Acts*, 30–31, for the "enigmatic" nature of these structural elements for Acts.

on "Paul's missionary outreach to the gentiles." [5] In a similar fashion, Scott Spencer states, "The book of Acts presents a dynamic story of the gospel's journey from Jerusalem to Rome, propelled by the earliest followers of the risen and ascended Jesus in the power of the Holy Spirit."[6] C.K. Barrett describes the primary interest of Acts as the progressive expansion of the gospel to the gentiles, stating that Luke "wished to show how the Gospel had been taken beyond the Judaism in which it was cradled into the Gentile world"[7] and that "the story of this expansion was known to [Luke] in terms of places—Samaria, Caesarea, Antioch, and beyond—, and in terms of outstanding men—Peter, Stephen, Philip, Paul."[8] And finally, Mikeal Parsons describes the plot as following: "Luke tells the story of the first followers of Jesus in such a way as to highlight that community's heritage in the scriptures and experience of Israel and at the same time to chronicle the new thing God has done through the death and resurrection of Jesus, Israel's Messiah, especially in terms of the inclusion of the Gentiles into the newly constituted people of God."[9] Thus, I would identify the constituent elements of the story of Acts as a divinely guided, geographical progression of the gospel by prominent disciples, especially Peter and Paul, with an emphasis on gentile inclusion. Visions and dreams certainly function in relation to the first element: divine guidance/directive.[10] But dreams and visions are strategically placed at critical moments in the plot of Acts, which contribute to the other elements as well. The critical moments are at the beginning with the Pentecost event, the middle with the transition from Peter to Paul and the corresponding turn to the gentile mission, and the end with Paul preaching unhindered in Rome.

Beginning: The Visionary Experience of Pentecost

In considering the Pentecost event as a vision at the beginning of the story of Acts, two important questions need to be answered: (1) is the Pentecost event at the beginning of Acts, and (2) is the Pentecost event presented as a vision?

5. Ibid., 28, 29.
6. Spencer, *Journeying*, 13.
7. Barrett, *Acts of the Apostles*, 1:49–56.
8. Ibid., 1:57.
9. Parsons, *Acts*, 7.

10. Dreams and visions as divine directives has been the primary way interpreters have identified their function within Acts. See, for example, Squires, *Plan of God*, 103–20.

Let us begin with the first question: is the Pentecost event the beginning of Acts? Though oversimplified, it can generally be said that interpreters of Acts usually identify the beginning of Acts in one of two ways. Either Acts begins with chapter 1, or it begins with chapters 1 and 2. For example, Scott Spencer reads Acts beginning with chapters 1 and 2, and he entitles this beginning "Orientation: The Journey Begins."[11] For Spencer, Pentecost is an episode connected with themes from chapter one and functions as an introductory climax that sets the stage for the global advancement of the gospel. As such, Pentecost can be considered a significant part of the beginning of Acts. On the other hand, Robert Tannehill reads chapter 1 as the beginning of Acts, entitling it "Transition and Preparation"; that is, transitioning from the Third Gospel to Acts and preparing for the narrative that is to unfold. And yet, in describing the function of the Pentecost event in chapter 2, Tannehill states, "Thus the promised Spirit initiates the actions of the plot by initiating the mission that continues through the rest of Acts."[12] So, though Tannehill does not place the Pentecost event in the beginning of Acts in terms of narrative structure, he does understand its initiatory function for the plot of Acts. Despite the differences in how they outline the book of Acts, Spencer and Tannehill both recognize the significant role the Pentecost event has in beginning the story of Acts: it is the divine initiative that prompts and empowers the church to begin its gospel-witnessing mission. It is an event that results in Jews from every nation hearing in their own language a testimony to the "mighty deeds of God" (2:11) and then hearing Peter's interpretation of the event and proclamation of the gospel. The Pentecost event is both preview and realization of the gospel mission to the world, and as such it provides a proper and dramatic beginning to the plot of Acts.

Now to the second question: is the Pentecost event a vision? Certainly the point of the Pentecost event is to narrate the coming of the Holy Spirit, which the Lukan Jesus promises in both Luke 24:49 and Acts 1:4–5.[13] But the coming of the Spirit is accompanied by phenomena that should be understood as a vision experience. Acts 2:2–4 reads:

> And suddenly there was from heaven a noise like strong, driving wind, and it filled the whole room where they were. And there appeared to them divided tongues like fire, and they rested on each one of them. And all were filled with the Holy Spirit and

---

11. Spencer, *Journeying*, 33.

12. Tannehill, *Narrative Unity*, 2:26.

13. The Pentecost event may also be the fulfillment of John the Baptist's statement, "He will baptize you with the Holy Spirit and with fire" (Luke 3:16b).

they began to speak in other tongues as the Spirit was giving to them to utter.

This account is reminiscent of another episode in Luke-Acts where the coming of the Spirit is narrated. Interpreters of Luke-Acts have long observed the parallels between the Lukan Jesus's experience of the Holy Spirit at his baptism (Luke 3:21-22) and the early believers' experience of the Holy Spirit at Pentecost.[14] Both experiences of the Holy Spirit are actually narrated in terms of visionary and auditory elements.[15] For Jesus, the visionary element is a "bodily appearance like a dove" (εἴδει ὡς περιστερὰν, Luke 3:22); for the Jerusalem believers, it is the appearance of divided tongues like a fire (ὤφθησαν ... γλῶσσαι ὡσεὶ πυρὸς, Acts 2:3). In terms of the auditory element, for Jesus there is "a voice from heaven" (φωνὴν ἐξ οὐρανοῦ, Luke 3:22); for the Jerusalem believers there is "a noise from heaven" (ἐκ τοῦ οὐρανοῦ ἦχος, Acts 2:2). This combination of visual and auditory elements is consistent with other vision reports in Acts. For example, in Paul's vision in Acts 9 there is a "light from heaven" and he hears "a voice." In his vision in Acts 10, Peter sees "something like a sheet" and "a voice" comes to him. In his speech in Acts 7, Stephen recounts Moses's vision (ὅραμα, 7:31), in which "an angel appeared to him in the flame of a burning bush" and he heard the voice of the Lord. Another parallel between Jesus's baptism and the early disciples at Pentecost is that both experiences of the Holy Spirit happen at the beginning of the recipients' respective public ministries. The parallel function of these two accounts, however, is achieved primarily by vision-laden language. Thus, Jesus's visionary experience of the Spirit at his baptism primes the audience to hear the Pentecost event as a similar visionary experience. In addition, an ancient audience would find a beginning vision or dream quite familiar. Luke himself begins his Gospel with a series of vision narratives: Zechariah's vision in the temple, the angel Gabriel's appearance to Mary, and the appearance of the angels to the shepherds. Matthew's Gospel begins the narrative proper with a dream scene: an angel of the Lord appeared Joseph in a dream.

---

14. For example, Polhill, *Acts*, 95-96; and Bruce, *Book of Acts*, 42 n. 57. Though, without explanation, Conzelmann, *Acts of the Apostles*, 14, states, "This manner of the 'pouring out' of the Spirit (cf. vs. 33) as Luke describes it, is qualitatively different from the manner in which the Spirit came to Jesus (Luke 3:22)."

15. Our modern distinction between audition and vision should not be overly pressed with this ancient text. In his foundational study of dreams and visions in ancient literature, John Hanson observes that in Greco-Roman literature "no specific terminology for auditions develop, but that even where the dream-vision proper is only auditory visual terminology prevails" ("Dreams and Visions," 1411). So, from an ancient perspective, auditions were considered part of the larger experience of what was called visions or dreams.

In Greco-Roman literature, Achilles Tatius also begins his romance story of Leucippe and Clitophon with a dream narrative (*Leuc. Clit.* 1.3.2–5).

In the interest of space, let me simply list other features that would make a case for Pentecost as a vision: (1) Luke's affinity for using the aorist passive of ὁράω for vision and dream reports, (2) Peter's interpretative role for the Pentecost vision (2:14–42),[16] and (3) the literary practice of connecting dream-visions with prophecies.[17] In summary, Luke has shaped his narration of the Pentecost event according to the literary convention of a vision, and by such a dramatic elaboration Luke has emphasized the significance of this beginning plot scene.

"Middle": The Visionary Frenzy Accompanying the Transition from Peter to Paul

In terms of the structure of Acts, most scholars recognize a major transition occurs at chapter 13, a transition not only facilitated by a so-called chain-link rhetorical device but also a transition from an emphasis on the ministry of Peter to the ministry of Paul. For example, Bruce Longenecker provides the following observation:

> Each figure holds prominence in relatively self-contained sections of the text. In Acts 1–12 the main figure is Peter, who evidently oversees both the Jerusalem-based community and the initial expansion into other geographical areas.... In Acts 13–28, however, the narrative focuses primarily on Paul, depicted as a great missionary working for the spread of the Christian communities throughout the Mediterranean basin.[18]

The dramatic prelude, or impetus, to this transition, however, occurs with the memorable visions of Paul and Ananias in chapter 9 and the visions of Cornelius and Peter in chapter 10. So, though the visions of chapters 9 and 10 are not in the middle of the Acts in a structural sense, they signify a pivotal moment at which the story begins its transition from Peter to Paul; and yet, this transition is unified by the connection of the visions with a central feature of the plot: the gospel's expansion to the gentiles. The visions in chapter 9 facilitate the conversion and election of Paul to take the name of Christ to the gentiles; and the visions in chapter 10 prompt Peter's witness to the non-Jew Cornelius, resulting in the Holy Spirit coming upon a

---

16. Miller, *Convinced*, 174–77.
17. Dodson, *Reading Dreams*, 151–52.
18. Longenecker, *Rhetoric at the Boundaries*, 171–72.

household of gentiles. So, the visions function to demonstrate the divine initiative and unity of Paul's and Peter's respective missions to the gentiles, though the narrative will move from the prominence of Peter to that of Paul.

The significance of these visions to the plot of Acts, including their conjunction with one another, is evidenced by their elaborate and parallel presentations. It has been observed by others that the visions of Paul and Ananias and the visions of Cornelius and Peter represent a sophisticated, literary device called a double dream-vision narrative.[19] A double dream-vision narrative involves two characters who each experience a vision or dream. The two visions can be identical, similar, or entirely different, but they are connected in some way, as John Hanson notes, to "produce what may be called a 'circumstance of mutuality' between the two [visionaries]."[20] Beyond a "circumstance of mutuality" between the two visionaries, a double dream-vision narrative can also produce what I have called a "circumstance of benefit" for someone else beyond the two visionaries.[21]

The visions of Paul and Ananias can be described as a double vision narrative in the following way. Paul's vision is a dramatic encounter with the risen Lord, which renders him blind and causes him to fast, features that signify a process of conversion. Immediately following Paul's vision, the disciple Ananias receives a vision from the Lord. There are three interesting features to note about Ananias's vision. First, the vision instructs Ananias to find Paul and heal his blindness. Though reluctant at first, Ananias obediently responds to the vision, healing Paul's blindness, baptizing Paul, and giving him food, thus completing the conversion. Second, the vision informs Ananias (and so the reader) that Paul is the one chosen to take the gospel to "the Gentiles, kings, and the children of Israel" (9:15). Thus, the significance of Paul's vision experience is actually stated in Ananias's vision. And third, in Ananias's vision the reader is informed that Paul is receiving a subsequent vision at the same time Ananias is receiving his vision. Acts 9:11–12 reads, "And the Lord said to him, 'Ananias, Get up and go to the gate that is called Straight and seek in the house of Judas one named Saul of Tarsus. For behold, he is praying and he sees a man in a vision named Ananias coming and laying his hands upon him so that he might see again.'" This double vision narrative is notable for the way a third vision is embedded in one of the vision reports. The two visions work together to create a "circumstance of mutuality" for both Paul and Ananias. The infamous

---

19. Wikenhauser, "Doppelträume," 100–111; Hanson, "Dreams and Visions," 1414–19.

20. Hanson, "Dreams and Visions," 1415.

21. Dodson, *Reading Dreams*, 160–61.

persecutor of the church is now received and served by a would-be victim. Ananias also benefits with the revelation that Paul is no longer a threat. But more importantly, there is a "circumstance of benefit" for those who will now hear the gospel of Christ because of Paul's mission.

The visions in Acts 10, which are experienced by a gentile "God-fearer" named Cornelius and the apostle Peter, also constitute a double vision narrative. Cornelius receives the first vision, in which an angel announces, "Your prayers and almsgivings have gone up as a memorial before God. And send now men to Joppa and summon a certain Simon who is called Peter. This one is being entertained by a certain Simon, a tanner, whose house is by the sea" (10:4–6). The scene then shifts to Joppa, where Peter is praying on a rooftop. And as he is praying, he falls into a trance and has the following vision:

> He saw the heavens open and some object descending like a large piece of cloth being let down upon the earth by the four corners. And on it there were all kinds of animals and reptiles of the earth and birds of the sky. And there came a voice to him, "Get up, Peter, kill and eat." But Peter said, "By no means, Lord, for I have never eaten anything defiled and unclean. And the voice again a second time came to him, "What God has cleansed, you do not consider defiled." And this happened three times, and immediately the object was taken up to heaven."
> (Acts 10:11–16)

As Peter is pondering the meaning of the vision, Cornelius's messengers arrive and relate the request to return with them to Cornelius. Peter accepts the invitation, and the gentile Cornelius describes his vision to him. Peter learns his own lesson, announcing that "God has shown me that I should not call anyone defiled or unclean" (10:28). Peter then preaches the gospel, after which the Holy Spirit comes upon all who heard Peter's preaching and are baptized. The "circumstance of mutuality" effected by these visions is Cornelius's hearing of the gospel, experiencing the gift of the Holy Spirit, and receiving baptism; and Peter is prepared for his encounter with the gentile Cornelius, which leads to a new understanding about the character of God and the implications of the gospel for inclusion of the gentiles. And like the double vision narrative in Acts 9, there is a "circumstance of benefit" beyond Cornelius and Peter. The Cornelius event becomes the critical impetus for the church recognizing the inclusion of gentiles among God's people.[22] In fact, the double vision narratives of Acts 9 and 10 function in

---

22. See Acts 15:1–28, esp. 7–11 and 13–18.

tandem to provoke the events that will ultimately determine the decision of gentile inclusion in Acts 15.

The importance of these visions for the plot of Acts can also be demonstrated by comparing how other ancient literature narrate critical moments by elaborate and multiple dream-vision narratives. Two examples will suffice. The first example comes from Herodotus's *Histories*. In book 7, Herodotus narrates a series of dreams to both the Persian king Xerxes and his advisor Artabanus. Xerxes was intent on leading a military campaign against the Greeks until Artabanus in a long speech convinces him otherwise (7.10). When Xerxes goes to sleep, he has a dream in which a "tall and handsome man stood over him" and exhorted and threatened him not to change his mind but to continue with his original plan. Xerxes does not change his mind, and so the same dream happens again the following night with both exhortations and threats. Xerxes is quite alarmed and decides to have Artabanus wear the royal attire and sleep in the royal chamber. For a third time the dream appears; though the dream visitant is not deceived it gives Artabanus the same message: invade Greece or else. One scholar has stated, "Xerxes' decision to invade mainland Greece is the most elaborately deployed, important, and over-determined decision in the *Histories*."[23] The three-time recurring dream to Xerxes and Artabanus stands at a critical juncture of Herodotus's *Histories*, initiating a turning point in the story that will occupy the rest of the narrative.

The second example comes from book 11 of Josephus's *Jewish Antiquities*, which just happens to be the midpoint of this work. It is an account of Alexander the Great's march into Jerusalem. The high priest Jaddus has received news that Alexander the Great with his army is approaching Jerusalem. Jaddus had previously defied Alexander and so was in fear of the impending encounter. Having called upon the people to pray, Jaddus also prayed and offered sacrifices requesting God's help. While in the temple he falls asleep and receives a dream that instructs him "that the people should be in white garments and he himself with priests should be in the robes prescribed by the laws, and that they should not look to suffer any harm, for God was watching over them" (*Ant.* 11.327 [Marcus, LCL]). Jaddus obeys the dream command and goes out with the people to meet Alexander and his army. The tension of the scene is heightened by Josephus's portrayal of the army, who "thought to themselves that the king in his anger would naturally permit them to plunder the city and put the high priest to a shameful death" (*Ant.* 11.330 [Marcus, LCL]). But when Alexander sees the people in their white clothing and Jaddus in his priestly garb, especially the priestly headdress with the name of

---

23. Fisher, "Popular Morality in Herodotus," 220.

Israel's God inscribed upon it, he prostrates himself before the divine name and greets Jaddus. Alexander then explains this highly unusual and unexpected act by describing a previous dream of his own, in which the high priest Jaddus, dressed in the same priestly clothes, encouraged Alexander to commence his military campaign, a venture that Alexander now believes to be under divine guidance. Thus, the dream of Jaddus inspires actions that cause Alexander to recall his own dream, which moves Alexander to spare Jaddus and the Jewish people. The "circumstance of mutuality" exists in the Jewish people's salvation and in Alexander's opportunity to worship the God that exhorted him to begin his military conquest. Josephus utilizes the double-dream narrative for this critical, momentous event, and it is a literary device by which he creatively writes the Jewish people and their God into the world history of Alexander and the Greeks.[24]

Thus, like other ancient literature, the visionary frenzy of Acts 9 and 10 signals a critical turning point in the plot of Acts: by divine initiative the two most prominent figures in Acts, Peter and Paul, are prompted and compelled to participate in the gospel inclusion of gentiles.

Ending: A Dream-Vision Contribution to the Suspended Ending of Acts

Let me be explicit: there are no visions or dreams at the end of Acts. But there are two dreams in 23:11 and 27:23–26 that predict events that conclude—or do not conclude as the case may be—Acts. The narrative of Acts comes to a close with Paul in Rome under house arrest, testifying to the Roman Jews (28:23–27), announcing that salvation has been offered to the gentiles (28:28), and "preaching the kingdom of God and teaching the things about the Lord Jesus Christ with all boldness and without hindrance" (28:31). This ending is consistent with the plot of Acts: the expansion of the gospel all the way to Rome by Paul with an emphasis on gentile inclusion; and the divine guidance for this witnessing activity is the dream in 23:11. In chapters 21–23, Paul has been at the center of several disturbances in Jerusalem (21:17–36; 22:22–29; 23:6–10) and is in Roman custody for his own safety. As he is in Roman custody, he experiences a dream:

> Now on the following night the Lord stood by him and said, "Take courage! For just as you testified about me in Jerusalem, in the same way it is also necessary that you testify in Rome." (23:11)

---

24. Gruen, *Heritage and Hellenism*, 193–99.

The function of the dream is two-fold: (1) to encourage Paul in his present circumstance and (2) to provide divine assurance of Paul's eventual arrival and testimony in Rome.

The other dream in 27:23–26 is similar in function. Paul is aboard a ship being taken as a prisoner to Rome. The sea voyage has proved to be quite difficult, and so he addresses those on board in order to encourage them:

> I urge you now to take courage, for there will not be one loss of life from among you but [only] the ship. For in this night an angel of the God to whom I belong and whom I worship stood by me and said, "Do not fear, Paul, it is necessary that you stand before Caesar. And behold, God has graciously given you all those who are sailing with you." Therefore, take courage, men! For have faith in God that it will be in the same way as it was spoken to me. (27:22–25)

Like the previous dream narrative, this dream functions to give encouragement and to signify the divine intent of Paul's testimony before the emperor in Rome. However, the fulfillment of this dream prediction is not narrated; there is no account of Paul testifying before Caesar. Most scholars now interpret this unfulfilled foreshadowing in terms of its rhetorical function. For example, Charles Talbert states, "narrative suspension is a literary device whereby the author, by failing to bring certain narrative data to their resolution, hinders the closure of the narrative world for the reader. The closure must be achieved by the reader, who does so by finishing the story in consonance with its plot."[25] Though the events are not narrated, the divine nature of the dream provides a secure basis on which readers know of Paul's eventual testimony before the emperor. More importantly, this narrative suspension also allows the author rhetorically—and theologically—to conclude the narrative with an emphasis on the unhindered, barrier-breaking gospel, which in many ways sums up the story of Acts.[26] Thus, it is two dream reports that anticipate and predict how the end of the *story* of Acts includes Paul's testimony in Rome and before Caesar; but the dreams also set up the rhetorical device of suspension that gives the *narrative* a proper thematic ending.

---

25. Talbert, *Reading Acts*, 231. See also Tannehill, *Narrative Unity*, 2:353–57.
26. Stagg, *Book of Acts*.

Conclusion

As stated at the beginning of this essay, the story of Acts is the divinely initiated and guided, geographical progression of the gospel by prominent disciples, especially Peter and Paul, with an emphasis on gentile inclusion. Visions and dreams contribute to this story, particularly at the critical moments of beginning, middle, and end. The story of Acts begins with the vision at Pentecost, a divine event that initiates and empowers the gospel mission of the early believers. This vision event also previews the geographical expansion of the gospel with "devout Jews from every nation" (2:5) observing the phenomenon and eventually being baptized (2:41). The visions of chapters 9 and 10 mark the transition from Peter to Paul in the narrative, yet the emphasis of the visions is the progression of the gospel to include gentiles. The significance of this moment in the narrative of Acts is evidenced by the use of the double vision literary device in both chapters, thus creating parallel scenes of divine enlightenment for Paul and Peter. And finally, dreams contribute to an assurance that the gospel will progress to Rome and to an awareness that Paul will testify before the emperor. Such knowledge, particularly testifying before the emperor, is not narrated, but this allows the narrative to end on a more appropriate note: the unhindered, still progressing gospel (28:31).

Works Cited

Barrett, C. K. *The Acts of the Apostles*. 2 vols. ICC. Edinburgh: T&T Clark, 1994–98.
Bruce, F. F. *The Book of Acts*. Rev. ed. NICNT. Grand Rapids: Eerdmans, 1988.
Conzelmann, Hans. *Acts of the Apostles*. Hermeneia. Philadelphia: Fortress, 1987.
Dodson, Derek S. *Reading Dreams: An Audience-Critical Approach to the Dreams in the Gospel of Matthew*. LNTS 397. London: T&T Clark, 2009.
Fisher, Nick. "Popular Morality in Herodotus." In *Brill's Companion to Herodotus*, edited by E. Bakker, I. de Jong, and H. van Wees, 199–224. Leiden: Brill, 2002.
Gruen, Erich S. *Heritage and Hellenism: The Reinvention of Jewish Tradition*. Berkley, CA: University of California Press, 1998.
Hanson, John S. "Dreams and Visions in the Graeco-Roman World and Early Christianity." *ANRW* 23.2:1395–1427.
Longenecker, Bruce W. *Rhetoric at the Boundaries: The Art and Theology of New Testament Chain-Link Transitions*. Waco: Baylor University Press, 2005.
Miller, John B. F. *Convinced that God has Called Us: Dreams, Visions, and the Perception of God's Will in Luke-Acts*. BibInt 85. Leiden: Brill, 2007.
Parsons, Mikeal C. *Acts*. PCNT. Grand Rapids: Baker Academic, 2008.
Pervo, Richard I. *The Mystery of Acts: Unraveling Its Story*. Santa Rosa, CA: Polebridge, 2008.
Polhill, John B. *Acts*. NAC 26. Nashville: Broadman, 1992.

Spencer, F. Scott. *Journeying Through Acts: A Literary-Cultural Reading.* Grand Rapids: Baker Academic, 2004.
Squires, John. *The Plan of God in Luke-Acts.* SNTSMS 76. Cambridge: Cambridge University Press, 1993.
Stagg, Frank. *The Book of Acts: The Early Struggle for an Unhindered Gospel.* Nashville: Broadman, 1955.
Tannehill, Robert C. *The Narrative Unity of Luke-Acts: A Literary Interpretation.* 2 vols. Minneapolis: Augsburg Fortress, 1990.
Talbert, Charles H. *Reading Acts: A Literary and Theological Commentary on the Acts of the Apostles.* Rev. ed. Macon, GA: Smyth & Helwys, 2005.
Tate, W. Randolph. *Biblical Interpretation: An Integrated Approach.* 3rd ed. Peabody, MA: Hendrickson, 2008.
Wikenhauser, Alfred. "Doppelträume." *Bib* 29 (1948) 100–111.

Cinematic Acts and the Triumph of Christianity

Richard Walsh

IN THIS ESSAY, I read a cinematic genre, the Christian biblical epic, alongside the book of Acts.[1] The epics tell the story of Jesus's post-apostolic followers as they face persecution for their faith under Nero (or Caligula). As the epics do not adapt Acts literally, they are not an obvious part of the reception history of Acts. It is the obvious differences, however, that make the similarities between these films and Acts enlightening.[2] My comparison claims that audiences of these films and Acts see/read similar patterns, learn similar lessons, and are invested with similar identities.[3]

    1. This essay is but a token of my respect and affection for my Doktorvater Naymond Keathley. I am grateful for all that he taught me as professor and mentor, but I am even more grateful for his continuing kindness and friendship over the years. I will always remember fondly his call or message, "let's have a coffee, Richard." I have chosen to write on Acts generally, and the triumph of Christianity therein specifically, because of Naymond's own academic interest in that theme. See Keathley, *Church's Mission*, where he often expresses his own dependence on and affection for one of his teachers and his work, Frank Stagg, *Book of Acts*.

    2. This approach understands texts (and films) and interpretations as intertextual and relies on Jonathan Z. Smith's comparative approach to religion. Smith has often said that one must pursue "difference" to find illuminating comparisons. For a theoretical explication, see Walsh and Aichele, "Introduction," vii–xiii.

    3. My approach ignores the wisdom of (some) biblical scholars, who, if they choose to interpret film at all, usually engage obviously biblical films. Such analyses typically have one of two foci. The most common compiles a list of the ways in which a film deviates from a biblical text. The other, which may also include a list of deviations, focuses on the film as a cultural production, interpreting the biblical text from and for a given moment. Both "close readings" and historical examinations are second-nature to most biblical scholars. The obvious exception to this "literal" approach is Christ-figure analyses. While they are quite popular, the fact that critics routinely lampoon them

Acts on Film

While "literal" films reprising Acts exist, they are low-budget affairs with little cinematic interest. Their raison d'être is devotional and evangelistic (e.g., *Living Bible Series: Acts of the Apostles* [1957], *The Visual Bible: Acts* [1994]). More cinematically interesting films move away from Acts toward the biopic or the Christian biblical epic genre.[4] The biopic presents the life of a great person, who has had a significant impact on the history leading to the audience's culture, in terms of that person's "call" (to a mission or idea), the character's subsequent struggle against a society not ready for this change, and a public trial epitomizing the protagonist's triumph and bestowal of benefits upon society (e.g., *Peter and Paul* [1981], *Paul the Apostle* [2000]).[5] The big-budget, Christian biblical epic—or TV miniseries—focuses on fictional characters created from the margins of biblical accounts (like the centurion [or tribune] at the cross [e.g., *The Robe* [1953], *A.D. The Bible Continues* [2015]) or on characters from a period slightly after the biblical accounts (like Neronian Rome) (e.g., the fifties epics [see below], *A.D.* [1985]).[6] These spectacular epics aim at shock and awe. Even if they sometimes avoid miracles, they focus on miraculous transformations (conversions). They add romance and violence—battles, persecutions, martyrdoms—wherever possible.[7]

---

underscores my claim that biblical critics prefer more tangible connections between Bible and film. See, e.g., Reinhartz, *Scripture on the Silver Screen*, 184–87; Reinhartz, *Bible and Cinema*, 129–253. In fact, any biblical scholar engaging in Christ-figure interpretations will take great pains to justify his/her approach—typically through appeals to "material" connections between the film and the Jesus story. See, e.g., Walsh, "Modest Proposal"; Reinhartz, *Bible and Cinema*, 148–74. Burnette-Bletsch's careful defense of the legitimacy of some comparative interpretations, which she calls "analogues," in her "General Introduction," 10, to her two-volume book on the Bible's reception in film is another indication of scholarly leeriness about such interpretations. On this debate and the history of biblical film criticism, see Walsh, "Introduction."

4. For an introduction to Acts and the apostles in film, see Walsh, "Paul and the Early Church in Film." Acts does not figure prominently in cinema. Reinhartz, *Bible and Cinema*, 231–33, has recently identified the cinematic biblical stars as Genesis, Exodus, Samuel, Kings, Esther, Ruth, Job, the Gospels, and Revelation.

5. On the biopic, see Custen, *Bio/Pics*.

6. On the epics, see Forshey, *American Religious and Biblical Spectaculars*; Babington and Evans, *Biblical Epics*; Solomon, *Ancient World in the Cinema*; and Reinhartz, *Bible and Cinema*, 17–127.

7. Roberto Rossellini's *Atti degli apostoli* (Acts of the Apostles [1969]) does not quite fit this spectrum of films. Downplaying the miracles and suspense, the movie has a neo-realist, intimate, and philosophical aura, focusing on the apostles' teaching. The "conversational" style is typical of Rossellini's oeuvre and of his so-called "historical" period particularly.

Significantly, these epic conventions tend to "bleed" into biopics and even into the most "literal" Acts films. Thus, both the *Living Bible Series: Acts of the Apostles* and *The Visual Bible: Acts* increase the aura of persecution and the violence of martyrdom found in Acts. The former adds martyrs (the widows of Acts 6 are so because of persecutions; the martyrdom of Stephen is repeated with more detail during Paul's conversion). The latter is more circumspect, but it opens quite dramatically with Luke in danger, tending an injured girl on board a ship in a stormy sea before narrating his Acts. Similarly, *Paul the Apostle* creates a character (Reuben) who hounds and tries to kill Paul. Many reviewers have observed that the recent, popular TV productions, *The Bible* (2013) and *A.D. The Bible Continues*, intensify biblical violence (as well as the spectacularly miraculous). After repeating Jesus's crucifixion and focusing in apologetic detail on the resurrection (particularly on the unsuccessful Jewish and Roman attempts to produce the body and stop this story), *A.D. The Bible Continues* sets the narrative of Acts 1–12, with very brief selections from the sermons, in the political struggles to maintain place and order in Jerusalem, a situation made particularly dangerous for Jesus's followers by a Pilate, who is more bloodthirsty than that in Josephus and who crucifies Jews constantly as state terror to achieve his goals, by a Saul, who is willing to use any means to have Peter (and other blasphemers) killed, and by Caligula's maniacal attempt to have his statue erected in the temple. The action/characterization comes from the biblical epic, not from Acts.

The Christian Biblical Epics and Acts

As these cinematic tropes have leaked into all the cinematic Acts, perhaps the consideration of the classic Christian biblical epics vis-à-vis Acts is warranted. The most famous of such epics are *Ben-Hur*, *Quo Vadis* (with its dark double, *The Sign of the Cross* [1932]), and *The Robe* (with its sequel *Demetrius and the Gladiators* [1954]). *Ben-Hur* (1907, 1925, 1959, 1988, 2003, 2010, 2016) and *Quo Vadis* (1902, 1912, 1925, 1951, 1985, 2001) are the most important—and virtual franchises, rather than individual films—because they have been produced repeatedly. They stem respectively from two nineteenth-century novels of the same names by Lew Wallace (1880) and Henry Sienkiewicz (1895).

The most well-known and, arguably, the best *Ben-Hur* is the 1959 film.[8] It tells the story of the ruin of a wealthy Jewish prince and his family

---

8. On the many iterations of *Ben-Hur* and their variations, see Ryan and Shamir, *Bigger than Ben-Hur*; Solomon, "Belief is in the Eye of the Spectator"; and Kreitzer,

at the hands of his childhood friend, the Roman tribune Messala. Framing an accident as an attempt on the Roman governor's life, Messala makes the Hurs examples of Rome's ruthless power. He has Judah's mother and sister imprisoned and Judah sent to the galleys. Fueled by his desire for revenge, Judah survives the slavery and a dramatic sea battle in which he saves a Roman consul's life. The consul adopts Judah who gains wealth and power and becomes a talented charioteer. Judah returns to Jerusalem to have answers from Messala. The Romans discover the neglected, imprisoned Hur women are lepers and expel them from the city secretly. Esther, a Hur family servant and Judah's love interest, finds them, but keeps the information from Judah, fearing what he might do in revenge. Angry with Messala, Judah enters a chariot race against him (and others). Judah wins and Messala is mortally wounded. Dying, Messala taunts Judah by telling him his mother and sister are in the Valley of Lepers.[9] Judah carries on past his grief because of his unfinished "business" with Rome. Ever angrier, Judah rejects the Roman citizenship arranged by his fatherly consul and turns Pilate, who has announced this "gift" to Judah, into a dangerous enemy. Meanwhile, Esther tries to turn Judah from vengeance to Jesus's message of love and laments that the kind man she once loved has now become (like) arrogant Messala. Finally, at wits' end, Judah agrees to take his leprous family to the healer, but Jesus's trial has already begun. At the cross, as he later reports, Judah hears Jesus forgive his enemies and has his sword taken from his hand.[10] As blood flows from the cross, mingled with rainwater,[11] Judah's mother and sister are healed, and the Hur family is restored.[12]

As this summary—and the novel's subtitle (*A Tale of the Christ*)—indicates, the setting of this story is that of the gospels, and Judah's story takes place around the edges of familiar gospel incidents.[13] Unlike many films and Acts itself, which reprise Jesus material in order to explore the tale of the resurrection (e.g., *Barabbas* [1961]; *Risen* [2016]; *A.D. The Bible Continues*),

---

"Ben-Hur"; as well as the literature listed in n. 6. The 1907 is notable because it was the center of a lawsuit over rights that both helped set the standards for acquiring film rights to stories and turned filmmakers toward material not protected by copyright, like biblical stories.

9. In the 2016 film, Messala survives the race, and Judah forgives him at the cross.

10. In the 1925 film, Judah sees Jesus on the Via Dolorosa and drops the sword in his hand, foregoing the armed revolt he has planned (having amassed and trained two legions of rebels) to make Jesus King.

11. For discussion of the role of (the cup of) water in Ben-Hur's transformation, see Kreitzer, "*Ben-Hur*."

12. The women are healed on the Via Dolorosa in the novel and in the 1925 film.

13. In the franchise, the 1925 film has the most gospel incidents.

Ben-Hur ends at the cross. Nonetheless, *Ben-Hur* does manifest the epic tropes:

1. Spectacle: The sea battle and the chariot race dominate.
2. Romance: Romantic love [Esther] is as important as faith in moving Judah from vengeance to love and forgiveness.
3. Violence/the oppression of the noble hero/heroine by ruthless Rome: Messala's desire to demonstrate the power of Rome catalyzes the story, and Ben-Hur and Messala represent respectively noble faith/freedom and imperial hubris.

The *Quo Vadis* franchise is more typical, if not prototypical, of the Christian biblical epic. As the title indicates, Peter plays an important, albeit minor, role, but the story focuses on the corruption and persecutions of Neronian Rome, as the novel's subtitle, *A Narrative of the Time of Nero*, clearly indicates. The 1951 film is the franchise's most famous.[14] It begins with a lengthy voiceover describing Rome as the world's undisputed, corrupt, cruel master:

> But thirty years before this day, a miracle occurred. On a Roman cross in Judea, a Man died to make men free, to spread the Gospel of Redemption. Soon that humble cross is destined to replace the proud eagles atop the victorious Roman standards. This is the story of that immortal conflict. In this, the summer of the year 64 A.D., in the reign of the antichrist known to history as the emperor Nero . . .[15]

Neronian Rome, then, is mere stage setting or, more accurately, the spectacle the audience wants to see as it watches the love story of Marcus Vinicius and Lygia unfold in the midst of Christianity's providential triumph.

In the story proper, the arrogant Marcus Vinicius leads his victorious legion back into Rome. He meets and becomes enamored of the Christian Lygia, a Roman hostage. He also meets the philosopher Paul, who is Lygia's tutor. Even though Marcus conspires to have Nero give Lygia to him, Marcus gradually learns she cannot be his property. Professing his love, Marcus promises Lygia that she can practice her faith and, if necessary, he will convert himself. The romance runs aground, however, when Paul explains that

---

14. On the versions of *Quo Vadis*, see Scodel and Bettenworth, *Whither Quo Vadis*, in addition to the literature listed in n. 6. The 1912 version is notable as it is sometimes called cinema's first blockbuster and is credited with motivating D. W. Griffith to produce the first U.S. biblical epic *Judith of Bethulia* (1914).

15. All film quotations are my own transcription from film DVDs.

Marcus should also free his slaves and give up violence (war) for love and forgiveness. Frustrated, Marcus demands that Lygia choose between him and the man Christ. When faithful Lygia makes the only choice she can, Marcus breaks Lygia's devotional cross and storms away.

Meanwhile, Nero has Rome set on fire, so he can create an epic about it and build a new, gleaming Neropolis. Marcus heroically saves many, including Lygia, from this conflagration. When the mob storms the palace to deal with "the incendiary," craven Nero blames the Christians, enemies of humanity who have predicted the end of the world by fire, for the arson and promises the mob the spectacle of Christian martyrdom as an appeasement. Marcus goes to the cells to have Lygia released, but is instead arrested and sentenced to the same fate. Peter has left Rome, but he sees a bright light in the shape of a cross on the road and asks Jesus where he is going (*quo vadis*). Jesus tells Peter that if Peter is leaving, Jesus is going to Rome to be crucified a second time.[16]

Returning to Rome, Peter stands in the arena seats and proclaims that the Christians facing the lions will be in paradise with Christ today and prophesies Christ's ultimate triumph over Nero. The mob laughs and Peter is arrested, which allows him to marry Lygia and Marcus. After Peter's crucifixion,[17] and that of other Christians, Marcus and Lygia face their own moment in the arena. Bound in the royal box, Marcus can only watch as Lygia's bodyguard, the Herculean Ursus, tries to defend Lygia, tied to a stake, from a wild bull with his bare hands. As Marcus prays, Ursus kills the bull. Marcus breaks his bonds and frees Lygia, while some of his loyal troops rush to his defense. From the arena floor, he inspires the crowd to revolt with news of the approach of Galba's forces. A craven Nero commits suicide, and the happy couple leaves Rome passing Peter's flowering staff at the *quo vadis* spot, where a chorus intones, "I am the way, the truth, and the life."

Like *Ben-Hur*, *Quo Vadis* displays the epic conventions:

1. Spectacle: The 1951 film has three major spectacles: Marcus Vinicius's triumph; Rome's conflagration; and the Christians' martyrdom. The last is thematically central, nicely balances the opening Roman triumph, and indicates the thematic move from Roman to Christian triumph. Rome afire, however, dominates the film cinematically.

2. Romance: The story focuses on Marcus's love for Lygia and its transformative effects on him, but the 1951 film also includes the love stories of Petronius and Eunice and Nero and Acte. Marcus's prayer

---

16. The *quo vadis* story comes from the second-century *Acts of Peter*.
17. Only the 1951 film shows Peter's martyrdom.

for Lygia in the arena represents his conversion; however, even at the film's end, Marcus is more concerned with the rule of Rome than that of Christianity.

3. The oppression of the noble hero/heroine by ruthless Rome: Lygia's callous enslavement by Rome and thoughtless pursuit by Marcus dominates the story line, until Marcus begins to change under her influence. The couple's subsequent suffering represents at a personal level Nero's persecution of Christians.

The other Christian epics also feature couples, comprised of a Christian and a Roman, who "converts" to Christianity. Roman intolerance and corruption always endangers the couple—although the real culprit is typically a vile emperor and a few henchmen. Rome itself may be salvageable by conversion to Christianity or by the adoption of religious tolerance.[18] While Marcus and Lygia live happily ever after, the epics' romantic couples sometimes die (e.g., in *The Sign of the Cross* and *The Robe*), but such films still reveal the martyrs' and Christianity's ultimate triumph through the exalted, transported looks on the couple's faces, by glowing crosses of light, and by triumphant music, like the Hallelujah Chorus—all accompanying their final moments.

These epics are based on novels, plays, legends, and cinematic precursors. Typically, their setting is later than that of Acts (although see, e.g., *Ben-Hur*, *Paul the Apostle*, *A.D. The Bible Continues*). Nonetheless, the epics have significant similarities to Acts.

First, like Jesus in Acts, an apostle plays a cameo role.[19] Nonetheless, the apostle has a significance beyond his screen time because he represents Jesus. For *Quo Vadis*'s Christians, Peter is a celebrity because he saw and heard Jesus. This status recalls the eyewitness requirements of apostles in Acts itself (Acts 1:21–22). Like the Paul of Acts, *Quo Vadis*'s Paul is respectful of this apostolic priority. In both Acts and the epics, the apostles are the material manifestation of the sacred and windows on both the sacred past and the sacred other. They center the epic's world morally. Like the apostles in Acts, stories of degradation and conversion swirl around them. The fall of the wicked (e.g., Judas, Ananias, Sapphira, Herod, and Simon in Acts; and Nero, Tigellinus, Poppaea, and others in the epics) and the conversion of the good (e.g., Saul in Acts and Marcus in the epics) provide both drama and moral satisfaction.

---

18. At the end of *Demetrius and the Gladiators*, Claudius, who has replaced Caligula, releases Demetrius from the arena, returns Jesus's robe to him, and tells him that Christians have nothing to fear from Rome if they do not disrupt Roman order.

19. Jesus also makes cameo appearances in some of the epics.

Second, the epics' new followers imitate the apostles and thus Jesus, as do the apostles, Paul, and the elders in Acts. Everyone's life falls into the same Christ-like (or biopic) pattern. After a miraculous call/conversion, they stake their lives for their new cause, escape certain death miraculously, or if they die, still triumph—at least symbolically.[20]

Thus, and third, dramatic, miraculous conversions are *de rigueur* in both Acts (see, e.g., Acts 2; 9; 10–11), and the epics. While there are crowds of Christians in the background and in the arena, the epics focus specifically on one conversion, that of the Christian's Roman lover. In fact, one might well describe the epics as the hero's (or heroine's) Christian "baptism" or coming of age. Acts does not focus on a conversion in this biopic fashion, but it relates its own tale of a converted Roman soldier (Cornelius).[21] As the later report of this event indicates (Acts 11:1–18; 15:6–11), however, Peter's attendant vision and the event's subsequent impact on the expansion toward the gentiles clearly overshadow Cornelius's "personal" conversion. In fact, after the initial account in Acts 10, Cornelius never appears again by name. The focus on Saul's miraculous, show-stopping conversion (or call), twice repeated (Acts 9:1–19; 22:4–16; 26:9–18), reflects a similar disregard for "person." While Saul/Paul is arguably the most important human character in Acts, as he has more text time than any other character, a biopic aggrandizement of Paul is not the point. For Acts, Paul is not an apostle; elders succeed him (Acts 20:25–38; cf. the Pastoral Epistles); and his fate in Rome is not even worth narrating.

In short, the epics have a more personal face (as do the biopic versions of Acts) than Acts does. The importance of romance in the epics also bespeaks a (modern) personality not present in Acts. For the epics, romance is more important and requires more screen time than conversion (or religious practice or teaching). What invariably happens is that the Roman "convert" proves a true, steadfast lover refusing to abandon the Christian love interest to Roman persecution. *Omnia vincit amor*. The epics do not discriminate at all between this true romance and (the workings of) divine love. Like ambition, lust is a different matter—and Poppaea is thereby villainess in both *Quo Vadis* and *The Sign of the Cross*. While romance plays no role in Acts, one could easily read its story as that of God's loving creation of a people (or gentile Christianity) for himself. And, one should not forget that biblical texts often bathe divine love in erotic language. Interestingly, even though the romantic duo is the

20. On the repeated characterization pattern in Luke-Acts, see Talbert, *Literary Patterns*, 15–26.

21. *A.D. The Bible Continues* develops Cornelius's increasing attraction to Christianity more than any other film of which I am aware. *The Robe* and *Risen* develop the tale of the conversion of the Roman official (not always a centurion) at the cross.

epics' main concern, the Christian protagonist's devotion to Jesus often has erotic (perhaps even masochistic) tinges, as actors portray their faith with awe-struck faces, swoons, and wringing of hands.

Further, the epics' "theology" expresses itself primarily in terms of Jesus's message of love and forgiveness. While not part of Acts, this message is quite Lukan (cf. Luke 6:20–49 with Matt 5–7). Not surprisingly, many epics recall that (Luke's) Jesus, in some texts, forgave his tormentors at the cross (23:34; see *Ben-Hur*, *The Robe*). Epics also feature Peter's memory of his forgiveness by Jesus (e.g., *The Robe*, *Quo Vadis*), which escapes mention in Acts unless it finds an echo in Peter's calls of others to repentance or in Peter's transformation from cowardly denier (Luke 22:54–62) to bold witness (e.g. Acts 4; 5:12–42), a stance that puts him and others in deadly jeopardy.

Fourth, then, both Acts and the epics create an atmosphere of deadly jeopardy for Jesus's followers. The epics simply raise the ante and the violence. Martyrs in Acts are quite few in number (see Acts 7; 12:2). Peter and Paul, particularly, are virtually "bullet-proof." By contrast their martyrdoms figure importantly in the epics, and the arena is the setting for the public trial of (all) the faithful. In *Quo Vadis*, Christians fall to the lions and die on burning crosses that light the night, in true epic fashion, beyond number. Among these martyrs, someone stands up boldly, like Peter in Acts, for the faith, whatever the cost. Peter and Plautius do so and, therefore, stand out in *Quo Vadis*, but almost all the martyrs meet their death singing, a matter that maddens and befuddles Nero (the martyrs also sing in *The Sign of the Cross*).

Acts and the epics do differ on the deadly threat's source. The jeopardy in the epics is almost always Roman (but, see *Paul the Apostle* and *A.D. The Bible Continues*). Despite the fact that Jesus was crucified and that Acts ends with Paul imprisoned in Rome, Acts never clearly identifies Rome as the threat (though see Acts 16:19–24). Instead, Acts infamously blames the Jews for Jesus's crucifixion (e.g., Acts 2:23; 3:13–15; 4:10) and (some) Jews for Paul's constant missionary trials (e.g., Acts 9:23–24; 13:44–52; 14:1–7, 19–20; 17:5; 18:5–6). Almost beyond belief, Acts says that Pilate would have released Jesus (Acts 3:13) and has Romans save Paul from certain death at the hands of a Jewish mob (Acts 21:31–40) and conspiracy (Acts 23:26–35). And, of course, Acts does not narrate Paul's (or Peter's) martyrdom by Rome.

Fifth, both Acts and the epics relate numerous near-escapes. Near escapes are one of the most common subgenres or type scenes in Acts.[22] In fact, if one considers the numerous "stories" of the suffering righteous in biblical narratives, one will find the miraculous escape from certain death

---

22. See Pervo, *Profit with Delight*.

more common than martyrdom.[23] Surprisingly despite the epics' high body count, near escapes are more prominent than death in the epics' story-lines. Even if the romantic couple dies, as in *The Robe*, part of the story's delight is how long it takes for villainy to finally "do in" the protagonists. Every epic features the hero's success in battle, and most feature thrilling races for freedom or the salvation of the loved one. Lygia and Marcus's escape from certain death in the climax of *Quo Vadis* then is hardly an exception.

Sixth, both Acts and the epics present symbolic victories. The resurrection (and attendant spirit) is the transformative, salvific moment in Acts. As the sermons in Acts repeat tirelessly, it is God's answer to the crime of Jesus's innocent death. The resurrection also transforms Peter from craven to hero and Saul from persecutor to missionary. This resurrection is, however, largely symbolic. At least, it is not the apocalyptic, kingdom-changing event that one expects from such an apocalyptic motif (cf. Acts 1:6). The glory of the Roman Empire remains in full force. The victory is private, spiritual, symbolic. Acts imagines God's victory over the empires—before it occurs. Matters are similar in the epics—at least, in terms of their setting. The introductory voiceover in *Quo Vadis* predicts Christianity's ultimate triumph over Rome. While the audience of the film looks back on that victory with historical certainty, the victory is spiritual or symbolic for the characters. As Scodel and Bettenworth say, the epics' stories of the martyrs simply ignore the centuries before Christianity conquered the Roman Empire.[24]

Unlike Acts and early Christian art, both of which focus on surprising deliverances, the epics use the cross to represent this Christian triumph. *Quo Vadis* is somewhat unusual in this regard. The film's most memorable cross scenes are Marcus's breaking of the cross, Peter's crucifixion upside down, and the martyrs' deaths on fiery crosses. All, but particularly the first, evoke Jesus's own suffering at Roman hands. The triumph is not yet even symbolic. The more typical conquering cross of the epics is visible only once, in the brief, heavenly cross of light that attracts Peter's attention on the road outside Rome and returns him to his martyrdom. The saving cross in the 1959 *Ben-Hur* is more typical, as it is in that scene that Judah emerges from his self-destructive vengeance and his mother and sister from leprosy. Perhaps, the scene in the opening sequence of *The Sign of the Cross* is most paradigmatic. There, a star/cross of light is gradually superimposed over a Roman eagle. Similarly, in the finale, as the Roman soldier

---

23. See Nickelsburg, "Genre and Function."
24. Scodel and Bettenworth, *Whither Quo Vadis*, 25.

and his Christian love march to their martyrdoms, a cross of light appears on the door to the arena.[25]

Finally, both Acts and the epics use this symbolic triumph to position their audiences as the end of history, as providence's children. As Acte, almost a Christian, says comfortingly to Lygia when Nero gives her as property to Marcus: "Bear in mind, your fate is determined by the greatest power in this world. His will be done." As Conzelmann famously put it, Jesus is *der Mitte die Zeit* in Luke-Acts.[26] Later Christian chronology similarly divides all history into BC and AD. Films, titling themselves *A.D.*, express this Christian destiny most concisely. The epics' audiences know that Christianity triumphed over Rome, as certainly as they know that liberal democracies triumphed over tyranny. They also know this history led up to and has created them. The epics, that is, celebrate a shared past that invests audiences with a mythic identity.[27] Acts does, too, although, in its day, it could have created a mythic identity only for a sect or sub-community within the larger Roman Empire. The epics' mythic identity is far more imperial.[28]

Acts as Epic Film: Concluding Questions

I have noted several similarities between Acts and the Christian biblical epics, but not in order to demonstrate that the films "get" Acts right (or wrong). Neither is my argument that the epics can be seen as interpretations of Acts—although I believe they can. My basic point is that if one reads Acts and the epics together certain similarities (and differences) appear. The result is merely an interpretation, situated in the intertext that is the interpreter. After engaging in this exercise, however, my concern is that my reading of Acts—and perhaps that of other academics, as I have not knowingly departed from defensible academic positions on Acts—is itself

---

25. Throughout the film, crosses haunt the Roman soldier, as Jesus's robe does the soldier in *The Robe* and all Christian symbols do Barabbas in the film of that name. Such hauntings suggest the cross's talismanic power.

26. The phrase is the German title of Conzelmann, *Theology of St. Luke*.

27. On the replay ad nauseum of the birth of the U.S. in U.S. epic cinema, see Wood, *America in the Movies*. The epics never challenge empire. Instead, they look for a good, just empire, rather than the corrupt one of Caligula or Nero. Despite the epics' emphasis on freedom (and rejection of slavery in *Quo Vadis*), they always advocate "law and order."

28. Audiences of evangelical films may see themselves, like the epics' protagonists and the putative audience of Acts, as a threatened sect or sub-community; however, the financial success of *The Bible* and *A.D. The Bible Continues* belies the contention.

overwhelmingly epic. I fear, then, that my reading and my Acts is in the service of spectacle and empire.[29] I look over my shoulder waiting for some Esther to appear to name me Messala. My concern is not that biopic and epic conventions bleed into the literal cinematic Acts, but that they bleed into modern readings of Acts, even if the interpretation does not consciously pair Acts with modern cinema:

1. Spectacle: Spectacle dominates Acts (or any reading of it), which moves from Pentecost through various miraculous conversions and near escapes to Paul's perilous, dramatic sea journey or any Acts whose end is shock and awe. In this process or end, what becomes of the normal and the ordinary?

2. Romance: Romance is far less obvious in Acts than in the epics. Romance, however, is often faulted for escapism and for narcissistically narrowing the world to the romantic duo. Read carefully, Acts does not support such narrowing as the individual never emerges from the community and destiny. Read in evangelical circles, however, Acts easily becomes a romance of divine love's pursuit of individuals, which climaxes in their personal conversions. There, one is not very far from the biopic or from everyone as epic hero.

3. Oppression of the noble hero/heroine by ruthless Rome: If one replaces Rome with empire, the connection to both radical and conservative readings of Acts becomes obvious. Acts easily supports those who see themselves as the currently maligned, but soon-to-triumph children of destiny—whatever their ideology may be. Imperial Acts, that is, make it easy to cloak oneself in divine certainty and to vilify, rather than take loving responsibility for, the surrounding society.

In short, spectacle, divine identities, and easily identifiable evil (others) are not very human territory. Such patterns/myths/readings aggrandize their audiences/interpreters. One rides in triumph as Marcus does as conquering hero in *Quo Vadis*. *In hoc signo vinces* indeed. Unfortunately, such interpreters lack the unnamed character who rides behind Marcus holding Marcus's laurel wreath crown and intones repeatedly, "Remember thou art only a man [sic]."[30] Without such reminders, it is very hard to see how *omnia vincit amor* in epic spectaculars.

---

29. On the perils here, see Debord, *Society of the Spectacle*.

30. My reading of Acts and the epics might be more (ethically) satisfying if I could find a meaningful connection between something/someone in Acts and Petronius, the amused cynic, of *Quo Vadis*. Petronius alone pesters and thwarts the oppressive, narcissistic Nero (empire). Scodel and Bettenworth, *Whither Quo Vadis*, 28–42, claim that

Works Cited

Babington, Bruce, and Peter Williams Evans. *Biblical Epics: Sacred Narrative in the Hollywood Cinema*. Manchester: Manchester University Press, 1993.

Burnette-Bletsch, Rhonda. "General Introduction: The Bible and Its Cinematic Reception." In *The Bible in Motion: A Handbook of the Bible and Its Reception in Film*, edited by Rhonda Burnette-Bletsch, 1:1–14. 2 vols. Berlin and Boston: De Gruyter, 2016.

Conzelmann, Hans. *The Theology of St. Luke*. Translated by Geoffrey Buswell. London: Faber, 1960.

Custen, George F. *Bio/Pics: How Hollywood Constructed Public History*. New Brunswick, NJ: Rutgers University Press, 1992.

Debord, Guy. *Society of the Spectacle*. Translated by Ken Knabb. London: Rebel, 1983.

Forshey, Gerald E. *American Religious and Biblical Spectaculars*. Westport: Praeger, 1992.

Keathley, Naymond H. *The Church's Mission to the Gentiles*. Macon: Smith & Helwys, 1999.

Kreitzer, Larry J. "*Ben-Hur* (2016): Jesus Finds a Voice." *The T & T Clark Companion to the Bible and Film*, edited by Richard Walsh, n.p. London: T&T Clark, forthcoming.

Nickelsburg, George W. E. "The Genre and Function of the Markan Passion Narrative." *HTR* 73 (1980) 153–84.

Pervo, Richard I. *Profit with Delight*. Philadelphia: Fortress, 1987.

Reinhartz, Adele. *Bible and Cinema: An Introduction*. London: Routledge, 2013.

———. *Scripture on the Silver Screen*. Louisville: Westminster John Knox, 2003.

Ryan, Barbara, and Milette Shamir, eds. *Bigger than Ben-Hur: The Book, Its Adaptations, and Their Audiences*. Syracuse: Syracuse University Press, 2016.

Scodel, Ruth, and Anja Bettenworth. *Whither Quo Vadis? Sienkiewicz's Novel in Film and Television*. Chichester: Wiley-Blackwell, 2009.

Solomon, Jon. *The Ancient World in the Cinema*. Rev. and exp. ed. New Haven: Yale University Press, 2001.

———. "Belief is in the Eye of the Spectator: Beholding the Other Actor's Reaction." In *The T & T Clark Companion to the Bible and Film*, edited by Richard Walsh, n.p. London: T&T Clark, forthcoming.

Stagg, Frank. *The Book of Acts: The Early Struggle for an Unhindered Gospel*. Nashville: Broadman, 1955.

Talbert, Charles H. *Literary Patterns, Theological Themes and the Genre of Luke-Acts*. Missoula: Scholars, 1974.

Walsh, Richard. *Finding St. Paul in Film*. London: T&T Clark, 2005.

———. "Introduction: Biblical Film Studies." In *The T & T Clark Companion to the Bible and Film*, edited by Richard Walsh, n.p. London; New York: T&T Clark, forthcoming.

———. "A Modest Proposal for Christ-Figure Interpretations: Explicated with Two Test Cases." *Relegere* 3.1 (2013). https://relegere.org/relegere/article/view/569.

---

the film's sympathetic portrayal of Petronius sets it apart from other biblical epics. See Walsh, *Finding St. Paul*, 186–92, for a comparative reading of *The Apostle*, Acts, and Paul that tries to find a more human place.

———. "Paul and the Early Church in Film." In *The Bible in Motion: A Handbook of the Bible and Its Reception in Film*, edited by Rhonda Burnette-Bletsch, 2:497–515. 2 vols. Berlin: De Gruyter, 2016.

Walsh, Richard, and George Aichele. "Introduction: Scripture as Precursor." In *Screening Scripture: Intertextual Connections Between Scripture and Film*, edited by George Aichele and Richard Walsh, vii–xvi. Harrisburg: Trinity Press International, 2002.

Wood, Michael. *America in the Movies*. 2nd ed. New York: Columbia University Press, 1989.

III. Interpreting Christian and Baptist Life

The Bible as Spiritual Friend

Charles H. Talbert

THE PURPOSE OF THIS address is to make a personal statement about the Bible as Canon within the context of the current controversy agitating my confessional community, the Southern Baptist Convention.[1] There are four parts to my remarks, each one dealing with a specific question.

What Is the Bible?

That is, what model best conveys Scripture's character as Canon?[2] The model that makes the most sense to me is that of a developing human personality. This model is preferable, for me at least, to the traditional paradigm of the Platonic idea, an eternal, unchanging reality. The Platonic model seems to lie behind most conservative thought about the Bible as a compendium of unchanging dogma, as a timeless ethical system, or as an unalterable pattern of church polity. For this model, the diversity within the Canon poses the gravest of challenges, so it is either minimized or denied. The model of the developing human personality is also preferable, for me, to the liberal evolutionary paradigm of the older natural sciences which sees a straightforward development from simple to complex, from primitive to higher ways of thinking, so that time is the basic clue to differences within the Canon. For this model, origins are an embarrassment and must

---

1. This essay was originally delivered as the Presidential address, NABPR, Anaheim, California, November 25, 1985, and subsequently published as "The Bible as Spiritual Friend," 55–64. I am pleased to include it in this volume honoring my friend and colleague, Naymond Keathley, and I am grateful to the editors of *Perspectives in Religious Studies* for permission to reprint it here.

2. Kelsey, *Uses of Scripture in Recent Theology*, has addressed this problem from a different angle.

be passed over on the way to the normative later developments. The model of a developing human personality is also preferable, for me, to that of Heideggerian *Dasein* in which the person-she-may-become calls to the person-she-is, urging decision to realize her potential, which in its Bultmannian appropriation becomes the call of the kerygma to the person-she-is, urging decision which results in authentic existence. For this model, only a very few parts of the Bible embody a kerygmatic summons and, by content criticism, must be distinguished from those that do not, the former constituting the canon-within-the-canon.

From my perspective, the Bible is best conceived as a living, maturing person who passes through a number of developmental stages, is involved in multiple cultural settings, and faces a variety of issues that call for diverse responses. Like any human being who lives so long, this self moves from childhood with its developing awareness (OT) to adult value decisions that constitute the self's personal center (Jesus), and then to adult life that attempts to embody the personal center with some degree of faithfulness (NT). In the various crises, amid the multiple cultural settings, it is hopefully the same personal center (Jesus) that shines through.

Although aware that such a brief sketch as this may raise more questions than it answers, I have used it because it allows me to make explicit, at the very beginning, my basic assumption. The Bible is best conceptualized in terms of a personal model rather than that of a timeless idea, an impersonal process, or a perpetual summons to self-actualization. From my perspective, the Bible is to be regarded as a living, developing person with whom the believer can be involved as a "spiritual friend."[3]

How Does One Approach the Bible as Canon?

That is, if the Bible is viewed as a "spiritual friend," what is the nature of the relationship between her and the believer? Does one approach the Bible as its superior, as an equal, or as one who is subservient with no recourse but to obey blindly?

It is not uncommon for modern readers of the Bible to consider ourselves the intellectual, moral, and spiritual superiors of the one with whom we are dealing. A number of cultural assumptions may cause us to approach her differences from us with an air of superiority: (a) the belief that the history of humankind is properly understood as a progress from dark, restricting superstition to reasoned liberating enlightenment; (b) the

---

3. The expression is taken from the book by Tilden Edwards by the same name and published by Paulist Press in 1980.

belief that since moral and spiritual versions of the human condition come to us from the past, they are necessarily infected with superstition, whereas scientific versions of our condition are myth-free; (c) the belief that modern technology, knowledge, and manners are so radically discontinuous with those hitherto known that there is no sense referring to traditional standards. If so, then our reading of the Bible will be reductionistic. We will listen only to those items that conform to our contemporary standards. Paul Minear comments:

> Indeed the guiding of travelers through the world of the Bible with a minimum of culture shock is often assumed to be the chief function of ministers and teachers. They are expected to limit the questions and to select the answers which will not threaten the self-assurance of their customers.... They remain blissfully unaware of how completely they have destroyed the integrity and independence of that other world.[4]

Reading the Bible with an assumed superiority to one's spiritual friend is hardly what the church has understood as listening to Scripture.

Neither is it uncommon for certain modern readers to go to the other extreme and relate to the biblical mind with the subservience of a slave, with no recourse but to obey blindly. Respect for the canonical authority of the Bible may be construed by some to imply blind, unthinking obedience to what she says or is believed to say. This, however, turns the Bible into what Paul Tillich called a heteronomous authority, that is, an alien external law imposed from without.[5] It would be what Rudolf Bultmann called formal obedience, that is, blind obedience simply because such and such is commanded, rather than radical obedience, the obedience that exists when one inwardly assents to what is required so that the whole person is *in* what she does. In radical obedience one is not *doing* something obediently but *is* essentially obedient.[6] Formal obedience to a heteronomous authority is not what the church has understood as listening to Scripture either.

How can one approach the Bible without either an attitude of superiority which leads to reductionism or an attitude of formal obedience that leads to heteronomy? The road between these two extremes is not that of approaching the Bible as an equal. That would miss her canonical authority. The road, however, must lead to radical obedience so that one inwardly assents to what is said by one's spiritual friend, that is, to a theonomous posture.[7]

---

4. Minear, *To Heal and to Reveal*, 4.
5. Cf. Hordern, *Layman's Guide to Protestant Theology*, 168–70.
6. Bultmann, *Jesus and the Word*, 65–66, 77.
7. The Westminster Confession of Faith, Chapter 1, "Of the Holy Scripture," item

A correct approach, I propose, is to regard the Bible as a dialogue partner. This dialogue partner is not an equal but rather a recognized specialist in Christian life and faith. She is not, however, the kind of dialogue partner who uses her acknowledged authority as a club to beat one into submission. Rather she functions as a spiritual director who is eager to talk with you until you are able to see more than you have ever taken in before. In a dialogue with the Bible, one's approach may take the form of questioning her or arguing with her. "I cannot buy that. Why do you take that position? That is difficult for a modern person to understand. It is even harder for one in our culture to believe or practice." If the dialogue is sustained over a period of time, the approach may bear fruit. The biblical intent may grip us as valid for us. The scriptural categories may undergo metamorphosis so that they are retranslated into equivalent ones within our culture. The biblical perceptions of Christian life and faith may become catalysts for the shattering of our preconceived notions about who God is, how he relates to us, and what he desires from us. When this happens, the Bible has become more than ancient Israelite and early Christian literature whose point of view one's study has described. She is functioning as a spiritual friend to whose insight we are able inwardly to give assent. In this experience of radical obedience a theonomous posture results, that is, a stance in which the law of God is recognized as at the same time the law of one's deepest inmost self. Our dialogue partner has enabled us to identify and follow the Spirit's movement in our lives.

Why Listen to the Bible?

That is, why invest one's spiritual friend with authority? The answer is, obviously, because of the benefits received. Without claiming to be comprehensive, I mention three areas in which my personal experience has benefited from listening to the Bible as a spiritual friend. (1) I invest the Bible with authority because what she said about Jesus proved true in my conversion experiences.[8] As a nine-year-old child raised in a Christian home and within an ongoing church community, I came to know about Jesus through the Bible. What the Bible told me was reinforced by the church's dramas (bap-

---

5, says: "Our full persuasion and assurance of the infallible truth and divine authority thereof, is from the inward work of the Holy Spirit bearing witness by and with the Word in our hearts." Only thereby can biblical authority be theonomous and not heteronomous.

8. The category of multiple conversions is standard in the literature of Christian spirituality: e.g., Kerr and Mulder, *Conversions*, 36 (on Pascal); Fuchs, "Sin and Conversion," 260.

tism and the Lord's Supper) and by the church's life (loving relationships), but the Bible was the primary source. When I made my profession of faith, it was in the Jesus about whom the Bible had spoken. My spiritual friend had introduced me to Jesus. As a twenty-year-old college student who had long since dismissed everything he had been told about religion by Bible, church, and family, I was suddenly and repeatedly ravished by a mystical presence so powerful I thought I must surely die, which turned to sweetness only when addressed by the name "Jesus." Out of that continuing experience I went back to the Bible to find that it confirmed what I was experiencing about the nature of the Living Lord. This time my spiritual friend confirmed what I had experienced about Jesus. In my first experience, I came to believe in Jesus because I trusted my spiritual friend. In the second, I came to trust my spiritual friend because I had first come to trust Jesus. Because of the Bible's participation in my conversion experiences, I invest her with authority.

(2) I invest the Bible with authority also because she continually helps me formulate what it means to be a Christian. As a seminary student in the late 1950s, due to the vital religious experience of my college years, I possessed a strong personal testimony but was not at all sure what, if anything, I believed. Imagine my perplexity when a church was willing to call me as a student pastor. What was I to say? What could I preach? After a while personal testimony gets stale! My recourse was to take the church and to try to do expository preaching, beginning with Paul's letters to the Romans and the Philippians. Sunday after Sunday I proclaimed "what Paul says." Sunday after Sunday driving back to school from the church field I was aware that what Paul says was what I thought. The Pauline theological structures gave concrete expression to my religious experience. They helped me formulate what I believed as a Christian. Over the years this experience has been multiplied indefinitely. Repeatedly, my spiritual friend assists me in the formulation of what I believe. Because of this ongoing assistance, I invest her with authority.

(3) I invest the Bible with authority, moreover, because she helps me discern error in belief and practice, both my own and that of others. My third conversion came at age forty-five in the midst of the mid-life passage. It consisted of a renewal of personal intimacy between myself and the Triune God, an intimacy that had been lost sixteen years before. It came as part of a wave of renewal in my area of the country in which many persons were experiencing new life in God. It was a rediscovery of the God who dwells within the believer. What soon became apparent, however, was that a great majority of those who had rediscovered the presence of God within and were trying to live out of that presence were being taught a heteronomous view of Scripture that robbed them of what they had just experienced

by putting a Law between them and God. It was in my study of Galatians during that period that I came to see that Galatians is not so much addressing how one becomes a Christian (justification) as how one who has experienced justification by grace through faith moves on to maturity: not by works of law (Gal 3:1–5). One moves to maturity the same way one comes to Jesus the first time, through faith. One is not justified through faith and then comes to maturity through works. It was this assistance from my spiritual friend, the Bible, that kept me from error and enabled me to speak to the eccentricity of others. Because she helps me discern error in my life and in that of others, I invest the Bible with authority.

To sum up: I listen to the Bible because she has been a spiritual friend, a recognized specialist in religious reality, who introduced me to Jesus, who helps me clarify that relation with Jesus, and who keeps me from eccentricity in my relationship with Jesus.

What Does One Listen For in the Dialogue with the Bible?

That is, what kind of assistance is the Bible qualified to give? For me, the Bible speaks with authority on relational or soteriological matters, not matters of fact. I am aware that this is the dividing line between myself and many of my Christian friends.[9] To my knowledge, however, this issue has not been addressed directly by Southern Baptist moderate leadership.[10] I aim to do that, though briefly.

Let me start with an analogy. We had met, dated, and made commitments. Then she went off to another state to teach for a year. I planned a trip to see her. Before I left, her letter arrived. It told me three things: (a) something about the history of the school; (b) how to get there, especially

---

9. The Evangelical debate is epitomized in two recent books. Rogers and McKim, *Authority and Interpretation of the Bible*, argue that historically the church has asserted the infallibility of the Bible for faith and practice, but that it has never held the inerrancy view in matters of science, history, and geography. Woodbridge, *Biblical Authority*, refuses to accept Rogers's distinction, claiming rather that in church history the central tradition has held both to the infallibility of the saving message and to the inerrancy of the Bible in matters of fact as well. Phillips, "Argument for Inerrancy," 84, contends that if modern inerrantists want to claim support from the church fathers, it is necessary to show not only that they viewed Scripture as inerrant but also that they regarded this as a first order doctrine (i.e., that they were foundationalists).

10. Note the complete absence of any conceptual engagement of the Southern Baptist inerrantists by the Southern Baptist moderates in *The Theological Educator*'s special issue on "The Controversy in the Southern Baptist Convention," 1985. This is representative.

the last stretch which was on state roads, and (c) that she loved me, still wanted to marry me, and was eager for me to arrive. Before I left, I read the catalogue of the school and saw it was not founded in exactly the year the letter said. It was close but not exact. It was exactly right about why the school was founded. Before I left, I got a map of the state where her school was located and checked the highways, including the state roads. All was correct about the directions in the letter except, when I got to the final crossroads, I needed to turn right instead of left. Just the one detail of geography was out of place. When I got there she was truly thrilled to see me. When we talked, she said she did want to get married and set the date. In our general relating to one another, there was no doubt in my mind that she loved me. I had the relational data in the letter verified by my experience with her. The factual data I checked against other sources, finding most things accurate but a couple of items slightly off target. So it is when I listen to the Bible. She is an acknowledged expert in the relational data (how God relates to me, how I am to relate to him, to others, to myself, and to the world). This data, moreover, is validated by my experience with God. Matters of history and science I check against other sources to determine their accuracy. Inaccuracies in matters of fact do not detract from relational truth which is validated in experience.

This I take to be the intent of the Abstract of Principles of the oldest Southern Baptist Theological Seminary when, under "I. The Scriptures," it says:

> The Scriptures of the Old and New Testaments were given by inspiration of God and are the only sufficient, certain and authoritative rule of all *saving* knowledge, faith and obedience.[11]

A position such as that just taken runs directly counter to the Chicago Statement on Biblical Inerrancy (1978).[12] Article XII, in part, reads:

> We deny that Biblical infallibility and inerrancy are limited to spiritual, religious, or redemptive themes, exclusive of assertions in the fields of history and science.

In the Short Statement preceding the 1978 detailed arguments, number 4 says:

---

11. *1985–1987 Catalog: The Southern Baptist Theological Seminary*, 2 (italics mine). Cf. The Constitution on Revelation of the Second Vatican Council, section 11: "The books of Scripture must be acknowledged as teaching firmly, faithfully and without error that truth which God wanted put in the sacred writings *for the sake of our salvation*" (italics mine).

12. Taken from Packer, *God Has Spoken*, 138–53.

> Scripture is without error ... in all its teaching, no less in what it states about God's acts in creation, about the events of world history, and about its own literary origins under God, than in its witness to God's saving grace in individual lives.[13]

An undated statement of 1982, article 6, reiterates the claim:

> We deny that, while Scripture is able to make us wise unto salvation, biblical truth should be defined in terms of this function.[14]

This insistence on extending the Bible's authority beyond the realm of religion into the spheres of science, geography, and history is focused on Jesus's words about the Old Testament. The Chicago Statement (1978), article XV, says:

> We deny that Jesus' teaching about Scripture may be dismissed by appeals to accommodation or to any natural limitation of His humanity.

What this means is that when Jesus speaks in the Gospels about the Old Testament, it is God speaking. What he says is infallible, inerrant not only in moral and spiritual spheres but also in matters of fact. Several examples should suffice. (1) In Matt 12:39–41 Jesus speaks of Jonah as though he were a historical person. The Old Testament book of Jonah, therefore, cannot be fiction but must be history. (2) In Mark 10:4–5 Jesus accepts the Mosaic authorship of Deut 24:1–4; in John 5:45–47 he speaks of Moses as author of parts of Scripture; in John 7:19 he says Moses gave the Law. Moses, therefore, must be the author of the Law. (3) In Matt 22:43–45 Jesus says that David spoke Ps 110:1. David, therefore, must be the author of at least this psalm. (4) In Matt 23:35 Abel is spoken of by Jesus as a historical figure; in

---

13. Stott, in an interview published as "The Church in the Modern World," says: "Simply to say that the Bible is inerrant may be misleading because there are things contained in the Bible that are not affirmed by the Bible. . . . What does it affirm in Genesis 1, 2, and 3? Is it affirming that the world, the universe, was made in six days or not? So we have to argue about the hermeneutical question." Inerrantists argue that the Bible affirms things about science, history, and geography. My contention is that the Scriptures affirm matters soteriological, not scientific, geographical, and historical except as these are inextricably related to its soteriological claims.

14. *Christianity Today* (17 December 1982) 45–48. Packer, "Hermeneutics and Biblical Authority," 3–12, and Packer, *Fundamentalism and the Word of God*, 94–101, follows the Reformers' insight, contending that the Bible's authority is grounded in God's ability to speak through it, disclosing himself and bringing redemption. The meaning of inerrancy is thus not determined in an a priori manner but is formulated on a secondary level, one relating to the primary intent and purpose of Scripture: salvation. Regardless of his posturing, therefore, Packer is close to Jack Rogers. Cf. Phillips, "Argument for Inerrancy," 87, 88, n. 50.

Luke 17:27 Noah is referred to by Jesus as a historical figure. These references guarantee that at least these two parts of Gen 1–11 must be historical fact. This all translates into the proposition: When Jesus speaks, even in the area of matters of fact, it is God the Son speaking.

It is not necessary to do more than scratch the surface of such a position to lay bare its christological presuppositions. They are Apollinarian at worst, Monophysite at best. Neither is in line with Chalcedonian orthodoxy.[15]

The Council of Nicea (AD 325) concluded that Christ was fully God and was made man. On the basis of this Nicene orthodoxy, the further question arose as to the relation of the divine and the human in Christ. One approach to the christological problem involved a practical absorption of his humanity into his divinity. This solution is best exemplified by Apollinaris, bishop of Laodicea in Syria (c. AD 390). Assuming a tripartite anthropology, Apollinaris said that Jesus had a human body and a human soul but instead of a human mind there was the divine Logos, the second member of the Trinity. Since this denied Christ's humanity, it was condemned by Rome in 377 and 382, by Antioch in 378, and finally by the so-called Second Ecumenical Council of Constantinople in AD 381. The solution that eventually won out was that decided at Chalcedon in AD 451. The creed spoke of Christ as "in *two natures,* inconfusedly, unchangeably ... the *distinction of natures being by no means taken away by the union,* but rather the *property of each nature being preserved,* and concurring in one person and one subsistence ... the Lord Jesus Christ."[16] The subsequent opponents of Chalcedon were the Monophysites, the believers in one nature. They contended that the human in Christ was real but that it was so subordinated that the ultimate reality was the divine. Whether it was Apollinaris before Chalcedon or the Monophysites afterwards, their position was such that Jesus's humanity was swallowed up by his divinity. With Apollinaris the focus was on Jesus's mind. It was not human or subject to human limitations but rather was the second person of the Trinity, God the Son. So when Jesus spoke, even on matters of fact, he transcended human limitations. Although this error was rejected decisively by Chalcedon (in two natures ... the distinction of natures being by no means taken away ... the property of each nature being preserved), it has reared its head again in these last days in the guise of biblical inerrancy. When inerrantists argue that when Christ speaks even about matters of fact it is God talking, we are

---

15. For what follows, see Lohse, *Short History of Doctrine*, 82–95. An argument similar to my own may be found in Brown, "And the Lord Said," 3–19.

16. Calvin, *Institutes,* 11.14.1 (italics mine), echoed Chalcedon when he said, "The divinity was so conjoined and united with the humanity, that *the entire properties of each nature remain entire,* and yet the two natures constitute only one Christ" (italics mine).

to recognize it for what it is, Apollinarian heresy at worst, Monophysite error at best. If Christ's humanity is not to be seen in his being a man of his own time in the area of matters of fact, then I fail to see where his humanity is to be found insofar as his human mind is concerned.

It is not difficult to understand why inerrantists cannot abide the orthodox Chalcedonian affirmation of Jesus's humanity, including the time-conditioned character of his human knowledge in matters of fact. It is because there is in biblical inerrancy a massive confusion about the relationship between finitude and sin. Edward J. Young puts the inerrantists' position succinctly:

> Yet if Jesus, in his human nature, was subject to fallibility, then, of course, he was not what he claimed to be. He was subject to sin (for *fallibility is the consequence of sin*) and so he cannot be our Savior.[17]

I cannot agree. In matters of fact, fallibility is not the result of sin but the natural by-product of human finitude (for example, Rom 6:19).[18] Our finitude, moreover, is not something that is evil but something good, because it was created by God (Gen 1:31). It is, however, sin to reject one's finitude and to grasp for divine knowledge (Gen 3:5–6). For Jesus to have been a man of his own time in his knowledge of matters of fact would not have subverted either his divinity or his sinlessness but instead would have guaranteed his full humanity, including finitude, even the finitude of limited knowledge in matters of fact. Only if he were truly human (including finitude), as well as divine and sinless, could he be our Savior. It is a soteriological necessity to maintain the Chalcedonian confession (in two natures . . . the distinction of natures being by no means taken away . . . the property of each nature being preserved) if we are to believe our own finitude, including our mental limitations, is not rejected by God but will be participant in the salvation of the Last Day, the resurrection from the dead.[19] Christological orthodoxy, therefore, argues for a distinction between matters of fact and matters of religion, not only in the Bible as a whole but also in one's understanding

---

17. Young, *Thy Word Is Truth*, 77–78 (italics mine). The same underlying confusion is implicit in the 1982 statement reported by *Christianity Today* (17 December 1982) 47. Article 2 reads, "We deny that the humble, human form of Scripture entails errancy any more than the humanity of Christ, even in His humiliation entails sin."

18. Although the identification of sin and evil with ignorance of the finite mind is very general in the pre-Augustinian period of Christianity, its source is Hellenistic culture, not biblical faith. Cf. Niebuhr, *Nature and Destiny of Man*, 167–77.

19. Warfield, *Person and Work of Christ*, 211, said, "No two natures, no Incarnation; no Incarnation, no Christianity." Warfield did not, however, see the implications of this correct doctrinal confession for his view of biblical authority.

of the Jesus of the Gospels. It is with a sense of assurance, then, that in my dialogue with the Bible, I listen obediently to what she says about relational or soteriological matters, and find in my ongoing experience with God her wisdom to be fully justified.

Works Cited

Brown, R. E. "'And the Lord Said'? Biblical Reflections of Scripture as the Word of God." *TS* 42 (1981) 3–19.
Bultmann, Rudolf. *Jesus and the Word*. New York: Scribner, 1958.
Calvin, John. *Institutes of the Christian Religion*. Translated by Henry Beveridge. Ontario: Devoted, 2016.
Edwards, Tilden H. *Spiritual Friend: Reclaiming the Gift of Spiritual Direction*. Mahwah, NJ: Paulist, 1980.
Fuchs, Joseph. "Sin and Conversion." In *Conversion: Perspectives on Personal and Social Transformation,* edited by Walter E. Conn, 247–62. New York: Alba House, 1978.
Hordern, William. *A Layman's Guide to Protestant Theology*. New York: MacMillan, 1955.
Kelsey, David H. *The Uses of Scripture in Recent Theology*. Philadelphia: Fortress, 1975.
Minear, Paul. *To Heal and to Reveal*. New York: Seabury, 1976.
Kerr, Hugh T., and John M. Mulder, eds. *Conversions: The Christian Experience*. Grand Rapids: Eerdmans, 1983.
Lohse, Bernhard. *A Short History of Doctrine*. Translated by F. E. Stoeffler. Philadelphia: Fortress, 1966.
Niebuhr, Reinhold. *The Nature and Destiny of Man*. New York: Scribner, 1955.
Packer, J. I. *Fundamentalism and the Word of God*. Grand Rapids: Eerdmans, 1972.
———. *God Has Spoken*. Downers Grove, IL: InterVarsity, 1979.
———. "Hermeneutics and Biblical Authority." *Themelios* 1 (1975) 3–12.
Phillips, Timothy R. "The Argument for Inerrancy: An Analysis." *Journal of the American Scientific Affiliation* 31 (1979) 80–88.
Rogers, Jack B., and Donald K. McKim. *The Authority and Interpretation of the Bible*. San Francisco: Harper & Row, 1979.
Stott, John R. W. "The Church in the Modern World." *Mission Journal* 19 (1985) 3–7.
Talbert, Charles H. "The Bible as Spiritual Friend." *PRSt* 13 (1986) 55–64.
Warfield, B. B. *The Person and Work of Christ*. Philadelphia: Presbyterian and Reformed, 1950.
Woodbridge, John D. *Biblical Authority*. Grand Rapids: Zondervan, 1982.
Young, Edward J. *Thy Word Is Truth*. Grand Rapids: Eerdmans, 1957.

Restoring the New Testament Church?

Baptist Self-Perception(s) in America from the Mid-Nineteenth to the Early Twentieth Century

C. Douglas Weaver

SOUTHERN BAPTIST E. Y. Mullins is often credited with providing the most definitive statement of Baptist identity in the twentieth century, surely for Southern Baptists, but also for many other Baptists during his era.[1] Mullins provided a set of Baptist principles, called axioms of religion, which he said were derived from the distinctive historical characteristic of Baptists, the competency of the soul in relationship to God. These axioms were: (1) "the theological axiom: the holy and loving God has a right to be sovereign"; (2) "the religious axiom: all men have an equal right to direct access to God"; (3) "the ecclesiastical axiom: all believers have a right to equal privileges in the church"; (4) "the moral axiom: to be responsible the soul must be free"; (5) "the religio-civic axiom: a free church in a free state"; (6) "the social axiom: love your neighbor as yourself."[2]

Mullins offered his axioms as a "fresh" restatement of historic Baptist principles, but the practice of identifying Baptists with a set of principles had begun in the 1840s and had roots among the earliest English Baptists.[3]

---

1. This essay is derived from a previous work by the same name. Permission to use from *Mirrors and Microscopes*, Copyright © C. Douglas Weaver 2015. Published by Paternoster, Milton Keynes, UK. Naymond Keathley has deep roots in Baptist life and it is with gratitude that this essay is published in his honor. I am grateful to be his colleague.

2. Mullins, *Axioms of Religion*, 76.

3. Weaver, "Introduction," in Mullins, *Axioms of Religion*, 1–35. Mullins's use of the term soul competency was new, but the present essay notes that the focus on personal direct relationship to God was already common in Baptist life. See the list of principles in "A Declaration of Faith of English People," 114–22. James Leo Garrett noted that the

The lists of distinctives are remarkably similar. For example, in 1846, William B. Johnson, first president of the Southern Baptist Convention, wrote that Baptists "hold the true fundamental principles of the gospel of Christ. These are the sovereignty of God in the provision and application of the plan of salvation, the supreme authority of the scriptures, the right of each individual to judge for himself in his views of truth as taught in the scriptures, the independent, democratical, Christocratic form of church government, the profession of religion by conscious subjects only, and the other principles of scripture truth growing out of these or intimately connected with them."[4] In 1857, Francis Wayland, President of Brown University, summarized Baptist principles as "the doctrines of the spirituality of the church, the right of private judgment, the perfect sufficiency of the Scriptures as a rule of faith and practice, and the absolute separation of Church and State." In sum, Wayland noted, "we have stood for apostolic Christianity and the inalienable rights of conscience."[5]

The goal of this study will be to analyze American Baptist self-identity from 1845, the date of Southern Baptist origins, up to 1925, or the Mullins era, particularly from writings of Northern and Southern Baptists that gave focused attention to a declaration of Baptist principles. The broad thesis is that these Baptists viewed themselves as restoring or embodying the New Testament church. They believed their principles were an emulation of the apostolic model of the church, and, in these decades of intense denominational competition, they believed they followed the model better than anyone else. Most Baptists did not assess their Christian neighbors as bluntly as Landmark leader, J. R. Graves, did when he called other groups religious societies rather than churches. Nevertheless, as Southern Baptist R. B. C. Howell declared, failure to honor any of the Baptist principles would cause "irreparable injury" to the faith.[6] In essence, Baptists agreed with New York pastor John Quincy Adams that they were the most thorough religious reformers, having alone restored New Testament Christianity.[7]

---

delineation of Baptist principles was a rarity in early Baptist life, but the genre of "the exposition and/or defense of Baptist distinctives or emphases" came into existence in the 1840s and 1850s. Garrett, *Baptist Theology*, 531–32.

4. Johnson, *Gospel Developed*, 16.
5. Wayland, *Notes on the Principles*, 138–39.
6. Howell, *Early Baptists of Virginia*, 10.
7. Adams, *Baptists*.

The Role of Scripture

Baptists were clear that one indispensable foundational identity marker was the centrality of Scripture as the sole authority for religious faith and practice. Most authors began their discussion of Baptist principles with a focus on Scripture. American Baptist missionary, W. B. Boggs, said that the "final authority of the Bible" was the great fundamental principle for Baptists.[8] A. E. Dickenson, a Virginia Baptist editor, called the Bible the "bedrock of Baptist faith ... The Word of God is the sovereign, and this sovereign has no parliament and no prime minister."[9] Baptists strongly affirmed the "all-sufficiency of Scripture" for religious faith and practice.[10] With hyperbolic flair, William B. Johnson exhorted that the "the Bible is the religion of Christians."[11] Francis Wayland concluded, "in all matters of religious belief and practice, (it is) the New Testament, the whole New Testament, and nothing but the New Testament."[12]

The description of Baptist identity in terms of Scripture was almost always accompanied by a negative assessment of church tradition as a source of religious authority. John Quincy Adams, for example, said that the first feature of a thorough reformation was the "exaltation of the Word of God over tradition." Tradition added the "innovations of men" like infant baptism which invalidated the "commandments of God."[13] The "all-sufficiency of Scripture," on the other hand, "eliminates the authority of councils, popes, synods, conferences, bishops etc."[14]

One aspect of tradition that Baptists gave extensive attention to was creeds. Baptists had long utilized confessions of faith to help identify themselves, but had only rarely used historic creeds. Southern Baptist John Broadus said that confessions of faith could be useful—his employer, Southern Seminary, used an "abstract of principles"—but that Baptists were not "bound" by them except by "voluntary agreement."[15] Other Baptists agreed, noting that creeds were acceptable as "expressions of belief" but were never authoritative because the Bible was the only standard for

---

8. Boggs, *Baptists*, 6.
9. Dickenson, "What Baptist Principles Are Worth," 267–68.
10. Gambrell, "Obligations of Baptists," 252.
11. Johnson, *Gospel Developed*, 15.
12. Wayland, *Notes on the Principles*, 86.
13. Adams, *Baptists*, 51–52.
14. Gambrell, "Obligations of Baptists," 252.
15. Broadus, *Duty of Baptists*, 6.

orthodoxy.[16] What could be called a striking characteristic, but in reality was an ordinary one, was that Baptists in America never appealed to historic creeds, or even Baptist confessions, to assert their commitment to Scripture or other tenets of the faith.

Most authors were strongly critical of "man-made" creeds because of the tendency to give them authority rather than to the Bible. Francis Wayland criticized the idea that historic creeds were the best basis for unifying believers. On the contrary, Wayland noted, creeds do not have the power to create or preserve unity. The use of creeds had not produced unity in Roman Catholicism or in Protestant groups that relied on them.[17] New York pastor, Thomas Armitage, had little use for creeds. Armitage noted that some, though not all, churches had articles of faith. In any case, creeds never had any ecclesiastical or theological authority for Baptists; a creed was worth nothing unless it was supported by Scriptural authority. "If the creed is founded on the Word of God," Armitage concluded, "we do not see why we should not rest on that Word which props up the creed."[18] Texas Baptist leader, B. H. Carroll, was perhaps the bluntest in the assessment of creedal tradition when he said that creeds were "as variant and conflicting as their composers and all are without a shred of authority."[19]

Dissenting voices were few to this self-understanding of Scripture and tradition in Baptist life. The development of more progressive Baptists associated with the social gospel and/or modernism joined the chorus against creeds and "dead authority." Wallace Buttrick of New York, a supporter of the new modern methods of critical biblical study, said that creeds of the fourth century were built upon philosophical assumptions of that day and only used Scripture as proof texts. Buttrick concluded that creeds erred in attempting to put Christian truth in some logical order, which was contrary to the ethical focus in biblical revelation.[20] At the same time, the development of new biblical critical study and liberalism in this era brought a different view of Scripture as well. Walter Rauschenbusch, for example, affirmed the centrality of the Bible over creeds but he warned against conservatives who made the Bible into "one huge creed" and who demanded conformity to their interpretation. Rauschenbusch concluded, "A creed tells you what you must believe; the Bible tells you what holy men have believed."[21]

16. Forrester, *Baptist Position*, 3.
17. Wayland, *Notes on the Principles*, 14–15, 44.
18. Armitage, "Baptist Faith and Practice," 33–34.
19. Carroll, *Ecclesia*, 14.
20. Buttrick, *Distinctive Views of Baptists*, 10–14.
21. Rauschenbusch, "Why I Am a Baptist."

The Nature of the Church

Baptists since their origins in the 1600s affirmed that following biblical authority included the command to restore and embody the New Testament church. Some Baptists disagreed with certain points in the Old Landmark system of J. R. Graves such as equating the kingdom with the aggregate of local Baptist churches.[22] However, no Baptist writer disagreed with the depiction Graves employed that Baptists, in insisting on a regenerate church membership rooted in personal voluntary faith and believer's baptism by immersion, "place Christ before the church while others place church before Christ." Non-Baptist religious societies, Graves added, "put the water before the blood and made it necessary to reach the blood through the water."[23] In other words, Baptists were the only Christians who affirmed the New Testament command to establish the church on voluntary profession of faith in Christ as Savior followed by believer's baptism rather than upon the involuntary nature of infant baptism and the heresy of salvific grace through sacraments.

Since their origins, Baptists rejected infant baptism based on their reading of Scripture. In this era of sustained denominational competition, Baptists never wavered from this principle. They never tired of expounding upon the proper meaning of the word baptize. Infant baptism was not biblical, they argued, but was a post-apostolic innovation of church tradition that sullied the purity of the regenerate visible church. With the adoption of infant baptism, the church was no longer separated from the world. The spirituality of the church, a phrase that Baptists used to denote a regenerate church, had been sacrificed to worldliness via the tradition of having church members who had never professed faith in Christ.[24] In addressing the idea that infant baptism had developed as a "discretionary move" to meet the needs of ministering to the pagan Roman world, South Carolina Baptist educator, Thomas Curtis, strongly objected by appealing to the Baptist commitment to embodying the New Testament church. According to Curtis, the church had no permission to add to the "original construction of Christ's visible church." Visible churches "are simply executive bodies, not legislative. Their duty is to carry out the laws of Christ, not to make laws of their own."[25]

---

22. Dargan, *Society, Kingdom and Church*. See also Mullins, *Axioms of Religion*, 49–58.

23. Graves, *Old Landmarkism*, 43, 51.

24. Adams, *Baptists*, iii, 71; Armitage, "Baptist Faith and Practice," 40.

25. Curtis, *Progress of Baptist Principles*, 235.

Not surprisingly, then, infant baptism was pictured as the root of all ecclesiastical evils produced by dependence on fallible tradition rather than the authority of Scripture. Francis Wayland called infant baptism and its "hereditary membership" "the great curse of the Christian church."[26] Baptist criticism of Roman Catholicism began with infant baptism. According to Texas Baptist leaders, James Gambrell and later G. W. Truett, infant baptism was the "cornerstone of popery."[27] William Whitsitt of Southern Baptist Theological Seminary explained that infant baptism was the "source of formalism in religious life and superficiality of religious experience, the Pandora's box of evil to the church and to the cause of piety and the main pillar of popery."[28] And in a bit of nativist flair, Northern Baptist fundamentalist, A. C. Dixon, referenced the growing "foreign problem" in America at the outset of the twentieth century to contend that infant baptism introduced a foreign element into the church and consequently wiped out the distinction between the church and the world.[29] The rejection of infant baptism seemed obvious to Baptist identity—the New Testament church did not allow it.

The Place of the Individual

Intertwined throughout Baptist history with the commitment to Scriptural authority and the restoration of the New Testament church has been a focus on the individual, especially an indispensable role for freedom of conscience. Brief mention has already been made of the centrality of believer's baptism based upon a voluntary personal profession of faith as a condition for church membership. Baptists called this the voluntary principle.[30] Several Baptists in this era actually found the distinguishing mark of Baptists in this individual faith. New Jersey pastor, Henry Fish, declared that the distinguishing tenet of Baptists was "direct personal and individual responsibility before God." Highlighting the direct, unmediated connection, Fish added, "to God each man, for himself, either stands or falls."[31] Walter Rauschenbusch gave as his first reason for being a Baptist "the primacy of personal religious ex-

---

26. Wayland, *Notes on the Principles*, 97.

27. Gambrell, "Obligations of Baptists," 251; Truett, "Baptists and Religious Liberty," 7.

28. Whitsitt, "Position of the Baptists," 7.

29. Dixon, *Points in the Baptist Position*, 8.

30. Howell, *Early Baptists of Virginia*, 100–101; Gambrell, "Obligations of Baptists," 245, 251; Burrows, *What Baptists Believe*, 19–34; Truett, "Baptists and Religious Liberty," 3.

31. Fish, *Price of Soul Liberty*, 20.

perience." "We are an evangelistic body," Rauschenbusch noted, "We ask a man: 'have you put your faith in Christ?' . . . We do not ask him to recite a creed." Spiritual experience is the "only essential thing in religion" and when Baptists insist on it "we are hewing our way back to original Christianity."[32] E. Y. Mullins continued this self-perception with his now well-known assertion that soul competency—each person had the God-given freedom and ability to have direct, personal relationship with God—was the historical contribution of Baptists to Christian faith.[33]

Baptists consistently declared without hesitation their commitment to the right of each individual to read and interpret Scripture without dependence upon external authorities. The gift of private interpretation of Scripture meant direct, personal accountability toward God; in other words, "no Pope, priest, council or creed should come between him and God." Put positively and confidently, A. C. Dixon implored, "In the spirit of love every Christian may ask all who would come between him and the light of revelation to stand aside, that the glory of God's truth may shine full upon him."[34] In language popular with all Americans, Northern Baptist theological educator, Albert Newman, and Southerner, J. B. Gambrell, declared this gift of individual interpretation to be an "inalienable right" which correlated with the principle of individualism in religion.[35]

The triangle of emphases on Scripture, church, and the individual were expressed in the Baptist identity markers of congregational church polity and the priesthood of believers. These were, of course, mandated clearly in the New Testament church, Baptists said, but they also were natural corollaries from the focus on personal voluntary faith, individual conscience, and personal direct accountability to God. Baptists asserted that the local New Testament church was a voluntary society of professing believers.[36] Each congregation, with each person having a vote as an expression of the equality of Christ's disciples, must be free to answer directly to God.[37] The church should be a Christocracy, argued William. B. Johnson, or a theocracy since God is to be sovereign, contended A. C. Dixon, but all Baptist writers believed that democracy was the best method of church organization this side

---

32. Rauschenbusch, "Why I Am a Baptist," 2.

33. Mullins, *Axioms of Religion*, 66. See American Baptist book editor, Philip Jones, who mentions and follows Mullins. Jones, *Restatement of Baptist Principles*, 13–17.

34. Dixon, *Points in the Baptist Position*, 1.

35. Newman, "Baptist Churches Apostolical," 240; Gambrell, "Obligations of Baptists," 250.

36. Curtis, *Progress of Baptist Principles*, 239.

37. Adams, *Baptists*, 112, 122; Armitage, "Baptist Faith and Practice," 38.

of heaven.[38] The local church with its democratic participation of professing believers, Baptists believed, was the most effective agent of church discipline and guardian of doctrinal orthodoxy.[39] Baptists had preached democratic church government since the 1600s, but not surprisingly, they uncritically viewed the progress of Baptist growth and American democracy in this era as a sort of Baptist monopoly. The growth of American democracy vindicated for them the triumph of Baptist principles.[40]

The Baptist insistence on equality before God was seen in a fierce aversion to hierarchy, especially the elevation of ministerial authority.[41] Sacramentalism bred sacerdotalism, the idea that those clergy who administered the sacraments were part of an elevated church hierarchy necessary to dispense grace to the laity.[42] Hierarchy was not needed, Baptists argued, because the New Testament was a "revelation to every person"; there was no church or minister set apart to interpret for everyone else.[43] New York pastor, Wallace Buttrick, said that the pastor was "first among equals" but he had no special authority. While ordinances were performed by ministers, they did so, Buttrick noted, because of order but the laity surely could do any ministerial task.[44] The church was a spiritual democracy, all Baptists declared.[45] As J. B. Jeter of Virginia noted, they practiced New Testament Christianity, not a hierarchical "churchianity" which focused on ecclesiastical power and salvation through sacrament.[46] In contrast to hierarchy, Baptists advocated the priesthood of believers. This biblical principle affirmed the direct relationship of each believer to God without the necessity of human mediators.[47] Benjamin True of Rochester Theological Seminary asserted that sacerdotalism, with its "mediatorial priesthood," denied every person's "fundamental right to have direct personal dealings" with God and assumes to "monopolize the application of saving and efficient grace."[48]

---

38. Johnson, *Gospel Developed*, 16; Dixon, *Points in the Baptist Position*, 10.

39. Whitsitt, "Position of the Baptists," 13.

40. Dickenson, "What Baptist Principles Are Worth," 275–76.

41. Jeter, "Distinctive Baptist Principles," 124.

42. Carroll, *Ecclesia*, 153; Curtis, *Progress of Baptist Principles*, 80; Truett, "Baptists and Religious Liberty," 5.

43. Curry, *Baptist Church Radically Different*, 2. See Wayland, *Notes on the Principles*, 123.

44. Buttrick, *Distinctive Views of Baptists*, 21–24.

45. Mullins, *Why Is Christianity True*, 351.

46. Jeter, "Distinctive Baptist Principles," 125.

47. Wayland, *Notes on the Principles*, 131; Eaton, *Faith of Baptists*, 16.

48. True, "Baptists and Religious Liberty," 241.

The focus on personal faith in Baptist identity was most strongly trumpeted in the insistence upon freedom of conscience and religious liberty for all. J. B. Jeter exclaimed that Baptists had been "unswervingly loyal to the principle of religious liberty" since "the liberty to worship God according to the dictates of conscience is the dearest of all human rights."[49] Francis Wayland said that religious freedom was the "peculiar glory of the Baptists."[50] Several authors like Thomas Armitage felt so strongly that they declared that if a Baptist ever denied religious freedom to anyone, that person would cease to be a Baptist.[51]

Most Baptists highlighted the role of Baptist predecessors, especially Roger Williams, to trumpet their legacy of commitment to religious liberty and freedom of conscience.[52] They often employed Williams's term soul liberty. In 1860, Northern Baptist, Henry Fish, dedicated an entire treatise to the topic entitled *The Price of Soul Liberty*.[53] In language reminiscent of the earliest English Baptists and foreshadowing E. Y. Mullins, John Quincy Adams used the concept of competence to get to the crux of the matter. Religious freedom "acknowledges no human authority competent to come between the conscience and its Maker in reference to his will and duty." When Christians departed from the authority of Scripture for church tradition, Adams added, the rights of conscience were crushed.[54] Baptists often emphasized that they were dissenters persecuted on behalf of conscience. Thomas Armitage employed another phrase from Roger Williams—"the bloody tenent"—to affirm that soul liberty was obtained at a great price of persecution.[55] Because of soul liberty, T. T. Eaton insisted, no one came "between the individual soul and Christ. He and He alone is Lord of the conscience."[56]

---

49. Jeter, "Distinctive Baptist Principles," 120, 122.

50. Wayland, *Notes on the Principles*, 137.

51. Armitage, "Baptist Faith and Practice," 47; Jeter, "Distinctive Baptist Principles," 122–23; Curry, *Baptist Church Radically Different*, 6.

52. Almost every author cited the importance of Roger Williams. For example, see Dickenson, "What Baptist Principles Are Worth," 265; Forrester, *Baptist Position*, 82, 87; True, "Baptists and Religious Liberty," 252.

53. Fish, *Price of Soul Liberty*, 19.

54. Adams, *Baptists*, 91. In addition to affirming the competency of each person to go directly to God, Mullins and early English Baptists said that the state, like ecclesiastical hierarchies, was "incompetent" to judge spiritual matters. Mullins, *Why Is Christianity True*, 166.

55. Armitage, "Baptist Faith and Practice," 36–37.

56. Eaton, *Faith of Baptists*, 12.

Modern historians quickly note that the relationship of Baptists and church-state separation is not monolithic, but is complicated. Yet in this era, Baptists argued their affirmation of soul liberty meant a strong declaration for "absolute" or "entire" separation.[57] Religious freedom was for all people of all faiths or no faith, and no civil government or church could take that God-given freedom away. G. W. Truett's 1920 sermon on the steps of the Capitol in Washington, D.C. became the most well-known statement of this Baptist self-perception, but Baptist leaders before Truett were all saying the same thing. In 1857, Thomas Curtis, for example, said that non-Baptists had accepted the Baptist-led truth of separation of church and state so there was little need to debate the point.[58] E. C. Morris, first president of the African American National Baptist Convention, preached that Baptists had been persecuted on account of their "unrelenting war for absolute separation of church and state" and the "absolute liberty of conscience" and Americans owed them a debt for this gift that could never be repaid.[59]

Could the Baptist principle of freedom of individual conscience be abused? Yes, Baptists acknowledged the possibility. G. E. Horr, President of Newton Theological Institute, and A. C. Dixon noted that some freedom is given up where there is cooperation with others. Individualism needed to be "married to fraternity"; independence and interdependence should work together.[60] The conscience was to be enlightened and guided by the Scriptures.[61] Walter Rauschenbusch and other social gospelers leveled significant attacks against an individualistic evangelism that ignored the social nature of the gospel message and the social nature of humanity. Even E. Y. Mullins was careful to defend his focus on soul competency from the charge of excessive individualism by noting regenerate individuals engaged in social ministry.[62] At the same time, Mullins captured the Baptist sense of the risks and rewards of preserving access to individual conscience when he discussed the Protestant/Baptist emphasis on reading Scripture:

> The right of private judgment is a dangerous word, but it is a winged and emancipating word. It is the sole guaranty that

---

57. Forrester, *Baptist Position*, 82; Whitsitt, "Position of the Baptists," 9; Howell, *Early Baptists of Virginia*, 10.

58. Curtis, *Progress of Baptist Principles*, 15.

59. Morris, "Infallible Proofs of the Perpetuity," 29–30.

60. Dixon, *Points in the Baptist Position*, 11. Horr said freedom was limited by the general position of the group to which a person voluntarily belongs. Horr, *Baptist Heritage*, 94.

61. Adams, *Baptists*, 108.

62. Weaver, "E. Y. Mullins," 445–60.

> man will pass out of the childhood to the manhood stage of religion... It was the hammer with which Roger Williams broke the chain which united church and state.... The right of private judgment; yes, a dangerous word, but a word which started man on a new voyage of spiritual discovery.... It is true it produced the sects of Protestantism. But these, after all, are not comets or wandering stars without central control, plunging blindly through space.... Loyalty to Christ balances their right of private judgment and is the guaranty that the faith of the New Testament shall not perish from the earth.[63]

In sum, Baptists of this era relied on a belief in a common commitment to Jesus Christ as Lord, to the final authority of the Scriptures, and to a common personal experience of grace. Individuals with these common commitments might express some diversity, but they could achieve spiritual unity.[64]

Whatever the creative or disruptive tensions between the relationship between Scripture, personal faith, and the attempt to restore the New Testament church, Baptists did not abandon freedom of conscience. Dissenters might be rejected by a local church but dissent was not silenced. Why? Because Baptist Christian identity was ultimately eschatological. Each and every person must have freedom of conscience because each must meet Christ face to face and be accountable to him in the Last Judgment. No church, no church leaders, and no civil magistrate would be there or be accountable in place of him or her.

This self-perception, an eschatologically formed ecclesiology, had been present among Baptists throughout their history.[65] Francis Wayland testified concerning access to the Scriptures: "they were given to every individual that he might understand them for himself, and the word that is given him will judge him at the great day. It is hence evident that we can have no standards which claim to be of any authority over us."[66] In exhorting Baptists who might be hesitant to obey God's command to do mission work, B. H. Carroll declared that the church could not absolve anyone from individual duty because "they do not stand before the great white throne of judgment. But thy soul shall appear before the Judge. Well did our Lord know that there could be no evangelization of the world if ancestors, families, customs, government, commerce, and priests could

---

63. Mullins, "Baptist Life in the World's Life," 312.
64. Mullins, *Christian Religion in Its Doctrinal Expression*, 346.
65. Weaver, "Early English Baptists," 141–58.
66. Wayland, *Notes on the Principles*, 14.

stand between the individual soul and God."[67] With rhetorical flair, A. E. Dickenson concluded, "soul freedom comes with the adoption of Baptist principles as day comes with the rising sun. It is the inevitable, local outgrowth of the doctrine that each must hear for himself, repent for himself, believe for himself, confess Christ for himself, and be baptized for himself that as we come one by one into the world, so we must go to Christ one by one for mercy, and at least go one by one out of the world, to be judged according to the deeds done in the body."[68] Belief in the Last Judgment, Baptist identity affirmed, required freedom of conscience. Thus, these Baptists practiced an eschatological ecclesiology that preserved and allowed conscience for authentic voluntary Christian identity.

Conclusion

There are, of course, other avenues toward assessing Baptist identity in the late nineteenth and early twentieth centuries. Baptist responses to slavery obviously reveal a large divide between Northern and Southern Baptists. A deeply rooted, pervasive sense of Anglo superiority is obvious and race cannot be ignored in telling the Baptist story. Some theological diversity was always present, despite Baptist protestations to the contrary, and increased with modifications to the prevailing Calvinism and the onset of biblical criticism and liberalism. The story of the Baptist move from rural to urban at different speeds, but in both North and South, is another nuance to the story. For example, David Benedict's 1860 book *Fifty Years Among the Baptists* reveals an angst about Baptist trends toward urbanization, centralization, and professionalization, themes already seen earlier in the nineteenth century in the writings of John Leland, the Anti-Missions Movement, and Landmarkism.[69] In one of the rare citations of social class in Baptist declarations about identity, William Whitsitt reminded an audience of seminary students that their heritage was one of being the "common people" rather than those that sought power through politics. To remember this, Whitsitt contended, was "better for the cause of pure Christianity."[70]

All of the issues that rightly fascinate historians, however, were not key themes in the intentional descriptions of Baptist identity that flourished in this era. When Baptists talked about who they were, they declared triumphantly that they were the best hope for Christianity; they were the

---

67. Carroll, *Ecclesia*, 150.
68. Dickenson, "What Baptist Principles Are Worth," 274.
69. Benedict, *Fifty Years Among the Baptists*.
70. Whitsitt, "Position of the Baptists," 13.

embodiment of the New Testament church. Even the more ecumenical and liberal trends among many Northern Baptists did not stop Walter Rauschenbusch from affirming that the Baptist focus on personal religious experience was "hewing our way back to original Christianity."[71]

Baptists did reveal some nuance in describing the heart of their faith. Some like Albert Newman and G. W. Truett announced that the doctrine of the "absolute Lordship of Christ" was the most fundamental characteristic of "apostolical churches."[72] It was thus the "nerve center," the "bedrock" of Baptist life.[73] Several authors cited the all-sufficiency of Scripture as the foundational Baptist principle. And others, before and along with E. Y. Mullins, saw the heart of the faith in the voluntary principle and the free, direct relationship of the soul to God. Baptists always affirmed believer's baptism by immersion but they never highlighted this ordinance—which they acknowledged was the distinctive non-Baptists cited—as their most important principle. Their practice of baptism was the "formal expression" or "external principle" of their more fundamental distinctives.[74] Indeed, Northern Baptist William Wilkinson defended the Baptist insistence on believer's baptism by immersion from charges of bigotry, intolerance, and self-conceit when he declared the essential Baptist distinctive to be obedience to Christ.[75]

In 1920, Kentucky Baptist leader, Victor Masters, revealed a Baptist sense of chosenness when he declared, "As goes America, so goes the world. Largely as goes the South, so goes America. And in the South is the Baptist center of gravity of the world."[76] Baptists in this era of religious competition were naturally conditioned by a need for certainty and an aura of triumphalism. They thought that they were either not really Protestant or the only Protestants that had logically followed through with the commitment to *sola Scriptura*. This was also the era when Protestants and Catholics engaged in cold war amid Vatican I statements about infallibility and Protestant nativist fears of rapid immigration of Catholics to America. While the ecumenical movement took root among Northern Baptist leaders in the early twentieth century, the anti-ecumenical posture of Baptists exhibited defensiveness about the rapid cultural and theological changes swirling

---

71. Rauschenbusch, "Why I Am a Baptist," 4.

72. Newman, "Baptist Churches Apostolical," 200; Truett, "Baptists and Religious Liberty," 4.

73. Truett, "Baptists and Religious Liberty," 4.

74. Horr, *Baptist Heritage*, 88; Howell, *Early Baptists of Virginia*, 9.

75. Wilkinson, "Baptist Denomination," 253.

76. Weaver, *In Search of the New Testament Church*, 66.

around them. Many non-Baptists revealed similar attitudes, though Baptists clearly expressed their sense of being the apostolic church with vigor and gusto second to none.

Ethical judgments or explanations aside, what is fascinating about Baptists of this period is their consistent pattern of self-identity in terms of a set of principles that they offered as a coherent, biblical understanding of Christian identity. These principles did not negate diversity; with their focus on voluntarism, they often provided for it. However, Baptists were unwilling to separate their distinctives; they viewed them as a seamless robe of obedience. If one held to the Lordship of Christ and the final authority of the Scriptures, then a focus on church and the individual was inevitable. What was most important was the (elusive) need to restore the New Testament professing, regenerate church, which was rooted in the centrality of voluntary personal religious experience of Christ. At the gates of heaven, each believer would be held accountable for his or her actions. Consequently, freedom of conscience was absolutely, eschatologically necessary this side of the pearly gates. Individual and community, Scripture and Christ—Baptists found them indispensably intertwined. It was never one or the other(s).

Works Cited

Adams, John Quincy. *Baptists, the Only Thorough Religious Reformers*. 1876. Reprint, Paris, AR: Baptist Standard Bearer, 2008.
Armitage, Thomas. "Baptist Faith and Practice." In *Baptist Doctrines*, edited by Charles A. Jenkens, 30–48. St. Louis: Chancy R. Barns, 1880.
Benedict, David. *Fifty Years Among the Baptists*. New York: Sheldon, 1860.
Boggs, William B. *The Baptists: Who Are They? And What Do They Believe?* Philadelphia: American Baptist Publication Society, 1877.
Broadus, John A. *The Duty of Baptists to Teach Their Distinctive Views*. Philadelphia: American Baptist Publication Society, 1881.
Burrows, J. L. *What Baptists Believe*. Baltimore, MD: H. M. Wharton, 1887.
Buttrick, Wallace. *Distinctive Views of Baptists*. Albany, NY: Albania, 1898.
Carroll, B. H. *Ecclesia: The Church, Bible Class Lecture, February, 1903*. Reprint, Paris, AR: Baptist Standard Bearer, Inc., 2006.
Curry, J. L. M. *A Baptist Church Radically Different from Pedobaptist Churches*. Philadelphia: American Baptist Publication Society, 1889.
Curtis, Thomas. *The Progress of Baptist Principles in the Last Hundred Years*. Philadelphia: American Baptist Publication Society, 1857.
Dargan, E. C. *Society, Kingdom and Church*. Philadelphia: American Baptist Publication Society, 1907.
"A Declaration of Faith of English People Remaining at Amsterdam, 1611." In *Baptist Confessions of Faith*, edited by William Lumpkin, 116–21. Valley Forge, PA: Judson, 1969.

Dickenson, A. E. "What Baptist Principles Are Worth to the World." In *Baptist Principles Reset*, edited by Jeremiah B. Jeter, 257–85. Dallas: Standard, 1902.

Dixon, A. C. *Points in the Baptist Position*. Philadelphia: American Baptist Publication Society, n.d. [c.a. 1907].

Eaton, T. T. *The Faith of Baptists*. Louisville: Baptist Book Concern, 1898.

Forrester, E. J. *The Baptist Position as to the Bible, the Church, and the Ordinances*. Baltimore, MD: R. H. Woodward, 1893.

Fish, Henry. *The Price of Soul Liberty and Who Paid It*. 1860. Reprint, Paris, AR: Baptist Standard Bearer, 2008.

Gambrell, J. B. "Obligations of Baptists to Teach Their Principles." In *Baptist Principles Reset*, edited by Jeremiah B. Jeter, 243–54. Dallas: Standard, 1902.

Garrett, James Leo. *Baptist Theology: A Four-Century Study*. Macon, GA: Mercer, 2009.

Graves, J. R. *Old Landmarkism: What Is It?* Texarkana, TX: Bogard, n.d. [1880].

Horr, G. E. *The Baptist Heritage*. Valley Forge, PA: Judson, 1923.

Howell, R. B. C. *The Early Baptists of Virginia*. Philadelphia: American Baptist Publication Society, 1857.

Jeter, Jeremiah B. "Distinctive Baptist Principles." In *Baptist Principles Reset*, edited by Jeremiah B. Jeter, 11–135. Dallas: Standard, 1902.

Johnson, William Bullein. *The Gospel Developed through the Government and Order of the Churches of Jesus Christ*. Richmond, VA: Ellyson, 1846.

Jones, Philip. *A Restatement of Baptist Principles*. Philadelphia: American Baptist Publication Society, 1909.

Morris, E. C. "Infallible Proofs of the Perpetuity of Baptist Principles." In *Sermons, Addresses and Reminiscences and Important Correspondence* (1898). http://docsouth.unc.edu/church/morris/morris.html.

Mullins, E. Y. *The Axioms of Religion*. Edited by C. Douglas Weaver. Macon, GA: Mercer, 2010.

———. "Baptist Life in the World's Life." *RevExp* 25 (1928) 310–14.

———. *The Christian Religion in Its Doctrinal Expression*. Philadelphia, PA: Roger Williams Press, 1917.

———. *Why Is Christianity True*. Philadelphia: American Baptist Publication Society, 1905.

Newman, Albert H. "Baptist Churches Apostolical." In *Baptist Doctrines*, edited by Charles A. Jenkens, 198–244. St. Louis: Chancy R. Barns, 1880.

Rauschenbusch, Walter. "Why I Am a Baptist," *Rochester Baptist Monthly* (1905–1906). http://abcrgr.org/index.php?option=com_content&view=article&id=14:why-i-am-a-baptist&catid=6:content12.

True, Benjamin O. "Baptists and Religious Liberty." In *Baptist Principles Reset*, edited by Jeremiah B. Jeter, 230–42. Dallas: Standard, 1902.

Truett, G. W. "Baptists and Religious Liberty." (1920). http://www.bjconline.org/index.php?option=com_content&task=view&id=4454&Itemid.

Wayland, Francis. *Notes on the Principles and Practices of Baptist Churches*. New York: Sheldon, Blakeman, 1857.

Weaver, C. Douglas. "Early English Baptists: Individual Conscience and Eschatological Ecclesiology." *PRSt* 38 (2011) 141–58.

———. "E. Y. Mullins: Soul Competency and Social Ministry." *PRSt* 36 (2009) 445–60.

———. *In Search of the New Testament Church: The Baptist Story*. Macon: Mercer University Press, 2008.

———. "Restoring the New Testament Church? Baptist Self-Perception(s) in America from the Mid-Nineteenth to the Early Twentieth Century." In *Mirrors and Microscopes: Historical Perceptions of Baptists: Papers from the International Conference on Baptist Studies VI*, edited by C. Douglas Weaver, 129–48. Milton Keynes, UK: Paternoster, 2015.

Whitsitt, William H. "Position of the Baptists in the History of American Culture, Inaugural Professorial Address, 1872." *The Whitsitt Journal* 13 (2005) 7.

Wilkinson, William C. "The Baptist Denomination." *New England Magazine* 6 (1888) 253.

Discipleship as Participation in Christ's Death to Sin

Sharyn Dowd

If the operative understanding of the Christian life held by the typical Protestant youth group member in the United States in the twenty-first century is "moralistic therapeutic deism,"[1] it might be because that is the dominant understanding of discipleship in U. S. Protestantism in general. If Christian adults display the same tendencies to divorce, to unreflective consumerism, to self-justification, to addiction, to judgmental attitudes, to racial prejudice, and to xenophobia as their unchurched counterparts it might be because we, their pastors and teachers, have no idea how to deal with these tendencies in our own lives, much less how to teach others to do so. Thus, discipleship in many congregations is reduced to Bible study and conformity to cultural expectations of appropriate behavior without any expectation of transformation.

This tendency is not limited to the "mainline" denominations. The charismatic revivals of the seventies led to personal renewal for many, but not to widespread transformed living as a sign of the kingdom that is to come. Only now, a century after Rauschenbusch, are evangelicals beginning to discover that there is "a hole in our gospel."[2] Christians on every part of the theological and political spectrum are equally vulnerable to cultural accommodation. Those who in the sixties began to turn toward the "social gospel" often reduced it to formulaic political correctness without spiritual disciplines, sacrifice, or any attempt at accountability through Christian community.

1. Smith and Denton, *Soul Searching*, 162–71.
2. Richard Stearns's powerful testimony, *Hole in Our Gospel*, is one of many examples of the evangelical turn to a more wholistic gospel.

This essay addresses the Pauline concept of Christ's death to Sin and his call for participation in that death by the baptized. It is an attempt to point toward an approach to discipleship that focuses on transformation and avoids the legalistic approach to spiritual maturity characteristic of both the right and the left. It is offered in honor of Naymond Keathley because an interest in the effectiveness of Christian teaching has been a central concern of his life and work. One can see this clearly illustrated in Keathley's *Discovering Romans*.

Paul claims in Rom 6 that baptism into Christ means baptism "into his death" (6:3), from which the baptized emerge to "walk in newness of life" (6:4). Further, he claims in Gal 2:19b–20 that the one who has thus "been crucified with Christ" lives, not the life of the former self, but the life of the indwelling Christ whose love for humankind is demonstrated by Christ's unwavering faithfulness to the point of "giving himself" up to death for women and men. Such a love-directed life would presumably be noticeably different from the lives of others, no matter how benevolent and generous those others might be.

What understanding of the cross is at the root of these claims? What kinds of discipleship practices might North American churches adopt that would help Christians grow in this direction? We will explore the questions in that order.

In Rom 5–8 Paul emphasizes the importance of Jesus's death on the cross as the destruction of the power of Sin. Paul uses the verbal and substantive forms of ἁμαρτ- fifty-five times in Romans, more than all such uses in the remainder of the Pauline and deutero-Pauline letters combined. In Rom 5–8 Paul uses the word repeatedly in a way that personifies Sin as a slavemaster. In these instances, the word translated Sin does not refer to specific human misbehaviors, but to Idolatry as an enslaving power. Paul understands specific instances of rebellion against God's rule ("trespasses," παραπτόματα, 2 Cor 5:21) as by-products or consequences of the reign of Sin/Idolatry over the self (Rom 7:14–25). This analysis is in line with the view of the prophets and the Deuteronomists that personal depravity and social injustice follow from false worship (Amos 5:21–26). When the god being worshiped is not the God with whom Israel is in covenant relationship, the correctness of the form does not prevent that worship from being idolatrous. Idolatry (seldom conscious or deliberate among Christians) is the source of all the negative human behaviors (sins) that destroy the self, others, and human community. Throughout this essay those instances of personification of Sin as Idolatry will be indicated by an initial capitalization.[3]

---

3. Some of these instances are obvious from the context but sometimes the

But how is Jesus's death on the cross a "death to Sin" if the New Testament regards the life of Jesus as perfectly sinless? In Rom 6:10 Paul writes, "The death he died he died to Sin once for all; but the life he lives, he lives to God." But in 2 Cor 5:21 Paul makes an assertion that has been interpreted to mean that the human life of Jesus the Messiah was one of perfect obedience/sinlessness: "For our sake [God] made [Jesus] to be a sin offering[4] who knew no sin, so that in him we might become the righteousness of God."[5] The author of Hebrews uses more explicit language: "We do not have a high priest who is unable to sympathize with our weaknesses but we have one who in every respect has been tested/tempted as we are, yet without sin" (Heb 4:15).

We find the narrative form of this assertion in Matt 4:1–11//Luke 4:1–13. In this tradition, Jesus is tempted by "the devil" to build his identity on displays of his own power and on his miraculous protection by God, but he resists these temptations, citing Scripture. In the logic of the Gospel narratives, Jesus's resistance to temptation demonstrates that he is the obedient Son of God empowered by the Spirit of God, just as the voice from heaven had announced at his baptism (Matt 3:16–17//Luke 3:22). Matthew, Luke, and John have to make significant adjustments to Mark's straightforward account of Jesus's baptism by John, apparently in order to make it clear that Jesus has committed no sins for which to repent, unlike all the others who receive John's baptism. How then, is Jesus's crucifixion a death to Sin?

On Rom 6:10 Robert Jewett writes, "Christ's crucifixion was an unrepeatable moment of being subjected to the power of sin . . ."[6] This is an important insight because if Christ were not subjected to the power of Sin in some way it is difficult to see how his death can be said to break the power of Sin. Indeed, if slavery to Sin is the human condition, how can Christ have been fully human if exempted from any aspect of the human condition?

Similarly, Robert Tannehill argues that Christ participated "in the human plight, which makes possible human participation in God's Son."[7] He compares the language of Rom 8:3 with that of Gal 4:4–5 and 3:13:[8]

---

capitalization will indicate my interpretation of the context.

4. Collins, *Second Corinthians*, 124, discusses the debate between "sin" and "sin offering" in this passage. He disagrees with my translation.

5. Second Corinthians 5:21 must not be understood to mean that God made Jesus, "who was not guilty of any wrong behaviors to become a sinner for us." When Paul refers to one who is guilty of wrong behaviors he uses the word ἁμαρτολος, as in Rom 5:8, not ἁμαρτία, as in 2 Cor 5:21.

6. Jewett, *Romans*, 407.

7. Tannehill, "Participation," 229.

8. Ibid., 227. On p. 228 Tannehill argues persuasively that Paul's use of "likeness"

Rom 8:3–4	God [sent] his Son	in the likeness of sinful flesh	so that the just requirements of the law be fulfilled in us
Gal 4:4–5	God sent his Son	born under the law	in order to redeem those under law
Gal 3:13	Christ . . . by	becoming a curse	redeemed us from the curse

While Gal 3:13 refers to the crucifixion as the point of identification with those cursed, both Rom 8:3–4 and Gal 4:4–5 apparently refer to the incarnation, suggesting that Christ's entire obedient life was lived out in the condition of idolatry-oriented existence common to all human beings "in Adam." Douglas Campbell also emphasizes that the incarnation means that Christ entered human existence, not as it was originally created, but as it exists historically: oppressed and enslaved.[9]

In the Philippian hymn Paul writes that Christ "emptied himself, taking the form of a slave, being born in human likeness." Since Jesus of Nazareth was not literally a slave, this synonymous parallelism again suggests that to be in the world as a human being is to be a slave, the very claim that Paul is making in Rom 6. Thus, it is possible to read the temptation narratives of Matthew and Luke and the claim of Heb 4:15 that Christ "in every respect has been tempted as we are, yet without sin" as affirming that although fully human, therefore enslaved to Sin, Christ's triumph was complete resistance to the slavemaster of all humankind, thus complete obedience to God, "even to death on a cross." Paul's readers would have understood that the revolt of a slave against the master meant certain death, probably crucifixion. Christ's death to Sin ended the inevitability of human bondage to Sin: a bondage in which he participated. As Gregory of Nazianzus wrote in *Epistle 51, To Cledonius*, "That which he has not assumed he has not healed."

In Rom 6:3–6 Paul identifies baptism into Christ with baptism into Christ's death, "so that the old self . . . might be destroyed and we might no longer be enslaved to Sin." It is because the Roman Christ-followers have died to Sin that it is absurd for Paul's critics to suggest that their baptism is license to "continue in Sin in order that grace may abound" (Rom 6:1). In fact, Paul claims that they already believe ("we know") that baptism

---

and "form" are not qualifications of Christ's identification with humankind. The "likeness of sinful flesh" is equivalent to "sinful humanity." Fitzmyer, *Romans*, 485, makes the claim explicit by insisting that the Son of God "came in a form like us in that he became a member of the sin-oriented human race; he experienced the effects of sin and suffered death, the result of sin."

9. Campbell, *Quest*, 58.

identifies them with the Messiah who broke the enslaving power of Sin. Because the Roman believers have changed masters by virtue of being "in Christ," Paul tells them "you must consider yourselves dead to Sin and alive to God in Christ Jesus" (Rom 6:11).

We turn now to our second question: "What kind of discipleship practices might assist Christians to consider themselves dead to Sin and alive to God?" Put another way, what practices might present an opportunity for the Holy Spirit to transform Christians from unreflective accommodation to their various idolatrous cultures to an unwavering commitment to becoming the gospel community that would present a recognizable threat to the dominance of Idolatry and its consequences in human life?[10]

Keathley writes:

> Enslavement to sin results in uncleanness, iniquity, and ultimately death. When a person changes masters, there is a resultant change in lifestyle. The consequences of enslavement to Christ are righteousness, holiness, and ultimately eternal life (6:19–22). Uncleanness and iniquity belong to the old master. Any behavior characterized by these qualities cannot be entertained or tolerated (6:21) by the believer who has been redeemed through Christ's death on the cross and set apart for service to the Lord.[11]

The verbs "entertain" and "tolerate" here stand for Paul's παραστήσατε (imperative plural), which the NRSV translates "present" ("your members"). Other translations use "offer" (CEB, NIV), "give" (Wycliffe, Geneva), "yield" (KJV, RSV), and "surrender entirely" (CEV). Eugene Peterson paraphrases: "That means you must not give sin a vote in the way you conduct your lives." (Rom 6:12, MSG). The challenge comes in helping Christians learn how to consider themselves dead to Sin. Few answers to this question are available that do not end up as moralistic exhortations to try harder to avoid behaviors that are unacceptable or to adopt behaviors that are approved in a particular Christian subculture. The results of this approach to discipleship recall what Flannery O'Conner wrote of the protagonist of her novel *Wise Blood*: "There was already a deep black wordless conviction in him that the way to avoid Jesus was to avoid sin."[12]

Of course, Jesus's call to "take up [one's] cross" has been understood by persecuted Christians as a call to actual martyrdom. Early Christian

---

10. Gorman's treatment of the church's mission in the series The Gospel and Our Culture is titled *Becoming the Gospel*.

11. Keathley, *Discovering Romans*, 71.

12. O'Conner, *Wise Blood*, 16.

writers saw martyrdom as a "second baptism" that provided forgiveness for all previous sins and (obviously) prevented all future sinning, thus becoming the ultimate "death to sin" in imitation of Christ.[13] And martyrdom continues into the present century. Self-preservation is instinctual for all animals, including humans. For Christians, however, self-preservation is a relative value. To the extent that self-preservation is allowed to become an ultimate value that supersedes all others, it has become an idol. What is true for literal self-preservation is also true for a Christian's reputation, financial security, social status, and job security. Bondage to any of these is Idolatry; freedom is found in death to Sin.

This works itself out for some in the response to a vocation to service to others at the risk of disapproval from family and associates. For some Christians such a vocation can in fact put their lives in jeopardy.[14] Examples might include participation in a group like Doctors without Borders[15] or the Free Burma Rangers.[16]

For those not called to risk their lives, other practices can help to crucify specific manifestations of Sin. Financial security is a relative good that can be turned into an idol by anxiety or greed. Making a practice of giving away more money than one believes one can afford to give can involve dying to Idolatry. Congregational leaders can make a significant contribution to the discipleship of their participants by teaching tithing as a way of dying to mistrust in the provision of God, rather than as a way for the institution to pay its bills. Radical generosity is modeled by a group of people who systematically give away large portions of their income annually. Some are wealthy, but others are people of modest means.[17] Choosing a minimum income to live on and giving the rest away is a way to crucify the Idolatry of depending on money for one's security rather than depending on God for "daily bread." Living on a very modest income can be achieved by sharing living space with others, thus dying to the idolatrous attachment to privacy

---

13. York, "Early Church Martyrdom, 29–31.

14. The call to protest injustice that led to beatings and murders in the Civil Rights and anti-war movements of the past century is again putting Christians in danger of injury or death. Harper, "Will America Pick Up Its Cross?"

15. *Médicins sans Frontiéres*, "At Least 11 Killed."

16. The Free Burma Rangers (http://www.freeburmarangers.org/category/reports/in-memoriam/) is a multiethnic humanitarian service movement working in conflict zones in Myanmar, Iraq, and Sudan to provide emergency medical services, food, shelter, and evacuation assistance to non-combatants.

17. See, for example, the testimony of teacher Boris Yakubchik at Bolder Giving, http://boldergiving.org/stories.php?story=Boris-Yakubchik_137.

and complete control of one's living environment and making the always difficult experiment in Christian community.

An example of bondage to Sin that goes unremarked in many Christian communities is the assumption that one's own nationality, gender, ethnicity, or social class is the norm by which other people and groups are measured. It is not the case that racial prejudice is never condemned from the pulpits of U.S. churches, but in most cases it is too easy for congregation members to exempt themselves. Bigots are always other people. Few Christians develop honest, self-disclosing friendships with people whose lives are vastly different from their own. A way to begin the crucifixion of prejudice is to deliberately locate oneself in social situations, churches, community groups, neighborhoods, or schools where one is in the minority. This practice can serve to undercut Christians' views of themselves and those like them as normative for human life.[18]

For some Christians this might mean developing relationships with people who have dramatically smaller incomes than they do. For others death to Idolatry might involve developing relationships with people who enjoy a material standard of living so luxurious that those who sympathize with the poor would be tempted to dismiss the wealthy as shallow or even inherently oppressive. In the polarized political situation here in the United States, just listening attentively to a person one regards as "extremist" might go some distance toward death to the Idolatry of unreflective self-righteousness.[19]

Suffering is a temptation to Idolatry for many Christians. The loss of relative goods such as health, comfort, fulfilling relationships, and employment can pull a Christian away from relationship with God in anger or unbelief. Or, instead of turning from God, one can be tempted to turn to an insistence on deliverance from suffering in a compulsive barrage of prayers of "faith." Of course, the Bible is filled with petitions for relief and assistance from God, both for oneself and in intercession for others; the Bible is also replete with dramatic examples of God's deliverance. The problem comes when prayer degenerates from trust in God's goodness and power into a firm commitment to the will of the supplicant and a refusal to explore other responses to suffering. The response to adversity, whether the adversity comes from an annoying co-worker, unemployment, or debilitating illness or accident, can become a tool for death to Sin if the response is focused on

---

18. Perkins and Rice, *More than Equals*.
19. Williams, *White Working Class*.

reflection and prayer about how the situation can be used by God to change course or to strengthen one's reliance on God.[20]

If Idolatry/Sin is an enslaving power, then its closest twenty-first-century analog is addiction. Although this point was made as early as 1987 by Keith Miller,[21] congregational leaders seemed unaware of or uninterested in exploring addiction recovery as an approach to discipleship until Rick Warren assigned John Baker to develop "Celebrate Recovery" at Saddleback Church.[22]

Like addiction, Sin depends on denial for its power; it is important for the idolater to deny that she has a problem, or that her problem is beyond her own power to escape. Paul claims that freedom from Sin includes surrendering all aspects of the self to God (Rom 6:11–14). Like Alcoholics Anonymous and other programs based on the "twelve steps," Celebrate Recovery ministries emphasize admission of powerlessness and the surrender of the will to God.[23] Death to Sin as enslaving power is also facilitated by the practice of making a searching and fearless moral inventory, admitting to God, to oneself, and to another human being the exact nature of one's wrongs, and making direct amends to all persons that one has harmed, except when to do so would injure them or others.[24] Participants continue the process of self-examination and amends and commit to deepening their relationships with God by prayer and meditation.

As Miller, McCormick, May, and Rohr all point out, understanding Sin as addiction includes many more addictions than substance abuse. This essay has explored just a few in the discussions of self-preservation, financial security, ethnic identity, and self-righteousness above. Celebrate Recovery expands the understanding of addiction to all "compulsive behaviors" and "defects of character." While making no claim to be a substitute for medical or psychological intervention, Celebrate Recovery provides the support and accountability of Christian community for those who are in the process of

---

20. Talbert, *Learning Through Suffering*, 92. Congregational teaching about Christian responses to suffering should be carefully planned. This educational approach is not usually appropriate as pastoral care for those in the early days of a life-disrupting event. "Why is this happening to me?" is almost never a request for a discourse on theodicy, or any other topic, for that matter.

21. Miller, *Sin*, and later *A Hunger for Healing*. See also McCormick, *Sin as Addiction*; May, *Addiction and Grace*; and Rohr, *Breathing Under Water*.

22. Celebrate Recovery, http://www.celebraterecovery.com/.

23. Celebrate Recovery is explicitly Christian in identifying the "higher power" of the twelve steps as the triune God.

24 The Celebrate Recovery adaptation of the twelve steps is on the website. Confessing one's sins aloud in the context of confidentiality produces immediate death to the preservation of one's preferred persona.

"considering themselves dead to Sin and alive to God." While most Celebrate Recovery ministries are part of the outreach programs of congregations that sponsor them, "open share" groups and "step studies" actually function to deepen the maturity of Christians as they come to recognize and surrender more aspects of themselves, becoming "freed from Sin and enslaved to God" (Rom 6:22).

Like its predecessors (monasticism, Wesley's "Holy Clubs," Keswick, the Oxford Groups, and Alcoholics Anonymous) Celebrate Recovery is not perfect. The use of Scripture in the written materials lacks attention to context. My present research and experience after a year of participation in a Celebrate Recovery ministry has uncovered no recognition of the corporate addictions that plague U. S. culture and churches: racism, white privilege, militarism, the sexualization of entertainment and advertising, and unreflective consumerism, to name but a few. In my opinion, however, Celebrate Recovery is a more effective tool for discipleship than any I have encountered in forty years of ordained ministry. But as long as salvation from Sin continues to be understood as the "confession of Christ as Savior" followed by Bible study and corporate worship or as participation in the Sacraments without additional practices of self-examination and community accountability, the transformation of the baptized envisioned by Paul will continue to elude us.

Works Cited

Campbell, Douglas A. *The Quest for Paul's Gospel: A Suggested Strategy*. London: T&T Clark, 2005.

Collins, Raymond F. *Second Corinthians*. Grand Rapids: Baker Academic, 2013.

Fitzmyer, Joseph A. *Romans*. New York: Doubleday, 1993.

Gorman, Michael A. *Becoming the Gospel: Paul, Participation, and Mission*. Grand Rapids: Eerdmans, 2015.

Harper, Lisa Sharon. "Will America Pick Up Its Cross?" *Auburn Seminary*, n.d. http://auburnseminary.org/will-america-pick-cross/.

Jewett, Robert. *Romans*. Minneapolis: Fortress, 2007.

Keathley, Naymond. *Discovering Romans*. Carmel, NY: Guideposts, 1985.

May, Gerald. *Addiction and Grace: Love and Spirituality in the Healing of Addictions*. New York: Harper & Row, 1988.

Médicins sans Frontiéres. "At Least 11 Killed." February 15, 2016. http://www.msf.org/en/article/syria-least-11-killed-another-msf-supported-hospital-attack-idlib-province.

McCormick, Patrick T. *Sin as Addiction*. Mahwah, NJ: Paulist, 1989.

Miller, Keith. *A Hunger for Healing: The Twelve Steps as a Classic Model for Christian Spiritual Growth*. New York: Harpercollins, 1991.

———. *Sin: Overcoming the Ultimate Deadly Addiction*. New York: Harper & Row, 1987.

O'Conner, Flannery. *Wise Blood*. New York: Penguin, 1983.

Perkins, Spencer, and Chris Rice. *More than Equals: Racial Healing for the Sake of the Gospel*. Downers Grove, IL: InterVarsity, 2002.

Rohr, Richard. *Breathing Under Water: Spirituality and the Twelve Steps*. Cincinnati: St. Anthony Messenger, 2011.

Smith, Christian, and Melinda Lundquist Denton. *Soul Searching: The Religious and Spiritual Lives of American Teenagers*. New York: Oxford University Press, 2005.

Stearns, Richard. *The Hole in Our Gospel*. Nashville: Thomas Nelson, 2009.

Tannehill, Robert C. "Participation in Christ: A Central Theme in Pauline Soteriology." In *The Shape of the Gospel: New Testament Essays*, 223–37. Eugene, OR: Wipf & Stock, 2007.

Talbert, Charles H. *Learning Through Suffering: The Educational Value of Suffering in the New Testament and in Its Milieu*. Collegeville, MN: Liturgical, 1991.

Williams, Joan C. *White Working Class: Overcoming Class Cluelessness in America*. Boston: Harvard Business Review Press, 2017.

York, Tripp. "Early Church Martyrdom: Witnessing For or Against the Empire?" In *Witness of the Body: The Past, Present, and Future of Christian Martyrdom*, edited by Michael L. Budde and Karen Scott, 20–42. Grand Rapids: Eerdmans, 2011.

The Abolitionist Pastor Who Left Providence "To Serve the Devil"

Rev. James B. Simmons of the First Baptist Church of Indianapolis (1857–1861)

Travis L. Frampton

> ... He was a man
> Who stole the livery of the court of heaven,
> To serve the devil in ...
>
> —Robert Pollock, *The Course of Time*

On 14 November 1857, the following announcement appeared in an Indianapolis daily newspaper:

> There is no more beautiful edifice in the city than the Baptist Church, South-west corner of Maryland and Meridian streets, since it has been repaired and re-painted.[1]

The meeting house of the First Baptist Church of Indianapolis was likely refurbished in anticipation of the arrival that same month of the congregation's new pastor, Rev. James B. Simmons.[2] The church had been without

---

1. *Daily State Sentinel*, November 14, 1857.

2. James Barlow Simmons was born on April 17, 1827, in the town Northeast, New York. He served as pastor of the First Baptist Church of Indianapolis from 1857–1861. Rev. Simmons, his wife, and his son are all buried in the center of the Hardin-Simmons University campus in Abilene, Texas.

Brief summaries of Simmons's life are located in "James Barlow Simmons," 198; "James B. Simmons," 337–40; "Rev. James B. Simmons," 12; "Simmons, James B.," 1059; "Simmons, James Barlow," 173. For a more extensive biographical account, consult MacArthur, *Foundation Builder*.

a pastor since April of that year when Rev. Sidney Dyer resigned from the pulpit.[3] The chair of the Committee of Supplies at First Baptist, Judson Osgood, wrote to Simmons, who was then pastor of the Third Baptist Church in Providence, Rhode Island, to gauge his interest in the position.

Unbeknownst to Osgood at the time was that his prospective candidate from the East Coast had, several years prior, enthusiastically expressed a desire to assume a ministerial post in a church out west. Shortly before graduating from Brown University in 1851, Simmons wrote to Benjamin Hill, the Corresponding Secretary of the American Baptist Home Mission Society, about the possibility of pastoring a church under the society's patronage. The response from the secretary was sympathetic and encouraging, but not exactly what the budding minister wanted to hear. Hill emphasized that all clergy commissioned by the society, "with scarcely an exception,"[4] were ordained, and Simmons at the time was not. His energy, aspiration, and promise were admirable, but, according to Hill's temperate counsel, they were no substitute for formal theological education, especially before entering into a mission field where "the western mind is keen, shrewd & discerning, intensely devoted to secular pursuits and occupied with fallacious religious pretensions."[5] Hill further advised, "The brightest and most enterprising of our citizens go West; if you would succeed there, you will need all the preparation you can acquire."[6] Simmons accepted Hill's recommendation, and the longing to "go West" was suppressed so he could complete his formal theological training.

Leaving Providence (1857)

By the time Osgood's letter arrived in the summer of 1857, Simmons had been ordained (1854); he had obtained a seminary degree from Newton Theological Institute (1854); and he had been pastor of Third Baptist Church for three years (1854–1857). Osgood's proposition was precisely the kind of opportunity Simmons had desired just six years prior.

In August, the young minister from Providence traveled to Indiana to meet with Osgood and the rest of the Baptist congregation. The visit was a positive one. Simmons was able to tour the capital city, to see the Baptist meeting house, and to learn of the immediate needs of the community. After his visit, he returned home to await the vote. News of the church's decision

3. Judson Osgood to James Simmons, June 18, 1857, Simmons Collection.
4. Benjamin Hill to James Simmons, February 6, 1851, Simmons Collection.
5. Ibid.
6. MacArthur, *Foundation Builder*, 25.

arrived on August 11. The Committee of Supplies voted by silent ballot and had made their choice. Osgood informed the reverend that he was elected with "entire unanimity" and implored, "This thing is of God . . . [God is] speaking to you to 'come over and help us.' . . . Our heart is enlarged toward you."[7] The chair went on to quote from the Book of Isaiah (32:8), intimating a radical vision of the kingdom of God shared between Rev. Simmons and the Baptist congregation: "We want to welcome you and your dear wife to our homes and our hearts, to our trials and our joys, and join with you in devising *liberal things* for the Kingdom, knowing 'that he who deviseth *liberal things*, by *liberal things* shall he stand.'"[8]

Since Osgood's first correspondence with Simmons, the idea of potentially leaving his congregation in Providence had weighed on him heavily. In his letter of resignation, Simmons wrote to his beloved members of the Third Baptist Church that the matter they were all aware of had caused great agitation in his own mind for several weeks:

> But much as I have loved you,—much as I love you still,—I am compelled to say that after a severe struggle, *one* of the most severe in my life, my heavenly Father has been pleased to settle it in my mind that it is my duty to remove to a more destitute section of his vineyard. Without his bidding I would not go. Without his bidding I should not *dare* to go. I only go, because I believe God calls. If I am mistaken, the calamity will be mine, not yours. You have done all that was proper for you to do to induce me to remain.[9]

Thus, Simmons's acceptance of Osgood's offer was not easy for him to make. Nevertheless, he resigned as pastor of the Third Baptist Church, effective 20 September 1857.

As for Osgood and the rest of the First Baptist Church of Indianapolis, they had a new pastor with whom they could—in the spirit of the Old Testament prophet—join "in devising liberal things for the kingdom." The exact nature of what "devising liberal things" *could* mean became clearer within weeks of Simmons's presence in the state capital.

---

7. Osgood to Simmons, August 11, 1857, Simmons Collection.

8. Ibid. Emphasis added.

9. Simmons to Members of the Third Baptist Church, September 13, 1857, Simmons Collection. Emphasis original.

Fugitive-Slave Trial (1857)

Simmons was thirty years old when he arrived in Indianapolis with his wife, Mary, and their two-year-old son, Robert. Just as he and his family were settling into their new home that November, Simmons encountered an individual who affected him profoundly for the rest of his life. More than likely, the two were never formally introduced, nor is there record they ever exchanged words. Yet, for the remainder of his adult years, Simmons's professional life charted a fixed course upon the chance meeting of a "young boy" by the name of West.[10]

Although the *Daily State Sentinel* paid little, if any, notice of Simmons's arrival to Indianapolis, the local periodical did not ignore the spectacular attraction West drew upon his arrival:

> About four years ago a black boy named West made his escape from his master, Dr. A. W. Vallandingham, living in Frankfort, Ky. Night before last the boy, having, a day or two since, been captured at Naples, Illinois, was brought to [Indianapolis] on his way home.[11]

Dr. Austin Vallandingham was a slave owner from Kentucky who sent his agent, Hezekiah Ellis, to retrieve West from Illinois. The doctor alleged that West was a slave of his who had escaped several years before. Vallandingham's son, George, travelled with Ellis in order to identify the fugitive properly. Upon their arrival in Naples, George Vallandingham remained in a hotel room, concerned that West might recognize him in public and flee before Ellis had an opportunity to apprehend him. On 23 November 1857, Ellis captured West, arrested and handcuffed him, and brought him to Vallandingham's son for proper identification. The three men then boarded a train for Kentucky later that afternoon. The party arrived in Indianapolis around 2:00 PM the following day where they were delayed awaiting a connecting train to Jeffersonville, Indiana, a destination situated on the Ohio River that provided a crossing to the southern shores in Louisville, Kentucky. During the lengthy rail postponement, anti-slavery advocates in Indianapolis worked quickly on behalf of West. Four attorneys initiated a legal proceeding in the city court against Dr. Vallandingham for kidnapping a free man. The judge's ruling called for the immediate release of West from Vallandingham's custody.[12]

---

10. Less than a decade separated the two men in age.

11. "Another Fugitive Slave Case," *Daily State Sentinel*, November 26, 1857.

12. Money, "Fugitive Slave Law in Indiana," 258–60; "Fugitive Slave Case before U. S. Commissioner Rea," *Daily State Sentinel*, December 5, 1857.

In anticipation of the judge's decision, however, the claimant's lawyers filed a legal countermeasure with the federal commissioner's office to ensure West remained a captive. West was taken into custody again, but this time by a federal official. Jesse Carmichael, a United States deputy marshal, acted upon the affidavit presented by Dr. Vallandingham. This case proved much more difficult for West and for his attorneys since it was brought before a United States commissioner. The Fugitive Slave Act of 1850 played a central role during the proceedings.[13] West now had to demonstrate he was a free man. He had no papers to present and was not allowed the time necessary to secure an admissible witness to testify on his behalf; his own testimony was, of course, inadmissible. Nevertheless, the commissioner allowed the claimant to serve as a witness on his own behalf, along with his son and Ellis.[14] Like West, Vallandingham was unable to provide papers. During the course of the trial, he did not submit any proof of sale regarding his previous purchase of West.[15] It was Dr. Vallandingham's word versus that of West. West's fate was set. The headline reporting the decision read:

> THE FUGITIVE SLAVE CASE.
> Before U. S. Commissioner Rea.
> INTENSE EXCITEMENT.
> A GREAT CROWD IN ATTENDANCE.
> The Commissioner's Decision,
> THE FUGITIVE REMANDED.[16]

Charles H. Money, in his article "The Fugitive Slave Law in Indiana," suggested that the lawyers for West attempted to accomplish at least one of three possible outcomes in their legal maneuverings: "First, they intended to do their best to liberate West. Second, they were for attempting a rescue, if they should fail legally to liberate him. [Third], they had it in mind to delay action in the trial in every possible way in order to make it cost the claimant the value of the slave or more. By making it cost the claimant a great deal, the abolitionists felt that they could discourage slave hunting in

---

13. The following articles from the *Daily State Sentinel* provide summary accounts of the trial (1857): "Fugitive Slave Case," November 28; "Fugitive Slave Case before U. S. Commissioner Rea," November 30; "Fugitive Slave Case before Commissioner Rea," December 1; "Charge against Dr. Vallandingham," December 4; "Fugitive Slave Case before U. S. Commissioner Rea," December 5. For a detailed analysis of the case, see Money, "Fugitive Slave Law in Indiana," 257–70.

14. "Fugitive Slave Case before U. S. Commissioner Rea," December 5, 1857.

15. Ibid. As part of his testimony, Dr. Vallandingham did mention as evidence of ownership a scar on West's back from an ax injury and that he had "cut off the first joint of West's right forefinger for a bone felon."

16. Ibid.

Indiana."[17] Although they were tenacious and resolute in their efforts, they failed on all three counts.

Several anti-slavery advocates, along with West's lawyers, did make arrangements for an attempted escape for the defendant during the course of the trial.[18] On Wednesday, December 2, Simmons was present and witnessed the events of that day, a day in which "devising liberal things"—as Osgood had intimated over the summer—took on new meaning.

Controversy Surrounding Simmons's Anti-Slavery Sermon (1857)

Although Simmons was openly opposed to the institution of slavery and supportive of anti-slavery causes, he was not an ardent activist from the pulpit. He kept those sentiments relatively close to himself, but the matter for him became clearer and more pointed when he accepted the position of pastor of the First Baptist Church of Indianapolis and observed West's unsuccessful exodus. Within weeks of arriving in the capital city, he was embroiled in his first major public controversy because of a sermon he preached after West's trial.

In January of 1858 the editor of the *Providence Daily Journal* wrote Simmons and inquired about rumors he had heard that there was an "incident" at the First Baptist Church and that as the recently-appointed pastor there he was given ten to twelve days to leave Indianapolis or be covered with a coat of tar and feathers. Several friends from Rhode Island had also written to Simmons relaying their concerns about enmity expressed via personal threats against him regarding his anti-slavery rhetoric from the pulpit. In response to these concerns Simmons sent a letter, dated January 23, wherein he described his experience, as witness to West's fugitive slave trial, an encounter which emboldened him to find a stronger, more active voice opposed to slavery:

> ... A fugitive slave by the name of West was tried here, soon after my arrival in this city. I attended the trial. The fugitive was a Methodist;—and the deputy marshal who held him in custody and who conveyed him each morning from the jail to the court room is I understand a member in good standing of the Third Presbyterian Church in this city. Once, during the progress of

17. Money, "Fugitive Slave Law in Indiana," 257.

18. For a synopsis of the attempted escape, consult "Fugitive Slave Case before U. S. Commissioner Rea," December 3, 1857; Julian, *Political Recollections*, 164; and Money, "Fugitive Slave Law in Indiana," 267–68.

the trial the fugitive broke away from the marshal at the jail door, and fled for the fields. The Presbyterian marshal pursued his Methodist brother with revolver in hand, shooting at him twice before he caught him. My soul was horrified. I said to myself,—"When, in the name of heaven, shall a man who fears God speak, if not now?" I *did* speak. My subject was "*The American Slave System tried by the Golden Rule*." . . .

My sermon of course, stirred up somewhat, the stagnant bile in the stomachs of those who differ from me in opinion. I should have been sorry had it not been so. It is a sign that pills are of the right sort when they create a *movement*. Certain papers, of course, gave me a gratuitous benefit of several columns in length;—but with invariable good courtesy. Private circles talked about me. And I am told, that there *is one* member of my own congregation, recently over from Kentucky, who feels grieved with me. . . . And in reference to the "coat of tar and feathers,"—if it comes, I shall sit down and scrape myself as patiently, and at the same time as expeditiously as possible,—and immediately thereafter be up and at them again;—not with a sword of iron, but with "the sword of truth." My impression is that a little persecution would benefit not only myself, but most of my brethren in the ministry. We need stirring up. We should be much more effective preachers, if we could be favored with a coat of "tar and feathers" say about once every twelve months.[19]

"The American Slave System Tried By the Golden Rule"

Simmons delivered a public address on Tuesday, December 8, just three days after West's future had been decided by Commissioner Rea. It is very likely that the subject that evening was the same he mentioned in his letter: "The American Slave System Tried by the Golden Rule." His extended discourse prompted a written response in the daily paper from someone writing under the pseudonym Publius, "a close and attentive listener," who was "surprised at some of [Simmons's] statements and startled at some of his conclusions."[20] Publius began by providing his reasons for engaging Simmons in a public discussion. He wanted to attract the pastor's attention to

---

19. Simmons to the Editor, January 23, 1858, Simmons Collection. Emphasis original.

20. Publius [pseud.], "To the Rev. Mr. Simmons," *Daily State Sentinel*, December 10, 1857.

some of the propositions touched upon in his sermon from the previous evening out of "an earnest desire to get at the truth."

One of the main points Publius disputed was Simmons's claim that "it was a sin against God, for one man to claim and exercise property in another man." Simmons also argued that "the Bible recognized slavery ... but did not establish it." Publius contended that slavery was never condemned explicitly in either the Old Testament or the New Testament. The Bible lists numerous prohibitions and sins, including moral and legal, including the substantial and the minute, oftentimes with punitive consequences and dire judgments following. According to Publius, slavery as a divine institution was never condemned by God, for "God never winked at wickedness," and "Christ never winked at sins." Moreover, if what Simmons said were true, that slavery was a sin against God, then "God yielded to the wicked passions of men, and *provided* [Old Testament laws regulating slavery] *by which they were to sin against His Great and Holy Name.* Impossible!!"[21]

When bringing his formal disputation to a close, Publius averred:

> We know that from the time of the encampment of the Jews at the foot of Mount Sinai until the overthrow of Jerusalem, a period embracing many centuries, that slavery existed among the Hebrews. Now, as the purpose of God never fails; if he had made a law for the abolition of slavery among his chosen people, slavery could never have existed within their borders. But as slavery did exist, we are forced to the conclusion that these laws were not incompatible with its existence.[22]

In the final sentence of the column Simmons's antagonist ends with the following line and valediction: "You doubtless know more of Bible teaching than I can claim; but no one is more anxious to get at the truth than, Your obedient servant, Publius."[23]

Simmons lost no time in his reply, choosing to respond, at least initially, in the same way he was addressed, i.e., through the local paper. He had ambivalent feelings responding to his opponent in such a public format, primarily because he was uncertain of his interlocutor's intentions, and secondarily because newspaper discussions, he remarked, "are generally endless things, and so far as I have observed, result in very little good. Besides, my professional duties are such as to prevent my entering upon this ground of controversy in the public prints, even were my inclinations

21. Ibid.
22. Ibid.
23. Ibid.

ever so strong in that direction."[24] Simmons refused to engage his opponent in public *printed* debate. Even so, he did offer an alternative. If Publius was indeed sincere when he said "no one is more anxious to get at the truth" than himself, then Simmons would extend to him an invitation to his sermon, that coming Sunday evening, when the two could meet to discuss their differences *in person*. If his anonymous challenger was unable to convene at that time, Simmons provided his home address as an alternative where the two could meet whenever Publius had availability. Simmons concluded his rejoinder: "If, as you say, '*no one is more anxious to get at the truth in this matter than yourself,*' this communication will satisfy you; but if on the other hand, your tacit purpose was to tempt me into a newspaper controversy, I shall probably have the honor of hearing from yourself or your friends through the same medium in the future. Your humble and ob't serv't, James Barlow Simmons."[25]

Publius hastily countered Simmons in print again. Since Simmons never proffered a theological or biblical point of contention, there was nothing to dispute except the form of the dispute. In his response Publius declared that pastors can make any assertion they like from the pulpit,[26] but pointed out that such a medium as the pulpit does not allow a proper exchange of ideas because the voice of opposition cannot be heard. Public journals, on the other hand, were a last resort by which, according to Publius, he could "either invoke the aid of the press, or permit . . . erroneous teachings [from the pulpit] to pass for Bible truths."[27] He goes on to accuse the Baptist pastor of advising his congregation "as to their political duties, from the pulpit. . . . That, as no one can speak in church, save yourself, you will take advantage of your position, and impress your political opinions on your hearers, and recognize the right of no one to assail them outside of the church."[28] Simmons remained true to his word and did not reply to Publius in print.[29] He did, nonetheless, continue preaching from the pulpit

24. Simmons, "A Word to Publius," *Daily State Sentinel*, December 12, 1957.

25. Ibid.

26. In a later article in the *Sentinel*, "To the Rev. Jas. B. Simmons," December 24, 1857, Publius defended his manner of communication by saying, "You chose to give your explanations to the public from the pulpit. I can only reply through the press."

27. Publius [pseud.], "To the Rev. James B. Simmons," *Daily State Sentinel*, December 14, 1857.

28. Ibid.

29. The early exchange between Publius and Simmons in the *Sentinel* did spawn other public debates over their published correspondence on the Bible, slavery, theology, and hermeneutics. For examples, consult Philo Publius [pseud.], "Theo. Hielscher, Esq.," *Daily State Sentinel*, December 25, 1857, and an anonymous article published in the *Sentinel*, lacking a title, on January 13, 1858.

against slavery and against any interpretation of the Bible that supported the institution of slavery. The dispute was one of perspective, of hermeneutics. Were the moral law and the letter of the law the same? For Simmons, the two were not.

After seeing no response in print, Publius again questioned Simmons a few days later, enticing him to debate through the pages of the *Daily State Sentinel*. Simmons's position on the question of moral authority versus legal authority in his sermon "The American Slave System Tried by the Golden Rule" caused considerable alarm for Publius:

> it was with pain that I heard you declare, in your sermon, that never, under any circumstances, would you yield your convictions of right, and comply with the requirements of the Constitution of the United States so far as the rendition of fugitive slaves was concerned. That you would make all the resistance in your power to prevent its execution. You gave, as a reason for this position, that the laws of God had a far higher and greater claim on your obedience than the laws of men. That, with the Constitution on the one side, commanding one thing, and the Bible on the other side, commanding in an opposite direction; the Constitution must give way, and the Bible be obeyed.[30]

Publius persisted with his argument, drawing attention to the fact that Saint Paul returned "the fugitive" Onesimus to his master, "unclaimed and unsought," and then questioned whether the apostle's own ideas of "right" in this matter should be ignored in light of a "modern and a new Christianity."[31] He charged Simmons with abusing his influence as pastor of a prominent church in Indianapolis by inciting the public "to swell this moral tide of mistaken enthusiasm, which is, as [Simmons] said, at this moment pressing this nation through the incipient stages of a civil war." In his remonstrance against the carelessness and rebellious spirit of the Baptist minister, Publius cautioned Simmons with an admonition the latter would ironically have accepted wholeheartedly, but for different reasons: "Before you counseled and advised that large audience to resist and rebel against the Constitution of the United States you should have counted the blood, the tears and the groans—that rich harvest of civil wars."[32] From Simmons's viewpoint, by using the Golden Rule—as a moral principle upon which to judge the integrity of the American slave system—he was

30. Publius [pseud.], "To the Rev. Mr. Simmons," *Daily State Sentinel*, December 17, 1857.
31. Ibid.
32. Ibid.

counting "the blood, the tears and the groans,"[33] not only of white citizens, but also those of American slaves. The fugitive slave case had emboldened him against what he considered to be an unethical, immoral, and ungodly institution. West brought biblical exegesis and the Christian gospel into clearer focus for Simmons.

"When in the Name of Heaven Shall a Man Who Fears God Speak, if Not Now?"

Simmons may have had Publius's article of December 17 in mind when constructing the letter he sent to the editor of the *Providence Daily Journal*. In recounting the scene he witnessed as West attempted his escape, he selected his words carefully. The handwritten narrative reveals an editorial decision made while crafting the letter. The relevant excerpt reads:

> The Presbyterian marshal pursued his Methodist *brother* with revolver in hand, shooting at him twice before he caught him. My soul was horrified. I said to myself,—"When, in the name of heaven, shall a man who fears God speak, if not now?"[34]

Simmons inscribed *brother* above another word that he crossed through several times. The original term is obscured but still legible beneath several lines and hashes of omission. Buried beneath the ink was *prisoner*. More than a mere editorial decision was made; it was also interpretive, theological, and political in nature.

By omitting the word *prisoner* and instead supplying *brother*, Simmons demonstrated sensitivity and understanding with respect to the power of language. These two words each denote a specific social relationship and speak to intrinsic obligations citizens have toward those relationships. The social obligation required of a person toward a prisoner is drastically different, less onerous, than the duty one has toward a brother. One label imparts judgment upon a person and exhausts human dignity; the other imbues a person with intrinsic value and worth.

On the one hand, Simmons humanized West by calling him a Methodist brother, that is, a Christian brother; on the other hand, he challenged American federal and state laws. Why was Carmichael, a Presbyterian marshal, pursuing West, his Methodist brother, with revolver in hand and shooting at him? In one respect, Carmichael was carrying out the law of the land; he was doing his duty as a citizen. Simmons, however, by opting for the

33. Ibid.
34. Emphasis added. Simmons to the Editor, January 23, 1858, Simmons Collection.

word *brother* instead of *prisoner* changed the dynamics of their relationship significantly, and in doing so, challenged the authority by which Carmichael acted. Why would one Christian brother chase and fire shots at another? By what authority was he acting, American or Divine? In the eyes of Simmons, West was created a free man by God and appropriately deserved liberty, not shackles; in the eyes of Vallandingham and the law of the land, however, West was a prisoner and bound to the American slave system.

State and federal laws were not the same as the gospel of Jesus Christ. A distinction between the two must be made for the sake of truth, for the sake of justice, and—most emphatically—for the sake of those like West: "My soul was horrified. I said to myself,—'When, in the name of heaven, shall a man who fears God speak, if not now?' I *did* speak. My subject was '*The American Slave System tried by the Golden Rule.*'"

Witnessing West's trial, especially his failed escape, called into question Simmons's own obligation to the American slave system with its concomitant fugitive laws. Seeing with his own eyes a man being shot at brought into sharper focus his calling as a pastor of the gospel of Jesus Christ and provided acute clarity: what happened to West violated moral law and was a moral injustice, irrespective of whether shooting at a "fugitive slave" was legal or not.

Regardless of how American law was defined by the commissioner and the judges or regardless of how it was understood by the attorneys on both sides of the case, according to Simmons, the legal system failed West. Simmons's opinion was resoundingly clear:

> West did not have a fair trial. . . . The commissioner received the master's testimony and excluded the fugitives [sic]. Could he not have extended the time of the trial to give West a fair chance for liberty? There was no protection to the black man. Any of them could be picked up in our streets and be carried off by the same process which consigned West to slavery.[35]

Given the impotency of the civil courts, Simmons deemed the pulpit the medium through which moral truth and moral justice must be heard. Perhaps this was another reason he rejected the newspaper column in his dealings with Publius as suitable enough for the seriousness of the weight of the matter at hand. If not the pulpit, then where? And, more importantly, if not the pastor, then who?

---

35. Money, "Fugitive Slave Law in Indiana," 270.

Controversy Surrounding Simmons, John Brown, and Jesus (1859)

Two years later, on 24 December 1859, Simmons again appears in the *Daily State Sentinel* amidst controversy over his anti-slavery stance. An opinion piece entitled, "Getting Sick of Their Hero," criticized several Abolitionist papers across the country for valorizing John Brown, who had been executed earlier that same month upon a gallows in Virginia for his leadership in the raid upon Harper's Ferry in October.[36] In addition to these periodicals, a sermon delivered by Rev. Simmons on December 18 also drew severe scrutiny for drawing parallels between Brown's execution and the crucifixion of Jesus. The editorial stated that Simmons has commented that "'Jesus Christ died like a hero upon the Cross—John Brown died like a hero upon the scaffold.' The Reverend Abolitionist in making this comparison between purity and crime is evidently unable to distinguish the difference, thus presenting to the community the most remarkable qualifications for a teacher of truth." Those who attempt to canonize "Old John Brown," the article declares, have "made the most consummate donkeys of themselves. . . . It is a compliment which the Reverend Simmons and his Brown coadjutors must appreciate."[37]

Within a week, Simmons demanded that the *Sentinel* retract the statements purported as having come from his pulpit. Attempting to clarify the matter and set the record straight, he explained that "No comparison *whatever* was made between the excellency of Christ and the excellency of Brown. The simple, and only design of the allusion, was to show that the death of Christ by crucifixion was held to be a disgraceful mode of execution."[38] This clarification, however, did little to convince the editors who, in their printed correction, queried with suspicion why Simmons, "with his well known sympathies," still compared the cross with the Virginia gallows. They admitted that they were glad to publish the correction, yet did so with a sarcastic, backhanded compliment: "we give [Simmons] the full benefit of the denial, and it gives us pleasure to know that he is anxious to disavow it. It is evidence that a diseased mind is returning to health."[39]

---

36. "Getting Sick of Their Hero," *Daily State Sentinel*, December 24, 1859.
37. Ibid.
38. "A Correction," *Daily State Sentinel*, December 30, 1859.
39. Ibid.

Controversy Surrounding Simmons, Governor Hammond, and Serving the Devil (1861)

The third controversy in which Simmons appeared involved the exiting Governor of Indiana, Abram Hammond. In his final gubernatorial address before the state legislature, in January of 1861, the Democratic governor blamed pastors like Simmons, whom he called "missionaries from New England,"[40] for agitating public sentiment, frustrating the South, and causing the present crisis. These clergy members had preached politics from the pulpit rather than the gospel. He accused them of being "profoundly ignorant of the political bearing of questions of social and political economy"[41] and for training the younger generation into a new "grand anti-slavery army against the Constitution."[42] The abolitionist "notions in regard to slavery" were not taught by the older generation. The fathers of the younger generation knew, so argued Hammond, that it was not a sin to make the slave "work and earn his livelihood as well as the white man."[43] Many of these Northerners from an earlier era had sold their own slaves for profit to plantations in the South. They knew it would be hypocritical to call Southern slave traders "traffickers in human flesh." According to Hammond's line of reasoning, the fathers knew why they sold their slaves South: they knew that most American slaves were "naturally lazy, and would not work for a living unless compelled to do it"; they knew that, if they had not sent them South, "hundreds and thousands would fill the prisons and poor-houses of the Northern States and become burthens upon white tax-payers"; they knew that, if they had not sent them South, it may happen that "instead of negroes being slaves, white men (assessed to meet such burthens) would become such."[44] The New England missionaries had caused a mighty rift between fathers and sons. The younger generation believed themselves to be "wiser, better and holier than their fathers." Taking one last parting shot at abolitionist pastors like Simmons, Hammond concluded his harangue with an oft-quoted line from Robert Pollock's epic poem, *The Course of Time*: "The men from the East, 'who wear the livery of heaven to serve the devil in', have done it all."[45]

40. "Messages of the Governors," *Daily State Sentinel* January 19, 1861; see also Thornbrough, *Indiana in the Civil War Era*, 98.

41. "Gov. Hammond and the Preachers," *Daily State Sentinel*, January 18, 1861; also Scott, *Visitation of God*, 21.

42. "Messages of the Governors."

43. Ibid.

44. Ibid.

45. Ibid.

After Hammond had bitterly denounced the pastors "from the East," Simmons capitalized on the opportunity, while in the midst of a sermon series on the "Sufferings of Christ," to use his Baptist pulpit to respond to the governor's criticisms directly. His subject on Sunday, 13 January 1861, was unequivocal: Jesus's trial before Pontius Pilate, Governor of Judea.

In his homily, Simmons incisively noted that one of the false charges brought against Jesus was his involvement in "raising insurrectionary excitements" in the province. Simmons asked his audience to imagine the scene where Jesus pushed off from the shore in "his floating pulpit" to preach to the multitudes.[46] The analogy was meant to draw a comparison with the throngs of people who would gather to hear the provocative anti-slavery sermons of the "missionaries from New England." Jesus's teaching caused a disturbance, especially among the religious and political authorities of the day, including Governor Pilate. Simmons exclaimed that Jesus was "in the strongest sense of the term, a dissenter—a reformer! He had substituted a right for a wrong interpretation of the Old Testament Scriptures. He had set aside old and dead rites ... and introduced new vitalities."[47] The problem the authorities had with Jesus was that

> he *had* preached, and the people were excited, and this was his crime! The mad throng, instigated by the corrupt hierarchy, the foundations of whose power his teachings had sapped, are now in eager waiting to lead him forth to martyrdom.
>
> Here we see the Son of God impeached, before the Governor of a province, for giving men the truth; the truth, which, according to Jesus' own words, if they had received, and not resisted, would have made them "free indeed." Truth resisted is a two-edged sword!! As well impeach God for giving us fire, because wicked men use it to burn houses! ... This case of Christ was not the last time in the history of our world in which preachers have been arraigned before a Governor, and accused of creating an insurrection. I am proud to-day, to stand side by side with Jesus my Lord, with the same accusation resting upon me as upon Him,—He accused by the Governor of Judea,—I by the Governor of Indiana, of making an uproar among the people. If I had my co-workers in the ministry before me, I would say, Brethren, Gov. Hammond, in his recent message, has honored us over-much! Let us send him our respects, with a copy of the New Testament, and ask him to study the history of Jesus Christ as a *preacher*, as well as an Atoning Savior—and not

46. "Gov. Hammond and the Preachers."
47. Ibid.

to forget to look into the character and fate of the Governor who pronounced His condemnation.⁴⁸

Around 5:00 AM, early Sunday morning on 27 January 1861, precisely two weeks to the day after Simmons admonished the governor to heed the example of Pilate, the "beautiful edifice" at the corner of Meridian and Maryland streets mentioned in the newspaper advertisement cited at the beginning of this essay, burned to the ground, spire and all.

The *Indiana State Sentinel* reported on the event three days later in an exposé under the title "Burning of the Baptist Church." The only suggestion put forth as an explanation as to the cause of the fire was that "The fire was evidently caused by a defective flue."⁴⁹ According to the article, the meeting house had burned for some time before being discovered. The destruction of the Baptist church that Sunday morning became a major topic of conversation that week. In the midst of much speculation and concern about the utter ruin— "burned out to the basement"—of the building "belonging to the congregation of the Rev. Mr. Simmons," the *Sentinel* reiterated the only possible explanation: "There is but one opinion about the cause of this fire, and that is that it caught from a flue."⁵⁰

Two days later the *Indianapolis Daily Journal* published resolutions adopted by the First Baptist Church, with Simmons listed as moderator. Lines from the resolution insinuate that the fire was more than a mere accident. The congregation openly proclaimed that from the very beginning God has "guarded us and helped us—led us when we were too feeble to walk alone, guarded us when we were in the midst of danger, and helped us when we were weak and our hearts fainted, and we were ready to fall by the way."⁵¹

In an unfortunate turn of events, the rhetorical remarks Simmons brought against the governor, only two weeks prior, had materialized and taken on new meaning a fortnight later: "As well impeach God for giving us fire, because wicked men use it to burn houses!"

Yet, the words carried more than the weight of unfortunate irony for Simmons personally. For most people in Indianapolis at the time, the reason provided by the *Sentinel* sufficed. The church burned because of a defective flue. Yet, in 1897, thirty-six years after he left Indiana, Simmons supplied another answer contrary to what was printed. In a letter he sent to the First Baptist Church of Indianapolis upon the occasion of commemorating the congregation's seventy-fifth anniversary, he reminisced about the

---

48. Ibid.
49. "Burning of the Baptist Church," *Indiana State Sentinel*, January 30, 1861.
50. Ibid.
51. "Church Meeting," *Indianapolis Daily Journal*, February 1, 1861.

work he and the congregation had done together when they were "blamed for favoring freedom." He stated with no degree of uncertainty that "our meeting-house was burned because the doctrine of emancipation was taught within its walls."[52]

The Confession of Rev. Simmons (1861)

As stated previously, Simmons left Providence with his family and moved to Indianapolis to begin serving as pastor in the Baptist meeting house that was "repaired and re-painted." Three years later that same building burned to the ground. Simmons believed disgruntled locals had torched the building because of his strong anti-slavery stance, and just three months after the "spire and all" fell to the ground in January of 1861, the Civil War commenced.

On August 12, that summer, President Abraham Lincoln appointed "the last Thursday in September next as a day of humiliation, prayer, and fasting for all the people of the nation."[53] Simmons, like so many Northern pastors at the President's request, preached a sermon that September 26. He later circulated a published version of the discourse which he entitled: *The Cause and Cure of the Rebellion*. The opening line reads:

> All true Bible preaching is corrective in its character. Its tendency is to displace error and give room for truth, and so to restore in man the lost image of God.[54]

A close analysis of *The Cause and Cure of the Rebellion* is beyond the scope of this essay, but here it is appropriate to mention that each of the three controversies, mentioned in the sections above, bear upon the contents of this sermon. For example, the burning of the Baptist church could not have been too far removed from his thoughts when Simmons stated: "Meeting-houses, too, have been burned, and ministers threatened with hanging, here in the free North, for defending the cause of the *black poor!*"[55]

The bulk of his sermon implicates Northern participation in supporting the institution of Southern slavery. For Simmons, Southern slavery was a national crime, a sin perpetuated by both North and South. Later in the text he identifies the cause of the rebellion as the American slave system and the cure of the rebellion as the abolition of slavery. He was dubious

---

52. Hoffman, *Light in the Forest*, 41.
53. Lincoln, "Proclamation," 482.
54. Simmons, *Cause and Cure of the Rebellion*, 1.
55. Ibid., 6.

that any other explanation could be offered with respect to the cause or that any other solution could be offered as the cure. Although earlier in his life he refuted any characterization of himself as an abolitionist, as in the case involving his sermons on John Brown, in *The Cause and Cure of the Rebellion*, so there could be no misunderstanding of his anti-slavery opinions, he strongly identified himself as an abolitionist with alacrity. In so doing, he publicly declared himself an activist. Interesting too is the way in which he announced it, by way of a public confession of sin:

> And just here I have a confession to make. I have publicly denied being an abolitionist; and as public sins should be publicly confessed, I now as publicly take it back. I do it out of deference to the following definition, which may be found in the "Southern Literary Messenger," a conservative organ of the South:
> "An abolitionist is any man who does not love slavery for its own sake as a Divine institution; who does not worship it as a cornerstone of civil liberty; who does not adore it as the only possible social condition on which a permanent Republican government can be erected; and who does not, in his inmost soul, desire to see it extended and perpetuated over the whole earth, as a means of human reformation second in dignity, importance and sacredness alone to the christian religion. He who does not love African slavery with this love is an abolitionist."
> In these times of war I welcome this whole congregation and the entire North to take shelter under this definition. The truth is, brethren, we have all been ashamed to be called abolitionists; we have flung it from us as a term of reproach; but by this definition it is saddled upon us and girded tightly to us, and like the unreconciled steed we may flounder all we please, but we cannot break the fastenings and free ourselves from the disgrace.[56]

Upon preaching his sermon twice that September, a caustic response, published in the *Indiana State Sentinel*, issued notice to Simmons by way of a threat:

> "Cause and Cure of the Rebellion."—We are indebted to the Rev. James B. Simmons, pastor of the First Baptist Church, Indianapolis, for a sermon preached by him at Masonic Hall, September 22d, 1861. Mr. Simmons evidently desires a notice by sending us his abolition trash "with his best wishes." The game is not worth the candle. Such men as he were the "cause" of the rebellion and the "cure" is to wipe them out, which is fast being done.[57]

56. Ibid., 8.
57. "Cause and Cure," *Indiana State Sentinel*, October 16, 1861.

Simmons moved with his family to Philadelphia that next month.

Upon Simmons's advent to Indianapolis in 1857, he arrived a strong anti-slavery advocate. By the time he departed the city in 1861, the Civil War had begun, and he left emboldened in his opposition against slavery as an abolitionist. In a manner of speaking, during his four-year tenure as pastor in Indianapolis, Simmons's understanding of his Christian calling had passed through the heat of several crucibles, whether the fire came from a deputy's revolver, from an incinerating church, or from impassioned public controversy. What remained after the fires was a lifelong commitment to uniting a divided country through Christian higher education and the gospel of Jesus Christ.

Departing Indianapolis (1861): A Postscript

Simmons departed Indianapolis in November of 1861, a month after circulating *The Cause and Cure of the Rebellion*. He became pastor of the Fifth Baptist Church in Philadelphia. After serving for six years in that capacity, from 1861–1867, Simmons stepped away from the pulpit and accepted the position of Corresponding Secretary of the American Baptist Home Mission Society. By the time he had assumed this position, the bloodiest war to date in our country's history—in terms of loss of American lives—had finally come to an end. In his role as Corresponding Secretary he went on to help start seven institutions of learning for freedmen in the South, five of which continue to thrive as vibrant campuses today: Virginia Union University, Benedict College, Shaw University, LeMoyne-Owen College, and Morehouse College.

The last college he helped establish was Simmons College (now Hardin-Simmons University), which he himself called "Christlieb College" or the College of Christ's Love. It was the farthest school west he founded, away from the political and social quagmire then still dividing the country along racial lines, even though America was again a united nation, but united in the most peculiar way as "separate, but equal." Christlieb was everything he dreamed a Christian college could become. Call it a place of hope. It was the culmination of his life's work, a vision he had for the future, Christ's love and a liberal arts education as an antidote to those things which had divided a nation.

Works Cited

Daily State Sentinel (Indianapolis), November 12, 1857–December 30, 1859.

Hoffman, Harold Richard. *A Light in the Forest: A History of First Baptist Church of Indianapolis, Indiana, 1822–1966.* Indianapolis: Joseph C. Collins, 1966.

Indiana State Sentinel (Indianapolis), January 30, 1861–October 16, 1861.

Indianapolis Daily Journal, January 18, 1861–February 1, 1861.

"James B. Simmons, D. D." In *Commemorative Biographical Record of the Counties of Dutchess and Putnam, New York, Containing Biographical Sketches of Prominent and Representative Citizens, and of Many of the Early Settled Families*, 337–40. Chicago: J. H. Beers, 1897.

"James Barlow Simmons, D. D." In *Andover Theological Seminary, Necrology, 1905–1906*, 198. Boston: Everett, 1906.

Julian, George W. *Political Recollections, 1840–1872.* Chicago: Jansen McClurg, 1884.

Lincoln, Abraham. "Proclamation of a National Fast Day." In vol. 4 of *The Collected Works of Abraham Lincoln*, edited by Roy P. Basler, 482–83. New Brunswick, NJ: Rutgers University Press, 1953.

MacArthur, Robert Stuart. *A Foundation Builder: Sketches in the Life of Rev. James B. Simmons.* New York: Fleming H. Revell, 1911.

"Messages of the Governors." *Indiana State Guard* (Indianapolis, IN), January 19, 1861.

Money, Charles H. "The Fugitive Slave Law in Indiana." *Indiana Magazine of History* 17 (1921) 257–97.

Pollock, Robert. *The Course of Time.* New York: A. S. Barnes, 1856.

"Rev. James B. Simmons." *The Brown Alumni Monthly* 2 (1901) 12.

Scott, Sean A. *A Visitation of God: Northern Civilians Interpret the Civil War.* Oxford: Oxford University Press, 2011.

Simmons, James B. *The Cause and Cure of the Rebellion: Or How Far the People of the Loyal States Are Responsible for the War.* Indianapolis: Werden, 1861.

———. Letters and Papers. Simmons Special Collection. Box 1:1.1. Research Center for the Southwest. Hardin-Simmons University Library, Abilene, TX.

"Simmons, James B., D. D." In *Baptist Encyclopaedia, A Dictionary of the Doctrines, Ordinances, Usages, Confessions of Faith, Sufferings, Labors, and Successes, and of the General History of the Baptist Denomination in All Lands, with Numerous Biographical Sketches of Distinguished Americas and Foreign Baptists, and a Supplement*, edited by William Cathcart, 1059. Rev. ed. Philadelphia: Louis H. Everts, 1883.

"Simmons, James Barlow." In *Historical Catalogue of Brown University, 1764–1914.* Providence, RI: Brown University, 1914.

Thornbrough, Emma Lou. *Indiana in the Civil War Era 1850–1880.* Vol. 3, *The History of Indiana.* Indianapolis: Indiana Historical Society, 1965.

Fidelity

Daniel G. Bagby

Several words in the Hebrew language prove difficult to translate. They often carry rich and multiple meanings, not often captured in English by a single word or concept. Such is the case with an unusual idiom that attempts to describe a cardinal characteristic of the nature of God in regard to relationships: חסד. The term refers to a particular characteristic in relationships, often specifically attributed to God. Over the centuries translators and translations have used several words in trying to "capture" the fullness of the word's meaning: faithfulness, lovingkindness, fidelity, unwavering loyalty, loyal love, boundless care, etc. (Miles Coverdale, translating the Bible into English in 1535, first chose the term "loving kindness" to interpret חסד).

The word began to appear first as an idiom to express God's determined faithfulness to God's part of the relational agreement with Israel.[1] Used also, however, to describe a unique commitment in relationships, the word carried both a positive and a negative connotation, depending on context and situation. While the Creator's relationship to Israel was defined as an unbreakable bond of mercy and affection, the same term, in describing one or two human relationships, intimated a closeness that exceeded proper boundaries of care (Lev 18:19).

What are we to make today of this intriguing term and its implication in divine/human relationships and human/human relationships? Do both positive and negative understandings of it carry a valid message? What are we to learn about what חסד says about God and God's purposes in relationships? In what way, if any, does the word reflect God's hope and purpose in human relationships? These questions, and perhaps others, lead us to an examination in the following pages of the etymology and meaning of the term.

1. Snaith, *Theological Word Book*, 136–37.

A starting place in the investigation immediately suggests an assessment of Yahweh's purposes in creating humankind. The first chapter of Genesis informs us of a very orderly and intentional process of creation, culminating in the creation of man and woman (Gen 1:1–31). Having already pronounced the "goodness" of all previous creation, the Creator next purposes to create Adam in the Maker's image, after God's "likeness." What does this action mean?

The Likeness of God in All Living Beings?

The animals of the field, the birds of the air, and the inhabitants of the sea show a remarkable protective behavior toward their offspring (their creation), often sacrificing their safety in order to preserve, feed, and protect their unborn and newborn progeny. Their allegiance and care sometimes extend beyond the first few months of life, but soon dissipate as the vulnerable "child" becomes an independent and self-sufficient adult.

Such a clear demonstration of protective allegiance and care may well reflect a beginning understanding of God's חסד in the created order of life. What is sometimes described and identified as a "maternal instinct" in those who generate life may also offer a clue as to God's nature and purpose in all creation: the Maker of life wanted all creation tended, nurtured, and cared for, and thus generated that impetus as a propensity in all creatures. God then shared that same capacity with the highest form of God's created order, human beings (Gen 1:27–31). Embedded in the nature of every living creature was the proclivity to create, to protect the fragile and unprotected, and to offer nurture and care in the process of being "fruitful" and multiplying.

The Likeness of God in Human Beings

Human beings were one of the last creations designed to offer this "likeness of God" at a higher level in relationships. Made in the image of the Divine, humans were designed to offer and provide a more permanent quality of relationship. The One Who made all men and women desired a different and distinct quality of endurance and connectedness in the human network of relationships.

How was the likeness of God to appear in the creation of human beings? According to Cuthbert Simpson, Semitic people of biblical days, keen on avoiding an anthropomorphic representation of "God," chose the concept of "image" as most likely a likeness in "spiritual powers"—the power of thought, the power of communication, the power of self-transcendence.² To the writer, such characteristics inevitably included the capacity of choice, the power to care, and the power of responsible behavior.

God's desire for human relationships centered on individuals and people taking creation seriously—and taking God seriously. From the beginning of creation, when the Creator offered a relationship to human beings, it was offered as a sacred commitment to nurture and protect them. The Maker of life designed the divine-human relationship with an affinity to care for and preserve its "offspring." Yahweh's intent was to remain faithful to an unbreakable covenant of care with all the humans God created. The Creator chose in the process to make indissoluble caring covenants as a characteristic both of Yahweh and of Yahweh's created "children"; human beings were purposed to keep relationships sacred and unbreakable also. This expectation of fidelity in a relationship with Yahweh became both a source of hope and faith for the early Hebrews.

Biblical Inferences of God's Fidelity

Early references to Yahweh's nature and character adorn the pages of the Pentateuch. God's response to human disobedience in the garden, and His enduring care of the generations that followed is a keen example of the Maker's חסד (Gen 3–4). God's grace in restoring a covenant with Noah (Gen 6–7) after human failure again reflects the forgiving and faithful nature of the Creator God. When the people Yahweh created failed to follow the likeness and purpose of God in their relationship with the Almighty, the Lord God still demonstrated a caring faithfulness to the created order and the scattered people of God (Gen 11).

Yahweh called Abram and Sara to a trusted set of promises and still protected and nurtured the fragile patriarch and his wife when they struggled to remain faithful to God's vision and call (Gen 12–17; 20). Abraham's son Isaac and grandson Jacob fared no better as followers who struggled to keep their promises in their relationship with God (Gen 25–34). Abraham's great-grandson Joseph was himself so consumed by his father's favoritism that he needed to be jolted with brotherly rejection and ostracism before he awakened to Yahweh's care as a slave in an Egyptian home (Gen 38–45). The Almighty's constancy was reaffirmed at each instance of the inconstancy of human beings in their relationship with God.

The second book of the Pentateuch delivered the same message at its outset. The faithful Creator sought out the people of God in slavery, never

---

2. Simpson, "Genesis," 485.

forgetting the divine commitment to an unbreakable relationship of care with Israel. Yahweh called a gifted leader to help the people of God walk to freedom (Moses), only to hear an unsteady and suspicious voice in reply (Exod 3–4). The chapters that follow reflect the stubborn faithfulness of a Creator in the face of repetitive opposition and disloyalty from the inconsistent children of God (Exod 14:11; 16:3; 17:2–3; 32:1–6).

Judges and kings soon joined the company of unfaithful relationships (Judg 2:1–2; 9:23; 13:1; 1 Sam 7:7; 16:1; 2 Sam 12:7–10), including Saul (2 Sam 21:1), David (2 Sam 12:7–13), Solomon (1 Kgs 11:4–6), Rehoboam, and Jeroboam (1 Kgs 12). The recorded history of Israel and Judah's leaders repeats a cycle of blessing and fidelity from God, and a cycle of infidelity and failure by succeeding kings.

Divine Fidelity and Human Brokenness in the Psalms

The psalmists employed חסד on several occasions to describe the unrelenting commitment of God to people and persons. In the seventeenth Psalm of the compendium, the writer enjoins the Creator to show "thy marvelous lovingkindness" and save the psalmist from the wicked (Ps 17:7–15).[3] The struggling believer appeals to God in Ps 25:6 to "remember thy tender mercies and lovingkindness" because they have been known "of old" and generate trust (25:2, 6). The follower of Yahweh in Ps 26:3 declares that the Maker's "lovingkindness" is ever before his eyes; and the writer of Ps 36:7 affirms that the חסד ("lovingkindness") of God provides safety and trust in the "shadow of thy wings," and hopes that such faithfulness can be continued in the relationship (Ps 36:10).

Yahweh's חסד is almost always translated as "loving kindness" (at least 231 times) in the King James Version of the Bible. The worshiper in Ps 40:10 declares that he has not concealed God's faithful love from those with whom he worships, and also employs the term "tender mercies" to describe God's grace and gift of preservation (v. 11). The despairing and disquieted soul (Ps 42:1–8) will still hear the Maker's faithful presence and song of hope in both daytime and night, as "deep calls unto deep" and a prayer of mourning is challenged. The seeking worshiper finds the gift of God's חסד both in the sorrow of the soul and in the praise of joyful gratitude (Ps 48:9).

The psalmist not only praised the Almighty in the temple, but sought comfort during confession in worship. The contrite believer of Ps 51 pleads for the tender mercies that accompany the "lovingkindness" of Yahweh, and

3. All citations from the King James Version (KJV) unless otherwise noted.

the thirsting soul celebrates the faithfulness of God (חסד) as more valuable than life itself (Ps 63:3). The translators of the KJV regularly connect the words *loving kindness* to the Creator's "tender mercies" (Ps 69:16), and each description of a faithful God juxtaposes that characteristic with the identification of loving kindness (Ps 88:11). The Israelite in worship is deeply grateful for the One who relates to him with loving constancy and unfailing mercy (Ps 92:1–2).

The biblical writer, by contrast, knows the inconstancy of human covenants, and pleads that God may strengthen the human resolve to be faithful in response to Yahweh's fidelity (Pss 103:1–4; 107:43; 119:88, 159). Worship leaders of each generation reasserted the security of knowing God's unfailing mercy and the tenuousness of human commitments. The contrast between God's unwavering faithfulness to relationship covenants and the regularity of human failure to keep those covenants is a persistent theme in the biblical witness of dealing with חסד.

The Prophets and Fidelity

Isaiah was one of several prophets who recorded the disappointment of God with Israel's failure to keep faithful to her promises (Isa 1:12–20). The prophet likened the people's infidelity to the actions of a harlot, and called the city, and the people, to repent and act righteously and responsibly with God (1:21–23). In an appeal to the people's memory of God's loyalty and mercy over the years, Isaiah reminded the people that God expected truth and faithfulness in return for those same qualities extended in Yahweh's relationship with them (63:7).

The prophet Jeremiah also interpreted the Almighty's "delight" in showing a merciful fidelity to the people of God, calling them once again to a right way of living and relating to their Creator (Jer 9:24). Warning those who believed in Yahweh and sought a proper relationship with God, the spokesman for God declared that the people stood in danger of losing what was most valuable in life, the removal of sorrow, and the infusion of joy, personal peace, and mercy in their daily living (16:5). The Creator was described by the prophet as possessing a tender and gentle affection for the people, having "loved them with an everlasting love: therefore with lovingkindness have I drawn thee" (31:3).

The prophet Hosea took pains to communicate the forgiving nature of a God that would not break ties with the children of God, but sought them out, with intent to establish a sacred covenant with them, as the exchange between a bride and groom (Hos 2:18–20). Speaking as a voice for Yahweh,

Hosea expresses the agony and determination of a Creator who seeks to woo God's people with "bonds of love" (6:1–6) and does not want to give up on them (Hos 11:8–9).

Jesus Christ and Faithfulness

The Creator of fidelity expressed the greatest form of faithfulness in the appearance of the child of Bethlehem, who was born out of the unflinching commitment of a God who wanted lasting relationships, and broken relationships restored. The promise of a Savior rings throughout the Israelite history of exile and oppression; the covenant that God made with the children of God was that they would not be forgotten, and that Yahweh would redeem the people—regardless of times when they would "walk in darkness" (Isa 9:2). The tangible presence of a Messiah was to bring hope and peace to a people often suspicious that they had been forgotten; the covenant set forth promised that his primary nature would be wrapped in both righteousness and faithfulness (Isa 11:5).

Jesus Christ was God's faithful response to a frightened people, yet many of them were so preoccupied or fearful that that they did not recognize him (John 1:10–13). The word became flesh, and lived among them, and defined the fidelity of Yahweh in human relationships. He shared the חסד of the Creator in his daily walk with people, and sought חסד in return. He declared clearly that his purpose was not to condemn and reject, but to reconcile and save (John 3:16–17). He called people to follow his nature and purpose (Mark 1:16–20).

The Messiah's message was clearly a call to a responsible and rewarding life, based on trust and grace. When asked what limits should be imposed on the initiative to forgive an infraction or to repair an interrupted relationship, he surprised one of his devoted disciples by stretching the limits of grace far beyond where that person had already added to their understanding (Matt 18:21–35). The Author of extended mercy knelt beside a woman already condemned to die, and asked whether her accusers were less in need of grace than she was, then declared that he did not accuse her either, and called her to live a life of responsible behavior and purpose (John 7:53—8:11).

The Master's initiative toward persons who had been devalued by society, religion, and individual prejudice (children, disabled, gentiles, women, etc.) is ample evidence of his mission of unlimited grace. In the face of misunderstanding or rejection, he extended a relationship of unending mercy. Even at the point of death on a cross, he looked at those who had condemned him and declared, "Father, forgive them, for they know not what they do …" (Luke 23:34). The Savior also extended unprecedented grace when he sought out one in his trusted circle who had betrayed him (Simon Peter), and offered him reconciliation, grace, and a renewed mission (John 21:15–19).

God's Purpose in Relational חסד

The whole witness of the created order speaks of intentionality and purpose (Gen 1). God moved through the beginning chaos of creation to provide meaning and direction for creation. Yahweh's purpose in shaping human beings in the divine image had both specific plans and tangible dreams. If the Creator desired to fashion the most advanced creatures, human beings, to reflect the "image" of the Maker, and the Maker was not a physical entity, the purpose and notion of "likeness" takes on a spiritual and emotional image. What purposes might the Almighty have designed for his highest form of creation?

1. Relational Accountability

The Maker of persons and families wanted accountability in relationships as an ingredient of *value*. Yahweh demanded a sense of mutual responsibility as Creator for those whom God made; the Almighty chose to be accountable in all relationships, and wanted human beings to respond with accountability themselves. An agreement between parties that expresses some sense of responsibility between them adds an important dimension of value to the relationship. Yahweh intended the same strength for human relationships when the Maker positioned a man and a woman to share sacred vows themselves, and added depth to that dynamic by sharing with them the capacity to create life (children), thus multiplying both the characteristic of responsibility and its inherent value.

2. Indissolubility as Security

A covenant which guarantees inviolability and permanence, regardless of circumstance, is a coveted assurance. To know that " … neither death, nor life, nor angels, nor principalities, nor powers, nor things present, nor things to come, not height, nor depth, nor any other creature, shall be able to separate us from the love of God which is in Christ Jesus, our Lord" is, in fact, insurance of the maximum quality (Rom 8:38–39).

Such safety can be misinterpreted as an invitation to abuse such a privilege by acting irresponsibly out of a guarantee of forgiveness. As intriguing as such a choice might be, it is potentially trumped by the power of gratitude and grace experienced in the relationship, which gently impels the recipient to a higher level of responsibility.

The safety of knowing that a relationship cannot be permanently damaged or destroyed provides a deep peace as a foundation. Since human relationships are permeated by the threat and reality of rejection or betrayal, many human beings struggle to believe that God would act otherwise. The promise of insolubility in their relationship with God was often a source of bewilderment and disbelief by the Israelites.

3. Care as an Expression of Covenant Love

The capacity to care enough about the establishment, the nurture, and the maintenance of a relationship so as to invest oneself in it *permanently* is another unique characteristic of חסד. The commitment of one being to another in such a dynamic defines the core nature of Yahweh's Self, who *is* love, and defines love as a voluntary capacity to care about someone else in a boundless and unreserved way. The God who provides that level of care embodies the foundation of who God is, and asks of the created beings that they also learn to express that care in a measure that reflects the likeness and nature of the Maker. Covenantal love resides in a promise to care enough about someone else enough to make them a priority in a relationship.

4. Reconciliation as Initiative

The very act of initiating any reconciliation in broken or damaged relationships speaks to another characteristic of *loving kindness*. Human beings are often self-centered, afraid, or incapable of reversing the wounding from betrayal or rejection. The ensuing result in many broken or distanced human relationships is that the negatively affected connection remains unrepaired. The untended dynamic between two persons not only often causes increased sorrow and impairment, but syphons the person's energy and attention in depleting ways.

Yahweh's answer to such a human impasse is to initiate the healing process by starting the dialogue of reconciliation in a damaged relationship. Without excusing or ignoring personal responsibility, the Almighty seeks out the offender (or offended), and begins the journey of relationship recovery by identifying the issues that have caused separation and brokenness, extending forgiveness, and providing an opportunity for healing and recovery of trust and affection.

Fidelity as a Gift for All Human Relationships

Made in the image of God, we carry the characteristics and design of the Creator in ourselves. A capacity to create, to initiate, to love, and to become responsible in relationships was part of the grand design of human creation. Provided for us as gifts of character, these characteristics were intended to enrich and define the quality of all relationships. The unyielding devotion of חסד was to provide security, dependability, and continuity in relationships—in an otherwise unpredictable and unreliable world of connections. In what ways can the unique and significant model of *loving kindness* provide valuable dimensions to human relationships?

1. Fidelity as Accountability

Designed by the Creator to live in secure human connections, all human beings were placed in families for responsible care. What God intended in the formula of creation was to provide a caring network of non-negotiable sacred ties for each person in the small constellation of connected blood relationships. Yahweh's plan was that the *family* would act as a center of reliability and dependability for all those who lived together, so that the secure and loving development of every human being would never be in doubt.

A foundational expectation in family relationships involves accountability. Husbands and wives, in becoming accountable to each other, form a mutually responsible and reliable partnership, which not only provides trust in their own relationship, but brings trust and commitment to the offspring of their marriage. Children born into the maturity of a responsible marriage covenant thrive and blossom as fledgling persons made in God's image, and become capable someday of responsible relationships themselves.

2. Fidelity and Security

The home as the nucleus of security and safety remains one of Yahweh's greatest gifts to human beings. The covenants of marriage and parenting assume an environment which God purposed in the first Garden, where protection and provision delivered a significant measure of peace of mind and predictable comfort. Yahweh purposed a world of inhabitants who would model the level and quality of stability that God designed at the outset of creation.

Human beings today can still take hold of the power of security and safety in relationships, adding a dimension of stability and comfort while living in a very unpredictable and often unsafe world. The practice of offering such security and peace resides still in personal choices and sacred covenant that individuals, families, and congregations can assume with each other.

3. Fidelity as Covenant Love

Love is a word too often used and more than often misunderstood. The God who defined covenant love as חסד introduced a level of care rarely properly experienced. The quality of personal investment and self-giving expressed in loving kindness transcends the boundaries of human self-focus and self-survival to the point of sacrifice and preference extended to someone else as opposed to oneself. The model for such care was most deeply lived out by Jesus Christ, of whom it was declared, "greater love has no man than this, that a man lay down his life for his friends (John 15:13 RSV).

God created human beings with a deeper capacity for caring and loving than we often impart. While we are sometimes distracted by our own needs and preoccupied by selfishness, the Almighty provided the greater capacity for חסד within human beings as a quality of the highest value in relationships—and available to all.

The voluntary link between persons who form a covenant of friendship was also designed as a sacred commitment. Beyond the nucleus of the immediate family, God designed social circles to provide nurture and care beyond blood ties. The biblical description of David's relationship to Jonathan stands as another model of God's purpose for profound human experiences of חסד, loving kindness.

4. Fidelity as Grace and Reconciliation

Yahweh introduced grace and reconciliation as central ingredients in the divine/human relationship. Israel's poor performance of keeping relational promises with God highlighted a repetitive exercise of initiative from the Maker of life in an effort to repair the damage of covenants broken by individuals and a people. God extended forgiveness and grace as a model, again, for human covenants to heal, recommit, and thrive.

From the outset of any fallible relationship mutual forgiveness and grace provide the only realistic posture for renewal and permanence. A man and a woman, pledged to each other with sacred vows, regularly fail and need healing. Parenting requires ongoing forgiveness, and children and adults learn together that family ties assume unending repair and renewal. Friendships, marriages, parenting, and communal loyalties, all require a strong measure of grace to survive the challenge of imperfection and fallibility. Covenants between persons find hope and resilience when practicing forgiveness in the same manner as God always has. Relationships grow stronger, resilient, and more rewarding through the exercise of חסד.

Is it possible to rise to the challenge of loving kindness? If so, there's a lasting gift in it for the people of God.

Works Cited

Simpson, Cuthbert A. "Genesis." In *The Interpreter's Bible*, edited by George Arthur Buttrick, 1:437–829. New York: Abingdon, 1952.
Snaith, Norman H. *A Theological Word Book of the Bible*. New York: MacMillan, 1951.

www.ingramcontent.com/pod-product-compliance
Lightning Source LLC
Chambersburg PA
CBHW071236230426
43668CB00011B/1455